MW00893256

Journey from Invisibility to Visibility

Journey from Invisibility to Visibility

A GUIDE FOR WOMEN SIXTY AND BEYOND

Gail K. Harris, Marilyn C. Lesser and Cynthia T. Soloway

Copyright © 2016 Cynthia T. Soloway
All rights reserved.

ISBN-13: 9781534751897
ISBN-10: 1534751890
Library of Congress Control Number: 2016910206
CreateSpace Independent Publishing Platform
North Charleston, South Carolina

This book is dedicated to our husbands, Ed, Norman, and Mark; our children (JD, Brett, Olga, Geoffrey, Elana, Alexandra, David, Jaye, Steven, Joy, Scott, Robert, Deanna, and Michael); our grandchildren (Jack, Eden, Stella, Evita, Jenna, Brett, Eric, Julie, Matthew, Mia, Sarah, Andrew, and Sophie); and our wonderful friends, who never faltered once as they gave us their love and support. We have grown so much as women, mothers, grandmothers, and professionals as we listened and challenged each other to share our most authentic selves. We have learned so much from the more than four hundred stories women shared and from their wisdom, courage, and candor. We could never have written this book without their voices.

"A Woman's Perspective"

Fifty years is but a glance
In our Creator's eye,
But to us it can be a lifetime
As our span of years goes by.

The years begin so slowly,
Birthdays eagerly awaited.
Attracted by adulthood,
We anticipate the fated.

The years are full, consuming,
To be greeted as a friend,
And then go "hurry scurry"
As we hasten to our end.

But we've gained so much along the way,
Experience hard earned.
So it is quite appropriate
To pass on what we've learned.

We were children of the '30s,
Depression born and bred,
But never poor or needy—
We were richly loved instead.

Growing up before the war,
We never felt deprived,
'Cause everybody did without
And struggled to survive.

When the war years beckoned,
The Depression came apart.
Our families went off to fight the war,
And we, too, did our part.

We became children of the '40s,
Despite the war, naïve.
Peace returned, the world was safe,
Or so we did believe.

High schools for girls reached out to us;
We eagerly responded.
Her job to teach, our role to learn,
And soon we all were bonded.

No mention of our role in life,
Its limits, its confinement;
Just study hard while practicing
Decorum and refinement.

Our minds and dreams expanded,
As did our core of knowledge.
Then off we went to compete with men
In the venue of co-ed college.

Compete we did, and we excelled,
And yet we lost the race.
Because with graduation
We assumed a "woman's place."

To some, the '50s meant marriage,
"Kuche and Kinder" understood.
Creativity and talent
Focused on our motherhood,

And on our volunteering,
The arts, civic affairs,
Social action, and religion—
All wanting, willing heirs.

Our spouses, consumed with professions,
Needing nurturing, attention,
While we were filled with children's needs
Too numerous to mention.

We grew up with our children,
With the sharing of our days,
While our spouses grew divergently
In far more worldly ways.

And then the '60s burst on the scene,
The world was bathed in strife.
Anger and rebellion
Became the way of life.

Civil rights and women's rights
And peace, the end of war,
As women we expressed ourselves
As we never had before.

Assassinations, lynchings,
Turmoil everywhere.
The safety of the familiar
Was now no longer there.

Some could not meet the challenge,
Others stared it in the face.
But all agreed that it was hard
To keep up with the pace.

Marriages were severed.
Families were crumbled.
The power of the moment
Made us hesitant and humbled.

And then, at last, the '70s—
The turbulence surceases.
Time for reconciliation and
For picking up the pieces.

Our children had survived the stress,
And we were filled with pride
As they were faced with choices
That we had been denied.

Some of us were grateful for
Another worthy fact:
We, too, had passed the frenzy
With our marriages intact.

Though we had grown in different ways,
We had remained together,
Strengthened by the very stress of
The storms we'd had to weather.

While others, who'd found themselves alone,
Be it by choice or fate,
Moved on to the more productive life
They'd wanted to create.

We all were optimistic
As the seventh decade waned,
Thankful for the wisdom and
Maturity we had gained.

And then we faced the '80s,
Quite a different scene:
Our children gone, our parents aged,
And we were in between.

A new and strange dilemma
To face and feel and see,
Perhaps the perfect time of life
To concentrate on me!

A time for new experiments,
Advanced degrees, self-worth,
New businesses, professions,
Renewal, and rebirth.

A time for much accomplishment,
To join the race and win!
Out in the world at large, as well
As in the world within.

And then the mighty **'90s**
Came whizzing, whizzing by,
A time for much reflection
On the past and on the why.

Bringing us to a new **millennium**
Where technology is king.
Instant communication,
Instant everything!

Our lives could be depressing,
Feeling empty and bereft
As we are faced with aging and the
Shortened life spans left.

But most of us feel gratitude
For all that we have learned,
For all of our accomplishments,
The plaudits we have earned.

For all the places visited,
Inconsequential things,
The simple pleasures of living,
The joy a grandchild brings.

The uniqueness of a husband
With whom you've shared so much—
His wisdom, understanding,
His warm and tender touch.

There is so much to be thankful for,
But one thing beats the rest:
Because we were born in the '30s
Our options were the best.

We had no choice but to stay at home,
Raise children sans distractions.
We didn't work, could concentrate
On motherhood's attractions.

We were stay-at-home moms at a time when this
Was honored and respected.
How fortunate to have had the chance
To do what was accepted.

When women's rights came on the scene
To enlighten and unfetter,
We were free because our children had grown—
The timing could not have been better.

So finally, in retrospect,
As I peruse my life,
My greatest satisfaction came
As a mother and a wife.

I've been a successful student,
A consummate volunteer,
I've had the opportunity for
An administrative career.

But I find my greatest pleasure,
I hope you understand,
When a grandchild says, "I love you,"
When my husband takes my hand.

Though I look back with nostalgia,
I look forward unafraid,
For I know I'm in the "last of life
For which the first was made."

—GW

Contents

Preface

ike many other women over sixty, we began searching for answers to the questions of aging in our early fifties, when we first struggled to cope with the internal voices of menopause. How lucky we were that at that time Gail Sheehy had written a new book, *Silent Passages*, which spoke to many of the hidden anxieties we had about our aging bodies. That book was the impetus for creating a group of *age fifty-something women* who could share concerns and together fashion some workable solutions. Voila! *The 50s Group* was born.

Twenty-one years later, *the group* still meets monthly, but our focus has changed. A few of the women are still sandwiched between the needs of their frail, elderly parents and the economic and emotional uncertainties of their adult children. Many are reevaluating their long-term commitment to professional life; most are navigating the thrills of grandparenting. Yet all, saddened by the memory of two members who lost their battles with cancer, impatiently wait at the crossroads wondering, "So what is yet to come?"

The 50s Group brought the three authors together. Within the group's safe and nourishing world, we explored so many of our milestone issues. Our level of trust and appreciation for each other's insight and wisdom made this book collaboration a gift. These three social workers whose career paths had taken quite different turns were now bound together by the recognition that our future, beyond the likelihood of health issues, could well be the most fascinating and rewarding challenge yet.

We began this project by questioning how best we could balance our desire to articulate a credible thesis on aging in women, with a competing interest to inspire women over sixty to explore their pasts, compose their personal narratives, and create their living legacies. As we began to examine the relevant literature, we recognized that there was an underlying theme in the narratives of older women that spoke to their sense of *invisibility*. It appeared that the media and the workplace had created immutable standards specifically for older women. As we researched, we were met with stereotypes and were introduced to discrimination.

It came as no surprise, then, that among those who were aging, thoughts at times turned longingly to the vibrancy of youth. Nor was it alarming that many of us had begun to feel we had lost some of the edge we had enjoyed in our younger adult years: our sense of being essential in the lives of our families and on our jobs. As women over sixty, we were questioning just what our social value was now.

The hundreds of hours the three of us have worked together have been a labor of love. Using the questions we crafted for the book, we challenged each other and hundreds of women to explore our pasts, to uncover our histories, to welcome new behaviors, and to begin to create our legacies—our *work* for the next thirty years!

Gail Harris, LCSW, MEd
Marilyn Lesser, PhD, LCSW
Cindy Soloway, JD, MSSW, MA

Introduction

We do not remember days, we remember special moments.
The richness of life lies in memories we have forgotten.
—CESARE PAVESE

Age is just a number, and agelessness means not buying into
the idea that a number determines everything from your
state of health to your attractiveness to your value.
—CHRISTIANE NORTHRUP, MD

A Note to Our Readers:

For the past few years, I have been on a remarkable journey!

Leading up to my retirement, I began obsessing about how I would spend the hours of my days. I knew that I had to have a plan in hand as I closed my office door—boxes overstuffed with pictures and trinkets and memories—never to look back. Twenty years in this one place was a long time for me, as moving had always interrupted whatever job I was doing. I was then onto something newer and more exciting, reinventing myself for my next adventure.

Well, all that was over now. No new city. No new challenge. And oddly, no sadness or remorse. Yet I did have a twinge of anxiety as to what I would do and how I would create structure in my newest world...my world of the future.

That is where my two wonderful social worker friends came in. Over the years, the three of us had discussed writing a book together. One year it was about building healthy families, another about marriage, children, and female sexuality. We never got very far because of the demands of our jobs and the weight of our role as caregivers for our parents, our grandchildren, and, of course, our husbands. But now that we were over sixty, we had more time and a desire to explore (as social workers are wont to do) who we had become over these last sixty-plus years. Here lies the essence of our book.

Some women reach our age and begin to feel invisible in the eyes of society. There are no clothes in *Elle* specifically for women our age, but there are countless pages of advertisements for lotions and Botox and surgeries to help us all recapture that blush of youth. But is that what we really want to do?

On reaching our age, we (and frankly everyone else around us) are seeing power in the vibrancy of being young. Even if we continue to work, we may be haunted by thoughts and fears of being incapacitated by the illnesses of aging. Maybe we're terrified by thoughts of some hidden gene we have little control over. On reaching our age, we reflect, "If age is just a number, and if we feel vital and energetic, why is it that younger generations rarely seek us out for the wisdom of our life's experiences?"

When women like us begin to question our own merits, it is time to stop and reflect on who we are as we have aged. By first looking back at our development into womanhood, by telling our personal stories, and most importantly by listening to the messages in those stories, we will begin to celebrate who we have grown to be and revel in the many invaluable lessons we have mastered along the way. It is essential, as proof that we value the meaning of our lives, that we share the gifts we have acquired and create a living legacy for the cherished people in our lives.

The *soul* of this book is revealed in the more than four hundred stories women have shared with us as they explored their past. The stories evolved as the women answered questions we posed. The three of us also answered the questions, and clearly that is why this has been a remarkable journey. Along the way, there have been heavy doses of laughter, some closure, and a newfound respect and appreciation for so many things in our past. I would love for each of you to answer the questions we are asking in the book and tell your stories so others in your personal circle can be emboldened by your honesty and the vitality of your lives. We have been moved by the vision and clarity of thought in the stories women have shared with us. We hope you, too, will be inspired. We want your voice to be a part of the chorus of women who have within their grasp the possibility to change the landscape of aging with the legacies they leave for their loved ones. We want your voice to be a part of the chorus of women who, with their words and their insights, can initiate a change in how our society views the woman over sixty.

Cindy Soloway

CHAPTER 1
Welcome to the "Afternoon" of Women's Lives

It seems to me that old age is only a costume assumed for
those others; the true, the essential self is ageless.
—Malcolm Crowley

A human being would certainly not grow to be seventy or eighty if
this longevity had no meaning to the species to which he belonged.
The afternoon of human life must also have a significance of its
own and cannot be merely a pitiful appendage to life's morning.
—Carl Jung

In the midnineties, while the "whatever" generation of women in their twenties and thirties were living out the hopes and dreams of Betty Friedan and Gloria Steinem, Gail Sheehy gave new voice to midlife women. Until then, many women had placed on hold their personal narratives on the physical and emotional changes of aging. Inspired now by Sheehy's new insights, the boomer generation of women was ready to challenge America's dismissive dialogue on aging. The folklore about aging, which had passed as truth, was finally being contested by a new generation of empowered women. With a newfound resiliency and inventiveness, the emboldened midlifers, as described in *Declining to Decline* (Gulette, 1997), argued that youth—with its image of fun, sexuality, energy, and hope—was really "cultural goods with a short shelf life." The midlife woman was shaping her new persona: one that exploited the wisdom of her years and her experiences. She was no longer a passive, culturally drawn figure but rather had evolved into a valued decision maker and an occasional warrior.

At that same time, a group of us fifty-somethings got swept up in the exhilaration of those nineties ideas and decided to meet together to discuss what Sheehy described as the women we were in the midst of becoming. The group became an exciting venue to discuss all the issues midlife had delivered at our doorsteps. We were encouraged by the similarity of our feelings and by our parallel experiences as women, wives, parents, grandparents, children, and professionals.

Now, twenty years later, we find ourselves at a new crossroads. Like many women over sixty, we have sadly said good-bye to the triumphs of midlife as we face the last and, what we hope will be, the most celebrated years of our lives. We recognize that what had been significant in reshaping our midlife years was a shared interest in demystifying and *demythifying* the cultural messages that had historically defined midlife women. Those same challenges remain; the myths regarding these later years may even be more devastating to women's psyches.

Just as midlife carried with it immense ethical, political, social, and economic consequences, the sixty-plus years present a similar burden. Unfortunately, today there is a scarcity of voices heralding a bright and meaningful future for us. What we discovered as we began sharing our own histories was that each of us has a unique path to that future. The direction that path will take finds its roots in our own personal narratives.

We were amazed to uncover a convergence of many positive themes on aging from the four hundred shared narratives. It is quite possible a change will come in the landscape of aging as a result of the strength of the refrain of women over sixty speaking out. Their voices may prove to be the incentive for redefining the societal view on aging in the twenty-first century.

The Invisible Generation

Our very first task in this book is to address a myth that has been sown and carefully cultivated in America over the last fifty years: as women age past midlife, we become the invisible generation.

> I have been an involved member of my community, serving in leadership positions as a board member and chairman of committees of the all the major organizations. For the past forty-five years, I have served and loved every minute, as I loved having some small part in

insuring the future of strong community organizations. Now that "I am elderly," my feelings are the same: to participate in this endeavor. But what has changed is how I am treated. I feel invisible, and what's worse—unvalued. I shared these feelings with the president of one organization and offered my resignation to make room for the younger leaders. He refused and implored me to stay. He said that they needed the experience and history I had to offer. So I stayed. Well, nothing changed. The responses to my remarks are received as outdated and irrelevant. Sometimes the behavior even borders on disrespect. Most of the board members are twenty to twenty-five years younger. There are almost none of my peers still involved, and now I understand why. I acknowledge that "times are different" and priorities have changed. I work hard reading and attending educational seminars in order to stay current on community needs, interests, and changes. I feel this is my duty in order to be a relevant board member. I have always felt that everyone on a board is of value and should be listened to and learned from. This appears to have changed somewhat in our society; for some reason people are disposable as they age. What a shame! Not just on a personal note but for our communities. Every generation has much to give, and there is so much to be gained by the giving and receiving from each individual. I did not know that devaluation, just as arthritis, comes with *age*! (Observations of an active, *alert* seventy-six-year-old woman).—IKH

Getting married at age nineteen shaped the way I was at that time—which was to be dependent on my husband for most things. I feel I went from my parents' house to my own house, with little time to grow up as a mature woman. Having children was certainly a game changer, and with little experience at that time, my views of parenting have changed, but not in time to make those changes with my children. I would have given them more of myself and would have been more attentive to their needs as individuals. My husband's death changed my life drastically but changed me slowly. I had to learn to be self-sufficient, to call upon assistance whenever needed and in whatever areas the help was wanted, and I had to make my own decisions, the biggest challenge of all.—Anonymous

> At eighty-two years of age, my life's experiences and wisdom are irrelevant in today's world. As a child of the Great Depression, my value system, moral code, and general behavior were forged by the need to survive in those perilous times. Getting *old* is a state of mind. Unfortunately it places physical limitations, but determination and desire to accomplish a goal keeps one moving.—JAL

This devaluation seems quite baffling. Many of us are emotionally connected to the histories of our immigrant grandparents and great-grandparents, and that connection is rooted in a tradition that revered the elders in the community for their wisdom and omnipotence. Fifty years ago, the matriarchs in our society *held court*, and their authority was rarely questioned. Sundays and holidays, cousins played while parents, aunts, and uncles paid homage to the grandmother.

> My first memories of a strong sense of connectedness to people outside of my parents and older sisters were of the summers we spent at a lake resort in the Midwest. I loved those summers because I felt an integral part of a wonderful, loving family. Interestingly, I am not sure even to this day if my older sisters had the same experience as I had. For me, I was always envious of friends who had grandparents, aunts, uncles, and cousins whom they regularly saw and with whom they shared weekends and special events. Our extended family lived five hundred miles away, and it was the summers at the lake or the excitement of holidays that brought me into what I sensed was a gigantic bubble of love and belonging. Maybe I loved it so much because in my eyes my parents were also so happy and connected there. My parents would spend the days outside what I am sure now was a very primitive cabin, sharing months of events with the sisters-in-law and brothers. The cousins were left to devise activities on their own...as the parents cautiously gave us the freedom to explore. Late at night as I tried to sleep, I could smell the scent of cigars and hear the endless laughter of my parents and aunts and uncles as they played pinochle and laughed uncontrollably as the brothers took turns telling jokes. The sound of that laughter was the blanket of protection that made me feel that everything was all right in the

world. At that moment the world was a promising place, and I was convinced that my family had the energy to make amazing things happen. There was an optimism that pervaded those evenings and an insight into the mysteries of the adult world. Not until I was married and a parent myself did I realize how much I had treasured those childhood memories of hope, of optimism, of positive energy, and how I wanted my children to feel enveloped in that same blanket of protection.—CTS

I had one aunt that was the most giving and nurturing woman. Although her accent was thick and, along with her kids, we often joked with her about her misuse of words, I knew that she would always love me and be there for me. The first floor of the duplex where my aunt lived was not very large. Even though the sleeping accommodations were always cramped, with cousins sleeping in the attic or on the floor next to us, none of that mattered because most of my happiest memories as a teen and young adult centered on those times we spent sitting around the table at her house eating and laughing. There I learned about sacrifice, I learned about unselfishness, I learned about devotion to family, I learned about loving and about respect. My aunt was not educated, a refugee who had left her sister behind in the death camps. She had a sadness at times in her eyes, but her heart was only filled with love and devotion for all of us.—ETG

So why may it be different now in our generation of women? The changes over the years appeared to be so subtle, hardly noticeable. Here we are in 2017, and the world is a different place. We must be prepared to do battle to regain our sense of worth as aging women; we must not be governed by how we match up physically to younger generations.

No matter what magazine we pick up at the grocery or what store window we linger by, we are prejudiced by an insidious societal obsession with youth and physical beauty. Coupled with that obsession is an explosion of antiaging crèmes and tempting cosmetic surgeries ostensibly designed to enhance our physical appearance and consequently ensure our social value in the world.

We have often wondered, as we become beauty-product consumers, are we not fueling society's bias toward the power of beauty and physicality? Are we not perpetuating these values through our behavior and giving voice to their social value? Should we then be surprised when resources and opportunities are strewn at the feet of the young and beautiful? No matter what our brain tells us we are able to do, how can we succeed when society and our *maturing* bodies often compete for our attention?

Just as stereotyping grew out of racism and sexism in the sixties and seventies, American thinking today is fraught with discriminatory notions about aging. Typically aging women are portrayed as physically, financially, and socially dependent. The assumptions of *ageism* (a term coined by Robert Butler) are that old age is bad and old women are inflexible, asexual, and unhappy.

Our aging population has been labeled, interestingly enough, *the Silent Generation*, a term coined in a *Time* magazine article published in November of 1951. Others have labeled the silent generation, nestled between the Greatest Generation and baby boomers, the *Lucky Few*. This moniker may be contrary to what our Generation X children and grandchildren may think of our emphasis on playing by the rules and planning for the future, but it has worked quite well for us both financially and professionally. A 2014 *Forbes* report confirmed that although we are few in numbers, we are the healthiest and wealthiest generation. The median income of those seventy-five-plus-year-olds is higher than any other Americans and five times that of those thirty-five to forty-four years old. All this is proof enough that younger generations may want to rethink how they have characterized us. We can be proud, as Woody Allen put it, that we were a population who felt that the importance of life was just showing up 80 percent of the time. We had few expectations except to work hard and few dreams of changing the world.

Throughout the following chapters, we will present questions we raised to other women over sixty and some of their answers to these questions. We ask that you take time to read the questions and the vignettes and then think about their significance in your life. It may not be easy, but please try to respond to the questions, using your own stories to help discover your me within.

As a woman over sixty, what are the messages you have received from television, advertisements, magazines, and your favorite stores regarding aging? How do these messages affect your feelings about your body image, your sexuality, and/or your attitude about growing older?

Designers have completely ignored the over-sixty-five-year-old market. We have plenty of time and expendable income, and we can't find anything to buy, because everything is designed for fifteen-year-olds. I mean, the youth market has been served, but not with five-thousand-dollar dresses.—Iris Apfel, *New York Times Magazine*, April 13, 2015

No messages other than we'll feel better if we take medication for our aging bones and laxatives for our aging guts. Most ads are pitched at younger women.—IWG

The messages conveyed by television, advertisements, magazines, and favorite stores clearly emphasize the glory of youth. As a woman of sixty-nine years, I feel more and more alienated by many of these cultural mouthpieces. I flip through fashion magazines on the rare occasions I encounter them; they bore me because they are so clearly not directed to me. The same is true with much of television, although that has more to do with the poor programming. My *favorite stores*, on the other hand, are my favorite stores because I can find clothing and products appropriate for my age and style. I do not dress in a matronly fashion at all, but increasingly I am aware of my desire to dress stylishly but with restraint. The emphasis on youth, on perfect bodies and faces, honestly does not affect how I feel about my own body. Yes, of course I wish I had less wrinkles and no jowls, and of course I wish I *liked my neck*, but I spend very little time thinking about it. I really feel gratitude for good health, wonderful family and friends, and I don't want to waste any time bemoaning the loss of youth. In addition, I have a loving husband, we still have sex, and I feel good about who I am despite the indifference of the media to a woman my age.—Anonymous

As a woman well past sixty, I know that as far as TV, ads, etc. are concerned, I am totally invisible. Truthfully, my own feelings about my body image and sexuality were formed many years ago, and age has not really changed that for me. I must admit that I was more than a bit put off a couple of years ago when I was shopping for a dress for a grandson's bar mitzvah and the saleslady brought out only "matronly" selections. I have never viewed myself in that light. I still wear jeans and sneakers just as I always have and pick clothes that I think I look good in. I still like to shop, and I really enjoy relating to the young people who live in my condo, where age doesn't seem to be a barrier to at least a casual give-and-take. I do think it is easier to have that kind of attitude in a large city where really anything goes. So in short (or long), I don't feel those messages (or nonmessages) have any particular relationship to my feelings about myself.—ETG

What does getting older mean to you, and how does it feel?

When you are eighty years old, you are *old*! A few months ago, while riding in the Amtrak dining car, a man leaned across the aisle and said, "Aren't you Mrs.—?" He reminded me I was his teacher thirty-four years ago. Getting old feels pretty good, although I would not advise rushing into it!—Anonymous

Getting older is an adjustment due to a bad back that inhibits some activity, and I have aching joints, wrinkles, and all the things my mother told me. And I thought, "Not me!" I am fine with age and am proud to have a young spirit, enthusiasm, and a sense of adventure each day. The years have flown, but with each passing one, I have gained more wisdom and tolerance.—CS

It means nothing, really. Thank the Lord I feel fine. It is amazing to see my kids so old, however.—EH

It feels shitty and that I don't have much time left. And I better do things that make me happy and educated.—DG

I would define aging as the realization one has when peering into a 5x magnified, lighted mirror and realizing that the reflection is actually you. I felt chronologically the same as when I was twenty, but the definitive reflection indicated differently and took some adjustment. As I look back over the years, I am thankful to have had so many opportunities and experiences: raising children; having friends, family, and business relationships; traveling; and the many interesting people I have encountered through the years. I still maintain friendships from elementary, high school, and college and remain active socially and physically. I would not change anything about the landscape of aging as long as I can remain healthy. With age comes more understanding, mellowness, and an appreciation for the things we tend to overlook when we are younger raising our families. I find this is the best time of life. It's a time of freedom without the responsibilities that come with being young. I have adjusted to my 5x mirror, and now I am grateful for the years it indicated because they have led me to where I am today.—MB

Age is like the *Tin Age* rather than the Golden Age, as everything gets rusty like an old car. Some parts you can fix and others you cannot. And you adjust to it.—MM

Dealing with getting older has been an interesting experience, especially as I have given it so little thought (being too busy living and dealing with day-to-day life). When I hit sixty, I thought to myself, "Wow. Sixty is really *adult!*" When I turned sixty-five, I thought, "Can it be possible that I am a senior citizen?" And then seventy came and it was something of a jolt as then I began to wonder how many more years I have to accomplish what I want to. Having said that, I realize that these years have brought a measure of serenity. (Strangely, as I've finally come to terms with not having a model's body, I also have reached a point of stability in my weight at the size I always wanted to be!) I look back with pride at all I've accomplished in so many different realms, and I feel blessed to have had the experiences I've had and the opportunities I've had to make a difference. I guess we all live with the wish we had *do-overs*, and there are many things I would change if I had it to do all over again, but of course "hindsight is twenty-twenty," and that is the operative reality.—TG

Getting older *sucks!* I hate to see my body showing signs of aging— wrinkles, sagging, ugly veins, etc. It feels limiting to know I cannot walk as far as I used to years ago. I sometimes worry about the possibility of contracting diseases that could be terminal. Seeing close friends and family members struggling with serious illness makes me very sad. I've had several close friends die in the past number of years, and it makes me think about my own mortality.—AH

In my opinion aging is in many ways a state of mind! From birth to death, all of our life's experiences define the woman and mother you become and how you cope with your "senior years." I have been very blessed with my goals, values, and morals from my parents. I have done my best to pass them all down to my children…honesty, integrity, education, religious affiliation and beliefs, philanthropy, careers, community service, and *family*.—BDA

As I look back over how I've lived my life, I realize that I am always exploring, traveling, and finding new ideas and challenging activities. When I was twenty-six, I learned how to scuba dive, an activity I enjoyed for almost thirty years. Through scuba diving, I met many new friends, including my husband. When I was thirty, I learned how to ski. Since we live in Florida, this has taken me to many parts of the United States and the world that I might not have gone to otherwise. When I was forty, I learned to fly. Piloting airplanes has given me a tremendous confidence and an unequaled sense of freedom. I've flown all over the United States and in six foreign countries. What a different perspective of the world. When I was fifty, I learned to Rollerblade, another confidence builder and lots of good exercise. Now in my sixties, I have learned mah-jongg and canasta. I also play Words with Friends. These all provide mental exercise, while my other activities provide physical exercise. What will I be doing as I continue my life's journey? I am not sure what my seventies will bring, but I am sure it will be interesting. So as I consider aging, I believe in living each day to its fullest. Life is a wonderful experience and a fabulous adventure.—TS

Growing older means to me, as Browning so wisely said, "the last of life for which the first was made."—AOC

The worst part of getting older is not the wrinkles or the bulges or forgetting an occasional word. It is in knowing that one day before long I will not be here to witness what will become of this family I love so dearly. It is like watching a marvelous movie or reading a favorite book and never learning how it ends. How cruel it is to have to leave in the middle. So how does it feel to get older? I cannot pretend that I would not rather be twenty-four, but I am both grateful and amazed to be where I am now, and with a little luck, perhaps I will hang around a little longer. Perhaps there will come a time when I will wish I were only seventy-four!—JW

It feels calmer. Able to enjoy things and events more. Being in good health and being able to afford things. We have been careful about planning financially for our older years. I spent my earlier years providing and giving to other people—raising kids, college, weddings, etc.—family, children, etc.—so they would be able to enjoy things. Now I feel I can allow myself to enjoy things just for me. Older people do not scare me. I am not worried about wrinkles, etc. I feel I have more to give based upon the experiences I have had. I am in good health and able to travel to wonderful new places. I do not feel as responsible for raising the kids. I still love them very much, but my primary job of providing for them is over. My job now still is to encourage and love them. I am very comfortable and have confidence in being me at this age.—FR

I appreciate my mind, and I hope I never lose it. My priorities have changed. What is most important in life is health, not material things. Love and tranquility. The same things do not excite me anymore. Enjoyment is tranquility and peace. A good word vs. a new ring.—AO

Dealing with aging has been a personal journey. Age has not been considered a problem, while of course I am not unaware of the process. My physical body knows exactly how old I am. I believe it is true for many of us that when we look at our longtime friends, we see them as they were when we were in high school. Our topics of conversation have changed through the years from boys to periods to marriages to children to grandchildren to a litany of medical problems. Physical changes and mental changes are definitely a challenge, as is the ever more pressing thought of our mortality. It is with some humor (a form of denial) that we realize we no longer need long-term guarantees on purchases. That we will never have to worry about the tree we planted having to be trimmed because it has grown into the overhead wires. Another thing that happens is that objects and their accumulation hold no more interest for me. The few items that hold sentimental value are of no value to my children. They hold my memories, not theirs.—JR

It means free to be me. I can appreciate who I am at this age. The journey has been an evolution. Liberated to enjoy what I have. Content and not striving for anything more. I feel it is as good as it's going to get. I hope not to go backward. I wish only for good health for me and my loved ones. I finally have the time to smell some roses—I hope I have many years to do so.—Anonymous

For the first time, I am feeling my vulnerability and accepting who I am...the good and the not so good. I am feeling more comfortable with myself.—Anonymous

Getting old is not for sissies. Physically there are increasing challenges and limitations. However, I like not having the responsibilities and pressures I had when I worked full time and was raising children. One downside is not having a mate to share emotionally and practically.—NL

I feel wiser and it feels good.—JK

I feel that getting older means being less appreciated by some if not many and becoming invisible in certain areas of my life. I also find that I resent (hate that word, but you are asking for truth) the fact that my hard-earned skills in my chosen career are minimized by the younger crowd feeling minimized is probably a reaction to past learned experiences and therefore my fault actually, and because I feel that it is my fault, it helps enable me to continue to work on my personal self as well as on my professionals skills—taking risks, stretching. Getting older then is simply another learning stage. Fortunately, I have a job I love, my health, and friends. My response might be different without health, regular income, and friendships. I do find, as I get older, that I am aware of death as an actuality, not a concept.—GB

I worry about my health and my husband's health. It feels scary at times.—Anonymous

Getting older means doing more of what I want, greater independence, inner fulfillment, and being wiser through experience. Savoring life and activities are positive results. On the negative side, I am in denial that I am going to be seventy-two; the number does not match the feelings, although my body is starting to give me reality checks.—ER

Getting older is a mental and physical challenge as we grope for the right word (or people's names) and fix the wear and tear on our bodies.—BC

Getting older is a phrase. My age is an eight followed by a figure. Yes, I may move slower, I have a few more aches, and I tire quicker (or is that the result of two bad accidents?). But I have untold wealth as a result of my knowledge gained over the past eighty-plus years.—JO

How do you think young adults would describe your life?

Younger adults are amazed at my energy level and surprised that someone my age can still do what I do.—ML

It is hard to describe, since young adults usually think they will never get old, but they usually appreciate my experience and wisdom.—NK

What has been most challenging about the aging process? What concerns, if any, do you have about your future and aging?

Lately, it is a concern for me. I am the primary caregiver for my elderly mother. It's a big responsibility and often very challenging. I sometimes wonder how many good years I may have left. I am beginning to see and feel physical changes. I do my best to adapt. I was hoping to have more time for myself at this stage of life. Now I don't see that happening.—RE

Trying to do what I always have done and realizing that I don't remember as quickly and cannot run as fast I once did. I do manage to travel around Manhattan by subway, and I see very few people our age because they can't seem to get up and down the stairs of the subway stations so easily. We need more accommodations for our aging bodies.—LP

I am closer to the end than the middle, and I feel so good I'm denying the fact that I am getting older. That is, until I look in the mirror. Before, when I would get on the train, some of the people would get up to give me a seat; now they jump!—LWS

The New Face of Aging

Our recommended course of action is that we readjust our focus. Together let us explore how each of us, by recapturing accounts of the past and fashioning our own personal stories (what we call "narratives"), can redefine the future. During the process of creating our narratives, we will discover our unique personal truths, truths that will serve as the foundation for defining the legacy we hope to leave behind. It is the effort to continually construct and reconstruct our legacy that will serve as the action plan for our twilight years—an action plan that will embrace our hope and optimism, our love, our originality and spirituality, and our wisdom of years. It is a journey that will debunk the myths of aging and make us quite visible and dynamic in the eyes of society's naysayers.

I don't consider it to be getting old. I consider it a blessing. When my age increases, my wisdom increases; I gain more knowledge and know-how. It feels great to be seventy years old. I enjoying having my golden passport—it allows me to go catch the metro transit anytime I desire at no expense. I also enjoy receiving the many discounts and special offers that are rewarded to me for reaching the age I am. Growing old is beauty and grace.—VP

Getting older means, more than ever, it is *so* important to enjoy the *now*—that is all any one of us actually has! For me, it also is a time to reflect on and respect the balanced journey I have lived. I love being this kind of seventy-four—I take no prescription medications, I play tennis four-plus times per week, add paddle tennis to the mix during the winter months, do some weight training, walk, do yoga stretches, and hope to get on my bike in the not too distant future. What is objectionable is society's stereotype of aging and the elderly. "It ain't necessarily so." I love my silver-gray hair and the laugh lines. There is no other age I would rather be *now*!—MP

Do not think that we are discounting the obvious and the unalterable. The aging process itself is likely to trigger a series of life-altering transitions that can be potentially debilitating. When a 2005 *USA Today* poll asked, "What do people fear most in old age?" over 70 percent of people responded that loss of health and loss of independence were the most devastating transitions.

We are women who are confronting our own demons about aging and challenging ourselves to discover the *light* within. What we have learned is that there is a very reasonable alternative to spending our aging years obsessing on our broken parts or on our changing status in the world. Rather than exhausting ourselves with attempts to escape the messages out there on aging, we must first discover what lies beneath the surface of those messages—the philosophical underpinnings of those messages that are so unique to our country.

Aging is defined differently depending on what part of the world we live in. In many other cultures, the aging individual is still celebrated and revered. America's devaluing of the aged is based in part on our culture of individualism and self-reliance. Who best epitomizes that individualism and self-reliance? The young! In contrast, those individuals who are older and need support only reinforce society's view regarding their loss of independence and autonomy. Those who provide support (financial or physical) for their elderly family members are overlooking the reality that their efforts are as essential to the well-being of their elderly family members as was the assistance they received at earlier stages in the family's life cycle.

Next, we need to ask ourselves, how we got to where we are today, and how that can give us direction for the future. By identifying the influential people and the defining events in our lives as the major sources of our most integral values, we are able to reconcile our past with an emerging sense of who we might yet be able to become. With the resolve and a sense of confidence that comes from a clear understanding of ourselves and how we relate to the world around us, we can challenge the cultural myths surrounding aging and create lasting memories in the minds and hearts of those most dear to us.

> The death of my father was a critical point in the shaping of my life. I can point to the moment (practically the minute) when I began to grow up. I suddenly had to care for my family in ways I had never done before, and I had to leave a pretty carefree time to accept more adult responsibility. I think that my anger at that time prevented me from making more creative and positive decisions about my life.—JR

As we accept our mistakes and failures and missed opportunities, we might then be energized to share the lessons we have learned with younger generations. It is through those connections that we can reignite that person within who is aware and engaged, centered and inclusive, and comfortable in her own skin. By continuing to nurture our positive feelings, we can also renew our sense of order, significance, and meaning.

> I am pretty disciplined and have a good sense of humor (which I consider an essential survival skill). I try to relate with others in a positive way. I am also an intellectually curious person, which always makes life an interesting adventure.—Anonymous

Merely recollecting and evaluating our personal past does not justify writing our narratives. It is an understanding that by sharing these recollections, their messages will have life in future generations. Aging, then, becomes an enormous gift: an opportunity to stop and seize the moment, the potential to intrigue and captivate younger audiences with our story, and the chance to face and embrace the coming years with enthusiasm and exhilaration. It is the gift of investing in a bank of memories of immeasurable worth.

The Influence of the Positive Psychology Movement on Aging

In January 2000, a revolutionary new concept in psychology was introduced in a special edition of the *American Psychologist*:

> The exclusive focus on pathology that has dominated so much of our discipline results in a model of the human being lacking the positive features that makes life worth living...Hope, wisdom, creativity, future-mindedness.—Seligman and Csikszenmihalyi (2000)

As therapists, these words grabbed our attention. We had been trained to examine pathology, to concentrate on what wasn't working. We were committed to healing the damaged psyche. Now *positive psychology*, as this theory of psychology was to be called, was leading us down a new and promising path. These new voices were asking us to simply concentrate on the feelings of (1) well-being and satisfaction we experience when we examine meaningful events from our past, (2) hopefulness and optimism as we look toward fulfillment in our future, and (3) delight from those moments we take the time to value in our present daily lives. What makes this theory so appealing is that it applauds the development of valued individual traits—courage, communication, determination, forgiveness, and the capacity to love—and of valued communal responsibilities as well. For many it brings definition to what our lives could be.

Thus, according to positive theorists, it is not what actually happens that shapes how we feel about things but, more importantly, how we interpret what has happened. Social scientists attempting to unravel the mysteries of aging independent of physical decline incorporated positive psychology into their arsenal and discovered that life satisfaction and well-being became new benchmarks. Today, this has become the theory of *positive aging*. Imagine if we adopted the values of positive psychology as guiding principles for interpreting our personal narratives and discovering our unique legacy. We could possibly map out an exciting and productive journey of self-discovery.

What is positive aging? It is discovering a more enhanced meaning of growing older, concentrating on the positive late-life experiences that transcend the mental and physical decline of normal aging. For most aging adults, the acceptance of what we are able to do as opposed to acting on what we want to do is a constant struggle. To successfully adapt to transitions while still maintaining dignity and achieving life satisfaction is the essence of positive aging. Growing old with grace is the mantra for positive-aging enthusiasts.

Thoughts and beliefs are the single most important indicators of our state of health. In a University of Minnesota longitudinal study, a group of nuns were asked to write life essays. Eighty percent of the nuns who were fully engaged in creative life experiences and demonstrated a healthy mind and spirit, on autopsy showed equal numbers of plaques as the nuns in the study with dementia. The power of an ageless attitude is that a healthy mind and spirit can exist in a less-than-perfect body.

The one step to grace that some have yet to master is an ability to let go and be hopeful. To fear the unexpected, as our mothers often preached, generates a negativity that has the potential to complicate our positive journey to a healthy final third of our lives. The graceful management of life—being open to the possibilities in new ideas and accepting change as a springboard for growth—is integral to our stability. Although change in appearance is another transition that can defy our ability to age with grace, it can never mask what lies beneath. Whether in our clothing, our professionalism, or our commitment to family and/or our work, there is one message that is beginning to emerge: the aging woman of the twenty-first century may not be willing to "go gently into the night!"

For many of us, maintaining intimacy by sharing personal experiences with other women is central to being a woman and has always enriched our lives. The stories shared by hundreds of women in this book validate the willingness of women to bare their souls to other women. Their level of openness will hopefully be the impetus for each of us to explore our own histories and summon up our most valued experiences and meaningful life-span relationships. By looking through the lens of positive aging, we can begin to create a more enriched personal narrative and reframe the challenging transformations of aging as opportunities.

When we look with a positive eye, we find that our life can be fuller and richer and therefore more inspiring than in the days when we were singularly intent on our career or on growing a healthy family. Do not forget how vital a sense of well-being and contentment are to defining meaning and creating a significant narrative. Remember, too, how critical our connectedness to others is to achieving that sense of well-being.

No, We Are Not Too Old for a Developmental Stage

We begin this personal exploration by unveiling the foundation upon which we will build our narratives: the series of developmental stages through which we have traversed. By knowing the parameters of each stage, we are inspired to write our personal stories with a greater understanding of ourselves. Most of all, we hope this will help us to recognize the extraordinary gifts that accompany aging and inspire us to approach life with joy and gratitude.

Dr. Spock, Haim Ginott, Erik Erikson, and others informed our parenting practices when our children were young and we were directing much of our energy toward raising well-adjusted, contributing adults. From the handful of life span theorists that have made major contributions to the field of psychosocial development, Erik Erikson is clearly the most celebrated, and his stages of development serve as the cornerstone for all other developmental research. Erikson saw development in terms of a continuum of human qualities that tracks our physical, psychological, and ethical strengths as we grow and mature. It is important that we turn to science to help discover our place on this continuum and how that place can shape the expectations we may have for the quality of our future.

As early as the midtwenties, a longitudinal study began following a randomized group of children, with the assistance and involvement of parents, from birth to eighteen years of age. By the forties, Erik Erikson was on the staff of the study and was committed to capturing the changes in psychosocial development in children and later in adults. From his observations and documented interviews, he created a road map to direct children and adults on the path of self-awareness and identity. To Erikson, matured development was the result of ultimately balancing the extremes of each life-stage challenge. From our success at mastering this balance blossoms a virtue or the favorable outcome for each of Erikson's eight stages of development.

The earlier stages of development will be very helpful as we look back to examine our childhood and our own children and grandchildren later in this book. Our first task, though, is to understand the adult life stages and how each of us met and adjusted to the challenges we faced as we grew to adulthood.

By interpreting the documented interviews of the parent group of participants in the study, Erikson was able to define four stages of adult development: identity, intimacy, generativity, and integrity. Quite simply put, we are unleashed into adulthood in the *identity* stage, where the most compelling task we have is separating from an ideological dependence on our family of origin: our moms and dads and extended family members. Early on, it is a continuous struggle to know where our family's value system ends and at what point our independent identity is revealed. The *intimacy* stage comes on the heels of establishing our independence. This newly developed sense of self begins as we learn to make commitments to lasting friendships, companionships, and love. With *generativity* comes an extension in midlife of our social radius. We find ourselves balancing our self-absorption with family and/or career with an expansiveness directed outward toward community building, mentoring, and caring for all that the world and we have created.

> Rabbi Yaakov Kamenetzky considered the age of sixty the demarcation
> between young and old. The Talmud relates that Rabbi Yosef had a party
> when he reached sixty, celebrating the beginning of longevity.—TA

In Erikson's last phase, the *integrity* stage, we fight a sense of despair at growing older by reintegrating and recalling events and past circumstances and accepting, with the wisdom gleaned from all our life's experiences, the inalterability of the future. For us, it will be our time for chronicling our personal histories and composing our living legacies.

Following Erikson, throughout the next twenty to thirty years, Dr. George Valliant, a psychoanalyst, and his wife, Caroline, continued to expand the vision of adult development. The study that began six decades earlier captured the adult life cycle from interviews of participants, many of whom were well into their eighties.

There were some startling discoveries about aging gathered from these interviews beyond merely understanding the genesis of adult development. Participants in these studies were continually reinventing their lives at every age. Today, this may be why the vast majority of older adults without brain disease have a sense of well-being until the final months before they die. As aging adults, the participants were found to be less depressed than the general population. Remarkably, 70 percent of the college-educated participants who reached the age of sixty were likely to live beyond eighty years. Yet the most striking findings contradicted what other theorists had earlier described. The aging woman was no longer defined as Daniel Levinson had characterized her: an empty vessel, devoid of energy, interests, and resources. Rather, in Betty Freidan's words, older women were now seen in terms of their possibilities for "intimacy, purposeful work and activity, learning and knowing, community and care."

Valliant, learning from the narratives of those he interviewed, built on Erikson's four adult stages of development and introduced two new ones on the timeline: career consolidation and keeper of the meaning. *Career Consolidation* emerges after the intimacy stage, when older women, according to Valliant (2003) integrate "a social identity within the context of our work." Work no longer is just a job; it is now a career that reflects contentment, commitment, and competence. Valliant introduces the *keeper of the meaning* phase following generativity. Here we are charged with "conserving and preserving the tasks of mankind" and the critical values that have served as our support throughout life.

There are many competing issues that may determine if we will, in fact, be the keepers of the meaning. First, there is the question whether our generation of women over sixty will be revered like earlier generations of matriarchs and if our words will be respected. As the first "me" generation to arrive at this place, our expectations may be that at some point biology no longer only flows downhill. We all have heard women our age assert, "I have already spent many years raising my own children. It is now my time to explore what I can do for myself...grand-children or no grandchildren." We may not realize that the seeds of love, as Anne Lindbergh said, must be "eternally resown." Some women may not be willing to devote the time and energy to cultivate that love.

Another assumption may be that our life's work had been to plant and nurture the love for our children. Like King Lear, though, we may think it is time for our daughters and sons to redirect the flow of biology upward in appreciation for all that we did as parents.

Valliant disputed all this, convinced from his research that success in the generativity stage is measured by our capacity to give ourselves away. Success is measured by our willingness to enrich others with the wisdom of our life's experiences.

In this contribution phase of our lives, the sharing of wisdom is more than a mere summing up of our own lives. As keepers of the meaning, we ensure the preservation of our culture and our value system. It is critical that after midlife, we work to relinquish our need to be needed. Hopefully, we have come to realize that we are more authentic than we have ever been before. And at sixty-plus, we teach our children, grandchildren, and/or our community what is meaningful about the past. Thus, it is a perfect time to reach beyond our present selves to explore our lessons learned and document them for posterity.

This book is the celebration of our arrival as keepers of the meaning. Although our words are often very powerful, it is our behavior that predicts our future and reflects our past. It is in our capacity and desire to embrace this responsibility that we uncover the answers revealed in our personal history. One important way to maintain our integration into generational life is by unveiling our times past, our value systems, and our talents to the young people in our lives—for some, our grandchildren. By doing so, we are able to substitute our less productive feelings of self-concern with those of responsible nurturance.

Dear Sophie,

I just have to send you a note to tell you how proud I was of you today. I felt so special that I had the privilege of taking you to your friend's birthday party because Mom had to work and couldn't do it. I hope you felt the same way about having me there instead of Mom. You might ask why I was so proud of you. It might have seemed like a small thing to you, but to me it showed what kind of values you have. It was so much fun to see the balloon man make all those interesting characters out of the balloons. All the kids were so busy showing off their balloons to each other. But as we were eating lunch, I noticed that you hopped out of your chair and ran over to the other side of the room where a boy from your class was sitting. You talked to him, that same boy that the kids are often making fun of because of what some have called strange behavior. I overheard you ask him if he had gotten a balloon, and he must've said no because you ran over to the balloon man and said, "My friend has no balloon, and he would really like one. Do you think you could make him one?" When I heard you say that, Sophie, I was so touched by your kindness and thoughtfulness. And you know what? Those acts of kindness will be helpful to you for the rest of your life. I hope you never lose the sensitivity that you have to your friends' needs, the spirit of kindness, and your love of fairness—even if it means feeling that everyone should have a balloon at a birthday party. So today I want you to know how really proud I am of the friend you are, the person you are. Please do not lose that. Life is going to be so much richer and more meaningful if you don't.

Love, Grammy

This may be called "grandgenerativity", or a second chance at generativity. With the force of positive aging at our backs, we can reflect on the joy in giving unselfishly to others. And equally important, we can learn to graciously accept help from others while saving enough energy to continue to develop our sense of self.

To Erikson each stage was built on the balancing of opposing values. However, Valliant recognized only the positive and constructive aspects of adult development. In his final stage, he suggests that we experience a sense of existential integrity: the grounding of behavior in our values and acquired wisdom and in our persistence to find inner peace and serenity. Valliant suggested that it is important to face the final stage with optimism and confidence as an example to younger generations. Self-discovery is one important area of growth in the final stages of adulthood that allows for optimism and confidence. Writing our stories is a path to that self-discovery.

A change in family structure, often separating parents from children and siblings from each other, can impede our developing sense of optimism and confidence. In earlier times, support and encouragement were fostered when multigenerational families lived within walking distance. Today, their significance has slowly been eroded and replaced by Skype moments in front of computers that might span hundreds or even thousands of miles. Because of these added complexities in the lives of adult children, plus financial and logistical restrictions, regular involvement in the daily lives of families may no longer be possible.

It may be quite difficult for us to sustain a sense of hopefulness and dignity in this circumstance. Without the intimacy provided through family support, women especially may develop a diminished sense of autonomy. Historically, the elders in our society were revered for their achievements and for building lasting relationships. Rituals were idealized because they brought certainty and mutuality of thinking. It was easier in the past to remain positive. With increasing longevity and the explosion of technology sometimes outside the reach and understanding of the aging adult, all the earlier values have been worn thin.

As we begin to explore our past, it is important not to get sidetracked by the poor-me syndrome. It might be helpful to know that when the worst childhoods were compared to the best, neither childhood had an impact on successful aging. The most meaningful correlate to successful aging was the extent of one's emotional riches. What went right in childhood is a better predictor of successful aging than what went wrong. Although grief over losing a parent at an early age can be devastating, in the absence of conflict, the grief does not make us ill. Valliant was able to quantify factors—such as regular exercise, an adaptive coping style, a stable marriage, and education—that contributed positively to healthy aging.

Women who are keepers of the meaning recognize the richness of their past and understand that their story will continue to be told if they cultivate that richness in others—children, grandchildren, and the community. Keeping life simple, appreciating laughter, and retaining our dignity are the foundations for positive aging as we seize the moment and share its meaning each and every day. This treasure trove of memories allows us to access a needed withdrawal from our emotional bank when life throws us a curveball and we want to remain positive.

No Don't Give Up on That "Old" Brain of Ours!

Oftentimes, women over sixty, when introduced to the idea of writing their own narratives, are convinced that they no longer have the patience or the brainpower to master such an exercise. Concern over how our brain is functioning consumes many anxious moments throughout our days. When we turned to brain-health researchers to question how realistic those fears are, what we learned was inspirational.

We can alter our aging process by both physical and cognitive exercise. People who are cognitively active can trigger more areas in the brain, growing new pathways, at any stage of life. Working our brain not only makes us smarter, but it promotes a longer attention span as well as helps protect against cognitive decline.

Unfortunately, the earliest of gurus helped to create a terrifying caricature of the workings of the aging brain that influenced our perceptions for close to one hundred years. Early twentieth-century thinking regarding the aging brain was inspired by the words of Sigmund Freud: "Old people are no longer educable." With Piaget at his heels, it would soon became accepted that psychological development came to a screeching halt at young adulthood, at which time there began a slow, menacing erosion of brain function. Although the first studies that challenged these notions were published in the early sixties, it is only in the last twenty years that researchers and clinicians have made inroads in dispelling these early myths about the decaying aging brain. The good news is that the twenty-first-century *aging* brain is much more flexible and adaptable.

Aging or not, the human brain is a complex organism. Imagine the intricate underground patterns of endless miles of fiber-optic cables that course through pathways beneath our cities. Millions of televised and telephonic messages stream at lightning speeds 24-7 across those pathways. Now minimize these cables, design a more complex grid, and multiply that system. What you have now created is the human brain with its billions of neurons working tirelessly to ensure that the entire body remains healthy and survives.

Unlike many other kinds of cells, neurons in the brain can live a long life—some say as many as one hundred years. In order for the cells to stay healthy, they are in a constant state of maintenance and repair. Researchers have been able to show that, in a few regions in the brain, physical and mental activities can stimulate new neurons to grow even in the aging brain. As we exercise, our bodies produce brain-growth factors. It is these brain-growth factors that trigger cells to mature into active neurons. Learning also initiates the metamorphosis of cells into neurons and, in addition, promotes the web of connections. See why you shouldn't give up on your aging brain?

Gene Cohen, MD, in *The Mature Mind: The Positive Power of the Aging Brain*, summarizes four dramatic findings related to the current state of brain research:

1. The brain "continually resculpts itself" as it assimilates new experiences and new learning.
2. New brain cells form throughout our life span.
3. The circuitry in the brain matures, and with that comes more emotional stability.
4. Both hemispheres of the brain (the left, controlling speech, language, mathematical competence, and logic; and the right, controlling intuition, visual-spatial strengths, and creativity) are used equally and more frequently as we age.

Another myth to dispel is that older adults have a higher likelihood of being depressed. Depression among aging adults is no higher than in young adults. And in fact, the morale among the aging population is higher than in early adulthood, even when you study the frail elderly. The structural changes to the brain again play a critical role in the emotional stability of aging adults. Human emotions are nestled in the area of the brain called the limbic system, where electric-like impulses respond to external cues.

The Limbic System

Interestingly, the limbic system is blanketed with a thick layer of brain tissue, the amygdalae, in which the seeds of self-awareness, goals, and aspirations grow. In younger adults, emotionality rules, and rationality is overwhelmed and unable to mediate its recovery in the limbic system.

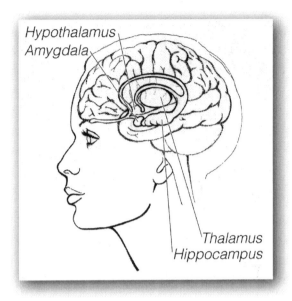

Why is there a possibility that this is different in the aging brain? When we are young adults, the amygdalae moderate the intensity of our emotions by intercepting sensory information and volleying off responses. If there is a threat, the amygdalae fire off a response before the blanket of rationality has time to process and respond. PET scans of the aging brain show that activity in the amygdalae declines over years, especially in regard to response to fear and anger. Studies have found that aging adults are less likely to experience negative emotions and more likely to remember positive ones. Now we have scientific proof to confirm why older adults may tend to be calmer in the face of life's harrowing events.

So what is the potential of the aging brain? Although women over sixty may bemoan the loss of their six-pack abs (if they ever had them) or tight behinds, we can celebrate that our brains have become more richly dense than they were as younger adults. In our early years, we tended to use one side of our brain at a time. Today, with the use of PET scans and MRIs, we have discovered that aging individuals use both sides of our brain. When three populations were studied (younger adults, low-performing older adults, and high-performing older adults), something quite amazing was revealed. Low-performing older adults and younger adults both used only the right prefrontal cortex for problem solving; high-performing older adults used both sides of the brain.

All this brain research validates what the authors of this book strongly believed when we began this project. For older adults, autobiographical narratives can capitalize on the use of both the right and left sides of our brain. We are able to create a work that is more thoughtful and poignant because of the melding of the language and sequential thinking of our left side of the brain with the creative and synthesizing skills of our right.

In order for us to learn about ourselves through our narratives, we must remember. Memories are created when thousands of neurons fire in a unique pattern. Focusing on the memory reinforces and strengthens the pattern. The more often the memory is activated, the stronger and more permanent the bonds are in the pattern. As we challenge ourselves, and our aging brains, with new experiences and with the task of remembering the old ones, we promote not only the reshaping and growth of our neural network but also an optimistic view of our potential as we age.

Contrary to what Freud predicted, the older adult is poised and ready to generate new ideas and cope better in stressful situations. To nourish brain "fitness," we quite simply have to embrace (1) mental exercise that processes and stores new information, and (2) physical exercise that increases our brain oxygen levels. How exciting it is to know that, contrary to current societal thinking on aging (that "older people are obsolete"), there is hope that the mentally active woman over sixty may still have quite a few good years left!

> **Thoughts to Remember:** As you read and respond to the questions, keep in mind the seven strategies for positive aging, adapted from Robert Hill, as a guide to writing our narratives:
> 1. **Find meaning in old age.** Discover one thing each day that is meaningful and purposeful and act upon it.
> 2. **Spend time learning.** We are never too old to learn. Take classes, practice on websites that stimulate brain activity. Master a new skill.
> 3. **Use the past to cultivate wisdom by writing our narrative.** Use the questions as a guide to telling our unique story.
> 4. **Strengthen our life-span relationships.** Use resources like Facebook or emails to reconnect with the special people in our past.
> 5. **Promote growth through giving and receiving help.**
> 6. **Forgive ourselves and others.**
> 7. **Possess a grateful attitude.**

How strange we are in the world, and how presumptuous our doings! Only one response can maintain us: gratefulness for witnessing the wonder, for the gift of our unearned right to service, to adore, and to fulfill. It is gratefulness which makes the soul great.

—Rabbi Abraham Joshua Heschel

Beginning the Narrative

As we begin creating our narratives, let us visualize ourselves as artists about to create a huge landscape that represents our six-plus decades. As we create our piece of art—the landscape that speaks to our distinctiveness, our individuality over time—we begin life's picture with the lushness of a nurturing soil that forms the foundation for our healthy growth and development, a soil that grows its roots in the enriched experiences of being and interacting with the world and its people—day by day, month by month, year by year. Each of our landscapes is enhanced with new vegetation and varying terrains; with highlands of celebrations and moments of joy and lowlands that reflect our most significant losses; with deserts that represent our thirst for something new or exciting; with mountains too steep to climb yet with accomplishments we never dreamed we could achieve.

Today, we begin with an empty canvas, as yet an unpainted landscape. The exploration of our life's works will fill our canvas. You alone will identify the large and small scenes in our design, our unique qualities that best define the people we have become. As the artist, we may be struck by the intricacies of our pictures. The twists and turns are now seen from afar. Each brushstroke will be chosen with care. Images of ideas, of relationships, of career choices, of risk-taking will be revealed alongside mistakes made throughout life. The open and closed spaces—our defined boundaries—speak to feelings of safety and trust in others. This twenty-first century offers many possibilities. Stand tall and appreciate our landscapes—the ones we created. They are originals, and they define us. They are priceless. We are priceless. Take pride in handing them down to future generations as works still in progress to be appreciated, respected, and cherished over time.

This book helps to guide us as we paint that landscape. We believe in the power of revisiting the events that formed the foundation, the lessons and values of a lifetime of encounters. We believe we can share this power when we communicate the memories in our narratives. To do this best, we must first appreciate the importance of our own uniqueness. In each of us is the artist's potential to create a magnificent landscape. The hidden stories of that landscape alone become a lasting legacy: a living connection to generations.

It is with a sense of connectedness to others, like that spoken in the first lines of Helen Reddy's song "I Am Woman," that we celebrate the importance of our lives with our narratives.

> I was sitting in the Social Security office with my number in hand, thinking about this new identifiable stage in my life. Now I was a card-carrying senior citizen, entitling me to monthly checks, health-care benefits, and an AARP magazine. I couldn't quite believe that I was now a Medicare patient and could walk into a movie theater with hopes that the person in the ticket booth will think that I cannot possibly be "that age"...a certifiable senior. Quite different than the proud senior of my high school years or that of college. At that moment, one of my high school friends entered the room for the same purpose, and for the next minutes we hugged, laughed, and reminisced about the then and now, still somewhat in shock recognizing that it had been fifty years since high school graduation and we could still remember our past like yesterday. Here we were...two high school friends that do not see each other on a regular basis, fond of our past and of each other, and now feeling a special connection through our combined history and common experiences as we enter this new phase of our lives together.—GH

The questions asked in this book will assist us in developing our unique stories. We will also read the narratives from other women over sixty. The strength of multiple single voices magnifies the accomplishments of each sixty-plus woman, ensures the triumph of the twilight years, and creates a new cultural discourse on aging. Restaging aging. Age sixty-plus will no longer represent what was and is no longer but rather, and more significantly, what is and what can be.

Our life cycles are an organic whole—each period contains all the others. Levinson said it beautifully: "The developing individual is like a long-distance traveler. From time to time he changes vehicles, fellow passengers, and baggage of all kinds, but the past does not simply disappear." For the aging woman, both the past and the future are in the present.

In the next chapter, we will reflect on our early childhood experiences and the meaningful relationships that were instrumental in developing our uniqueness. As we think about the stages of development, we find ourselves in what may be euphemistically called our late adulthood. We would like to believe that we are prepared for predictable jolts: changes in health, retirement, career endings, sexual issues, and financial concerns, to name a few. Yet with these endings, there are also new beginnings, new opportunities, and a new sense of freedom. Old roles will fade away as new ones take their place. It is the selves of sixty-plus years who have the distinct pleasure of becoming the *keepers of the meaning* for our children and their children as well as for our families and other women—as we all learn to value our lives!

LIST OF QUESTIONS TO REVIEW

As a woman over sixty, what are the messages you have received from television, advertisements, magazines, and your favorite stores regarding aging? How do these messages affect your feelings about your body image, your sexuality, and/or your attitude about growing older?

What does getting older mean to you, and how does it feel?

How do you think young adults would describe your life?

What has been most challenging about the aging process? What concerns, if any, do you have about your future and aging?

PERSONAL REFLECTIONS

_____

_____

_____

_____

_____

_____

_____

_____

_____

_____

_____

_____

_____

_____

_____

_____

_____

_____

_____

_____

_____

CHAPTER 2
Our Unique Selves

*People are like stained-glass windows. They sparkle and shine
when the sun is out, but when the darkness sets in, their true
beauty is revealed only if there is light from within.*
—Elizabeth Kubler-Ross

As we begin to tell our personal stories, we may struggle to decide where to start and how much of ourselves to reveal. For many, creating our narratives will likely entail reconstructing a past buried beneath layers of hidden memories. Some of these memories we might have stashed away, thinking we would never have to go back to them. Others may even have been fodder for comic relief at regular family get-togethers throughout the years.

We three authors have been there ourselves as we unearthed our own precious memories. We experienced a flood of emotions as we began to untangle the roots of those fundamental principles that have guided us since childhood. We invite you to revisit your memories. We encourage you to awaken the "light from within", and fuel the energy to transmit the values you have embraced.

As we navigate through the last third of our lives (Erikson's generativity and identity phases), many of us will encounter an irresistible urge to find more meaning in our worlds. To have the patience to follow through, we must first believe in our own distinct worth, knowing that we have a story that is ours alone to tell and that the many lessons we have learned throughout the ages are worth repeating and sharing.

When we the authors explored our own answers to the questions in this book, we felt empowered by a renewed sense of excitement that celebrated our authenticity and individuality. Maybe this powerful exercise was possible because we were tapping into both sides of our aging brains, and that provided us with waves of insights that were more profound than ever before. Maybe it was possible because we now had time or were just more comfortable in our own skin to process it all. Nevertheless, one of the important things we learned was that to discover our uniqueness within, we had to take the plunge into our past. So let's begin!

Each of us has the potential to create an amazing personal canvas. The initial broad splashes of color on that canvas represent the artistry of our parents, grandparents, and siblings—what we know as our family of origin. Their mastery in creating images served as a lens through which we viewed the world and the world viewed us. It is the only lens we knew in our earliest years, and as we grew, it influenced many of our initial decisions about how we defined our unique selves.

During our formative years, we may often have felt ineffective in the face of the overwhelming presence of our parents, of the pressures of our social and cultural communities, and of our own internal biological needs. At this time the struggle began, pitting our DNA-defined selves against the self that mirrored the attitudes, behaviors, and strategies of our parents. Many of us emerged into young adulthood still searching for our own answers to "Who am I?" and "Where do I fit in the world?"

As we look back, some of our most basic life lessons may reflect our parents' unresolved issues. This leaves us slumbering throughout our own lives in what has been dubbed "history's unmade bed."

Once launched into the throes of adulthood, life quickly became very complicated with careers, relationships, and our new families. Many of us did not have the energy or, frankly, the inclination to tap into our personal resources and do battle with those early messages now imprinted into the very fabric of our lives.

Exploring and Defining the Self

The concept of a unique self is abstract, and defining it is not an easy task. Listen to the words of other women as they explore their uniqueness.

How do you perceive your unique self?

> Feeling authentic is when some action, some thought, or some idea is triggered from the outside and I respond with my inner core values.—Anonymous

The stories I heard from my parents about their families left behind in Europe who did not survive molded my uniqueness and my need to someway somehow make a difference in my generation. And now, as I look at the younger women so different than I was and yet so very much the same, perhaps that is what it is all about. My involvement has brought self-awareness, strength, peace of heart and mind—I did make a difference, and there is no greater reward than that.—MC

I am an aging Jewish woman who thinks of herself as a young woman with unlimited potential. When I look in the mirror, I don't respond to the reflection that is facing me.—Anonymous

I do not know who I am anymore, and I am not the person I used to be. I'm afraid if I look in the inside, I won't find anything.—Anonymous

When I was twelve or thirteen, I knew my mind always remembered. I questioned things whenever something was said. I gave things thought. I always had confidence and I could remember. I always had an answer.—AO

Each of these statements speaks to important elements of the self: one's thoughts, feelings, and perceptions. Each self is a composite of who we think we are (cognitive), how we feel about who we are (affective), and how we act based on our perceptions of who we think we are (conative).

Our cognitive self reflects our social roles and identities. We may be moms, doctors, grandmothers, coworkers, or girlfriends, or, more importantly, we may be all of them. We may define ourselves according to our traits. We may be introverts, closed, or argumentative; we may be open, honest and caring, loving and hopeful.

What inner strengths have helped to define your unique self?

My ability to keep going despite my feelings/belief of not having achieved my potential. My recognition that I am a valuable human being capable of change, understanding that some of the things that others may not like about me are actually my strengths.—GB

Being raised in England in World War II, I learned very quickly the value of life, looking at a pile of rubble and realizing this was my home and that life would never be the same again. However, I also found out that it was "not the end of the world." Harsh but true.—JO

I don't know if I have inner strengths—but for sure, I have commitment and passion, devotion, integrity, and lack of hubris. I am also focused on the goal but noncompetitive. I also like to laugh.—EH

Doing what I think is right and moral.—DG

My husband, my family, my work, and my bout with cancer. Surviving two battles with breast cancer and going on to enjoy life.—BHK

I guess my ability to cope with and handle difficult situations. —Anonymous

I listen intently when others talk to me. I am trustworthy and loyal—I keep a secret when asked of me. If someone wrongs me, I look at all the good qualities they have, and I forgive them. I believe in the golden rule. I feel I am a loving and caring human being.—JK

My strengths are some of my values: honesty, empathy, loyalty, trustworthiness, respecting friends and people, sharing, dependability, and responsible.—ER

1. Attitude—the glass half full
2. Coming back from great adversity: breast cancer and the death of my younger daughter at seventeen in an automobile accident. I have learned to deal with this on a daily basis. I think of her with every breath I take.
3. Disciplined and fair
4. Persistent
5. Good natured and warm
6. Caring and responsible

7. "Live and let live"—most of the time I live in the gray area. However, when I feel an injustice has been done or I feel I am correct in my view, I will act accordingly. But I also can listen to another point of view.

8. Deal with problems and don't run away.

9. Sense of humor

—ANONYMOUS

I think that the inner strength that has not only defined me but helped me to enjoy all the ventures I have tried is one of energy and optimism. I think that I have been blessed with a happy and optimistic nature that always works for me. I believe that strength helped me to adapt to the move that we made twenty years ago. It was not easy to think of leaving our home and community to come to Florida, but I know that I was able to adjust and find a new life here with the inner strengths that keep me going.—BC

There may be nothing more critical to the development of our psyches than the value judgments we make of ourselves. The depth and complexity of our answers to the question "How do I feel about who I am?" are a function of what we understand about the affective component of our self: our attitudes, values, beliefs, and morals. By creating daily experiences that tap into our core values and beliefs and that expand our social consciousness, we can enhance our mental and emotional well-being.

Throughout my life, I've had several professional careers that I like to believe I have excelled in. I am planning to meet with my one adult son to initiate a family foundation for the sole purpose of purchasing cochlear implant equipment to be used for profoundly hearing-impaired individuals. As a former speech therapist, it gives me great joy to share this idea with my son and have him participate with me in decision making that will make the world resound for those individuals who have lived in silence.—LWS

I like my honest self-confidence and self-respect. I like my positive attitude and gratitude for the life I enjoy. I like my curiosity about everything.—BC

I have lived through three miscarriages, metastatic cancer, the birth of a grandson who faces a difficult life, hundreds of tenuous situations, and the loss of beloved family and dear friends. Nonetheless I reach this point in my life remarkably whole and full of well-being. There is a certain freedom I feel in being older. For one thing it is too late for me to die young, and there is a certain perverse comfort in knowing that. My inner strengths astound me. Each loss, each crisis, each monster I have faced, I have met with dignity and optimism. I believe we cannot guess what our strengths are until we need to bring them forth in order to confront each challenge.—JW

Not everyone is generative, though. There are those who instead of reaching outward may dwell within themselves, suffering from persistent feelings of inertia and being less willing to develop fulfilling interpersonal relationships. Those people are at risk for impaired mental and physical well-being. To avoid feelings of anxiety and uncertainly, they buoy their sense of self by ignoring any feedback that is inconsistent with how they like to see themselves.

If you treat an individual as he is, that's all that he will be. Only if you treat him as he ought to be will he have a chance to become what he ought to be and could.—Johann Wolfgang von Goethe

Self-concept is often referred to as the reputation we have of ourselves. How satisfied we are with that self-concept colors how successfully we navigate our lives. The following scales ask you to briefly evaluate satisfaction with who you have become at this moment in time. After you have completed the scales, you can tally your scores and then turn to the end of the chapter, where there is a guide to what the score means. If we are satisfied with ourselves, we are more likely to interact positively with others, take pleasure in all of life's experiences, and feel confident in our own uniqueness.

SATISFACTION WITH LIFE SCALE (SWLS) (Diener 2009)

BELOW THERE ARE FIVE STATEMENTS THAT YOU MAY AGREE OR DISAGREE WITH. USING A SCALE FROM 1 TO 7, INDICATE YOUR AGREEMENT WITH EACH

ITEM BY PLACING THE APPROPRIATE NUMBER ON THE LINE PRECEDING THAT ITEM. PLEASE BE OPEN AND HONEST IN YOUR RESPONSE.

7—STRONGLY AGREE
6—AGREE
5—SLIGHTLY AGREE
4—NEITHER AGREE OR DISAGREE
3—SLIGHTLY DISAGREE
2—DISAGREE
1—STRONGLY DISAGREE

1 _____ IN MOST WAYS MY LIFE IS CLOSE TO THE IDEAL.
2 _____ THE CONDITIONS OF MY LIFE ARE EXCELLENT.
3 _____ I AM SATISFIED WITH MY LIFE.
4 _____ SO FAR, I HAVE GOTTEN THE THINGS I WANT IN LIFE.
5 _____ IF I COULD LIVE OVER, I WOULD CHANGE ALMOST NOTHING.

SCALE OF POSITIVE AND NEGATIVE EXPERIENCE (SPANE) (Diener et 2009)
PLEASE THINK ABOUT WHAT YOU HAVE BEEN DOING AND EXPERIENCING DURING THE LAST FOUR WEEKS. THEN REPORT HOW MUCH YOU EXERIENCED EACH OF THE FOLLOWING FEELINGS, USING THE SCALE BELOW. FOR EACH ITEM, SELECT A NUMBER FROM 1 TO 5 AND INDICATE THAT NUMBER IN THE LINE PROVIDED.

1—VERY RARELY OR NEVER
2—RARELY
3—SOMETIMES
4—OFTEN
5—VERY OFTEN OR ALWAYS

1 _____ POSITIVE	5 _____ PLEASANT	9 _____ AFRAID
2 _____ NEGATIVE	6 _____ UNPLEASANT	10 _____ JOYFUL
3 _____ GOOD	7 _____ HAPPY	11 _____ ANGRY
4 _____ BAD	8 _____ SAD	12 _____ CONTENTED

What creates that sense of uniqueness in each of us? It is such a personal question, and it may be something we try to protect for fear of being exposed.

> I had to think about the many ways I could respond to questions of my uniqueness. My first thoughts to describe myself were common words, nothing so special, that others use for their own descriptions. But it does not negate the meaning of our individuality. So it is my curiosity about life and my sense of inquisitiveness about others that have guided me. I am proud to say that I am compassionate, kind, honest, genuine, and passionate about the human condition. I appreciate my strong commitment to what I believe speaks to social justice. I become an advocate for causes that speak to me for persons who cannot speak for themselves. I truly value the power of my voice, be it in writing or speaking. I am an action-oriented person filled with energy and a desire to make a positive difference it this world. I owe a debt of gratitude to my years of aging that have afforded me the confidence to be an emotionally stronger person than I was as a young adult yet still defining myself with common words that serve as the basis for my uniqueness.—GKH

When, as individuals, do we begin crafting our unique self? Let us not forget our canvas. Our earliest defining moment is at birth. We are born into this world with a temperament: each individual's nature, or style of approaching and responding to situations. According to Gordon Allport (1961), a founding father of personality psychology, temperament is the internal weather from which our personality evolves. It is our emotional nature that embraces all the peculiarities, fluctuations, and intensities of our moods. Within months of birth, the individuality of our *personality* begins to take shape as our inherent disposition interacts with the attitudes, expressions, and behaviors taught to us by our parents and influenced as well by other cultural and environmental forces.

Here is where it gets a little complicated. When we start our life, our temperament may be similar to or different than that of our parents. If a parent is expecting a child who is outgoing, motivated, and open to new experiences and instead their little Johnny is shy, reserved, and cautious, the parent-child relationship could be challenging. The parent may place subtle pressure on Johnny to be different than he is. Yet from its earliest infancy, a child is an individual with a unique temperament and personality. It is the parents who may have to make adjustments to their own expectations to ensure their child feels secure within the protective "cocoon-like" family of origin and in sync with his own being.

The family of origin is a unit distinct from any other in its membership, culture, personality, and theme. It is within our family of origin that we are first introduced to connectedness, and if we are fortunate, from there we will be launched into a lifetime of relationships based on love, honesty, respect, and truth.

Our Family of Origin

We all grow up within some kind of family system. The twenty-first-century family, possibly different than the families we grew up in, can take many forms in terms of number and gender of adults, children, and extended relationships. Yet no matter what generation we are talking about, we all share in defining ourselves by the following parameters: circumstances of birth, age of parents and siblings, economic conditions, cultural values, and type of nurturing, discipline, and parental expectations. All these factors will have an effect on what our future will look like post childhood.

We have to agree there is no one single quality that best describes the ideal family. For most of us, the family is a social unit of individuals bonded together and aligned by our genetics and influenced by economics, individual rights and needs, religion, culture, and the natural forces of life. In order to survive and flourish, it is important for us to understand that we live within a complex social system. Imagine the many ways culture impacts our families, and yet family systems thrive with their own unique personalities.

What messages did you receive from your family that influenced your view of yourself?

> I grew up in a small town in the interior of Brazil (a chauvinist country).
> As the third of four children, I had to decide to do something different
> than my siblings. So I excelled in school. My dad, who was a special,
> loving person, thought that I was the smartest girl in the world and that
> I could be anything I wanted to be in life. I did not want to disappoint
> him, and his encouragement made me into what I am today.—NK

I grew up in Columbus, Ohio, and had a fabulous childhood, glorious teenage years. My life to date has been mostly filled with blessings. I was the oldest of two children and had parents and grandparents who were nurturing, encouraging, and beyond loving. I learned kindness from my entire family. They were considerate of others and participated in their community with their time and generosity. My mom was the "Ann Landers" of the neighborhood, and Daddy was a hardworking and generous man in the community. I always knew I could talk to my mother about anything and everything! For example, after my honeymoon, my mother asked me how I liked sex. She was open and I was fine with it. I am not sure that I was quite that open with my daughter. She preferred more privacy, and I do respect that.—SC

From my family, the message was so simple: namely, be honest and know that there is always a tomorrow. My family seemed not to be involved in the community, and yet it was from them that I learned the ethics by which I live even today.—JO

I came from a very religious home where kindness and being a good person were major themes. My father taught us that being "kosher" taught us not to demand instant gratification and to show restraint. My mother was a strong, unselfish, and extremely capable person. She worked in the business with my father, took care of our home, and gave my brother and me top priority. I remember my friend's mother in elementary school whispering in my ear, "You know, your mother sacrifices things for herself so she can give things to you." My mother made me feel safe and secure, very protected, very loved. At sixty-five, I see that one of my strengths is not having envy or jealousy. I am very conscious of my traditional past, and today I am a loyal and devoted human being.—Anonymous

My mother taught me how to be thoughtful, kind, and loving. She was a nurturer and a worrier. She taught me how to be strong and to believe in myself, which served me well as my life presented a variety of challenges. So it was my mother who conveyed many life lessons to me. I was the only daughter of four children. To say I was outnumbered would be an understatement. But I had three female cousins who were always there for me and treated me as a sister. When my life would take a difficult turn, one cousin in particular was there to set me straight again. And when things were wonderful, she celebrated with me.—RTM

My father was dedicated to improving the world around him. He was intellectual and public spirited. He did not pass opinions on people who did not have his talent or his skill. He wanted me to do the right thing always. And he wanted me to never give in to mediocrity. He told me to rewrite and rewrite and rewrite—and he was right.—EH

From my uncle: be a person of great integrity and character and all it entails.—DG

It is within our family of origin that we begin to make sense of our world. It is there we begin to define ourselves and what we can or cannot expect of others, especially those around us whose job it is to nurture, provide safety, and make sure we are fed, clothed, and taught the rules. As infants, we do not know whether our personal experiences in our home are positive or negative or how they correspond with other homes. We don't know if our parents are treating us well and giving us all the nourishment needed to love and to teach us to take pleasure in humanity. Therefore, as we summon up these memories of our past, we have little to go on other than vague recollections or clouded perceptions of our family of origin and our own level of comfort or distress.

Our Family of Origin and the Culture That Affected Us. As we begin to slowly unravel our tangled memories, it may be helpful to look back at the world as it was when we began to grow our roots and the cultural boundaries that enveloped us. *Culture* is defined as the "integrated human pattern of knowledge, belief and behavior that depends on man's capacity for learning and transmitting knowledge to succeeding generations" (*Merriam-Webster*). Now we need to consider the impact of culture on our family of origin.

Even if we were born in the United States in the forties or fifties, many of our parents may still have been haunted by the effect of the thirties, like the decline of democracies in Europe, the unsuitability of immigrant traditions, or the horrors of the Great Depression. The visions of the American Dream were replaced with the nightmare of life in desperate and unstable times. Survival was key as America transitioned from a failed private-sector economy to the "alphabet soup" of federal programs (e.g., WPA, FHA) that were destined to dominate our country for the next decade. Although the educational system was bankrupt, the arts flourished, and we saw the explosion of great American writers like Hemingway, Fitzgerald, and Steinbeck capture the lives of the times. Although some of the music spoke of hardship, people were able to escape by dancing to the Big Band sound and listening to the antics of Amos 'n Andy and George Burns and Gracie Allen on the radio.

The forties were dominated by the events of World War II. As our men went off to war, women replaced them in factories and businesses throughout the country, triggering a monumental shift from the woman's role in the home to her necessity in the workplace. The federal government reclassified jobs so that single and married women and blacks were now eligible to fill them. The status of teenagers was also advanced as they took on menial jobs to help support their families. Food, clothing, and even toys were rationed. With the arrival of the refrigerator, women were able to store vegetables and fruits cultivated in the family victory garden, and the frozen dinner was created to help working women provide quick meals for the family at the end of a tiring workday. Movies were in their glory days as the Department of Defense promoted their importance as morale and propaganda boosters.

With the end of the war, the United States and Russia became the two superpowers. After seeing the world, our enlisted men came home with a new sense of themselves and goals for a better future. Communism became an anathema, and the United States engineered the rebuilding of Europe with the Marshall Plan. Working the family farm was no longer the ideal as the GI bill allowed more capable men to seek a college education. Although women gave up their jobs to the returning soldiers, they had tasted independence. Blacks, who had served alongside whites in the armed services, no longer accepted the lesser status of the past and were empowered as the Supreme Court awarded them the right to vote. Although commercial television was launched in the midforties, radio still was the link to American news and entertainment. As the horrors of the Holocaust were exposed, Americans became sensitized to the abusive power of prejudice. There was an awakening in our cultural consciousness to the significance of human rights in the struggle for freedom and survival. The Baby Boom followed the soldiers' return, a population explosion that has dramatically affected the lives of the women over sixty of today.

With the "fabulous" fifties came peace and a growth in prosperity. Everyone was out buying goods, and jobs were being created as corporations addressed our peacetime needs. Remarkably, two out of every five jobs were now filled by women. Life expectancy for women had increased ten-plus years to age seventy-one (men to 65.5 years). The country had learned the lessons of World War II with the displacement of millions of people throughout Europe and had expanded its immigration laws by removing ethnic and racial barriers to becoming a citizen. At the historic moment when Rosa Parks refused to sit in the back of the bus, the barriers of racial segregation began to disintegrate. In 1954, the Supreme Court struck down the notion of separate but equal as unconstitutional. Yet the tone of the fifties was to be more conservative. With the rise of McCarthyism and anti-Communist sentiments, Americans quickly took to the addition of "under God" to our Pledge of Allegiance. The focus was on the family and gender roles were strictly defined. Roads were expanded to superhighways, and vacations, no matter how brief, became an integral part of family life. It was through music and the creation of rock 'n' roll that American teenagers resisted the conservatism of the time and asserted their independence. This would prove to be the harbinger of what was to come in the sixties.

The sixties signified change—change in the values, lifestyles, educational goals, and laws—as American youth, the children from the postwar baby boom, who were now teenagers and young adults, revolted against the prevailing conservative character of the country. Universities were centers of protest: marching for civil rights and marching against the draft and the war in Vietnam. It was at this time that the notion of the generation gap was first conceived. American youth were the predominant force of the sixties and because of their growing numbers became a dominating cultural power. The country was in transition: the civil rights movement, the women's movement, and the rise of the Hispanic and Native American protests altered the face of America forever. The iron fist of Communism was still poised as Americans faced off with Fidel Castro and competed with the USSR for supremacy in space. It was in the midsixties that health warnings were placed on cigarette packages and the first concerns were advanced about the relationship between our health and our environment.

This historical framework sets the backdrop for how we developed as women. It influenced our view of our parents, impacted our educational goals, and determined the setting in which we have chosen to live.

Our obsession with youthfulness had its genesis in the forties, when youth were empowered as an economic force for the benefit of their families and as many became the link between their immigrant parents and the American society. In the fifties and sixties, the numbers and influence of our youth exploded as they defined the cultural milieu of the country: its music, its political focus, its elevation of gender and racial equality. Let's not forget this as we look to our family of origin and piece together our past.

The Family of Origin and the Child's Developmental Stages. Family life throughout the animal kingdom has much in common. The universal goal is to care for and nurture the young to secure survival. With the exception of humans, the family responsibility is short lived, as maturation is rapid. But for the human family, the ties and connections that bind us last forever. If we are successful, these relationships help us to fly when the appropriate time comes.

> I grew up in a loving, middle-class apartment community in Chicago (1932), one apartment building after another with tons of kids. My brothers played baseball and football in the street. They played ball in one park that adjoined the osteopathy hospital, and between their turns at bat, they often watched the residents perform surgery on animals. Today I look back and think of these as such good, safe times. Both my parents worked; Mom ran the show as dad traveled Monday to Friday most weeks. We three kids each had house chores and were expected to share in the burden. Education was important, and college was expected. As relatives lived in other areas, neighbors were like family. At age seven, two of us had health issues, and we moved to Mobile for several years, where we lived with my grandparents, with whom we then developed a close relationship. Dad would come and visit as the job allowed. When healthier, we moved back to Chicago, so I learned early that hard work is to be respected, and I learned the importance of friendship and education and that unforeseen issues may dictate changes in one's life, then and now. We learned to adapt. My family personality was one of flexibility and hope, with appreciation of what was and what could be in the future.—BH

> I traveled a great deal and never had a real home and, for some reason, no religion either. Religion depended on my girlfriends at the

time—if one was Presbyterian, so was I. Methodist—I'm in. I spent one year attending a Catholic boarding school. When I married my husband, we belonged to a temple, but I did not attend. When we had children, I knew I must give them something to connect to—to believe in—to create a sense of belonging. I decided to teach Sunday school. I had never been in a Jewish temple. I was hired anyway, and for ten years I got up every Sunday morning, and naturally my daughters came with me. One daughter was bat mitzvahed and the other confirmed. Today both girls are married and active temple goers. Three of my grandchildren have already been bat mitzvahed. Who says you cannot teach by example!—Anonymous

The understanding of who we are as individuals is rooted today in our family of origin. As older adults, we have traversed many stages in the life cycle. We are now reaching a time when reflecting on our family's foundation can help us understand the complexities of how we arrived at age sixty-plus. Reflections may also spark our sense of fulfillment as we continue to grow older and relate to aging parents, adult children, grandchildren, and friends.

Many of us have spent our years parenting and even perhaps grandparenting. With each step, we made an effort to build a cohesive family unit and/or meaningful relationships. With each step, we have hopefully learned something of value and given back something of value. Ideally each step strengthened our core relationships in our family and the broader community. What we have learned about ourselves from these experiences will guide us to find meaning and direction in our golden years.

The life cycle can be seen as a circle: from birth through infancy, early childhood, latency, adolescence, young adulthood, middle age, and into the aging years. In each of these stages, there are tasks, lessons, and issues to confront and resolve. What we are doing in this book is looking through our adult eyes at the stages of our own development: the dilemmas we encountered along the way, and how problems and crises were resolved, as well as those that were left as challenges to work through. When we scrutinize our earliest memories, we can begin to grasp how they have framed who we are today.

As we read in chapter 1, Erik Erikson's model examines development from a life-span perspective. Curiously, often it is not until we reach later developmental stages and have the luxury of time to look back that we consider our individual timelines. Those snapshots of ourselves at various stages allow us to observe which behaviors, thoughts, and feelings we have repeatedly owned and, equally important, which aspects of our personality and temperament we have passed on to our children and grandchildren. The beauty of analyzing development from this perspective is that it permits us to explore past and present relationships with tools to rework old issues that persist.

Development is a process, and humans mature in the context of meaningful relationships and cultural influences. Earlier, we discovered that we began life at birth with the essence of our unique temperament, making us different from anyone else. The adults that surrounded us, especially our mothers (or mother figures), responded to us on the basis of our temperament and their own. But relationships are a partnership. The mother-child relationship could very well serve as the template for all later relationships, for with it comes an internal mental image of how we feel about ourselves and what our expectations are of others.

The Family of Origin and the Early Stages of Child Development. Let us take a moment to review the early stages of development. Not only may it be helpful in putting our own childhood memories into perspective, it may also give us a paradigm or framework for what we can realistically expect from the younger generations of children in our families. Although it's likely we will not remember our infant stage, we can think back to the earliest childhood memories of our relationships with our parents and siblings and other extended family members. It is remarkable what we can learn.

In Erikson's model, the first stage, occurring in infancy and through the first year of life, centers on building trust. That sense of trust is strengthened by the positive and secure relationship an infant develops with a consistent, loving caregiver, usually the mother. It is the infant's behaviors coupled with the mother's sensitivity to accurately interpret and respond to those behaviors that build trust. A secure foundation is built as the infant comes to trust Mom. If the care is predictable for the infant, then the infant will have expectations that the world will be predictable and secure. It is this sense of security in the first year of life that gives an infant hope and optimism for the future. If that sense of security is severed, trust may be eroded.

Describe the women who were most influential in shaping your life.

> I always had the feeling that Mom was going to do it. I never felt that I was in limbo. I never felt in an unsafe place. I never felt insecurity.

I always felt this big calm that my mom spread over my life and my brother's. I left Hungary when I was six years old. Up until the age of sixteen, the four of us, my mother, father, brother, and me, slept in one room. Even when we got a larger apartment, I never had a room for myself. What you do not have, you do not miss. There was always a sense of calm. I was never afraid. I had the sense of togetherness that came with my family. Even though I did not speak the language when I came to Austria, I do not have bad memories of those times. I do not have the memory that we were refugees, that we were poor. I do not have the memory of that. I know that my parents could not afford to buy me nice clothes, so my mother would sew all the clothes that I had. They were still beautiful. I never felt as though I was not a member of my group of friends. I never missed anything. All this was true even though my mom was an explosive person like I can be. But when it came to her children, she instilled peace within us. She told us that every person has a function in this world. Mine was to be a good student, to bring home good grades so I could go to a better high school and university. I never felt poor. That is the one thing that defines me to this day. When I was eighteen, for my graduation gift from high school, my parents bought me a "beautiful" dress from a store. It probably was not as beautiful as I remember it, but I remember being so excited. The fact that I had something bought in the store felt good. When I looked back, I laugh because it is so unimportant now, but at that time it must have been very important.—VB

Born the third daughter in our family eighty years ago, I was raised by a very hardworking dad who commuted to NYC five and a half days a week and by a caring, creative mom who cooked, baked, and made many of our clothes. We lived next door to our paternal grandmother, who shaped my development in my early years. She was an honor student in high school, and at graduation in 1890, she presented an essay entitled "Byways of Women's Life," in which she urged women to strive for recognition and equality—two very contemporary objectives. I still read her paper, even though its pages are yellowed and its print faded. She had a ritual. Each afternoon she took a brief nap, followed by a bath and a change into a fresh dress and crisply pressed apron. When I arrived home from school, our wonderful conversations ensued. Her influence has helped define my inner strength of humor coupled with a large serving of curiosity and an abundant love of people.—Anonymous

My mother was certainly a strong influence in shaping my character. A product of the Lower East Side of New York, without a college education, my mother was remarkable. She could quote poetry by heart—Edna St. Vincent Millay, Robert Frost, and Elizabeth Barrett Browning were her favorites. And she could launch off into reciting one of their poems with no strain. She adored nature and literature of all kinds. I learned to love those things, too. She was not at all interested in jewelry, fancy clothing, fancy hairdos, etc., and was a strong influence in that regard. I was shaped particularly by her love of our summers in Vermont as a child, as a young adult, as a mother, and, in the last years, sharing the joys of the summer there with my grown children and my grandchildren. A second woman who influenced me was Millicent McIntosh, who was the president of Barnard College when I was there. She stressed to us all that we could "do it all," that we could have both family and career. This was just on the cusp of the women's movement. I graduated in 1959, just before *The Feminine Mystique* and the rest that followed. So although I was definitely reared with the idea that marriage and family was the proper role, I also always had a strong belief that we could "do it all"!—BC

These are the women who were and are the most influential in shaping my outlook on life. Grandmother Frye, in brief, was a worker bee! Had a dozen or more pregnancies and had more of them die that those that lived due to lack of medicine. She ran a wonderful hospitable home with a huge open house on Sunday afternoons. And her breakfasts would fill this page. The bookmobile, in later years, would come by every six weeks. The simple farmhouse stairs to the attic then gained banisters from all the books she took. She acted the power of love! Mother was always learning, teaching: a scholar.—AOC

As the mother of three boys, I was always interested in hearing daughters describing their moms as their best friends. I am in awe... and I listen. I do not remember feeling that when I was spending time with my mom, but as I think about the nurturance, the unselfishness, the desire to put herself second and me first, I often ask myself, "What was I expecting from her that she did not have?" I believe the answer lies within me. I did not see her as worldly or sophisticated, someone who may have all the answers to life issues. My friends filled that void. How foolish of me when I think about it now. Now she is no longer with me. She had the essence of what a best friend is. She was present in her own way, interested in me, and proud of my life. We often sat in my kitchen, she doing the prep work for a dish, telling me stories of how she almost baked her cat, Nunny Apples. We would become hysterical with laughter. Or she'd tell about the times her piano teacher would get her twin sisters mixed up and give the lessons to the wrong one. She made herself available to me and my family at a moment's notice. I can say now that I was deeply loved by my mother, and that is a wonderful feeling. I miss her often and would love to be able to tell her that she was a wonderful friend to and for me.—GH

My mother, who was fun and sincere, and died of cancer at forty-six, leaving a void.—BHK

Growing up in a home where values were practiced daily, not just spoken about in the abstract, provided me early on with a desire to practice and refine my value system as I lived my own life. My mother served as my most important role model and mentor in this area. My father was an active visionary, and my mother's value system helped enable the dreams of both of my parents to become reality. Worldwide anti-Semitism, coupled with the establishment by Nazi Germany of concentration camps in Europe, provided the impetus for my father to take an active role in helping create the state of Israel in 1948. My mother had "the courage of her convictions" and urged my father to work actively toward creating the birth of the state of Israel regardless of obstacles or criticisms placed in his path of action. A second example where my mother's active value system worked to encourage him was to translate a dream that my visionary father had to trade a downtown Miami commercial office building for a mangrove swampland in Biscayne Bay to develop a town where South Floridians could live a quality life. For over a decade beginning in 1947, my mother worked alongside my father, developing the town of Bay Harbor Islands, which continues to be an inviting place for people who wish to live in South Florida and call it home. Women showing their "courage of convictions" can pass on their visionary values and ideals to future generations.—AB

My grandma lived with me. She was kind, sweet, and always positive. I talked with her a lot about how things were for her growing up. I felt very comfortable talking to her. She was by far the greatest influence on me to want to be like her. I have tried to model myself on the way she was. Positive—treat all people like I wanted to be treated. No matter what their status. I am very uncomfortable being mean to other people.—FR

My mother, from my earliest childhood, taught me how to be and how to always be neat despite having very little to wear, and she taught me a Jewish way of life.—AO

I realized that both having a good sense of humor and being aware of avoiding the intrusion of the follies of life have been the mainstay of both my formative years and especially now that I'm reaching eighty-eight. I emulate my mother in this respect. She left Europe at age sixteen, "schlepping" her younger brother, to seek the good life, as many Jewish girls did, in order to avoid the dangers of attacks by the Cossacks. She said she never lost a sense of the ridiculous, even though she faced many untenable situations. Since both my professional and volunteer life have been in partnership with the most involved, committed, and intelligent women who have chosen to serve their community, I find, in retrospect, that I have had my thoughts and actions molded by women almost as often as I have guided them. I also had the advantage of living and working in eleven different states. This contact with regional thinking has helped me be aware of different attitudes and to be patient with those who haven't had the benefit of a wider geographic exposure. (Although now, with all the cyberspace gadgets and TV, the world can enter our homes as often as we let it.) I most value advice I have received freely from my association with those strong women who let little deter them. This has helped me achieve what I now realize has been a most purposeful life. I'm accused of been strong-minded, and there have been days that I might have been incautious and even rash, but when I think of all those forceful women who make things happen, I know I am among them and can set an example for my four granddaughters.—TFS

My mother was not necessarily a positive influence but left messages in my head that I have lived with and that are difficult to erase. Those would be something like, "Look nice so that people will like you" or "Be a teacher so that you have something to fall back on if you have to work." I was always striving to please, but it was never enough. My mother-in-law was a very positive influence on me for her acceptance of me as I was. We had a loving and happy relationship, and she thought of me as the daughter she never had. That was the epitome of acceptance. My voice teacher in college was another wonderful influence because she had so much confidence in me— something that I lacked. She too had a great love and respect for me, and I think she saw a small bit of herself in me. One maternal aunt and two other women, friends of my mother's, had an impact on me for their unconditional show of their love for me.—ER

Of course my mother had a great influence in my life. She was a strict disciplinarian, so I did not get to know her very well. She found social graces to be very important. She was honest and caring. She was serious and made my childhood a struggle.—EP

My grandmother was a divorcee with three small daughters. After being alone for thirty years, she met and married a wonderful man whom she lived with for twenty-five years. She showed me that you should never give up and that one does not know what the future has in store.—JK

My mother gave me an interest in the nursing profession and was a loving person. My stepmother gave me life lessons and loving qualities. My sister taught me about happiness. Six special women taught me what friendship is. One sister-in-law taught me what an in-law should be.—PH

I grew up in a privileged, old-world family. Gender roles and expectations were very rigid. I broke most of the rules. Probably my way of fighting back. I didn't get a lot of encouragement, generally. I did get a lot of criticism, usually. This really impacted me negatively, I believe. Oh, I would get attention for the superficial things, how I looked, how I dressed. Never for an opinion or thought. I think it made me fearful in some ways. I still have to really push myself sometimes. I was always very close to my maternal grandmother. Luckily, I had her until I was forty-three years old. She was somewhat narcissistic and critical in her own way. But I knew she loved me. That made all the difference. My grandmother was a real lady in the old-world sense. She really taught my sister (two years younger) and me how to navigate various social situations. We often spent summers with our grandparents and had a wonderful time. My mother is a graduate of the University of Pennsylvania, College for Women '46. She was the first in the family to go to college. She liked to tell us that my grandparents sent her to school to keep her out of trouble. It was during the war, and there were a lot of soldiers and sailors floating around. I'm sure they floated around in Philadelphia as well as in New York. Anyway, because of her good education, she always read to us. She introduced my sister and me to the public library at an early age. My mom would take us to the zoo and tell us about the animals and where they came from. She always had a keen wanderlust and traveled whenever possible. So my mother gave me an inquisitiveness, a thirst for knowledge, a love of a good story, a passion for travel, a talent for cooking, and probably much more.—RE

My grandmother loved me more than anything. Her love was comforting and made me feel special. I never had a mentor.—EH

My mother. She was very dynamic and a strong woman. She was a single mom who brought up two very happy, loving daughters. She was a very successful businesswoman and a very loving and generous mother. She gave my sister and me strength and courage and taught us how to deal with difficult situations.—Anonymous

As we examine our earliest years and the half-remembered stories of important women in our lives, we can piece together our earliest childhood connections and discover the possible reasons why a complete trusting relationship might or might not have occurred.

Who were the people in your family who were most supportive of you during your childhood, and in what ways did they show their support?

I was brought up as an only child, having lost my little sister when I was only four. One would think that I would have been petted and protected, but the opposite was true. I had extraordinary parents, and their messages, both subtle and conscious, set me on the path to successful adulthood. Throughout my youth I was given great freedom. I remember vividly hearing other mothers calling out to their children at play, "Be careful," "Don't run," and so on, but never my mother. At an early age I was allowed to go, with my friends, on public transportation—buses and subways—to distant destinations. It never occurred to me that this was anything unusual until I had children of my own. Then I asked my mother, "Mom, after losing a child, and having only one, how were you able to give me such freedom?" She answered that because I was an only child, my dad and she felt that I needed to be independent in case anything happened to them. What insight! Because my parents were both very educated—my mother graduated from Hunter College, and my dad had a PhD in geology and was an oil-mining engineer—it was simply expected that I would follow in their footsteps. And so, even though I married at eighteen (after finishing two years of college), as did so many of us in those days, and had children right away, I went back to school as soon as I could and continued my education. Ultimately, I completed a master's degree and PhD in English literature and taught at FIU for twenty-three years! Perhaps the most important quality my parents endowed me with was the idea that I could do anything. Throughout my young life, they praised my accomplishments, encouraging me in everything I did. I was made to feel that, within reason, all that I wanted to do, all that I desired to do, could be done. I have lived my life on that principle. What a gift to give your child! I believe that my parents had a great and positive influence on my life. Their love, their determination to bring me up as an independent person, their expectation of my educational achievements, and their attitude that their daughter could accomplish anything helped me to become a highly confident, successful, and happy adult.—ES

My parents, grandparents, and extended family fostered an ambiance of togetherness and concern for one another. Respect, accountability, integrity, work ethic, and community service were expected character traits.—LAP

For me, I was always envious of my friends who had grandparents, aunts, uncles, and cousins close by. Our extended family lived five hundred miles away, and it was the summers at the lake or the excitement of holidays that brought me into what I sensed was a gigantic bubble of love and belonging. Maybe I loved it so much because in my eyes, my parents were also so happy and connected. The sound of their laughter was the blanket of protection that made me feel that everything was all right in the world. I didn't know that the war had taken the lives of my parents' families in Russia and Poland. At that moment the world was a promising place, and I was convinced that my family had the energy to make amazing things happen. There was an optimism…in contrast to the usual fears I had seen at home in my mom's eyes. One of my aunts was the most giving and nurturing woman. Although her accent was thick and we, along with her kids, often joked with her about her misuse of words, I knew that she would always love me and be there for me, "her beautiful blue eyes"! I was so right. After my dad died when I was fourteen, my aunt was our grounding. My aunt and uncle's house in Milwaukee was much smaller than our home, and the sleeping accommodations were always cramped. But none of that mattered, because most of my happiest memories as a teen and young adult centered on those times we spent sitting around the table at their house eating and laughing. That was the only time I heard my mother laugh during those years. I felt so safe there; I felt my mom was so safe there. There I learned about sacrifice, I learned about unselfishness, I learned about devotion to family, I learned about loving and respect. She was not educated, a refugee from Poland who had left her homeland alone and her sister behind in the death camps. She had sadness at times in her eyes, but her heart was only filled with love and devotion for all of us.—CTS

I was raised in an Orthodox Jewish home and environment. Although I did not have a father in my home, the message was that a wife obeyed her husband, took care of her children, and worked hard to do the right thing. Because I did not have a father in the home, I did not experience the roles of parents interacting with each other or the interaction with a father. I married at the age of eighteen and had my first child when I was twenty-three. I had very little guidance about how to handle being a wife and mother. I did enjoy my two children most of the time, when they were younger. When they were teenagers, both boys became difficult to parent.—NL

I remember hearing from members of my family that when I was born, my mom suffered from the "baby blues." That's what postpartum depression was called in those days. I was the first child, and no one expected my mom to be like that. There were obviously no daycare centers, so my aunts and grandma took turns taking care of me at their homes. My aunts had small children of their own, and my grandma had some health issues. My dad was a traveling salesman, so he was gone during the week. Later he told me that he would take care of me on the weekends the best he could. I am sure he was very worried about my mom. Supposedly things got better after a few months, and strangely she did not have that problem when either my brother or sister was born. I don't know for sure if those early months had anything to do with it, but I have spent much of my adult life not having much faith or trust in the world around me. I know my mom did the best she could, but it seemed that those early months set the tone in our relationship. She seemed to always have a difficult time responding to me in a consistent and loving way.—JG

Elements of trust and mistrust reappear throughout all the stages of personality development. Because of fractures in our ability to trust, we may look suspiciously at the motives of others and have difficulty in maintaining successful future adult relationships. What can be both exhilarating and life-altering is that as we reexamine our history now, we have the power to change the messages we give to ourselves, rewriting our life script to project a more positive outlook.

The second of Erikson's stages rears its head in toddlerhood. This is the stage that coincides with a child beginning to walk. With this increase in mobility and independence, the toddler moves away both physically and emotionally from the parent. The objective for the child is to develop autonomy and feelings of adequacy and self-control. Parents, by allowing their children to move away, return, and move away again, encourage independence. If parents are unable to promote the independence needed, the child may have doubts about his ability to become self-reliant. Consequently, this stage provides fertile soil for the development of self-worth.

This can be a challenging stage for parents, as they may fear independence. Possibly the parents' own unmet needs for love and security prevent them from letting go. The toddler's need to practice becoming autonomous and build a sense of will can set off power struggles that may negatively impact the parent-child relationship and create issues of control that are carried forward even into our adult life struggles.

I grew up hearing my mom telling everyone who wanted to listen that I was the most difficult child when I was two. I think my mom was worried about me because all her friends' kids were already toilet trained. She always describes those times as the war of the wills. No matter how hard she tried to cajole and bribe me for the two years, I would not give up the struggle, I guess. I imagine that many of my control issues might have had their beginnings in those early power struggles with my mom. I still do not handle arguments too well. I always need to win.—ST

I was the youngest of three children and the only girl. My mom had had a couple of miscarriages between my older brother and me. I guess I also had asthma as a small child, so my mom was really fearful about letting go of me and allowing me to have any independence. The family story is that when I would start to run, my mom would pick me up and run with me. She was afraid I would get short of breath or something. I guess it is not surprising that I felt totally dependent on my parents, even after I got married and had my own children. Even when my husband wanted to move out of town when he got a great job offer, I just couldn't even imagine what it would be like living apart from my family.—BL

Erikson's third stage begins around age three, when children develop initiative and purpose as they cultivate relationships with new adults and peers. If encouraged, this sense of initiative gives the child a positive outlook on who they are and what they can do. A positive self-image is cultivated through meaningful relationships with important adults and significant peers. By the age of five, children have a good notion of themselves and what they can achieve. If development is positive, they will move out of early childhood with a sense of trust in the world, independence to think on their own, and the initiative to learn.

The fourth stage of childhood emerges in kindergarten, or about five or six years of age. During this time, children are expanding their horizons and continuing to include relationships with adults outside the family and with their peers. This is the stage of initiative because the young child increases the capacity for investigating both his physical and social worlds. Hopefully, children learn to control their behavior and take responsibility for their actions as they develop morals and internalize rules of discipline. Behaviors and thoughts that are not consistent with learned values or cultural prohibitions bring feelings of guilt or anxiety. At this age, children begin to internalize these ideals, and because of that, they can experience a sense of confidence that allows them to have the courage to take initiative.

Socialization during this stage can either mirror initiative and a sense of competency or it can be overwhelmed by a fear of new ideas. Between the ages of six and twelve, the child's focus is on developing a sense of industry.

What events (e.g., moving, a death, peer exclusion, parental issues) from your child-hood and adolescence were significant in shaping your adult life?

I had a horrible childhood, really. My dad was very abusive to my mom and my two siblings. I tried to hide and become invisible when he started on one of his rampages when he returned home after a week on the road. It is no wonder my mom suffered from depression. But her inability to cope affected my ability to function in school. From the earliest grade, I remember sitting at my kitchen table trying desperately to figure out my homework. I would call to my mom, who was in her room glued to the TV, to ask her for help. Her response was always the same: I do not know how to help you. In school I was too shy to ask the teacher for help and too embarrassed to ask even my closest friends for fear I would be labeled dumb...even dumber than I knew everyone thought I was. Although every year the teacher would call my parents to come in for a conference, my mom and dad were one of the few who simply ignored their responsibility and did not come to school ever. I grew up thinking I was stupid, and not until I was an adult did I have the courage to go to the university. I was totally amazed that I flourished there.—SK

If I had to name one part of my life that influenced me most, I'd have to say it was summer sleep-away camp at Camp Seneca, in Pawling, NY. These were eight-week sessions at what I realize now was a truly unique camp. Because of the polio epidemic in Miami and the fact that my older brother (at age seven) was going there, my parents allowed me to go as well, after hearing me beg them (age four!) to let me go. My father had been a camper and a counselor at this camp, and I ended up going there every summer until I left for Europe for my junior year in Paris, then returning afterward, graduating from camper to junior counselor to counselor to head counselor. In later years, my own children became the first third-generation campers at Seneca. What made this camp special was its emphasis on character development. We lived by the "seven Ss"—spirit, sportsmanship, service, sisterhood, skills, sincerity, and squaw character. (The squaws were inductees into the honor society for the older girls, membership in which was highly coveted.) There also was an emphasis on leadership, creativity, and of course teamwork—all of which gave me a solid background for adulthood.—TG

I arrived in Miami in 1965 with my mother. I was an only child, and my father had died the year prior to our departure from Cuba. Most of our relatives and friends were leaving the country due to the revolution. While in Cuba, I graduated from the Pre-University Institute and also as a professor of piano and theory of music from the National Conservatory of Music of Havana. In the United States, I learned that I must improve my knowledge of the English language and started attending classes in the language center. My wish was to continue in the music field, but it was not possible at this time due to the high cost of this career in the United States. I also enrolled in high school, and with big sacrifice, I graduated high school. One day, one of my cousins told me about a part-time job. The hours were good, so I went for an interview, and they hired me. This was my first job in the United States, and I was thrilled. But at the same time I was afraid. Finally the entire family was able to come from Cuba, and we reunited again. One day, I read an ad in the *Miami Herald* for a position at a bank. I went for an interview and obtained the position. I was delighted to have this new job and was ready to give it my best. I worked very hard because I knew this was necessary for my advancement. I started as a clerk but advanced to the position of assistant vice-president. I had the privilege of working with the most respectful and knowledgeable bankers who taught me day after day, and this I can say was a fantastic journey of learning that lasted twenty-eight consecutive years. After forty-five years of work, I thank G-d for keeping me on his land, allowing me to learn about different fields, people, and experiences, all without regrets and only with memories that helped me through this beautiful journey that is life. I expected to live in a free country like the United States of America. With freedom and justice for all. Obey the laws and respect this with profound gratitude to the ones that could not live in freedom. G-d bless.—MV

In my early years, I was very ill and learned that life can be very threatening. I learned to find strength with the help of fine parents, friends, and doctors who cared.—MB

The events that shaped my life were dictated by my fifty-year marriage to a great individual and fine artist and also by cracking the executive and managerial ceiling in international banking in the 1960s.—JAL

The Holocaust. What hate can do to people and how not to judge a whole community or whole nations for their sins.—AO

I was well provided for as a child, without financial worries. I had a lot of positive reinforcements for whatever I was trying to do. Enjoying vacations as a family. I was fortunate to be able to enjoy many advantages. I learned that I was a good team player and enjoyed it. My father always put my brother and me first. He always complimented me no matter how I did. Getting married early (at twenty years old) forced me and my husband to take responsibility for starting a family. I was no longer depending on my father financially or emotionally. I was fortunate to find a man who shared my dreams, goals, and high conscience and who was willing to live within our means. My husband would be the breadwinner, and I would stay at home and raise the kids. My senior yearbook said that I "radiated sunshine" with my positive and cheerful personality. My best friend in high school wrote this in my senior yearbook: "You are the type of person good things happen to..." Having a positive attitude has always helped me.—FR

I was the only child/daughter of two older immigrant parents from Belorussia who arrived before 1920. Both parents worked, and I was a "latchkey" kid at seven to eight years old who lived in a beach community that was deserted during the nonsummer months. Although my parents were very devoted and loving to me, they overestimated my ability, and as a result, I was unsupervised during some frightening times. I walked from the bus stop alone, passing the derelicts, who were called hoboes then, and I'd wave to an imaginary parent so these scary men would not approach me. I also was able to protect myself and escape other dangers. I know my parents did their best, and in the long run, I was grateful not to have early financial dilemmas and other challenges to meet. That all fast-forwarded me to have healthy fears, be sure there are definitely no bogeymen, and become confident but shy. They instilled an adult behavior in me. I now feel compassion for my parents, whose hands were tied, and very grateful for the many sacrifices they made on my behalf.—Anonymous

A nun in grade school used to have students stand in the front of the room and answer questions. Sometimes she allowed us to stay seated, and we were supposed to remember the questions, recite the questions, and respond. I was not able to do it, and I remember the first time she gave us a written test. I felt that she did that for me, recognizing that I was afraid to talk, not that I did not know the information. It meant a lot and to this day helps me to see beyond reactions. My mother? I loved her but did not like her to hold me—I would become stiff. I never understood my reaction. As an adult, after her death, I became aware that the smell of smoke nauseated me and realized that the reason I pulled away from her was because of how she smelled—she was a heavy smoker. I wish I had realized that prior to her death because I would have told her. Female colleagues have influenced me simply by positive interactions.—GB

Macro: John Kennedy's death had such a big impact—of unexpected sadness and lack of control. And the Vietnam War...Micro: my father's illness when I was twenty-one—both the war and my dad's illness made me change my expectations about my future.—EH

My father passed away when I was nine, and my mother had to care for four children. We had our own home, but money was always scarce. I felt quite privileged that I was chosen to spend a year in the United States with a family in Michigan as a high school foreign-exchange student in a program called American Field Service. We could not afford the costs, but the sponsoring school raised the money for my scholarship in 1967. I spent a phenomenal year with a wonderful family and learned so much about another culture, other ways of thinking, respect for freedom, and in some way empowerment of being a woman. After my return, I started studying with a friend of mine who had also studied in the United States under the same program. Taking stock of our situation, we realized that I was good in biology, she was good in physics, and we were about the same in English and chemistry. I moved to her house for two months, and we studied methodically for the entrance exams from 8:00 p.m. to midnight, from 2:00 to 6:00 p.m., and from 8:00 a.m. to noon. The rest of the time we slept, ate, bathed, and even did one hour of exercising listening to the *Abbey Road* and *Sgt. Pepper's Lonely Hearts Club Band* albums. I went home on weekends for a few hours to get clean clothes and bring in my laundry. I remember, many times, my mother would say that what I was doing was a waste of time. I was a girl and would not get into medical school. It was pretty grueling studying, but we stuck to it. The entrance exams took several days. Since we had studied together, we tended to answer the questions and solve the problems the same way. So the professors thought we were cheating and separated us, sitting us in different corners of this indoor football arena where seven hundred students took the tests. We passed in seventh and fourth place. So even though I did not get a direct message from anyone, I think my independence from my family at age seventeen, my own strong personality, my confidence in myself, the regular study hours, and the fact that G-d endowed me with some intelligence were all forces that allowed me to get into medical school, finish it, and eventually come to the United States for my medical training. And my stubbornness helped, because while my mother thought I should have left medical school to "the boys," I knew that I could be as good as they were.—NK

My mother's lack of self-worth. I think that was common in the women of her generation. She defined herself by what she wore, how she looked, and how she perceived what others thought of her. She was very emotionally needy. It was difficult as a child to constantly have to tell her how wonderful she looked and how wonderful she did things.—Anonymous

What important lessons have you learned from the mistakes you or others important to you have made?

My mother was a dear. Her philosophy was "turn the other cheek," which I adhered to for far too long. After my decision to leave a humiliating marriage, I realized that my mother had endured a similar relationship with my father. Actually, I'd guessed it before my first marriage. I confronted my father the night before my first wedding. I asked him if he had ever had any affairs. He said, "Shall we say, I have known other women. Don't ever let yourself go." I was twenty-one years old—I said "You *bastard*! And you blame *my mother* for your flaws?" The next day he walked me down the aisle. I thought no more about it until I admitted the state of my own marriage. No more turning the other cheek. I was getting dizzy—literally and figuratively! Early messages were to be faithful, meaning go to church weekly, trust the clergy and teachings. I tried to believe it all, hook, line, and sinker, until I discovered my religious father's hypocrisies and those of the family minister. Now Buddhism speaks to me deeply. Studying it even on an informal basis brings me great peace and comfort.—MP

I think the lesson I have learned is that each person must take responsibility for himself, be accountable, and learn life by experiences. I continue to support and love but encourage independence.—CS

I learned to become stronger in my opinions.—BHK

One of my young friends was recently diagnosed with cancer. In a spiritual group meeting, I was overtaken by her statements of thankfulness and blessings each day. I then realized that I might have moved from a home I loved, but it was the memories made in the home I could not let go of. I needed to reframe a new perspective of my new home and all of its possibilities.—HKH

One of the most important lessons I learned in my life was in observing my mother-in-law as she was dying of breast cancer. Even though my relationship with her was not the best, I could not help but be really moved by her courage and her dignity. She was not a complainer. She was a person who wanted everyone to have the space to do their own thing. Perhaps because I misinterpreted that, I did not give her the time or the respect someone else might have gotten who was more demanding (i.e., like my mother). Therefore, I have always had my regrets that I wasn't more intuitive and understanding of who she was. I was too busy thinking about who I was and my needs and never really listened or thought about her needs. For that I feel very sad.—CTS

I learned that it is not offensive to say no when you really do not want to do something. Saying yes to please creates major anxiety!—Anonymous

Lessons learned from miscalculations, errors, and omissions were: don't assume anything, do not take anyone for granted, and always apologize for offenses.—Anonymous

Not enough appreciation for the kindness given me in times of stress.—AO

All of life is a learning process. I like to think that I did the best I knew how with the knowledge and experience I had at the time. So although I have had disappointments and pain from death, divorce, and other setbacks, I think I have become a more tolerant, accepting person. Also I try to look for the positive in situations and people. That helps a lot in making life more enjoyable.—NL

I try to see the consequences of my mistakes. Mistakes are hard, if not impossible, to undo. For example, dropping out of my PhD program just before completing it was a major mistake, though I understand what motivated me to leave the program. I try not to allow myself to have the same reactions in other situations. Bad relationships? To recognize red flags prior to entering a relationship as well as during it, and to respond, not to react. One behavior pattern that I feel is a mistake is to gossip or to partake in "he said, she did" stories with coworkers, friends, or neighbors. I feel that spreading negative tidbits is gossip, which I don't like. I attempt to focus on what can be learned from the event. My mistakes have taught me that mistakes happen; that they do not end situations but offer opportunities to change; that it is okay to express and be yourself; that you have to keep trying to evolve, even if you find that there are little breaks along the way.—GB

Lessons learned from mistakes. There have been mistakes too numerous to count, but from some of them I've learned that I cannot change what happened. That's particularly hard as it is still difficult to remove the guilt associated with errors. However, since there is nothing I can do about those situations, I have to move on. I have also learned that I cannot correct the mistakes my kids make; they have to do that on their own.—ER

The most important lessons that I have learned are that forgiveness is a gift to oneself and to society. The fewer angry folks we have walking around, the more positive and healthy the walkers. "It is as it is AND it becomes what you make of it." The choice is always yours. You can accept it—you can get over it—you can make changes within yourself—you can be happy—you can be grateful! Very little is *really* important. Stereotypes and generalizations usually offend someone, so they ought to be discouraged and/or ignored. Most importantly—it is not about me!—MP

Aaah. Thank goodness not too many major errors. Friendships with the wrong people? Giving too much? Those are mistakes I am willing to make again. Some mistakes are okay with me. And it is really important to always remember how imperfect people are, but that's free will. Still, being nice can never be evil.—EH

Be aware going into a situation so you do not have to figure how to get out.—DG

I think that although I enjoyed all the things that I did in my life, I did make a mistake in not pursuing a graduate degree in something that could have provided a professional path that I would have enjoyed. The year before we were married, I taught in a middle school on the Lower East Side. In 1960, that was quite an experience. At that time there was a television program call *East Side, West Side* about life in the city. My cousin was friends with the producer of the show, and he needed some advice on one of the programs that was set in a school. He needed to know "how the kids spoke," "what they said," "how they behaved," etc., and he hired me to help write the scenes. It was really fun to work on. About two years later, when my oldest son was a baby, he called me to see if I could work on another show in the same capacity. But the hours were crazy. They could run late. We lived in the suburban New Jersey, and the job was in the city. It seemed *impossible*, and I did not even consider it. Of course, I hadn't read *The Feminine Mystique* yet. There really were not any "nannies," and the thought of leaving the baby with a babysitter and making my husband be in charge if I had to work late—it just wasn't anything I could even consider. That being said, I still feel it was a mistake not to have a "profession."—BC

The Family of Origin and the Adolescent Stage of Development. Between the ages of twelve and eighteen, children face the challenge of finding an identity. Some researchers have concluded that this is a stage that can be divided into two phases on the continuum of maturation: early adolescence (twelve to eighteen years) and later adolescence (eighteen to twenty-four years). In early adolescence, there is a search for a group identity with peers that helps the teen ward off a sense of alienation.

We were very different than today's adolescents. We were in a beautiful new school, and we felt safe and cared for. Families were not so scattered over the United States, and with them and our community, we were free to experience independence. No fear of walking alone to a friend's house or carrying your record player. Dysfunctional wasn't known to us till we got much older and looked back on our family situations. We were happy, good girls whose friendship meant the world to us and have held the test of time.—IWG

In early adolescence, puberty, with its rapid physical changes, is surfacing. Raging hormones create a new sexual awakening and, along with it, possible anxiety and confusion.

Later adolescence brings with it the crisis of individual identity and often identity confusion as well. The passage through adolescence is fraught with the pressure to complete the journey of independence begun in toddlerhood, and to emerge self-sufficient and yet not isolated from a social context. During this phase, young adults make critical life-altering decisions with regard to their educational goals, careers, and love relationships.

While adolescence has often been described as a period of strong emotional upheaval (attempting to resolve the conflict and confusion between dependence and independence), it can also be a time of excitement, new experiences, and new insights. Although one's peer group and intimate relationships may often monopolize an adolescent's thoughts and motivations, they do not necessarily trigger a complete break with the family of origin. Strong family support and understanding is critical to guide the adolescent through this stage successfully. Economic pressures have changed how young adults move toward independence today, as they may no longer be able to afford to live on their own.

As young women, our relationship with our core family was adjusted as we transitioned into adulthood and began to grapple with how we would fashion our own uniqueness and yet succeed in building strong, intimate relationships. The next chapter will speak specifically to that stage in our lives.

The Family of Origin and Gender. Beyond its impact on how we evolve throughout the stages of development, the family of origin also influences how we define ourselves as women. Those of us growing up in the forties, fifties, and sixties did so with a set of rules and expectations from our families of origin regarding achievement that were quite different from women of later generations. Many women of our generation accomplished great heights despite the fact that we were not raised to assume the role of career women. The norm of the day was to aspire to be a wife and a mother. College, if possible, was a stopgap measure until we found the man of our dreams!

Most of us were socialized to be nurturing mothers and dedicated wives. Despite all those messages, women now over sixty were instrumental in changing the face of gender roles through feminist activism and actual competency in their careers. As we look back at our own personal histories, we can see how traditional as well as changing gender roles played themselves out in our families of origin and how they shaped our goals and aspirations.

> When I was in college, I had no idea about becoming a career woman. Most of the girls I knew opted for teaching, nursing, or social work. It was a very small number who aspired to become businesswomen, doctors, or lawyers. Teaching was a career where women could actualize their goals for work and homemaking. It was consistent with the goal of helping others, being a good wife and mother. So I chose it. I'm not sorry, but at the time the choices were limited. Maybe I would have been an archeologist or something. The truth is, I never thought beyond the limits society imposed.—MCL

Gender is a primary factor that influences the contours of our family of origin. Societal views of gender have changed dramatically over the last forty years and, with that, an apparent growing sense of equality among the sexes. Yet boys and girls are still treated differently within family boundaries. These differences begin when parents lovingly look at their newborn girl and describe her with adjectives such as adorable, petite, and sweet, while their baby boy is often portrayed as tough, athletic, and resilient. Although some researchers have found that fathers are more eager to share in caregiving activities for their crown prince, both moms and dads have a more affectionate relationship with their baby girls. Thus, as females, we are programmed at birth for the feminine role. When we create our own families, the parent-daughter relationship remains the strongest as the daughter is encouraged to stay close and emulate her mother. On the other hand, sons are encouraged in their efforts to be resilient and self-supporting.

As a child, what were your dreams about your future, and were those dreams fulfilled?

> As a child, I loved dancing. My parents sent me and my brother to dancing school. He was a natural talent. I got the reputation as a "klutz." Since my mom thought it was a waste for me to continue, we were both removed from dancing. So forever, until this very day, I think of myself

according to those early messages and wonder why she just wouldn't let me think I could do it.—MCL

I came to the United States after completing two years (of the usual six years) in medical school in Brazil. When I arrived in Philadelphia, I could barely speak or understand English. My high school English had been very basic, and I felt like a deaf-mute person must feel. But my dream of becoming a doctor was so strong that nothing could deter me from it. Six years after arriving in the United States, I graduated from an Ivy League medical school, the University of Pennsylvania. I am convinced that the American dream is real and anyone with enough effort and self-esteem can achieve it.—NK

The Family of Origin and Sibling Order. Birth order has been known to have an effect on both the personality and behavior of children.

What was your birth order within your family, and what impact did that have on your relationship with other family members?

My older sister was always in charge, and to this day, when she speaks to people, she often is aggressive and discounting. When I am around, I can feel my face beginning to flush. I begin to find it hard to speak coherently. My body retreats and my voice begins to *fade*. I feel *insignificant*. After the confrontation, I do not like how I was silent and how it brought me back to my childhood, when I was taught not to answer back. I got a lot of points for doing what I was told. I only felt comfortable pleasing and mollifying. I realized that I was agreeing by remaining silent. My body language screamed that I was helpless and that I felt worthless. Many days I hated my sister, and even today we have a very distant relationship.—SP

Parents and family units respond differently to the order and circumstances of each child's birth, and that response profoundly influences personal development. For most families, the birth of the first child is a monumental event. As preparations are made for the baby's arrival, everything about parenting is new. The doting parents may put all their energy into making sure that the child is the recipient of everything they can possibly give. The expectation that this child will rule as the center of the universe is set, and Mom and Dad's anxieties about being inexperienced parents factor into their heightened tension and intense dedication as they negotiate the uncharted waters of parenthood. No doubt mothers spend more time feeding and nurturing the firstborn. Then the next child arrives. Not surprisingly, that child will not experience the oldest child's totality of attention but is likely to adapt more easily to established family patterns. In the hierarchy established by birth order, the firstborn appears to wield more power and dominance within the family, while the other siblings are acculturated to develop the interpersonal skills that help them build more successful peer relationships in the future.

The Family of Origin and How We Learn to Communicate. We know from our own histories that growing a healthy family is one of the most difficult jobs we have as parents. No matter what the configuration of the family, our first acquisition of language, values, behaviors, rules, and socialization comes from our family. A healthy family provides a loving atmosphere where every family member is valued and communication is open, honest, clear, and direct. By the time we are merely a few years old, we have already experienced many thousands of interactions through the process of communication. As unique individuals with unique temperaments and personalities, we cultivate our own interpersonal style based on how we communicate with others.

Virginia Satir, a celebrated family therapist, wrote that communication is the single most significant factor determining the success of relationships. We depend on our communication skills to manage our lives: when we seek to belong, when we develop intimacy, when we problem solve, when we make decisions. Our family of origin was the proving ground where, early on, we learned from observing the many styles of communication around us.

What we learned might have helped us or gotten in the way of our connectedness to our families, friends, and significant others. Through language, were we groomed to be the keepers of our family's secrets? Were we expected to be respectful of our elders at all times? Were we taught to share our feelings? To say, "I love you"? As we read what other women have to say about their styles of communication, we can ask ourselves if we hear our own voice in their words.

> The earliest sounds of my aunt and my mother arguing with each
> other have stuck with me my entire life. I can remember many

conversations where my mom accused my aunt of not being a good sister. It was obvious that she did not take into consideration how my aunt felt. She would berate her and say, "You never even call me to ask if I am free. Don't call yourself a good sister if you never make time for me. I feel like I am the only one working on our relationship. I always include you in everything." I find even today, when anyone in my family or any of my friends play the blame game, I shut down.—VJ

My sister was an incredible human being. She was probably one of the smartest people I ever met. She was knowledgeable about everything. Yet when it came to talking about her deepest feelings, I always felt that she was reticent to share. I was always a big sharer and tried to get her to open up about her feelings. It wasn't until I was much older that I realized that she could not let go emotionally because she would be too vulnerable and she needed to be in control.—FE

We can all recognize some of ourselves or others whom we love in these women's voices. It is not uncommon for patterns of communication to become embedded in how we relate to others, as oftentimes we mirror early memories of our own family dialogues. Over time, we gradually begin to distinguish which patterns no longer work for us, which bad habits deserve to be discarded. It is an endless reformulation of our communication style as we adapt and grow. For example, if SP could only have recognized that if she capitalized on her ability to be sensitive, caring, loving, and empathic, she would not have felt threatened by her sister's aggressiveness. If VJ's aunt could have been given enough support to feel comfortable in voicing her own defense, or if FE could have addressed her own feelings openly and then spoken directly to her sister's feelings, how different their connectedness would have been. Each time we speak, we are expressing our unique selves. If we value our connection to others, we become aware that the sending and receiving of messages is an art, and we must be mindful of our words and the way we convey them.

The journey back into our childhoods, beginning at the time of our birth into our family of origin, can provide some insight into the development of our personalities. As we examine our personal growth as a unique being, we are provided an opportunity to make sense of our development and to understand how past issues can lead to today's unfinished business. Some memories we recapture might have been life changers, such as an early marriage or early parenting, choices of careers, etc. Each memory may close some doors and open others.

While everything we have written may be true in a theoretical sense, it is difficult to predict absolutes about any individual's personal trajectory from childhood. Nevertheless, it is extremely helpful to examine our own families of origin and explore how gender, birth order, and communication styles have impacted who we became and how we coped as we matured into adulthood. Looking back allows us the time to reflect on our significant life events. What we choose to remember is as significant as the event itself. There is no purpose in conjuring up the past if it does not serve us for the future. While we cannot rewrite our history, we can try to use it as a catalyst to influence our future experiences, relationships, and the legacies we attempt to write.

Thoughts To Remember: 8 Ways in which we discover what makes each of us unique, distinctive and exceptional.

1. Identify who we think we are today and how we feel about who we have become.
2. Acknowledge the most significant messages that guided our life and have the courage to discard those that no longer are beneficial to our well-being.
3. Explore the skills we have developed over our lifetime and those hidden skills that we may not have tapped into as of yet.
4. Emphasize those qualities within us that highlight the most positive sense of self.
5. Let go of any negative family baggage and assume responsibility for creating our own landscape of life.
6. Be mindful of the "woman" within us and capitalize on the power that has been afforded to women in the 21st century.
7. Create daily activities that represent our core values and expand our sense of connectedness to the world around us.
8. Appreciate the qualities within each of us that make us unique, distinctive and exceptional.

For those of us hung up on the cultural dialogue on aging, we may not appreciate the multitude of choices we still have that can positively affect our years to come. We may still have some difficulty reconciling the early influences of our family of origin with how we approach relationships in the present. We may be victims of early messages and patterns of behavior from childhood we cannot seem to abandon. Allow the narratives women shared to be a vehicle for examining and understanding ourselves within the context of our parents, our childhood, and the early relationships we created. Consider the eight ways to discover what makes us unique, and allow what we discover to be an incentive for continuing to strengthen our most intimate relationships with partners (chapter 3, "When Love Beckons"), children, grandchildren (chapter 4, "Now Our Children Are Grown"), and/or our female friends (chapter 5, "The Richness of Sisterhood"). We can begin writing our living legacies here as we acknowledge our past and how our sense of uniqueness has been sown. The value of the lessons learned is immeasurable.

Understanding Our Scores on the Satisfaction with Life Scale (SWLS):

1. First total the score given for each question.
2. Read the explanation given regarding the scores.

30–35: Very high score—highly satisfied

If we scored in this range, we are loving our lives and have positive feelings about how our lives are going. We recognize that nothing is perfect and that our lives are as good as we can possibly expect. We are not complacent, and it is likely that welcoming growth and accepting challenges is a part of our nature and why most aspects of our life are going well.

25–29: High score

If we scored in this range, things are good, and we are mostly satisfied with our life. Like the highly satisfied, growth and challenge continue to make us feel good about the way our life is going. We may be motivated by those things that we need to change.

20–24: Average score

If we scored in this range, we are likely to be satisfied in some areas, and there may be some areas that we would like to improve. All of that is quite normal. Those of us scoring in this area are likely to want to score higher and to make some life changes.

15–19: Slightly below average

If we scored in this range, it is likely that we may have a few areas in our lives that are not going well, and they present a more significant problem for us. This score might help us be motivated to make some changes. Although feeling this way at any given time is quite normal, if we see that we feel dissatisfaction across many areas of our lives, we may want to sit back and reflect on how we can improve our feeling. Being dissatisfied in a number of areas can be a distraction and make us feel unhappy.

10–14: Dissatisfied

If we scored in this range, we may be very dissatisfied with our lives. Sometimes our dissatisfaction can have to do with a recent event (a death, divorce, or illness), and over time a feeling of higher satisfaction will return. If the feeling of dissatisfaction is chronic, a change in attitude, patterns of thinking, and activities is in order. Getting guidance to move in a more positive direction can be extremely helpful.

5–9: Extremely dissatisfied
If we scored in this range, we are likely to be extremely unhappy with our lives. Again, it could be in response to some bad event. If the problem has some underlying cause, like addiction, alcoholism, chronic depression, it would be helpful to seek guidance from a friend, a member of the clergy, or a helping professional. This dissatisfaction with life may prove to be a distraction and make it difficult to manage our lives on a daily basis.

Understanding Our Scores on the Scale of Positive and Negative Experience (SPANE)

Positive Feeling Characteristics: Positive, good, pleasant, happy, joyful and content

Add all these scores, with 6 being the lowest positive feeling and 30 being the highest positive feeling

Negative Feeling Characteristics: Negative, bad, unpleasant, sad, afraid, and angry

Add all these scores, with 6 being the lowest negative feeling and 30 being the highest negative feeling

Affect Balance: The negative feelings score then is subtracted from the positive feelings score to give you a score than measures your affect—your feelings about your life.

The score can range from -24 (unhappiest possible) to 24 (highest affect balance possible). Those of us who score 24 rarely or never experience any negative feelings and are very often or always positive.

These scores can give us good data about ourselves that we may want to stop and reflect upon. They give us some fundamental information about who we are as unique individuals and why we respond to life in the way we do.

LIST OF QUESTIONS TO REVIEW

How do you perceive your unique self?

What inner strengths have helped to define your unique self?

What messages did you receive from your family that influenced your view of yourself?

Describe the women who were most influential in shaping your life.

Who were the people in your family most supportive of you during your childhood, and in what ways did they show their support?

What events (e.g., moving, a death, peer exclusion, parental issues) from your childhood and adolescence were significant in shaping your adult life?

What important lessons have you learned from the mistakes you or others important to you have made?

As a child, what were your dreams about your future, and were those dreams fulfilled?

What was your birth order within your family, and what impact did that have on your relationships with other family members?

PERSONAL REFLECTIONS

_____

_____

_____

_____

_____

_____

_____

_____

_____

CHAPTER 3
When Love Beckons

When love beckons to you, follow him
Though his ways are hard and steep.
And when his wings enfold you yield to him,
Though the sword hidden among his pinions may wound you.
—THE PROPHET, BY KAHIL GIBRAN

And don't be frightened; you can always change your mind.
I know: I've had four careers and three husbands!
—NORA EPHRON

Growing from Adolescence to Young Adulthood

The post–World War II fifties and sixties served as the backdrop for many of our adolescent years. The country was hopeful as our parents recovered from the horrors of a devastating Depression and world war and attempted to offer us a more peaceful and less complicated life. Nevertheless, they could not control for the challenges faced by all generations: the emotional upheaval that accompanies adolescence and young adulthood. During our adolescent years, hormones raged as our need to take flight as independent adults often proved to be the wedge that separated us from parents who were not always willing to let go.

In every generation, parents and teens have battled over what is the appropriate level of independence to strive toward, over the ideal balance to strike between internal and external messages concerning adult life. Throughout our adolescent years, when oftentimes we were bewildered by the onslaught of social, psychological, and biological changes, our parents could be relentless—questioning us on the benefit of our friendships, on the sincerity of our commitment to learning, and on the selection of our ever-fluctuating love interests.

> Maybe I was more surprised than I should have been when I discovered just how universal the issues of adolescence are—how each generation of teens and their parents face the same conflicts, albeit each with slightly different window dressing. As a freshman in high school, I was left at home with a babysitter when my parents went to visit my sister at college for her sorority's parents' weekend. I was given strict orders to stay at home and *no parties*! I interpreted that to mean no boys at the house, so when a group of my girlfriends decided to spend the night, I never thought I was doing anything wrong. We were all sitting in the living room doing what teenage girls did when the last friend to arrive came rushing through the front door, bounded down the few small steps to our living room, and crashed down on the couch— breaking the fragile leg that supported the rose-colored Baker couch that framed the back wall. There was silence. Although I was quick to report the damage to my parents, I spent the next six weeks grounded. Fast-forward nearly thirty years. My husband and I were out of town attending the wedding of a friend's child. My college-aged son and his girlfriend were staying with my sixteen-year-old daughter. Knowing that she had spent the day with friends at a concert, I called to make sure she had arrived home safely. She was definitely safe at home but "unable" to come to the phone to talk. The times were different, but our motivation to test the boundaries of adulthood was no different. And neither was the punishment!—CTS

Throughout generations, parents have felt emboldened by imposing controls, convinced those controls insured their children's protection from the evils of the world. Similar to what happens today, their teens fought against being shackled by a set of rules they no longer felt was applicable to them. Inevitable conflict. Historical conflict. No quick fixes.

More than one hundred years ago, G. Stanley Hall wrote what continues to be a seminal work, *Adolescence*. Although more contemporary psychologists have tweaked and infused the world of modernity into his basic principles, many of the findings from his research are still universally accepted. He began by describing the storm and stress that Erikson spoke about later as oscillating thoughts and feelings—vacillating between "humility/conceit, goodness/temptation, and happiness/sadness." For Hall, there were certain characteristics that were universal among adolescents between twelve and eighteen. A love of novel and intense sensations is one that is very familiar to us all. We can hardly forget how we felt the first time the boy we were hoping would call asked us to the school dance.

> As strange as it sounds as I am repeating this, I can remember my feelings so vividly. It has remained as one of the few memories I have of those years. There was one boy who I had the hugest crush on. I thought he was so cute and so smart. Every time he looked my way, I wondered how he felt about me. It was after a huge snow, and we were all acting silly outside a friend's house after school, dodging snowballs. He came up from behind and stuck a huge handful of snow in my face. That convinced me he really cared. We were so innocent, and it took so little to make us feel connected.—MCL

Our sensations, both pleasure and pain, were intensified at this time. Craving that intensity, we might have been more susceptible to risk-taking behavior. Although for us the risks might not have been fraught with the consequences of today's dangers—drugs and sexually transmitted diseases, to name just two—our feelings were equally strong.

Erikson described this time in adolescence as the "Crisis of Identity vs. Identity Confusion": the ongoing struggle between creating our unique selves and our concern that our uniqueness will be acceptable to others our age and, of course, our parents! If we could not see our way clear to balance those two, we might well have felt socially disconnected. We might have lost confidence in our ability to fit in. If we could not uncover inner resources that allowed us to excel as independent individuals, we might have become dependent on others for our happiness.

What have you learned from your adolescence that has influenced your growth as a woman?

> Is it possible to take a sanguine look back to one's adolescent self? I'm not so sure. I can vividly recall the warmth and laughter of good friends, but as an adult, the essence of true friendship is still with

me. If it weren't, would I remember it so well? I can revive the thrill of starting a new class, meeting new teachers, and opening new books while at the same time relive my anxieties associated with a school large enough to have "up" and "down" staircases. My adult self's experiences are similar. I may indulge myself with travel and learning, but noise and crowds still unnerve me. To my adolescent self, I can relate and I'm comfortable with that. But I'm not so sure that I can look back at me then without the scrim of having been a mother. I caught on to my mother's insecurities when I had two adolescent daughters of my own. I'm discomfited by the sight of my adolescent self pushing boundaries laid out by a beautiful, intelligent young woman fearful of the paths her firstborn might take. I know now that she needn't have been fearful. I followed rules, but her lack of insight into that made for a cantankerous child (me) and colors my memories of who I was, and would have liked to have been, in my teens. Digging through the bits and pieces of my adolescent self has been a learning adventure, too. It has reminded me to be watchful of my *grandmother* self, whose work is not done. Her job is to cull and transform lessons learned into wisdom. May such wisdom enrich the lives of her/my three adolescents-to-be.—TRS

When I turned twelve, I began menstruation and was totally developed as a woman. I started junior high school and found that a lot of boys wanted to carry my books home. In those days we walked to school. In high school I was very popular. Sometimes I had two dates on the same day. It seemed like I dated millions of guys. I didn't like any of them that much. One boy took two buses to come to my house. I had no idea the sexual power I had over boys. Most of high school I had one significant boyfriend, which was an exclusive relationship. He was a twin. When he went off to college, we both dated. I went to his college prom, which was the first time I ever flew on an airplane. It was extremely exciting. He was an athlete and was on all the teams. He was crazy about me. When he went off to college, I didn't want to wait for him. I was having too much fun. In those days we "necked" a lot but nothing more. We were warned by our parents about sex and unwanted pregnancy. My mother was worried about sex but didn't discuss it. Somehow it was communicated to me that you just don't do it. My mother never told me anything about sex, but I had two older sisters who did. My friends and I had lots of parties, and we all went out together with a gang of boys. It was all good clean fun. I talk with my friends now about what a great adolescence we had. We were allowed in nightclubs without drinking. My adolescence occurred during the war years. There were air raid drills and worries about the war, but this had no effect on us. We were having fun, and I remember this time as a great one in my life. I think my daughters also had an innocent adolescence—that is, until drugs came along. If they were using any, I didn't know. They had boyfriends, but I was more of a disciplinarian than my mother and kept closer watch on them and what they were allowed to do. I worried if they were out late. I attended college for a year after high school. I had to quit because my parents could not afford it. I went to business school. I met someone who was handsome and charming but also mentally unstable. I only knew him for six weeks before we got married. I was only nineteen and he was twenty-seven. We were married for many years before I finally divorced him. We raised four children. I was married twice again, but I never ever met my soul mate, if there is such a thing. I don't think that all the male attention I received during my adolescence gave me confidence or built my self-esteem. When I think about my granddaughter and the world she is growing up in, I think it is very different. Girls today finish college, can earn their own money, and don't feel they have to get married young as I once did. Having said that, I think they also miss out on the respect once given to the female. She and all her friends still want what girls in my time did—marriage and a family.—Anonymous

Ready or not, most of us were catapulted from adolescence into young adulthood when we went to college or off to work. As we navigated our way, we began asking the most important question: "Who am I?" Finding our identity came as a consequence of our ability to integrate our sexual, social, and occupational roles as an adult. Answering "who am I?" allowed us to commit to others even if there were differences. It allowed us to find our sense of balance between, as Erikson points out, giving and receiving love and support. For young men, the move toward independence might have begun earlier and was accomplished with fewer traumas. For young women, achieving emotional independence might have been a lifelong struggle.

Developmental psychologists have defined late adolescence/young adulthood as a transitional stage. Encompassed in the transition are tasks that can be unsettling even to the most secure of us: redefining the character and meaning of the relationships we have had with family and friends in earlier adolescent years, untangling our childhood self from our blossoming adult self, and initiating new romantic relationships in our adult world.

Late adolescence is the time when we may be transitioning from believing that the important truths in the world are primarily externally driven through the voices of our parents, teachers, friends, and community. It is the time to believe we have now gained a sense of autonomy and the authority to define those truths within ourselves.

Abraham Maslow, a humanistic psychologist, focused on an individual's route to self-actualization. Maslow supported the belief that maturity and autonomy are achieved when our truths are not bound by conventional thinking alone but also grow out of our ability to integrate all we have learned to solve problems. Many women over sixty have listened to external voices the majority of our lives, and for us the move toward greater independence and self-direction might not have been tied to any specific age—even the *coming of age* in adolescence. Our parents, watching in the wings, agonized over the degree with which they should welcome or dread our approaching adulthood.

> There were very well-defined codes of behavior set out by our parents and by our communities when we were growing up. If I would share those codes of behavior with my children, they would respectfully laugh in my face and say that I grew up in some prehistoric age. But those codes were so embedded in our social structure that there was no room for even the slightest deviation—at least on the surface. Remembering back to my teen years, it seemed that the kids that were the most rebellious were those whose parents were the most rigid about curfews, etc. It figures, I guess. One of the biggest things our parents worried about had to do with having sex before marriage. Our adolescence and early adult years were years without oral contraceptives. Something we never really talked much about was getting pregnant before we

married. Months after starting college, I found out that a friend was pregnant and was leaving school to spend the rest of her pregnancy at a "home for unwed mothers." The name and the place said volumes about how our culture felt about young women who got pregnant outside marriage. She gave her child up for adoption. I am not sure she ever recovered from that experience. How the world has changed. Reading over this, I realize how archaic the values were and how severe our punishments.—Anonymous

Even after we began to rely on our own intuitions and to question the external directives that seemed to have dominated our lives, we would be dishonest if we denied that we still turned for answers to our mothers and sisters and girlfriends. Why? Because those women had answers that were grounded in firsthand experiences most like our own. Their messages rang true. Dorm rooms and workplace cafeterias buzzed with intense conversations; as young women we agonized over what our futures would be. Oftentimes we were just testing the waters, throwing out ideas and waiting to see if they caught traction with our peers. At the same time, we were struggling with the eternal questions: "Do I want to be like my mother or other women of her generation and live life as they did, or do I want something more, something different?" No matter what our answers were to that question, we know now it took a good five to ten years (or a lifetime for many of us) to withdraw totally from the comforts of our family homes and emerge, with or without kids, with or without husbands, into the world of independence *we* had created.

Searching for a Partner

The pursuit for both young men and women of any generation is to find that one individual to whom we can reveal our dreams and connect our destinies. Scenes from the movie *Shall We Dance?*, starring Richard Gere and Susan Sarandon, speak to the positives of lasting relationships. When asked at one point what is good about marriage, Sarandon's character replies,

> In a marriage, you're promising to care about everything. The good things, the bad things, the terrible things, the mundane things…all of it, all of the time, every day. You're saying, "Your life will not go unnoticed,

because I will notice it. Your life will not go unwitnessed, because I will be your witness."

For women our age, it was all about finding a male partner who was that *witness* and who wanted to share in the fulfillment of raising children and building families. The process of finding that person is and was an arduous one, no matter in which generation we find ourselves. It may take many broken hearts until we find our life partner...or, at least, a partner for a time in our life.

> I have been blessed the second time around with a marvelous partner and husband who was a childhood friend. We connected after thirty-five years and previous lives. Perhaps everything is so sweet because not only are we well suited for one another, but also because we have gotten the working part of our lives and child-rearing behind us. We can now indulge in each other and have a complete and beautiful life.—CS

> I didn't think much about what I would do as a career when I started college. I thought I would be like the rest of the people in my family and get married when I finished school...that is if I did finish. Although there were times, even after I started dating my husband when I was nineteen, that I secretly thought about a career (besides teaching) and grad school. I knew that my mother expected me to graduate and get married. Of course the expectations were very, very different for my husband. He was onto grad school while I taught to support us as a couple. I wasn't unhappy then. I thought it was the perfect thing to do. Marriage after graduation was definitely what most of my friends did. By our midtwenties the majority of my friends were in the same position I was in. Most of us did not look back—well, maybe not until our kids were teens.—CTS

Many of the building blocks for these lasting relationships are set in place during adolescence. Although generations of parents have tried to trivialize "high school romances," we know that adolescent relationships represent an essential piece of the social scaffolding on which lasting young adult romantic relationships rest.

Major changes to our social scaffolding in the last fifty years transformed what we experienced personally as the normal transition to responsible young adulthood and to building healthy significant relationships—changes to a more transient society, with family members separated by large distances; changes to the use of oral contraception; changes to living together before or in place of marriage. Fundamental changes that few of us were daring enough to attempt in the fifties or early sixties.

While some have hailed cohabiting as informal marriage, others have found that the bonds are much looser. Couples who went on to marry after living together were not necessarily prepared for a more committed marital relationship.

> I have a wonderful son and daughter-in-law and two granddaughters. Their experience with adolescence has been so different than mine, and although I am open minded, I am not sure I believe how girls are living their lives now is something I agree with. They have had many boyfriends and in some cases have lived with them. Times are very different.—MG

Along with these changes, there has developed over the last ten years a greater understanding and cultural acceptance of homosexuality and same-sex marriage. Now the term "significant relationship" has a plethora of meanings. What we had accepted as givens for our generation has changed, and now new dimensions have enhanced the definitions of love, faithfulness, financial security, and the other values associated with intimate relationships and sexual practices. Notwithstanding these changes, young adults still find the same stressors described by Erikson in their search for independence and autonomy.

Changes, though, are not unique to the twenty-first century. The concepts of romance and marriage, first appearing in the twelfth century, have been transformed repeatedly over the last nine hundred years. Even after their introduction, marriages continued to be arranged for reasons not romantic at all but economic, social, and political in nature. There was not the ecstasy of the romantic love we found as young adults in soap operas or TV series, or in what Denis DeRougemont, in *Love in the Western World*, describes as the passion in love, the "privileged form of suffering" that makes us feel vital, as though we are living on the edge. As odd as it may sound, it is the drama enveloping the passion—to love love more than the object of love, to love passion for its own sake—that seems to make us feel so alive, that makes us feel compelled to be connected.

What were the influential messages you received about romantic relationships?

There were so many "forbiddens" when my husband and I were dating and after we were engaged that I always felt we were living on the edge. I was a good girl. And a virgin before I got married! It was the fifties, and although I couldn't say for sure, I think most of my friends were just like me. So our sexual relationship was all about romance and excitement and anticipation. That is what I thought romance and passion were supposed to be. I felt so powerful because I was entering into the mysterious world of adulthood with the person I had chosen to spend the rest of my life with. So much drama...that drama only added to the passion. Although things have radically changed for the generations that followed, I wouldn't trade those early years with all that mystery and desire.—Anonymous

I have been married three times. When I married my first husband, the father of my four children, I was influenced by the role my mother played in her marriage to my father. Her role was very typical of women in the forties, fifties. My first husband was a verbal abuser, and although I didn't realize it, it became clear when he left our home (and our four children) that life was much simpler without him. We all pitched in...cooking, laundry, gardening, cleaning...my kids were ages four, six, ten, and twelve, but no one was too young to participate in some way to keep our new family of five moving forward. And so there was no way that I could have been the same kind of wife and mother as the generation that preceded mine, and so I rejected that in favor of being head of household. My second husband is someone I knew from my childhood and was likely the love of my life. My mother shared with me that she left her love back in Poland. I knew I had a wonderful opportunity when he proposed to me, even though it meant I would need to move my four children from everyone they knew and all of their family to Iowa City, Iowa. Today each one would tell you that although it was hard at the time, each of our lives became far better than we could have imagined... both then and now. That was one of the many gifts he gave to us. Today I still have a close relationship with three of his four children. Wonderful! Unfortunately my husband died of cancer only four years after we married, but my children have always considered him to have been more of a father in those short years than their biological father ever has been. After sixteen years, I began seeing other men again at the insistence of my granddaughter, who was four years old at the time. She thought it was unfair that my ex-husband had a wife and I had no husband. She insisted that I needed to try in order to be happy. One could say that this granddaughter of mine pointed out something that I had overlooked. I was working hard; all of my kids had finished college and were on their own. Was I unhappy? She held up the "mirror to my face." Two years later I was married to husband number three. And that has been a blessing.—RTM

Unless our marriages were arranged, our generation of women was a captive audience held hostage by the ideal marriages of beloved fictional couples. As modern women of the fifties and sixties, we were choosing our own mates, and it is likely that we never doubted that we would find fulfillment and emotional euphoria in our marriages.

It is important that you know you cannot change a person. It's personal. You just have to click. My husband and I had a very happy marriage of thirty-three years. I would rate it in the top 1 percent on a rating scale. It is important to get the right person in a relationship. My husband was smart, kind, and a very good person. He had a quick wit, and he and I shared the same values, placing great importance on education, having good morals, and treating others as we would like to be treated ourselves. We established a family fund and supported many charities, schools, and colleges. We tried to live a good life and believed in getting the most out of life. It was important for us to strive for as much as we could reach. My husband's philosophy, which influenced me as well, was the saying "It will work out or it won't." If I were to say at night that I was worried about something, he'd say, "I'll let you worry. You can do it for the both of us." My mom's belief, which I live with each and every day, is that if today is a bad day, tomorrow will be better.—Anonymous

My husband and I have had a glorious, love-filled life together. We have two remarkable daughters and two precious grandchildren with whom we are very close. We just celebrated our fiftieth anniversary with a beautiful and meaningful renewal vows ceremony in our home, surrounded by our children and grandchildren.—BW

For many of us, the archetype was our own parents' relationship—for good or for bad. Also, in the fifties and sixties, girls were fairly innocent and naïve. Unfortunately, the rise in the divorce rate in our own generation was only one symptom that we might have been bursting with unrealistic expectations.

As Daniel Levinson wrote in *The Seasons of a Woman's Life*, "The romantic ideal holds a magical promise and a heavy burden: it promises a marriage that is loving and fulfilling for both partners, but it demands great wisdom in choosing a mate and engaging in a marital relationship." Looking back, we may have to admit that some of our expectations were a bit ingenuous. It may be that we never appreciated just how hard it was to build a solid marriage.

The pool for our dating relationships, either at college or on the job, might have been relatively restricted. For women over sixty, these relationships likely included limited sexual experiences and a roller coaster of emotions. Because of our gender-defined lives (separate dorms in college, limited work relationships between genders), much of our knowledge of what actually made males tick was limited, and those mysteries took many of us a longer time to unravel. Because the majority of our interactions were within a strict, circumscribed social context, it took more time and effort than it appears it takes today to develop intense emotional ties to men. Compared to the days and weeks it may take to create the intensity of the relationships experienced by our children and grandchildren, our connections to men were months of weekend dating that may or might not have developed into liaisons with the potential one or ones we could or would marry.

If we take a long look back at our own histories, the number and the intensity of our relationships might have been restricted to those that offered real possibility for the ultimate marriage proposal. Once we narrowed the field, rather than looking at the human qualities that might be essential for a happy marriage, many of us were consumed with identifying the essential traditional qualities imbued by our parents:

the knowledge that our partner would be a good provider, a strong head of household, and a person of value. The influence of social context in assessing our lasting relationships was often overlooked. Many of us were so smitten that we might have ignored how our own social group gauged our relationship. Many of us were clueless of whether our friends approved. Interestingly, a couple hyped as a good match by their friends is more likely to see themselves as a good couple with enhanced possibilities for a sustainable romantic relationship. Some would argue that therein lies the wisdom behind arranged marriages. Arranging a marriage entails a more objective assessment of individual qualities, personal histories, and other factors such as social and religious constraints. It introduces a rational process divorced from excessive sentimentality, emotion, or passion. It is likely that our search for the right partner might have lacked the same degree of scientific examination.

Once we were the generation responsible for choosing our own partners, it is likely our choice was based on the innocent notion of romantic love, with little benefit of a variety of male-female relationships to give us the wisdom we needed to create lasting marriages. In the end, in our ignorance and inexperience, we might have settled for someone who fulfilled what we assumed were essential requirements. Even though we were in our late teens or early twenties, some of us may still have been troubled by the fear that if we did not get married soon, we would be *old maids*. Of course, many of our mothers only helped to perpetuate that fear! We might have seemed so sure when we accepted that marriage proposal, yet there might have been those of us who had real doubts right up to the time of the wedding march—and beyond!

> I will never forget the conversation I had with my mom the night before I got married. I was finishing my degree and was prepared to go out and work. I did not feel the tremendous need to get married in order to make it independently. So that was not part of my equation for getting married. I had only dated my husband-to-be for less than six months. He was older and already settled in his profession. I thought I loved him but was unsure whether it was him I loved or whether it gave me the chance to be totally independent of my parents. I was convinced that the second was definitely not a good enough reason to get married. The night before I got married, when I told my mother about my fears, she looked at me as if I had lost my mind. "Where do you think you will find such a good

man in the future? I promise, you will learn to love and appreciate him!" And off she went. I did get married the next day. But I never forgot her words. I guess she did not have too much confidence in my ability to find another "Mr. Right." As it turned out, I have had an amazing marriage, but I learned my lesson that my mom was not the person I needed to go to for help to solve the monumental problems I had in life!—Anonymous

Early Years of Marriage

We did not focus much energy on evaluating our relationship in the early years of our marriages because we were very busy, weren't we? Working, then raising children, was the norm for us. Many of us continued to socialize with familiar couples, so there were few changes in our lifestyle after we married.

In the beginning, our husbands were often responsible for our support, and as young women in our twenties and thirties, we took on community responsibilities, volunteering in school PTAs, women's organizations, and religious groups. There was a well-defined division of labor and an unambiguous split between the private and public faces of our partnerships.

John Gottman, PhD, has provided positive insights into the misconceptions many of us had, and continue to have, about what is a successful marital relationship. Gottman contends that, in contrast to the dicta of many therapists, it is not important to resolve major conflicts in our marriages in order to have healthy marital relationships. Problems are unavoidable in marriages. When we choose our partners, we are choosing a set of long-standing problems that we will deal with at regular intervals throughout our marriages. What can be destructive is creating interminable gridlock by refusing to accommodate to these problems and by failing to create strategies to deal with them.

Though some of us were unaware of it, there might have been a festering problem at the core of our marriages. Even women who recognized that there were problems adhered to society's message: "You made your bed, now sleep in it!" Women remained in their marriages. Only later, when women found their voice, did the divorce rate begin to grow.

Daniel Levinson compared the family structure many of us had created in those early years to a small business. Outside of the simple *family business* decisions we needed to make, there might have been little exchange or collaborative decision making between our husbands and us. Usually during those years, we did not have too many life-altering decisions to make; our lives might have seemed so simple. The *owners* in this scenario were too busy just managing the store to take a step back and analyze and evaluate whether our management styles were effective. It could very well have been that our family business was understaffed and hobbled by a scarcity of resources. Oftentimes, as a couple, we might not have been entirely connected. We were merely leading parallel lives—just getting through the days. We probably never thought about it in such a way then, but now we can see how critical it was to building our future. As young married women and new mothers, we were totally immersed in family life. We were facing a multitude of decisions that, unknowingly at times, affected the choices we made about our marriages, our education, our values, and our sense of self.

Dedication to our family might also have limited our possibilities for exploring life outside our marital microcosm or for defining what being an adult woman meant. What many of us discovered was more important: our family life promised us, as Levinson said, "greater stability, continuity, and rootedness." And that was our number-one priority.

During those early years of marriage, we also asked few questions, and for those we asked, we did not necessarily have many of the answers. Although some of us were half-listening to the emerging voices of feminism, overwhelmingly we felt our first obligation was to create the best homes for our families.

Surprisingly, statistics from today's mothers echo some of our same concerns. A *New York Times* article called "Why Gender Equality Stalled," by Stephanie Coontz (February 17, 2013), reported that in 1977, two-thirds of Americans believed that it was "much better for everyone involved if the man is the achiever outside the home and the woman takes care of the home and family." It looks like we might have foolishly thought that the movement toward gender parity had been victorious in the seventies, eighties, and nineties. By the time we moved into the twenty-first century, women had begun to voice similar concerns. In 2007, nearly 60 percent of full-time working mothers said they would prefer to work part time, and only 16 percent of stay-at-home moms said they would prefer to work full time.

How did the stressors in the early years of your marriage affect your relationship with your husband/partner?

> I do not often think about the years I lived away from our families.
> I do not like to think about those days because I felt so vulnerable.

I had thought that I was used to being alone with our child while my husband traveled for his job. I guess I never realized how much I depended on my parents and my friends back home for support. Those first few nights in a strange city, an unfamiliar home and neighborhood, when my husband wasn't there, I felt so alone and disconnected. I honestly felt that I was not emotionally capable of taking care of our child. I had never felt so alone, and I knew that I really could not count on my husband to bail me out. I realized that I had so sublimated my every want and desire for the past four years that I was on empty. I thought I had totally lost it and would never recover. Those years were real turnaround years. I saved my own life and my marriage. I made some critical decisions about my future, about a career, about my need to have my own identity. I could no longer feed off the fruits of my husband's labors. I had to grow my own fruits. When we moved again, I had a plan and the confidence that I could do it all—family and career.—JF

My childhood experiences have helped me to be resilient during my fifty-one years of marriage. My husband's company sent him to work in Holland for two years, and the family moved there. It was difficult, but in the end my children felt they learned a lot about other cultures. However, it was difficult for me. I enjoy new experiences. After being a successful executive for many years, my husband's company was downsized, and he was terminated. This was a very stressful period in our marriage, and my first response to him was that I would go back to work and help financially.—AK

Even so, as we endured the internal tug between family obligations and personal fulfillment, career decisions for women might not have been made as simply as the statistics seem to indicate. In his study, Levinson calls this time in our early marriages, when we were in our late twenties with a pack of children and a husband totally absorbed in his job or career, as the *rock-bottom years*!

As our children grew, we had more time and a growing feminist perspective to reflect on ourselves. We felt both vulnerable and passionate about our potential opportunities. Many of our husbands felt threatened by the mere idea of any transformation in us or in our marital roles. We had heard the feminist voices assert gender equality, but years of dependence on our partners and of mothering our children could not drown out our inner messages of gender inequality.

Were we really equal? For the majority of us who ventured out into the work-place, *we were not!* The jobs that were initially open to us—teaching, nursing, library science, social work, secretarial work, cashiering—did not come with great financial reward. Maybe for women of our generation, equality was not the most important issue. Even though many of us were looking for personal fulfillment outside the home, it might have been enough to actually do what we set out to do and be just a financial *contributor* to the household. Studies have shown that with employment came a newfound sense of well-being. We experienced a change in status within our own family units that might have had a profound influence on our marital bliss—for better or for worse! For our generation of conventional women, equality in the workplace, or anywhere else for that matter, might not have been the barometer we used to assess our personal growth.

All these changes might have had consequences affecting the stability of our marriages. They might also have had consequences affecting the confidence we felt regarding the direction in which our lives were going.

Impact of Separation and Divorce

Rather than face separation or divorce, many in our generation might have been more likely to choose what we knew and so embraced "'til death do us part"! For those of us who did that, we banked on the years invested in our marriages and in our families for strength to meet the challenges we were apt to face as our partner-ships aged. Intuitively we knew what researchers studying aging populations later revealed: the well-being of many older adults is dependent on having a partnered relationship. Not age, health, income, support networks, or educational level can obviate the sense of loneliness and despair that aging women can feel when alone. Since more of us are living longer and are remaining mentally and physically fit longer, our significant relationships need to be more meaningful longer and inti-mate longer.

Most women our age made the decision early on to stay in our marriages. Yet now there are a growing number of women who reach their fifties, sixties, and seventies and decide to divorce after thirty to fifty years of marriage. In fact, this age group has become the fastest-growing population to divorce and the most successful in adjusting to the break-up of the marriage. The divorce rate among couples fifty years and older roughly doubled between 1990 and 2013 (Miami Herald, February 28, 2015).

Why now? Thirty percent of these women say that there was not enough of an emotional connection in their relationships. Once their children arrived at adulthood, they were able to identify strains of dissatisfaction in their marriages, and with as many as twenty or more years of an active life ahead of them, they were not willing to sacrifice those precious times by remaining in an unhappy marriage.

> I married my high school sweetheart—met him at sixteen years and loved him since...married for twenty-seven years and three children later, and his death at the age of forty-nine was a horrible, devastating, traumatizing event. It certainly was a tremendous challenge to "move on." Two years later I met someone who knew exactly the right words... saw how vulnerable I was and told me everything I would ever want to hear. Two years later I moved and we got married. It was a miserable mistake. I stayed married for thirteen years, and really, looking back, I should have ended this horrible marriage many years before. In the beginning it was fun, but then a few years later, it started going downhill...Loneliness is not a good thing, but as my family and friends know, I have told them all many times I would rather be alone than live with my second husband.—BDA

> Several years ago, in the midst of a turbulent second marriage, I found myself living a lifestyle that was so far removed from anything I had ever experienced. Making this marriage/relationship successful was very important to me. Every step of the way, I questioned myself and considered that the challenges in the relationship were being set before me in order that I might spiritually grow. I thought that it was incumbent upon me to figure out how I could glean a positive from every negative situation. My lifestyle had changed dramatically. The idea of using what I thought to be a "G-d-given gift" of leadership no longer had a place in my life. I considered that in order for me to make the situation better, I needed to do "tzim-tzum"—that is, to shrink a little, giving my partner more space. Little by little my space diminished, and when a special girlfriend suggested in passing that she was worried about me, that I had changed, I recognized that in fact

all my inner struggles were far more apparent than I had thought. My life, once so busy and full of activity, which included endless meetings with dear friends, a passion for community activism, the desire to be close with my children/grandchildren (who lived far away), and exercise, now was very different. Most of the time, it was about being available and agreeing to live, eat, and play according to the rules (often unspoken) that my husband lived by. My feelings or needs were not given much attention, and the idea of seeking out counsel was a *no-no*...not a possibility in this relationship. Feeling trapped and with no way of finding solutions, a thought came to mind. Was this the life G-d wanted for me? What was my unique purpose, and could it be solely to be this man's wife? Wasn't I supposed to be able to use some of my unique blessings and find ways to live a life with meaning and purpose? The answer became clear, as did the next steps, given no alternative in the absence of a partner who could not get past the idea that it was "his way or the highway," a direct quote. I knew it was time to move on. A year and a half later, waking up every day filled with gratitude, I know that I did the right thing by leaving a relationship that was so dysfunctional. I have moved on to explore how I can use the gifts I have been given and make that difference. Living every day with the challenge of asking, "What is on today's schedule?"—allowing me to make a contribution, according to G-d's will, as I continue to better understand how to accomplish that challenge—grappling with my soul's curriculum.—FG

When I told my family—my adult children and sisters—that I was leaving my husband of thirty-seven years, they were shocked. "Why now?" they all asked. I have no doubt they thought that I was totally out of my mind. I couldn't say I didn't love my husband anymore. I just didn't like him and how I felt about my life. I had had some health problems. I guess that is when I began to think about my life as having some finite end. Maybe sooner than later. I felt my life was strangling me. There were thirty-seven years of arguments, probably no different than other people had. There was family friction...also not that different than other people's. I needed peace in my life. I had enough money saved so that I would not be a burden to my children. I could not stop thinking about the time when I could be free from feeling tension every hour of every day. I want to be free to think about me first. That may sound selfish, but I wanted to spend whatever days I had left losing myself in the things I loved best. Maybe it was selfish, but I was doing it anyway. It was time.—Anonymous

In my growing-up years, sex education was not a topic of conversation in my family from parent to child, nor was it spoken about with my friends. I married at age twenty and had a child one year later. I guess I knew a lot about sex, right? I knew zero. I was married for forty years and divorced at age sixty. I found out that my husband had been a philanderer. In one day my life fell apart and I threw him out. I went for therapy for about two years. I kept thinking, is this possible? Life had seemed so wonderful—a beautiful home with beautiful things. Lots of travel and a beautiful family, and then this. When the therapist asked me what was in my own name, I said, "Nothing." I was never concerned about this in the past. It was suggested I open my own bank account, which I did. My therapist recommended that I attend a three-day support group with her in another state, called "Tangled Vines," for women who had relationship problems. This was the first time I was able to talk about my situation. I worried I would never recover. In our relationship there was his life, his relatives, your life, your relatives. It looked impossible to survive. It was amazing how I made it through. I went back to school and became a Realtor. I walked into a prestigious firm on a prestigious street. When the woman interviewing me noticed my home address, she said, "What are you doing here?" And I said, "I'm applying for a job." I returned within a few days with over twenty listings, and that is where I began to work. Now I would have my own earnings to put in "my" bank account. A few years later, it was suggested I move out of the city—a city I loved, the place where I was born and raised until now. I finally did decide to move to give myself a new start. One of my children lived in my new city with her family, so it was with family support and much love that I began the next chapter of my life. I joined a temple. Began to make new friends and gradually became involved in activities within the community. And it was not long after my move that I learned to accept the fact that I was going to have to pump my own gas, as it was always done for me up north. Yes, once again, it's worth repeating: it is amazing how I made it through. When I think about it now, how did I ever manage? But I think I came out as a stronger person with a stronger personality. My mom was strong and I got her genes.—Anonymous

Fifty percent of women over sixty agree that it is now their time and they want to have the freedom to explore it all. Most remain in their marriages but begin to search out additional routes to happiness.

Intimacy and Communication in Our Significant Relationships

For those of us committed to working to ensure and to preserve the viability of our significant relationships, we now are under growing societal pressures, even at our age, to adapt to changing beliefs about intimacy and communication—beliefs that were and are different from those we cherished as a couple for the last forty to fifty years. Even the number of sexual encounters per month is governed by studies found in women's magazines and TV interviews. No matter what our personal inclinations are about sexual relations, we are bullied by Viagra and Cialis ads, feeling it is our responsibility to perform when our husbands are ready! We are now under societal pressure to become a new *we*.

In the past, intimacy, for many of us, had triumphed in our marriages when our partner validated and accepted us the way we were. Intimacy reflected that ultimate comfort level and being at one with each other. What David Schnarch suggests in *Passionate Marriage: Keeping Love and Intimacy Alive in Communication* is that there are flaws in that definition. As aging women, it may be even more important for us to reevaluate the whole concept of intimacy—its meaning in our significant relationships and how our patterns of communication may ultimately impact that intimacy.

In earlier chapters, we talked about how critical it was to an infant's development to bond or attach emotionally with the caretaker. In order to safeguard against interfering with this process of attachment, we as mothers are driven to nurture and comfort our helpless and dependent newborns. For those of us who grew up with a fifties and sixties mentality, we expected that we would have that same connection, that same attachment, to our significant partners. We safeguarded the notion of attachment and interdependency in our relationships by assuming that we shared with our partners the role of making the other feel nurtured and secure. Recent literature on the resiliency of infants has altered how developmental psychologists look at young children's needs. A belief in the resiliency of our partnerships may also be valuable in substituting old beliefs about attachment and intimacy. Surprisingly, a mindset that nurtures autonomy and individual freedom may replace the dependency and neediness that interdependency has ultimately created in many of us.

Converting those established patterns that have operated in our significant relationships for years seems to be an insurmountable task for many partners—especially when it relates to the areas of communication, intimacy, and sexuality! If we think about it, so much of what we have focused on is technique:

1. The technique of how we speak to each other
2. The technique of solving problems together
3. The technique of mastering intimacy
4. The technique of how we make love

Schnarch writes that we need to replace these techniques and learn to accentuate "the tone and depth of our connections rather than [mere] techniques."

Schnarch references the Greek mythological figure Procrustes as a marvelous example of how best to understand our approach to committed relationships, especially as we age. Procrustes was the son of Poseidon, and his stronghold was the sacred path between Athens and the important trade route to the Peloponnese peninsula. Procrustes hosted guests traveling this pathway, offering them a night's sleep on his iron bed. What was problematic was that Procrustes would either stretch the traveler or amputate his legs to fit the size of the bed.

At times, aren't we all guilty of being like Procrustes in our relationships? Haven't we all tried to make changes in our partners to make them be the way we think it is best to be—as they have done with us? Haven't we all attempted this, with varying levels of success?

It is fashionable to think that communication problems are at the core of today's relationship issues. Why? Because we hold the belief that we can argue, cajole, understand, and express ourselves out of any argument or dilemma as long as we continue to talk and communicate our wants and needs! One of our motives in doing so is to try to get our partners to validate who we are. If we cannot resolve our problems and receive the support we crave, we believe that our partnership desperately needs an overhaul.

> How often have we heard parents say, when making toasts of advice on marriage at their children's weddings, "Don't go to sleep angry!" In the early years of my marriage, I followed that advice. I would go into these long discussions about what was bothering me and what my husband had to do to make things better. When I would take a breath, I would have to ask if he was still awake. There were many nights when he slept through half of my rants. He might not have gone to sleep angry, but I sure as hell did. Either way, my discussions did not solve any of those problems. I would stay up then and question whether there was something terribly wrong with our relationship. I think back now, and I haven't had one of those discussions in about twenty years. I guess it was twenty years ago that I realized I had to find a different solution to handling my marital problems than getting him to say he agreed with all my complaints.—SW

Differentiation: A New Model for Improving Relationships

Murray Bowen, a twentieth-century psychoanalyst, offered a slightly different model for relationships. He recommended the concept of *differentiation* for improving relationships. His notion was fairly revolutionary. It was certainly contrary to the widely held principle, at the time we were building our partnerships, that intimacy was achieved in significant relationships when partners' belief systems were mutually validated and fused as one. In this earlier model, each partner was expected to maintain support and reassurance for the other's beliefs, thereby achieving what some relationship experts have labeled *truly intimate unions*. Bowen disagreed and argued that the opposite, or *differentiation*, was what was essential in our families, our workplaces, and our significant relationships. The success of differentiation is measured by a person's capacity to manage his/her own emotions, thinking, and individuality while maintaining a connectedness to his/her loved ones. Differentiation becomes the true signal of emotional maturity and of a mutually satisfying relationship for many.

It is that ideal balance between our need for individuality and our need for attachment that ensures equality and meaning in our relationships. It is striking that it is balance that permits us to preserve the authenticity of our self when we are both physically and emotionally enmeshed with our partner. The key to maintaining differentiation is our ability to be totally connected without being totally consumed. And with differentiation comes the ideal—interdependency without a sense that we are totally suppressed. Differentiation fosters the belief that we are in control of our own destinies.

We achieve differentiation when we uncover the presence of our own inner resources. It embodies what *we* know to be true and valued, not exclusively what our partner holds to be true and valued. Differentiation is the exact point in time when we are captivated by that still, small voice within us and yet can be open and unafraid to share our love and commitment with the one significant person in our lives. Differentiation represents the true intimacy. Total connectedness without differentiation does not always feel good. Most of all, it can be suffocating if we do not take ownership of who we are and who we are becoming.

So many women in our generation struggle each day with the idea of intimacy in their relationships. Because we have historically defined intimacy as an attachment that grows out of intertwined and mutually validated beliefs, it is not surprising that women in our generation may feel frustrated, disconnected, and incapable of asserting our own viewpoints.

If we alter our definition of intimacy and incorporate self-validated beliefs that contribute to our pleasure and make us feel whole, will the inner core of our forty-plus-year marriages be resilient enough to support these changes? More than likely, the boldness of our newfound respect and confidence in ourselves will become the key element that keeps the ship righted.

> My children's pediatrician probably never knew how profound an impact he had on my marriage. I was too immature to really appreciate what he was saying at the time. I had gone to meet him about a month before my first child was born. Within a short time, we had finished talking about baby stuff, and he began asking what I thought were very intrusive questions. Here I was nine months pregnant, and he was asking me what I was planning to do with my life? Initially, I thought he was kidding, so I said, "I am hoping to finally

have this baby!" He shook his head and repeated, "What are you planning to *do* with your life?" I became very angry and said, as I got up to leave, "I am planning to be a mother!" And that is when he said those prophetic words: "Your husband is going to be a star. You do not want to be a parasite, do you?" Indignant, I walked out the door. I was hoping I would never have to see him again. I had forgotten about all this until one day when my son was about eighteen months. My husband came home from work, and I started "interrogating" him about what he had done at work. He turned to me and said, in as kind a voice as he could muster at the end of a busy workday, "I just would rather leave work at work at the end of the day." At some level, I felt that I had been rejected. I looked at him, and the word "parasite" was reverberating in my head. I was so unsure of who I was at that time in my life that I was using him to fill in the huge gaps. It wasn't right for either of us, and I knew then and there that I had to find something within myself to change things.—CTS

Female Sexuality

Two Competing Principles. The core of our generation's understanding of sexuality is rooted in two competing yet persuasive ideologies. One is attributed to Sigmund Freud (1905), the father of psychoanalysis, and the other to Alfred Kinsey (1948, 1953) and Masters and Johnson (1966), the renowned researchers in male and female sexuality. In Freud's work, sex is partially removed from considerations of physical activities. Rather Freud focused on the psychological aspects of sex—the psychosexual energies of the libido—tangentially related to the bodies that perform the sexual acts. In Kinsey's and Masters and Johnson's works, the body, its positions, and the ultimate orgasm were what were encompassed in the rubric of sexual activity. The source of much of the ambivalence women specifically often feel about their sexuality rests in these two opposing positions. The conflict we struggle to resolve between the emotional component of our sexuality and the physical is a remnant many of us have carried over from our adolescent years. And it seems that this conflict is only exacerbated as both our bodies and we age.

As soon as our hormones kicked in at adolescence, so did that giant spotlight that appears to be fixed on our bodies. Cultural pressures to look a certain way put undue pressure on us to conform in order to be acceptable and attractive to others. Coupled with these new emotions and the fantasizing that came with our physical changes, we as young adults had underlying concerns that were quite real and produced tremendous anxiety: Were our bodies going to be pleasing, and then, would any uncurbed passion lead to pregnancy or sexually transmitted diseases?

As Sharon Lieblum, PhD, and Judith Sachs write in *Getting the Sex You Want*, adolescent girls must also contend with all the emotions that come with physical changes. Here is where all our earliest fantasies were rooted. Here is where we imagined being swept off our feet by a boyfriend who passionately pleads that he can no longer go on living without us. From our earliest years, we were acculturated to be pleasers. As young women, we were caught in that proverbial catch-22 where we wanted to please our boyfriends, who were begging for a sexual relationship, and our parents, who were cautioning us against it.

Lieblum and Sachs characterize this as "the crux of women's sexual conundrum." From these earliest years of sexual awareness, the only people we were probably not worrying about pleasing were ourselves. Women of our generation never put ourselves first when it came to our sexual behavior. Many of us grew up without an integral sense of what we should expect from our partners or from ourselves that would ensure we would have satisfying sexual relationships.

Therefore, our teenage and young adult years were probably filled with emotional turmoil. Many of us were the victims of deep internal battles between unresolved sexual issues and the external standards set up by cultural and parental values. Fueling the cultural constructs were Freud's teachings that our sexual drive was so deeply rooted in our biology that its intensity must be curbed before it threatened our stability and ultimately the mores of our society—thus the many prohibitions we experienced as teens! To Freud, sex was a potential addiction.

Fortunately the salvation for our generation came with the popularity of competing viewpoints that held that our sexual drive was much more variable and not nearly so destructive. Even in earlier cultures in which sex was defined within the construct of procreation, scholars postulated that sexual intercourse was not sinful but rather essential to the growth of societies. Thus, the inconsistent nature of human sexuality, its historical origins, and the diversity of its societal definitions were all at the root of our confusion.

Our sexuality was a driver of our emotions throughout adolescence, young adulthood, and beyond. As older adults, our sexual attitudes and behaviors continue to drive our emotions as well as represent societal viewpoints and our own physical and emotional evolution.

Societal Expectations. Societal expectations about sexual activity in the elderly play a part in how we perceive ourselves as sexual beings. Both men and women suffer, although as older women, we are likely to suffer more. While there may be less pressure on aging women to perform sexually, there is the constant burden to remain young-looking and sexually attractive. As Butler and Lewis so aptly write in *Love and Sex after 40*, "Our culture reinforces these notions at every turn, with a youth-oriented ideal of beauty that lacks the sophistication to include character, intelligence, expressiveness, knowledge, achievement, warmth, style, and social skills—those personal traits that make each woman unique and are found at any age."

Especially in our generation, men had their own set of problems as a result of societal expectations. Men had the role as the initiator of sex. To be a real man, he had to be able to have sex at any time and with any partner. Those may have been realistic expectations in his younger years, but with aging and the introduction of medications, alterations in health status, etc., that level of sexual activity may no longer be possible. Viagra and Cialis ads still offer hope for every man while continuing to foster the societal pressure of performance.

More profound, though, are the cultural influences that portray the elderly basically as nonsexual, or worse, castigate those who remain sexually active. Cultural myths abound about sexuality and women and men of our generation: myths about decreased desire, about our inability to make love even if we want to, and about our physical unattractiveness and sexual undesirability. Yet the most troubling myth is the one that regards the elderly as too fragile to attempt sex. All these myths have historically been promulgated by a culture grounded in religious doctrine that views sex mainly for procreative purposes and even by women over sixty whose parents and communities instilled strict boundaries regarding the parameters of our sexuality.

> Sometimes I want to shout out to all those young people who think they have cornered the market on satisfying sexual relationships. I would if I had a little support from my age group. But all my friends seem to go quiet or make pitiful but revealing jokes as soon as sex is mentioned. I want to say to them that my sex life with my husband is

so much more meaningful than it was when we were younger. We have time to really enjoy each other and to make sure that we are satisfying each other's needs. I think we are much more creative than we ever were...maybe because we have to be. And that is a really good thing. I guess those young people will find out for themselves in about thirty years, and then hopefully they will not have been prejudiced by the views they held earlier.—Anonymous

The Physical and the Emotional. We also need to understand how the physical changes pre- and postmenopause might have impacted our sexual lives. Some postmenopausal women feel a sense of freedom, liberated from the worries of pregnancy, and the beneficiaries of more private time as a couple. Those women have suggested that their reproductive aging is the "good old." Yet for others, the physical changes and health issues might have prompted a search for a gynecologist or alternative medicines as solutions to vaginal dryness or what we perceive as decreases in sexual desire.

Slowly, as we aged, we began to redefine sexual intimacy, while characteristically our male partners continued to identify it in terms of sexual intercourse. For some, this may be the first chink in the armor of mutually validated beliefs. Holding, hugging, and caressing may become the most intimate and exciting exchanges for women postmenopause. Many husbands do not call that sex!

How have the physical and emotional changes in both you and your partner over the years affected your sexual relationship?

You asked what I find to be the most sexually arousing act. Being held and cuddled. It yells, "I really adore you! I always want to be this close and connected to you."—Anonymous

Not much has changed for women, though, because sexuality has always had an emotional and mental component that drives our desires. For men, sex is mainly a physical activity. Some say this is a function of the differences in our anatomy. Whatever marks the difference, it is quite understandable why there are differences and how those differences are only exacerbated as we age!

The first challenge to our sexual relationship might have come long before menopause. It might have come at the very beginning of our significant relationship. The male partner most probably defined the issues of sexual intimacy, and more than likely it was all about intercourse then, too. We were happy that *our man* found us so desirable. As women, we had been acculturated to believe that intercourse was the essence of intimacy. After all, the sexual revolution and the pronouncements from feminists about women's rights in the bedroom came years after many of us were married. Birth control might have freed us from the worry of pregnancy, but it might have also intensified the sexual rift, as men felt less apprehensive about the consequences of intercourse. Many women capitulated, and men continued to be the dominant sexual force in the relationship and determinant of our sexual activities.

We might not have been unhappy with the status quo. Nevertheless, many of us might also have had hidden worries, wants, and desires. For many women, a faulty body image continued to be an ongoing problem, often having its roots as far back as adolescence. But it did not end there. At the time of each of our milestones—menarche (our first menstruation), pregnancy, menopause, post-menopause—our body offered overt signals that they had arrived. Oftentimes it was growing breasts, expanded waistlines, and widening hips that were the signals. All might have had a negative consequence on how we saw our bodies/ourselves. It didn't help when we opened the latest fashion magazines or turned on the television or watched our favorite movie stars on the big screen that we saw through everyone's eyes (male and female) the epitome of body perfect. Many of us knew then, and certainly understand now, that we cannot compete with that; few of us feel comfortable enough in our own skin to ignore these body images.

Some have said that the most important sexual organ for women can be found between our ears. There are endless numbers of examples of how as sexual beings we are influenced by what is in our brains, in our thoughts. In our younger years, our brains were calculating and organizing the numbers of carpools, the grocery lists, and the phone numbers of the handyman, electrician, and plumber. But primarily we were the managers of the "family business," as well as of the additional activities related to the stressors of our careers. When faced with addressing our husband's sexual wishes, we hid the pressures we felt and might not have always shared equally his desires. As we aged and some of the mental demands of the home and of our careers lessened, we still might not have felt as excited as our partner over the prospect of sexual activity as he defined it.

Today, we may be preoccupied (mentally) with how we are adapting to aging, to our changing bodies, and to our changing lives. Our brains continue to be in command. Thus, sex becomes only one of our compelling brain activities. Many have cited this as a reason for the complaints we have about lowered sexual desire.

Although our partners may also be experiencing physical issues with aging, they continue to define and associate sexual desire and satisfaction primarily with the act of intercourse, with or without pharmacological aids. Oftentimes little consideration is paid to what this provokes in us or how it intersects with the mental component of our sexual drive.

It is important to know and understand our bodies. In studying brain physiology, researchers have found that the band of fibers that covers both hemispheres of the brain is larger in women than in men, making it easier for communication between the thinking and emotional spheres. Leiblum and Sachs have suggested that orgasm is the time when our thinking takes a backseat to our emotional needs. Like many who work in the area of female sexual function, they believe that mindfulness, a special technique, helps to quiet the brain, quiet our thinking, in order to welcome feelings of sexual desire.

According to Jon Kabat-Zinn (2011) at the University of Massachusetts Medical Center, mindfulness is "the regular, disciplined process of moment-to-moment awareness, the complete 'owning' of each moment of your experience, good, bad, or ugly." The key to the success of mindfulness is to continually monitor our thoughts and bring ourselves back to what is actually happening in the present, rather than what is our perception of what is happening. In the sexual context, we need to focus on the sights, the sounds, and the touches without processing their meanings. It takes practice, but mindfulness may be something to embrace in order to enhance the enjoyment in our sexual relationships, especially as we age.

Although women of our generation have always been open to sharing our thoughts and experiences with other women, rarely have we revealed our sexual concerns. Many of us have remained silent on this subject throughout our lives. Inside we might have wrestled with our concerns of inadequacy, thinking that somehow there must be something wrong with us. We might also have felt that we were the only women in the world feeling like this. We might have felt alone, half-dead inside. Rather than feeling less pressure and relieved as health issues changed the sexual function of many of our mates, we longed even more for the physical closeness, the "intimacy" we craved at our core. Intimacy remains the pure sexual desire that excites us: the feeling when we lie in each other's arms, when we face each other as valued individuals and not as appendages of one another or as dutiful lovers. Nevertheless, it may be difficult to disclose our desires for this kind of intimacy to anyone for fear of being misunderstood.

An article by Daniel Bergner in the *New York Times Magazine* (May 26, 2013) addressed the potential for pharmacological solutions for female low sexual desire (or what physicians term hypoactive sexual-desire disorder, HSDD). Although there have been other experimental drugs that have come down the pipeline, none has yet to gain the Federal Drug Administration's approval. Drug management of sexual desire issues can become a management nightmare.

In recent years, it has not been uncommon to find aging women being treated with antidepressants at the onset of menopause. Most of the antidepressants are very successful at mitigating our moods, but unfortunately they calm the very hormones that help generate our feelings of sexual desire. With the proliferation of drugs like Viagra for men, researchers have begun to experiment with sex-enhancing medications for midlife women and beyond. We have become a nation of people who look to pills as a cure-all for every ill. Finding an effective medication to solve the problem of sexual desire in women may be years in the making, so we need to look outside the traditional medical model for our solutions.

Not only do we need to recognize that our brains may be the center of our sexual being, but we also ought to factor into the equation how our lives have evolved and our bodies have responded to changes in hormonal levels and aging in general. Add to that the influence *differentiation* could have on the dynamics of our personal connections as we discover the power of our inner resources as individuals and as partners in our significant relationships.

We have evolved so much over our lifetime as we have had to adapt to changing family dynamics, volatile economic constraints, and redefined social practices. However, many women are still silent and not confident enough to change the definition of one of the most central issues in our relationships: intimacy. Without betraying the confidences of our marital unions, we may be able to find strength from our women friends, who are likely to share many similarities and frustrations.

Both male and female partners deserve to have an authentic connection. This is the goal for all relationships but especially for aging couples, who have invested the largest amount of capital in growing strength from each other's sense of independence and centeredness. Clearly, no one promised that it was going to be easy! Critical is the understanding and recognition that intimacy, as we define it, is not constrained by physical or medical limitations. The dynamics of intimacy are concentrated in the emotional realm of our partnerships.

> I imagine that my relationship with my husband is not so different
> than lots of other women in our sixties. It seems like I have been with

my husband my whole life. And our life has been good, for the most part…Since the very beginning, my husband and I would have never described us as a "touchy-feely" couple. We never missed it, maybe because we never saw it in our own families. Our sexual relationship was satisfying. I think it is natural with aging that sexual relationships can change. Maybe there are more physical illnesses and changes that affect sexual performance. But honestly, I do not think about it very often because there are many other things we share together that we enjoy and that make us happy. But there have been times over the years, when I was sad or anxious about family losses and illness, that I could have used some hugs and tenderness. I guess I was not comfortable to ask him for what I needed. I still think about those times, so I guess it was a lot more important than I thought it was.—Anonymous.

I was not interested in having a serious relationship again after my second husband died. We had a loving, passionate, intimate relationship. Then I had a bout with cancer, and after the treatments, I definitely had no interest in anything sexual. I always joked with people that I was a "born-again virgin"! I had lots of friends and activities, and I was very satisfied with my life. Because of all the things that happened, I did not take anything for granted. One of the things I like the most is taking adult classes at the local university. There are always a lot of "eligible" men, but meeting a man was low on my priority list. I guess when you least expect it, things just happen. One tap on the shoulder, coffee, lunch, dinners, and now a trip to the Berkshires. Everything has changed. I realize that I am again a sexual being. Joking with a friend who reminded me about my age and stage, she said, "Remember, don't overanticipate—the Berkshires are hills, not mountains."—Anonymous

Now: How Culture Impacts Significant Relationships

As parents (or frankly as anyone who has loving relationships with young adults), it may be a good idea to cast aside any notion that adult children or their children will follow the clearly defined, gender-based guidelines for significant relationships, sexual behaviors, or family definitions that were at the core of what we held sacrosanct when we were their age. As our grandchildren so appropriately put it, "Duh!"…or its translation, "Get with the change in generational beliefs, Grandma!" And that we must!

Although the prevailing stereotype may be that aging populations become more inflexible and conservative with time, science has totally disproved that concept. In fact, studies have shown that aging adults show a greater tolerance than younger cohorts of adults, and again, this may be a function of those brain changes we talked about earlier. We are capable of making the necessary mental adjustments to changing mores regarding our significant relationships.

Today, for many middle-class young adults, opportunities have steadily diminished in the face of an unstable and ever-changing economy. This has played havoc with their role as young adults. As a consequence, parents have had to modify their expectations that their young adult children can afford to live independently as they quickly become casualties of the *returning young adult syndrome*. This alters what many parents have come to enjoy as their empty nest! The return of the young adult impacts the process of reconnecting with our partners that is designed to come when our adult children take flight and are totally self-sufficient.

Younger generations of adults between the ages of twenty and forty-five operate in a world that does not look all that similar to what we knew. For example, the fundamental principles of marriage have been altered. Our society has expanded the traditional definitions of marriage to include civil partnerships between same-sex couples and heterosexual couples who live together without marrying. But along with these changes has come a general sense of diminished obligation and commitment in young adults to the formal constructs of marriage. For young women, this might have had its roots growing up in the shadow cast by the feminist movement. While the traditional value of becoming a parent and achieving financial independence is inherently an adult behavior, today's young adult women are equally committed to meeting their own personal educational and career goals. And with that education, they are less likely to emphasize marriage as part of their future. The latest studies have revealed young women are apt to believe that both men and women can have satisfying lives without marriage, while for men, only women can have a satisfying life. Interestingly, young adults who are more religious and are already married with children believe that neither men nor women can have a satisfying life without marriage. In the fifties and sixties, marriage was the only mainstream, socially acceptable option for committed relationships. Today, in our rapidly changing landscape, even the expression "committed relationship" has been redefined.

In February of 2012, the *New York Times* Style Q&A printed an interview with Eric Klinenberg, NYU sociology professor and author of the book *Going Solo*. Klinenberg's findings were astounding. In the fifties, he states, when we were making decisions about our future relationships, only 20 percent of American adults were single. Today, the number of single adults is nearing 50 percent. Clearly Dr. Klinenberg made the distinction between "living alone" and "being alone," between being too self-absorbed to let others in and focusing on knowing how to take care of oneself. Furthermore, he pointed to the teachings of Dr. Spock, which might have impacted middle-class and affluent parents, who offered their children endless opportunities that met their individual interests and needs. According to Dr. Klinenberg, little was done to coordinate any of these activities between siblings and help them learn to live effectively together.

> It is hard for me to accept that my son can be happy single. I think that as parents we have failed somehow because he doesn't want to be married. I think I raised him to treasure his alone time and to be independent. We must have gone way overboard, because now he just doesn't want to make any kind of commitment that will make him have to compromise about anything. Maybe we made him so self-centered because we always were there to figure out a way to give him what he wanted. I cannot imagine that he will never have children, either. As he is nearing forty, he doesn't seem to feel he is missing anything in his life. I worry about what will happen when he gets older. Who will be there for him?—PR

Although there have been critical changes that have affected the status of our significant relationships in the twenty-first century, young women's perception of their sexual rights still might not have changed radically. For women of all ages, the level of sexual empowerment is contingent on their level of education, history of sexual experiences, and ethnicity. As strange as it may seem, young women share some of the same beliefs we did fifty years ago. Certain women continue to feel they do not have the right to make their own decisions about (1) whether or not to have intercourse; (2) whether to have intercourse without birth control;

or (3) whether they can dictate what is sexually satisfying to them. Even if gender equality is apparent in the workplace or in admission to universities, there is still a percentage of young women with the perception that they do not have the right to control their own sexual behavior.

When We Focus on Our Significant Relationships at All Ages

Whether we are in relationships that have spanned our entire adult life or whether we are looking to find new and meaningful ones, we are probably all governed by the same rules of engagement and quite similar needs and desires. *As we age, what seems to be most relevant to maintaining or creating an intimate relationship has little to do with length of years. Rather it is dependent on how well we communicate, understand, respect, and have trust in our partner.* Remember, we have more time to devote, a willingness to change, and an ability to accept and understand differences. These are the qualities that come with age if we are open to integrating them into our daily lives.

In an article in the *Wall Street Journal* (July 2012), Elizabeth Bernstein writes, "Want great marriage advice? Ask a divorced person!" Bernstein uses the book *Finding Love Again: 6 Simple Steps to a New and Happy Relationship*, by Dr. Terri Orbuch, and the data collected from over 350 couples (46 percent divorced over twenty-five years) to give "marriage advice learned the hard way." The advice emphasizes the importance of building trust by complimenting, cuddling, and kissing, and by encouraging partners to feel good about the kind of people they are and about the ideas they hold. For men in this group, not having a partner that showed love and affection was reason enough to lead to divorce; this was not true for the women. Women might have been acculturated over the years not to expect that from a man. Disputes over money and past events also triggered divorce. Dr. Orbuch writes, "By getting your partner's perspective, and marrying it with your perspective, you get the relationship perspective."

<u>Thoughts to Remember</u>:

1. Acknowledge who we are----our shortcomings and all.
2. Be accountable for past and present actions in the relationship.
3. Listen actively to our partner's words without assuming we know   what he/she might say.
4. Think about what we are saying and how our words are being received.
5. Respond in the present without bringing up past experiences and disappointments.
6. Avoid "if only" statements, blaming, and criticisms.
7. Steer clear of trying to change our partners into the people we think they should be.
8. Be mindful of the moment and enjoy the sights, sounds, and feelings of our sexual experiences.
9. Offer our definition of intimacy to our partners and, along with that definition, the sexual activities we find most stimulating and satisfying
10. Learn to accept our aging bodies and work to promote a healthy body image.
11. Find one thing to celebrate with our partners each day.

As we said earlier in the chapter, we can interact with our partners, through the use of differentiation, as independent and capable women. By continuing the practice of celebrating, acknowledging, supporting, nurturing, and respecting each other, we continue to build the strongest of emotional connections. In chapter 4, we will examine how we established our own families and just how we tapped into those same significant practices in order to forge enduring bonds with our children and their children.

Maybe because I was sitting in the third row, I could not help but to connect to the words of the song. I had heard that song hundreds of times, and the piercing melody always spoke to me. But that night it was the words that resonated in a way that they never had before. Why then?

Memories...
May be beautiful and yet
What's too painful to remember
We simply choose to forget.

Maybe it's because at my age, so much of what is stored in my brain are memories, memories of the life-altering experiences and the meaningful, significant relationships nurtured along the way. Memories...the high school loves, the college romances that each seemed to be Mr. Right at the time, the man I committed to spend the rest of my life with, in sickness and in health. Coming of age—that is what I did then, and isn't that what I am doing again now? I am retracing the paths those significant relationships took me down. But what is "too painful to remember" I cannot let myself forget! I am older and wiser and more sure of who I am now. So many things have changed me and the direction I have taken. I do cherish the memories of those early "loves." What is most important is that I can look back without any regrets because of what I learned about myself from each relationship. I am so lucky to have chosen a life partner who has provided me with so many adventures and so many incredible memories that my biggest fear is that I will forget. "It is the laughter," the shared laughter, that has carried me over the roughest patches. I hope I will always appreciate how profound is the love I share and that I will continue to appreciate it like I do at this moment.—CTS

Love recognizes no barriers. It jumps hurdles, leaps fences, penetrates walls to arrive at its destination full of hope. Maya Angelou

LIST OF QUESTIONS TO REVIEW

What have you learned from adolescence that has influenced your growth as a woman?

What were the influential messages you received about romantic relationships?

How did the stressors in the early years of your marriage affect your relationship with your husband/partner?

How have the physical and emotional changes in both you and your partner affected your sexual relationship?

PERSONAL REFLECTIONS

_____

_____

_____

_____

_____

_____

_____

_____

_____

_____

_____

_____

_____

_____

_____

_____

_____

_____

_____

_____

_____

_____

_____

CHAPTER 4
Now Our Children are Grown

Your children are not your children,
They are the sons and daughters of life's longing for itself.
They come through you but not from you.
And though they are with you.
Yet they belong not to you, you may give them
your love but not your thoughts.
—KAHIL GIBRAN

As we continue to reflect on our histories and to question our potential power to write our personal narratives, we are struck by how often we are enticed by the memories of our past relationships to help define our present ones. At times we may be discouraged by what we find. Maybe there are unmet expectations; maybe terrible disappointments. Or on the other hand, we may rejoice as we revel in the memories of the families we have created—families bound by strong commitments and shared values. Our challenge is to understand just how these memories carried forward from our past impact how we behave in our present. It is memories linked to our relationships with our children and their children that we explore here.

I have long subscribed to the idea that the most important role many people play in life is that of being a parent. And it is the one for which no one ever is trained beforehand. I've often wondered whether the fact that, for most, it is a prime example of on-the-job training is the reason so much of our society is dysfunctional.

It seems to me there should be a required course for both girls and boys in high school that is involved with what is required and what the challenges and aggravations will be. I had a particular challenge with a husband whose parenting philosophy was diametrically opposed to mine, making for a very difficult family situation—one that carried into my children's adulthood. It is only now, when I spend so much time and put so much effort into grandparenting, that my children have come to appreciate me more. I was always the disciplinarian while their father was not, and I remain so to this day. I am particularly pleased to see that my grandchildren have no problem with that.—MP

By the time we reach our sixty-plus years, we might imagine that our relationships with our adult children would now be fixed and unshakeable. Those relationships have been shaped over years by the emotional ebbs and flows we shared together. Those relationships have been influenced by both our successes and our failures at overcoming obstacles and by the possible chasms resulting from unresolved disagreements. At this stage in our family's development, we all come to the table with complex histories, and if we are honest with ourselves, we come entrenched in our own perspective. Confounding what we had envisioned as our ideal family tableau is the reality that our children have transitioned into adulthood in charge of their daily lives and their own decision making. They are figuring out life's challenges *on their own*! As well they should be…unless, of course, by some small miracle they might be willing to consider our thoughts and ideas!

To succeed as five-star moms, we have made accommodations and have regularly adapted to the ever-changing circumstances in our families' lives. Nevertheless, at this time, we may be finding it more difficult to negotiate our new relationships with our adult children. We may even want to ask when, if not now, our children will begin to adapt to our changes and acknowledge our needs as we did for them…and for our parents.

Our Adult Children

When we looked back at the character of our own parent-child relationship in chapter 2, many of us discovered we may still harbor our parents' long-standing expectations, most of which are charged with both positive and negative emotions. Many of our own early family lessons were infused with hopeful dreams. Yet at other times the messages were mixed:

> "Get an education!"
> "Marry well, since girls do not need to be educated,"
> "My mother always told me I was pretty, but I didn't believe her"
> "I could have been a great athlete, writer, singer..."
> "I could have been a doctor, but my father always said I was lazy and I should have tried harder!"

We can see how our own personal histories could have influenced who we were—and continue to be—as parents.

The history we share with our adult children could be either a history that will provide joy and hopefulness for the future or one filled with unfinished business that could easily color our feelings and expectations, especially as we age. As mothers, we invested extraordinary physical and emotional capital in our children when they were young. Who made sure they were nurtured, secure, and well fed? Who worried when they were sick, when they did not eat, had disappointments with friends, did poorly in school, or suffered trauma—real or imagined? Who raised them day after day, inputting respect for values, ethics, moral standards, and religious beliefs? Who worked tirelessly, at times to no avail, to ensure a future world that might be better than the one we had dreamed of for ourselves? At the time, all that might have seemed so critical.

Sharing her insight into her relationships with her adult children, CJ put it beautifully in the following analogy:

> Now our children are grown. I often think about my relationship with my adult children as the pigs in the "Three Little Pigs," who have gone off to seek their fortunes. Just like Mama Pig, we sit home wondering, Will they ever come back home? Will they ever send messages so we know how they are? Will they invite us to their homes once they get settled? Will our story be a "happily ever after" story? Although we want to believe we are writers of our own stories, we really do not have full control over how they will end. It

could go so many ways. Some little piggies could go off with feelings of resentment and frustration about us as parents. They might naturally blame us for all the things that have gone wrong. They are so happy to get away that they never call. We may get angry because we feel they are ungrateful, so we do not call. They have moved so far away that it isn't easy to pick up and visit. For them or for us. We make excuses. We say that it doesn't bother us but...The other option is that they leave with all their resentments. We could try and understand where they are coming from. We could push back our pride and decide that we are the adults and admit that sure, we probably made some big mistakes. We share that feeling with our children. Even so, the path to "recovery" is still bumpy, but we know that as the mom, it is our job to continue making the effort to reach out. We do not want to die knowing we had too much pride to try to rectify our relationship.—CJ

Now our children are grown. We speak with them as they move forward in life, and we try to maintain our relationships even though they have, like in the "The Three Little Pigs" analogy, gone off into the world to seek their fortunes. If we remove the drama that oftentimes surrounds our parent–adult child relationships, we can see that our adult children do remember all the things we have stood for, both good and bad. They do keep us in their memory banks—just as we did our parents. For certain, our past informs our present—and it informs our adult children's present and, most importantly, their future.

What are the most satisfying qualities about your relationships with your adult children?

Word to the Wise on Mothers
If we are available, we encourage dependency.
If we are busy ourselves, we are detached.
If we offer advice, we are controlling.
If we refrain, we are disinterested.
—RUTH HARRIET JACOBS, WELLESLEY COLLEGE CENTER FOR RESEARCH ON WOMEN

What was your concept of an ideal parent, and did the reality of parenting measure up to your expectations?

I had no preconception and never thought about "an ideal." I gave all the love I could, and I tried to do my best. And I always put my children first and trusted in what they did and said. They have never disappointed me.—EH

I liken it to making a cake without a recipe. The variables are limitless but must include patience, nurturing, listening skills, and unending love. There are many ingredients, but without a recipe, who will say how the cake will taste, let alone if it will rise? As parents, we have the responsibility to be sure our children get the best education. While the quality of teaching in the classroom is critical, we made sure our boys saw America. We traveled to (and sometimes camped in) most of our national parks as well as visiting Canada and Alaska. Family vacations built character and memories. Don't raise children without them.—Anonymous

This is a very good question. For an ideal parent, I would want one who made their child feel loved and affirmed; who always provided for their needs, both spiritual and material; who offered guidance and wasn't afraid to set limits; and who "provided" the child with a good example for living a useful and happy life.—MB

I feel that my husband and I were ideal parents. When the children were younger, we always did everything as a family. We were always very supportive of our children in "almost" everything they wanted to do. As a stay-at-home mom for eighteen years, I was always available for carpool, room mother, volunteer, Girl Scout leader, etc. I was involved in every aspect of our children's lives.—AH

We always listened to our children and respected their thoughts and wishes. We did not always agree, but they always had an opportunity to express themselves, and we expressed ourselves. Our children were all treated fairly and equally, and we never showed any favoritism. We taught them the importance of family and caring for each other. Our children are there for each other and are very close.—Anonymous

To allow one's children to feel free to be and do whatever they are capable of. Yes, the reality of this measured up to my expectations.—JK

I had the best parents in the world who exposed me as a young child to a Jewish religious and secular upbringing simultaneously.—AO

I do not recall having formulated any concept of an "ideal parent," therefore I didn't have any specific expectations—other than for my kids to be happy, healthy, and successful. TV families might have presented fantasized images of perfect families, but I don't think I put myself in the position to be in those images. The time and frustrations of figuring out how much to parent, much of the time by myself, were unexpected, with many mistakes made. Looking back, there are many things I would have done differently.—ER

1. To be calm with my children
2. To help my children instill in themselves a sense of worthiness
3. To introduce my children to experiences such as the arts, team sports, sleep-away camp, and different travel adventures
4. To teach my children to respect themselves and others
5. To allow my children to have and make choices
6. To have fun with my children
7. To have my children obtain a religious education

Most of these goals were eventually accomplished. However, life happens and it interrupts life, causing each of us to not be able to be in control, causing some negative consequences that hopefully you can work on to overcome.—Anonymous

The parent-child relationship, according to Kira Birditt, PhD, is "one of the longest-lasting social ties human beings establish." It is also the most dynamic—from the birth of our child to our death. Initially, we were inextricably connected to our child those early months and years. Within the mother-child relationship, there existed room for satisfaction, hope, struggles, tensions, and a myriad of challenges.

Once a parent, always a parent...in our children's eyes, no matter their age, and in our eyes also. Yet it is our flexibility and our openness to continuously redefine our parental role that shapes the success of our relationship with our children. It is our resourcefulness, as "moms forever," in triumphing over our imprecise sense of boundaries that portends the success of our connectedness to our adult children.

The social landscape in our country has changed dramatically over the last forty years and has further complicated the construction of those boundaries. The issues that we might have faced with our children as they navigated their way toward adulthood were either nonissues in our parents' generation or taboo subjects about which we had never spoken openly. The political power surrounding the issues of HIV and AIDS, homosexuality, marijuana, and sexual freedom, to name just a few, have redefined our society and our personal sensibilities on many different levels. Eating disorders and autism were not in the vernacular of the forties, fifties, and sixties. Today, every household has been touched in some way by one of these issues (and many more), and that has heightened our apprehensions as parents and grandparents. And because of our enduring concerns as mothers, we continue, unabashedly at times, to blur the boundaries with our adult children.

The emotional investment we make in our children does not end when our children mature into adulthood. As nurturers of our family system, we are the eternal jugglers, helping the family to survive and thrive by attempting to provide balance in relationships oftentimes disrupted by events. With each new adjustment, the balance must be reestablished; with each new tension, the life of the family may be forced to reassess how to regain its equilibrium. As a result of weathering those critical times, we have the opportunity to grow and develop—each of us and each of our children.

Although expectations may change, our emotional investment, no matter how we try to trick ourselves into believing otherwise, never changes. However, life circumstances obligate us to rethink our relationships with our grown children.

Oftentimes, new family members (spouses, partners, and/or grandchildren) transform our established parent–adult children interactions. No doubt a major readjustment is necessary to incorporate new family members and, frankly, to explore how we may fit into the landscape of the nuclear families they are creating.

Let us not forget that our relationships with our own parents and in-laws may continue to shape our behavior.

> Recently, I made a wedding for my daughter-in-law. The relationship between a mother-in-law and a daughter-in-law is the most difficult of all relationships. I resolved that when my older son got married, I would love his wife no matter what.—FM

If the relationship with our in-law children is good, we say we are lucky. If it fails to meet our expectations, we might not be surprised.

How would you describe your relationships with your adult children? How does that impact family relationships?

> I try to walk on eggshells. I try to keep my mouth shut unless I am asked!—Anonymous

> I do not know if I love my daughter-in-law more or respect her more than I love her.—EB

> Unlike many of my friends, I offer advice to my children whether they ask for it or not. Our children are in their forties to early fifties. My comments come from respect and love, and they do not have to take advice from me, but out of respect, they must listen. This is the way I grew up. I would weigh my parents' advice and then make the best decision for us.—JJ

> I don't voice my opinion unless I am asked. And even then, I have to be careful about what I say!—Anonymous

> Being a grandparent has filled my life from the moment my daughter-in-law invited me into the birthing suite to join in the birth of our grandson. My children live out of town, so it was particularly gratifying that they bought a house with a guest room so that we might be comfortable when we visit and spend as much time as possible with them.—LF

I love my son and we get along well. The only problem is my daughter-in-law. She holds the reins and she does not like me. I went to visit and wound up staying in a hotel. I felt so unwelcome.—Anonymous

I like to go to my daughter's home, but before I go, I always ask permission. I feel like a visitor, not part of the family. My son-in-law's mother is there every day. She is definitely part of the family.—Anonymous

There isn't a thing I do that I do not discuss with my daughter.—RL

I recall shortly after my daughter married, she said something to me that has lingered through all these years. It was a time when I was supplying too much information as to how she should run her home and life. She looked at me and said, "Mom, you are you and I am me. I am never going to be exactly like you; please let me be who I am." This comment gave me a new perspective on how I view my adult children. Now I give my children their space to be who they are meant to be, each different in many ways. I try to refrain from criticism unless absolutely necessary. I have turned into the agreeable mother and try to compliment when I can. This has worked well. We all get along and see each other whenever we want—dinners, holidays, birthdays, and special occasions—and are able to enjoy our time together. It's working for us.—MB

At times, our expectations seem to resurface. We may sense a loss of control that triggers a host of emotions.

I used to call my mother every day. I managed to find the time. But sometimes days—no, maybe even weeks—go by and no communication.—Anonymous

I don't expect to be the center of the family anymore. But as I age, I sometimes I think I am not even part of it.—Anonymous

Intellectually, we understand that as our children age, they are making new lives, and we delight in their independence. We ask ourselves, "Isn't that what we have spent our entire lives as mothers trying to achieve?" We know they are busy with children, with work. We even may have come to accept that a text is the new communication tool of choice.

Nevertheless, women of our generation operate within a different milieu than that of the generation of their adult children. Marriage and family were the cultural norms of the fifties and sixties. We often spent the early years of our marriages as homemakers, and our careers came later, once we felt our children were carefully launched into the world. Why? The prevailing culture around us defined our primary purpose and sense of self as being rooted in the perceived successes and failures of the mothering and wife-ing we provided.

Many of us fashioned a cocoon around our children. We attempted to meet their every need and, if we are honest, derived tremendous satisfaction from their achievements and experienced much angst when they failed. Even for those of us who subsequently defined additional roles to include important careers, meaningful volunteering endeavors, or sports activities, we were conscious not to abrogate our responsibility in order to be available and supportive. At a moment's notice, we might have morphed into superwoman, addressing any and every family demand. There is very little doubt, for many of us, that we felt our most self-actualized when we were serving those people in our lives to whom we had made a lifetime commitment. Sadly, for many of us, we still may be stuck in that mindset, trying to follow the same set of rules.

And, too, the world we inherited from our mothers is a far cry from the hectic, multitasking world of today. A part of that other world included the commitment to ensure the well-being of our aging parents. Be it weekly or even daily, our connection was the key to remaining respectful and caring daughters. Especially as our parents aged, our thoughtfulness was an important source of their comfort and security. For us, it was an act of love and concern—and of responsibility.

What generational differences, if any, affect the communication between you and your adult children?

I always thought I was a good daughter, and I was. I made sure that my mother had everything she needed. I made sure to spend time with her, call her weekly, take her places, and never leave her out. All my friends, to this day, say I was a good daughter. But in my mind I didn't give her enough. Upon examination, I think I know what was missing. I didn't give her enough of what she needed emotionally. She needed more assurance than I was capable of giving. She needed more nurturance. She needed me—not what I could do for her, but just me. Me to listen to her talk about things in her life that truly did not have much meaning in my life then. When I think about my own progression as I have aged, I understand the aging process so much better. I also understand that grown children have a life of their own.—MCL

Even if we were not perfect in our efforts, we tried because we were part of a tradition of nurturers. We were doing what had always been done. Somehow we believed that as we aged, our adult children would follow our lead.

In the beginning, I expected my daughter-in-law to call me frequently. After all, I called my mother-in-law frequently. Not only that, my mother-in-law was overbearing and had definite ideas about child-rearing, coming to her house for weekly dinners, and spending all holidays with them. Either I did not have the strength or I just thought it would be disrespectful to disagree, so whatever she said went! In the beginning, when my children were too busy to spend time with us, I felt bad and let them know it. Now even if I feel bad, maybe just a little disappointed, they think that I am angry or hurt. I may be, but I have come to realize that it is okay. I can take a little disappointment and move on.—MCL

The traditional model has been altered because of geographical separations and life-style changes. A new model of "family" is developing that might include whomever the family defines it to be: friends, coworkers, neighbors, or religious groups. The Norman Rockwell ideal—mother, father, children, grandchildren, aunts, uncles, and cousins living in close proximity for support and shared family activities—is now, for many, just a recorded moment in history. Even if distances do not divide families, gone are the days, for many, of weekend dinners with the grandparents—many generations talking, laughing, and sharing priceless lessons about life.

Could we, in fact, be part of the reason for the disappearance of traditional roles? The culture of our time celebrates the idea of independence and self-sufficiency; our children were educated to view the adult world through this lens. Imprinted on the psyche of women of our generation has been the idea that youthfulness and vitality were the secret to societal acceptance and eternal adoration. Our parents, products of the Great Depression and World War II, were not lured by the power of a youth-oriented culture, whereas we, along with our peers, might have been seduced by its popular message.

As a generation, we are committed to a high-energy life. Maybe the message we ultimately wanted to communicate to our children was that we were self-sustaining. Consequently, our children began to see us not as needy but as vibrant, active, and independent adults. To them, we could easily make a life for ourselves and did not need their daily support or attention.

The disconnect is that our children's perception of their mother and her needs as she ages is likely not to be the same as the perceptions indelibly imprinted in our memories of our own aging mothers. And whether or not we are always willing to admit it, our imprinted model is the one by which we judge the quality of our relationship with our adult children. It is therefore not surprising that we often struggle with what some have characterized as the essence of the generational divide between over-sixty mothers and adult children of the twenty-first century: the excessive demands and dangers of our current geopolitical world and the lack of a sense of security in the future that makes our adult children focus on successes in the here and now and the sustainability of *their* nuclear families.

Thus, over the past decades, the fabric of the American family has been redesigned, woven with new compositions—mobile families, *yours, mine, and ours*, same-sex parents, foreign adoptions, unmarried parents, *sixty being the new forty*. These assorted combinations might not have been available or, more likely, acceptable in previous generations. It is not new to our generation that change is inevitable. Some of us have been master change artists. What many of us have found is that one of the greatest challenges change creates is the necessity to continuously reexamine the dynamics of all our relationships. Most significantly, it is the relationship with our adult children that repeatedly tests our flexibility to adapt to change.

My daughter moved back in with me with her two children. It's my house and I love having them all. I am a widow with a rather large house. But I find myself disagreeing with many of the child-rearing practices I see. I think she is making some bad decisions. And since they are not my children, I feel it is better just to keep my mouth shut.—DG

Any interpersonal friction experienced by the early parent-child relationship may be predictive of the quality of our connection to our children throughout the life span of our families. As mothers, we might have seen our children as extensions of ourselves and therefore had a huge investment in their future achievements and/or failures. Our children, especially by the time they had reached adolescence, consciously attempted to separate from the family and identify their differences in values and interests. Those differences helped to establish our children as independent entities.

As difficult as this act of disengagement often was, preparing our children to be launched into the adult world was a stated goal throughout their development. Even though all our efforts were directed at launching self-sufficient and self-actualized adults, when they achieved a sense of autonomy, some little voice inside us was still calling out for them to need us...just a little. We might have even expected them to make a small investment in our lives, too. One of the leading researchers in the field of parent-child relationships, the above-mentioned Kira Birditt, aptly describes the social ties between our children and ourselves as "often highly positive and supportive" but also including "feelings of irritation, tension, and ambivalence."

While those tensions and irritations are normative in families, they can create rifts that are pervasive throughout the life of the parent-child relationship. "Relationship problems, like basic personality differences or parents providing unsolicited advice, tend to cause problems," Birditt says. "It may be that these kinds of tensions are longer term and reflect deep-seated conflicts that you just can't escape[,] whereas conflicts of lifestyle, education, finances can be put off to the side if you make an effort." We must never forget that our adult children have full control over their choices, and if we wish to develop and maintain a positive relationship with them, we need to communicate the confidence we have in their decision-making abilities. Nevertheless, because of our historical investment in these relationships, we may still experience emotional tensions.

Many of us reigned as *benevolent dictators* throughout our children's early years. We set the rules, and we guided our subjects with our values and standards. On closer examination, those rules and value systems were likely handed down, in part, from our parents. As a result, another layer of past benevolent dictators and their voices were added to the dialogue. Understandably then, we were rooted in those rules and even more convinced that our parental guidance would ensure a gateway to successful adulthood for our children.

Most probably, underlying the seemingly normal family life we might have thought existed are unresolved conflicts. In addition, as our children reached adulthood, they found significant others and began to create their own nuclear families. As parents of adult children, we become the supportive ring around the nucleus of this new family...and not an integral part at its epicenter. Many of us may have a very difficult time digesting that.

I'm a busy person, working full time, but two very important things hold my time. One is spending time with my grandchildren, because I want them remembering me for having given them "her time when she is not at work." The other thing that holds my time is my work, which represents who I am. When I put my name onto something, I give it my best. While it is not always perfect, what I put into it is what I want others to get out of it. In the relationship I have with my daughter, body language is very apparent. When I overstep my boundaries, she lets me know. But still we are very close. I know she loves me even though I am demanding and I like things done my way. I am independent and responsible, much like my mother was. She is not me! She is more like her dad. More passive and calming, yet she still has a mind of her own. Honesty is important to me. I don't have time to waste because I always had to work, and I accept that I have one daughter, and she knows that I am there to get stuff done. My grandson says, "Gaga, you are so right!" Maybe it skips a generation.—CS

It was not easy to hear that plans were being made that did not include me. I always saw myself as the head, the center of the family. When I wasn't included, I felt left out. It took a long time to understand that I always need to be there for my children, no matter what. That is my essence. But my children have their own families, and that is their essence. I know they will be there when I need them. And I hope not to need them, but I know someday I will. I think once you really understand this, it helps you to define your relationships with your children. For me, this was an "aha" moment. I want to share this because I spent much of life disappointed from unrealistic expectations.—PM

To what extent will these interpersonal tensions ultimately affect the relationship with our adult children?

Looking back and realizing how being a "latchkey" kid affected my life. I wonder how my choices were so similar to my mom's regarding career, working with my husband (number one), and being absent from the home (number two). I thought I could do it better—run my home, have good help, organize schedules, and find "good quality time" with my children to do parenting par excellence. There is always a price to pay, and yes, the outcome does have positives too. Like me, my daughter and my son became quite independent and capable of often navigating life without parental guidance. Yet the result is that there is an emotional distance that evolves when a parent, a *mother*, is not home to give comfort and caring to a child of any age. We don't know when and where the challenges for our children will occur...and if they had to endure moments of hardship without us when they were young, for sure they will not include you in their decision making when they are older. My takeaway is that the relationship that I wish existed between me and my mother, and now my daughter and I, is absent because the key foundational element was absent in those critical years of development. We never learned how to be together. I never made time to stop and *listen*, as no one had demonstrated that for me. I'm not blaming anyone. Yes, I was available for the big challenges. But I've learned it's the time invested in a relationship. The simple unstructured moments, often quiet, and the desire to set aside time that was lacking. Yes, I had the love, caring, and desire, but I didn't create the time necessary for our relationship to grow and for my daughter to realize I wasn't too busy for her "small" problems. Different for me growing up as a child of survivors, the silent message that no problem I might experience could be of consequence compared to what my own parents had experienced in the *Holocaust*. Ultimately I repeated the patterns of absentee parenting, although I thought I could be a *supermom*.—FG

We may not realize that we have the power to set the relationship right. Our years and our life experiences have helped to temper our emotional volatility. When our adult children act in ways that go against what we may believe are essential family values, the strategies we adopt to respond may very well affect our long-term relationship not only with our adult children but with their families as well.

We always have to be mindful that our children, as they become independent adults, may not share our perception of the specialness of our relationship or the intensity of our feelings of connectedness. Because we gave birth to them and have made a huge emotional investment in their growth and well-being, we may expect that our grown children feel that same level of attachment. They may or may not, but their primary investment is, and should be, their own family and its healthy, independent development.

Thoughts to Remember:

1. Encourage open dialogue with our adult children; be cognizant of what we are saying as well as what we are hearing.
2. Begin by acknowledging what is likely to be the consequence of our behavior.
3. Encourage discussion of the expectations we and our adult children (and their spouses/partners) have of each other.
4. Encourage discussion of the expectations we and our adult children (and their spouses/partners) have of our role as grandmother.
5. Be open-minded and nonjudgmental when asked our opinion and realize our adult children (and their spouses/partners) may not agree with it.
6. Avoid taking sides between our adult children and their spouses/partners. Discuss important rules that both we and our adult children may have in our homes and come to a mutual agreement as to what is acceptable for us both.
7. Be respectful of differences in political, social, religious practices that our adult children may have created in their homes.
8. Maintain healthy boundaries between ourselves and our adult children's family.
9. Encourage our adult children by recognizing their positive parenting skills.
10. Be mindful and respectful of in-law and extended family differences.
11. Embrace an ex-spouse as they will always be a father or mother to our grandchild/grandchildren.

The benefit of years and countless discussions set the stage for us to be more candid with our adult children…as long as they perceive what we say as constructive. If the situation is emotionally charged, we may choose to avoid any confrontations at all. Unfortunately, when we are not so measured, our responses may be more negative, and that will only exacerbate the tension and lead to interpersonal conflicts that may not easily be resolved.

With our daughters, it seems so natural to transition to a meaningful woman-to-woman relationship. If we have nurtured a strong connection, our daughters may always cherish that sense of involvement with family and a defining need to maintain that bond even after marrying.

> My daughter and I may speak several times during the day. We are both guilty of wanting to hear what is happening in each of our family's lives. When she calls, it is usually to ask for advice and support. I know that she values my opinion. Sometimes that becomes a huge responsibility because I never want any of her family's decisions to be made based on what I value or think is important. I try very hard to step back and help her find the solutions herself. She is an accomplished woman. She really doesn't need my help, but I can remember calling my own mother when I had a dilemma. I might have had more degrees, but she had the wisdom of life, and I valued that so much about her. So I understand where my daughter is coming from, but different than my mom, I really try not to convince her that my way is the only right way. I do not feel quite so comfortable with my sons because, frankly, they do not ask that often about daily dilemmas. When they call, it is more about issues outside their personal problems. They are more private.—Anonymous

With our sons, the connection may be more tenuous because their most meaningful relationships are often developed and cultivated outside the family's sphere of influence. Once married, for example, it is difficult for them to juggle two important female voices. Since daughters-in-law come with their own set of family values, it may be shortsighted of us to jockey for power over any differences that could easily push our sons to make choices that will have negative consequences in the lives of our family.

While we have had the pleasures and disappointments of shared experiences with our children, a new dimension of joy as well as tension may be added to our lives as they strive to form permanent partnerships with their significant others. The potential for satisfying relationships with our children's partners adds a new layer to the family fabric.

Our children's partners may also come into the marriage with their own expectations. For them, "mother-in-law" may be synonymous with the movie version, "monster-in-law." Dueling standards of behavior and family definitions may add tension to what may be a tenuous relationship between mother-in-law and in-law children to begin with. The in-law relationship requires a lot of hard work and a dedication to open lines of communication.

> I am always conflicted about my relationship with my adult children and their spouses. First and foremost, I want my own children to feel that they can come and speak to me about anything without worrying that I would breach their confidence. Sometimes I feel at odds with myself, because I had an open and honest relationship with my kids. I didn't try to push my beliefs on them, but they certainly knew what my beliefs on most subjects were. Now the dynamics of our relationship have changed, and I avoid most every conversation that is controversial or where I know that my honesty will make me at odds with them. So I bite my tongue, turn the other cheek, laugh at myself so that I won't be tempted to say what I am really thinking. I have seen it with my friends' kids. When their parents are honest and tell them what they really think, you can kiss that relationship good-bye until everybody cools down. Life is short. I do not want to waste a day. I ask myself, "Is there anything that is worth that when it comes to our relationship with our kids?"—PD

For each new addition into the family, an adjustment must be made. Remember that even the children you have raised come with knapsacks of unresolved family issues. So, too, for newly inherited in-law children, who appear with their own set of rules and instructions, personality differences, and expectations.

As the elders in all these relationships, sustained by a long history of interpersonal know-how, it is our responsibility to seize the leadership here—understanding that it is never too late for us to make adaptations and changes. The melding of generations in families is rarely smooth or uncomplicated. Each time a new relationship is added and solidified, a new family system is born, requiring revisions and readjustments from all its members. In the end, the viability of future connections with our adult children, their spouses, and their nuclear families may rest on our ability to navigate through these transitions as seamlessly as possible.

To move forward successfully, we need to look back at those issues that seem to be at the core of our conflicts with our adult children and then at the stressors and tensions manifested from these conflicts. Then...*just let go!* Let go of the hard and fast rules that we found essential to governing our own years of child-rearing. We must stand back and search our souls to determine what is most important at this time when our adult children begin to build their own family units: to insist on enshrining our historical family mores in perpetuity, or to appreciate each family's right to develop its own unique and blended traditions and customs—its own unique and blended nucleus. Our willingness to stand back, to have confidence in our adult children to do what is best for their families, may influence any future role we will play with our children and grandchildren.

GRANDPARENTING

> Grandkids help us to rediscover the wonder of it all...Like them, we can live in the eternal present, rejoicing in what is rather than bemoaning what was or will be. Whenever we measure a growing adolescent against our own shrinking frame, we learn through them to accept both stability and change. They will take whatever we have given them into the future, giving us sufficient hope for our own promised immortality.—Donna Lund, "Grandchildren Give Us Hope for Immortality," *Pittsburgh Post-Gazette* (September 7, 2013)

Reaching grandmotherhood is a milestone for many of us and one of the final opportunities we have to explore powerful new associations and to create enduring attachments. It offers an opportunity to reflect on our own experiences as children and identify those older adults who helped us or hindered us as we grew. Grandmotherhood is the consummate joy that our adult children, through their children, bring to our lives.

What special satisfaction do you get from grandparenting?

My special satisfaction comes from knowing that my daughter, whether she admits it or not, has carried on the same good job I created for her. Knowing that for now they are on the right road, being given every opportunity to fulfill themselves.—MS

Grandparenting is the best! There is unconditional love both ways. As a grandparent you know that the little bumps in life will work themselves out and that average is wonderful!—Anonymous

None. I am not allowed in their lives.—PH

Grandparenting is a hoot and a holler—short visits, few real responsibilities, and they return home. That has been the case for the first six grands. The latest grand is eight months old and only minutes away. I am positive at seventy-four that I am the luckiest nana in the world because I've the distinct pleasure of babysitting for him between two and four days per week since my daughter-in-law returned to work. The little bundle of joy will be attending a childcare program when he turns nine months, and I will still have a one-day-a-week treat! Practicing simple yoga poses while rolling around on the floor with him is great fun. Even greater is getting to my feet while picking him up! Grandparenting has simply made me extremely proud of my children and their own parenting skills. The world is in some good hands.—MP

Grandparenting is wonderful. I've heard the concept that we all should have started out as grandparents first(!), and there is a lot of truth in that fantasy. I am partial to babies and small children, so pouring out lots of love to them has been divine. (I continue that means of expression by volunteering at the neonatal intensive care unit at Nicklaus Children's Hospital.) Seeing grandchildren grow and mature has been beautiful. Since each of my sons is very different, their parenting techniques are unique and special to them and their situations. So I have to accept where they are coming from and interact with them and their children accordingly. Sometimes that is positive. Sometimes I do not agree. Sometimes it is frustrating, and many times the rewards are to see the positive accomplishments in my grandchildren. I had my turn; now it's theirs.—ER

When given the question about what satisfaction I get from grandparenting, it made me laugh. I immediately thought of myself when I was younger. I did not allow my children to get away with much of anything. I was a very strict single mom. As I matured, I began to develop a strong passion and love for the grandchildren in my life. It feels as if my heart grows weaker when I am asked for something from any one of them. I cannot tell them no. I also have gained a special sense of knowing when things have happened, positively and negatively, in their lives. It is a grandmother's instinct.—VP

Having grandchildren has changed the depth and breadth of my life. For many years my daughters and I had led strong, independent lives. We are connected in many ways, but their becoming parents has done more to gather us into a vibrant family unit than could possibly have been achieved by all the phone calls, family vacations, and visits we made since their college graduation. I feel especially appreciated and cherished as the grandmother of their children, and they've made me feel needed. As a sixty-three-year-old woman, I joined a club that I knew existed but had no idea as to the meaning or the extent of its services. The world looks different with grandma eyes. Crying babies don't bother me on planes. Stores have departments that I had somehow passed by. Time is even more precious, and what I had thought was important really isn't anymore. Even my relationship with my husband has grown. These three little people have provided us with whole new areas of conversation. In addition, I find that I think about my deceased parents more and would like to believe that they are here, too, watching out for and finding pleasure in these precious children. Ultimately, I like knowing that when I am no longer here, something of me will go on in the individuals G, K, and Z will become. For a while, I saw my life and the lives of my daughters as one day ending with a period. Now it's a comma. There's wonder in that.—TRS.

The "softa," the grandma, the "BB" (Bubbe Barbara) is my name. I have five blessed grandchildren. They are healthy, gorgeous geniuses and an extreme joy to me. We play well together. The most satisfying to me is watching my children parent. They each have a partnering spouse parenting with them in harmony. It wasn't until I saw each of them function as a parent that I completely understood their capacity for tolerance, patience, teaching, nurturing, loving, selflessness. Who we are, how we're put together, isn't chiseled until we're challenged in complicating and tough roles with huge responsibilities. I'm just so proud of my children as I watch them in their expanding adult roles raising my happy grandchildren.—BGP

Grandparenting is a wonderful reward. I have six grandchildren of my own and four of my husband's. They are precious and have their special gifts. Though miles separate us as we live in separate cities, I try to impart things to them. I find them uninterested in my stories or personal history, but they love me a lot. And we have a warm and loving time together. I think some of them see me as a role model.—CS

My grandchildren are the best gift that G-d could give. I think they are my reward for being nice. They are the love of my life. And the reason that I am so happy is that they are so absolutely wonderful, and I am so grateful that they are near me. I thank G-d every day for their health and their normalcy. I hope my family will be proud of me, and that when I am gone, my grandchildren carry some of my values and passions with them. And that they will remember me as I remember my grandparents.—EH

We adore all our grandchildren and speak to them frequently. Most of them are away at college, but we keep in touch and are aware of what is happening in their lives. When they were younger, we attended almost every activity in which they participated, including sports events, dance recitals, concerts, shows, awards assemblies, etc. We were always there to cheer them on. Our children know this and appreciated our involvement. It gave us a joint experience.—Anonymous

Knowing that they know how much I love them and they can always come to me whenever they want or need to. Watching them grow up to be magnificent human beings.—JK

For those of us who are not grandmothers, we can find a similar sense of fulfillment when we nurture relatives, students, or other young people in an effort to reveal the wisdom that helps bridge the eternal generational gap.

The Change in the Historical Meaning of Grandmother

Because of increased longevity, it is possible that we may spend more than one-fifth of our lifetime in the most important role of grandmother. The meaning of grandmothering has also taken on new dimensions in the twenty-first century, as we have had to adjust to changing world events, new technologies, and a shift in our social fabric. These new dimensions have advanced our growth and motivated us to evolve beyond what we could have dreamed.

Sociologist Jean Giles-Sims, PhD (2005), herself a new grandmother and struggling with what that identity really meant in her life, interviewed a multiethnic and socioeconomically diverse cadre of fifty twenty-first-century grandmothers to understand what makes us tick. Coaxed by her own confusion as to how our culture looks at its grandmothers, she found that little had changed as yet in the national dialogue about grandmothering, even after we ventured into the new century. Today, the American grandmother continues to be trivialized as society romanticizes every aspect of our *youth-oriented, consumerist culture*. Giles-Sims's prediction is that the baby boomer generation, a generation of grandmothers who in 2020 will number 40 million by some calculations, will begin to initiate changes in that public discourse.

When we study the role of grandparenting throughout the last hundred years, we can see that there have been many changes. In the late nineteenth and early twentieth centuries, many grandparents were immigrants who might not have spoken English well and were still clinging to the customs of their native lands and their memories of persecution and poverty. For their adult children, these grandparents were often a troubling influence, with their old-fashioned ways and rigid guidelines for parenting.

By the time we had reached the fifties, there was a more balanced view of grandparenting, although boundaries might have been difficult to establish, especially when there were multigenerational families living together within a quarter-mile radius. Once the sixties arrived, grandparents were already seen as fun seeking and served a supportive function without excessive interference. To Giles-Sims, "grandmother goodness," a historical phenomenon that speaks to a loving and critical involvement in grandchildren's lives, still flourishes, albeit with a different twist.

So who are the grandmothers of the twenty-first century? Many of us grew up as part of the population explosion following World War II. We marched against the inequalities in civil rights in the fifties, sixties, and seventies and the horrors of the Vietnam War. We fought for equality for women and for empowering a woman's right to choose in *Roe v. Wade*. Giles-Sims writes of both the traditional grandmothers and those enlightened women who bridge the gap between the older and the more modern roles grandmothers play in their grandchildren's lives. But it is truly the enlightened grandmother, with her growth of social and economic power, who has changed the landscape of grandparenting for women. Today those same grandmothers advocate for women's contributions outside the family as well as inside.

The grandmother of today is caught in a time warp, fighting the personal images of our own grandmothers and living the twenty-first-century life as a relatively transformed "Nana," "Mimi," and so on. These are similar battles we spoke about earlier with regard to conflicting images our adult children face when viewing each of us. When we reflect back to the past images of "grandma," do we picture a sweet, nurturing, wizened woman in sensible shoes and a housedress who lives close by and whom we visit frequently? That grandmother might have told us stories with life lessons and stories about family and was sure to invite us into the kitchen to smell and taste her goodies, if not to cook alongside her. Grandma was most likely a stay-at-home mom, although she might have worked in a factory when the men went off to fight in Europe in the forties. Or do we conjure up Little Red Riding Hood's sickly grandma, who must be protected from danger? That grandmother may well be the grandmother of our past. As an icon, like the Model T, she might have been replaced long ago with a newer model.

> My most vivid memory of my grandmother was from my early childhood. We only visited our grandparents for the holidays because

the drive in the car took over nine hours. I was jealous of my cousins who lived in the same city as she did. I had no grandparents living near us, and so I was always envious of those kids who could be with grandparents often. My memory unfortunately is a caricature of a grandmother...the flowered housedress, white apron, black lace-up shoes, a wig fashioned in a low bun at the nape of her neck, always slightly askew on her head. She spoke in broken English, but I understood her excitement in seeing us arrive by the warmth of her hug and the tears in her eyes. The table was always set with lots of dishes...everyone from the family would be coming in anticipation of seeing the Cleveland cousins. I loved the smell of the foods she was cooking on the stove. But most important, she had cherry Life Savers and candy corn wrapped and filling the candy dish in the living room. It was either Grandma's sweet tooth or her attempt at being the all-American grandma that prompted her to put those cherry Life Savers in the living room. My grandma had twinkling eyes, as though she was always up to some mischief. What freaks me out is that those memories are of a grandmother who was the exact same age I am right now. We may look very different, but I am not sure what differences we might find beneath the surface. I wonder if my grandchildren see something different through their eyes.—CTS

I adored my maternal grandmother, and I could never imagine a more wonderful grandmother than my mother was to my children. When I became a grandmother, I saw I had a chance to relate to children in a different way than I had with my own. I spend more time playing with them, following their lead in what we do together. It has also allowed me to see my grown children as patient, thoughtful, loving parents. I love seeing the connections between the six adults and eight children (ages four to thirteen)...the kids with their cousins and aunts and uncles as well as their parents. It makes me confident that they will continue to enjoy each other as time goes on.—DSG

Today's grandmother is a composite of that nurturing grandma of our past and a woman with a new blend of skill sets and responsibilities. As grandmothers, we may still bake cookies, babysit when needed, prepare family get-togethers, and knit baby blankets. But we do this in addition to busy work schedules, athletic pursuits, travel plans, book clubs, continuing education courses, and a myriad of other active pursuits.

> My husband and I made every effort not to exclude our children from the benefits that came with our careers. They traveled with us on business trips, and they always pitched in to help on projects when we needed extra hands. I like to believe that they were proud of our accomplishments. I needed to have away time with our kids because both my husband and I worked fifty-to-sixty-hour weeks. Since most of my friends did not work, I needed to try to level the playing field by doing special things with my kids. Now my husband and I are doing the same thing with our grandchildren. Our grandson is always so busy with afterschool activities that the only real alone time is when we take him away with us. I find that exploring a new city provides a wonderful chance to have incredible conversations about feelings, about family history, about cultural differences among people. I never thought I could be lucky enough that my children would allow us the freedom to take their children on these adventures. I am hopeful that the memories of those journeys will be permanently etched in the memories of their happiest days.—CTS

We may see the role of grandmother differently than grandmothers in the past saw their role. *Does the world see us differently? Do our adult children and grandchildren see us differently?*

In her book *Grandparenthood*, Dr. Ruth Westheimer maintains that although cultural messages espouse that grandparents today play a less significant role in their family's life due to geographical distances or career demands, grandparents are more vital than ever before. To Dr. Ruth, grandparents are in a position to provide a list of necessities money cannot buy, including "continuity, trust, stability, love, understanding, and unconditional support." In her opinion, grandparents should focus more on the symbolic aspects of their role and their meaning to the family. These attributes serve to ground our grandchildren, who are being reared in a mobile twenty-first-century family.

New Grandparenting Roles and Responsibilities

> It occurs to me that grandkids connect us to the future, and because of them, we must care what happens to the world.—NR

As we have shown, parenting styles and family dynamics have experienced major historical and philosophical changes over the past one hundred years. It is not surprising, then, that just as we had different views on child-rearing than our parents did, our adult children have their own notions of how to successfully raise their children. While some of today's parents have rejected the views of their elders, others have woven their parents' and grandparents' principles into the fabric of their family life.

My sister called me from New York and told me she and her family were coming to town and staying at my house for four nights. She has a five-year-old daughter, G. While I was fixing my morning organic green juice filled with organic kale, spinach, broccoli, ginger, beets, blueberries, and other amazing garden delights, I imagined the joy G and I would have together doing my morning chores and fixing my magic potion. Essentially I have a cat shelter at my home, with twenty-seven cat rescues and other outdoor strays that I feed. I clean the little boxes and change their water. I have a dog rescue that I walk, and she has a boyfriend dog rescue that she plays with every day. I have a broken dryer that I have committed not to replace, so I hang my clothes out in the yard on the clothesline to dry to save the environment, and it all feels good. I feel so close to nature, and I was excited to think that G would enjoy these activities with me, felling close to nature too. Then it occurred to me that I am a grandmother of twelve children who have never had the pleasure of and would never have the privilege to share in these earthly experiences with their grandmother because of their parents' limited belief system. My children have much more stringent religious practices than I do, and they put tight limits on what the children can and cannot experience. I don't have the right food and lifestyle, and so most of my experiences with my grandchildren are on their turf and/or out of my home. It is unfortunate, I think, and sad when I think about all that could be expansive and healthful for them. But grandparents have deep and expanding influences on their grandchildren in this way. And just for the final upshot, G did come. And we did all the things I imagined we would do together. The first morning out when we walked the dog together, G, coming from life in Manhattan, looked around the neighborhood and exuberantly exclaimed, "This is a jungle!"—RA

The Impact of Divorce on Grandparenting. Since the time many of us married, the rate of divorce has rapidly grown to over 50 percent. The high rate of divorce may have definite implications on the lives of our adult children and our grandchildren as well as on our grandparenting role. Our support can be invaluable and may prove to be essential in sustaining the family of divorce through its most difficult times. We may be called upon for those tasks ordinarily shared by both parents. We may be called upon to provide needed day-to-day care. We may be called upon to provide stability and emotional support to the family.

The divorce may put us at odds with one of our grandchildren's parents, but if our grandchildren reside with our biological child, we may likely have greater access to them. In *A Boomer's Guide to Grandparenting,* authors Kathryn and Allan Zullo boldly describe grandparents as the "other victims" in the divorce arena, and they place great importance on maintaining a relationship with the parent who is not our child for the well-being of our grandchildren.

Grandparents may play a major role in the ultimate adjustment of their grandchildren during and after divorce. As grandmothers, one of our biggest challenges is to remain neutral with the ex-spouse, especially when that spouse has threatened the very fabric of our grandchildren's lives. Grandparents who are there through the troubled times and are supportive can be the critical factor in the successful adjustment of their grandchildren to divorce.

What role do you think you have in shaping your grandchildren's sense of self?

The Impact of Being the Keepers of the Meaning. How agile we are as grandparents in adapting to change is the challenge we face as we relate to our adult children and grandchildren. Naturally, we may differ philosophically, but we should not expect we have the right to insinuate our beliefs into their lives.

For me, grandparenting is a dynamic experience that requires an ever-changing role as our grandchildren develop and change throughout

147

the life span. My recollection of the birth of my first granddaughter and how she laid on my chest and allowed the full weight of her sleeping body to relax on me in a soothed, comforted state fills my heart with deep love and satisfaction. The fun and reverie we have now, fourteen years later, shopping for school clothes, backpacks, the latest boots and fashionwear, is an expression of my understanding of her developmental changes, current needs, and wants. The grandchildren are so excited when "Nana" comes to town. What was once an unconscious learning on their part of a loving person in their lives, "Nana," who loves them, understands them, and has fun with them, has become a conscious awareness and an additional source of love and support in their lives. To keep the connection across generations, I called my daughter several weeks ago after thinking about my mother, who had died this past Mother's Day. I told my daughter I would bring her my mother's pearls and asked her to make sure that each one of my granddaughters wears these pearls at their wedding, a symbol and bond between the beauty and love of past, present, and future.—RA

More importantly, before we share our *wisdom* with our adult children, we must recognize that there is a possibility that no one is interested in listening to what may be perceived as outdated views of the world. We must begin by listening. Listening to what *they* are interested in is the very first step in developing a meaningful relationship with our grandchildren and, frankly, with their parents as well.

Even when our adult children ask for our advice about parenting or other family-related issues, they may not really want it. Giving unwanted advice can ultimately come between our adult children and ourselves and potentially cause irreparable discord in the parent-grandparent relationship.

What can we do that will prove to be helpful? Acknowledge the problems and dilemmas our adult children and grandchildren may have to face. Understand that the problems and dilemmas are their problems and dilemmas to resolve. Be empathetic, and certainly ask questions that may help clarify the issues. We may even suggest that we have some ideas about solving the problems *but* only after we ask if they are interested in hearing them. The only thing we know for sure is that telling our children what to do about their families will almost always get us into trouble. We need to ask ourselves, what if the solution we propose is wrong and does not work?

What can we do to optimize our role as *keeper of the meaning*? Share our histories and the legends that make each of our families so colorful and unique. Share the values and ethical constructs that have guided our lives and the lessons we have learned from living by them. Share our perspective. Through storytelling, weave a narrative they can understand and appreciate. Then hope and pray (if you find solace in that!) that they are listening, and later, when they are in search of a philosophical construct by which to live their lives, they will be reminded of our words.

The Impact of Becoming a Grandmother. Becoming a grandmother may signal the first signs of aging, something we may not be psychologically ready to accept. What may be most shocking is that the arrival of a grandchild has transformed us into a card-carrying member of that *third* generation. As Jackie Highe (2008) reflects in her book *The Modern Grandparent's Guide*, "Becoming a grandparent for the first time is a leap into the unknown. You wake up one morning to find you've moved up the generation chain...It's a shock to your system." We may indulge our grandchildren in order to feel loved and needed and to be explicitly connected with and integrated into their world. As we have described it, this stage in the older adult's life, generativity, is a time when we search for and find meaning in our lives in order not to stagnate. Grandparenthood is one pursuit that allows us the opportunity to find satisfaction and joy from sharing our lives and histories with our grandchildren. The increased responsibilities of being a new parent may have an impact on our one-on-one time with our adult child, and too, our focus on the new grandchild may also change the parent–adult child dynamic.

As expected, differing child-rearing practices frequently creates escalating disagreements. Yet we often hear grandparents say how much they enjoy and feel successful in the grandparenting role. Our children may even comment on how different we are with their children than we were with them.

> Being a grandmother is such fun! I love spending time with my daughter's three girls. I'm always looking for cute things to buy them. The most fun is to take the children *without* their parents: to shop, for lunch, to the theater or a museum. My relationship has improved with my daughter over the last number of years since she has had her three children. I think she realizes how much we love the girls and how much they mean to us. It is so very interesting to see what "kind of parent" your children become!—AH

> I just want to be there for them when they need me and hope it's enough. My reward that I never asked for is they always tell me how

lucky they are to have me. But of course I tell them I am the one who is so lucky to have them.—LKS

The years have helped temper our emotional volatility, and at this stage of our lives, we can see how our perspective has been shaped. Grandparenting may still be parenting, but without the heightened emotionality that came when we were positioned as parents in the first line of defense. Someone else has the final word now, and we can just focus on enriching our grandchildren's lives with unconditional love, emotional support, and unforgettable memories. It is no wonder being a grandparent is so rewarding!

Dear E,

The other day when you arrived from camp after being away for seven full weeks, the first thing you did when I visited you was to give me the most delicious hug, and then you said, "Come here, Grandma." You immediately took out several things from your backpack, and lo and behold, one was a canister of little plastic circles. You immediately said, "Grandma, I want to make this bracelet for you." You opened up a little canister that was filled with little elastic rubber bands of all different colors, and you made me a bracelet that I have worn the last few days everywhere I went. You then proceeded to tell me you had more things to show me that you had in that backpack, and you pulled out a little box that you had bought for your sister. It was the most precious little bear on a chain, and I wondered how you could have purchased it, knowing you were given only a few dollars to spend. I was curious, so I did ask about how much you spent, and you said two dollars. I was in awe. And then you brought out a gift for your brother—a little box of stones for his collection. Your enthusiasm for giving and sharing with others has been demonstrated to me as I watch you grow up! Thoughtfulness is such a beautiful quality, and I hope that you will continue to be appreciative of being a giver as well as a receiver with all the wonderful people you will meet over your lifetime.

Love always, Grandma

In today's world, our adult children are very mobile. They may no longer stay close to home or raise their children in the same neighborhood they grew up in. When grandchildren arrive, it is likely that travel plans may not center on how often we are able to visit as much as how often the parents are willing for us to come. Now, though, because of incredible advances in technology, we can FaceTime distant grandchildren regularly or Skype them on the Internet. Clearly, however, this is not the same as giving them a giant hug or rocking them to sleep in our arms. Distances still make it more difficult to maintain these meaningful relationships.

<u>Thoughts to Remember:</u>

1. Understand that there may be disparities between our adult children's and our own viewpoints regarding childrearing practices due to generational and personality differences.
2. Respect our adult children's role as the PARENT of our grandchildren.
3. Communicate with adult children any conflicting rules we may have when our grandchildren are in our care.
4. Discuss any activities we may want to do with our grandchildren with their parents first.
5. Discuss presents that we may want to give our grandchildren with their parents first, especially if we think the gift may be controversial.
6. Nurture our grandchildren with unconditional support, trust, consistency and love.
7. Share our family history through photos, conversations and storytelling.
8. Listen to our grandchildren's words and appreciate the "special gifts" they add to our life.
9. Be proactive in maintaining our relationships with grandchildren in a mobile and complex world.
10. Be accepting of the technological advances that are integral to our grandchildren's ever-changing world.
11. Be receptive to learning new technology to be able to communicate in your children's and grandchildren's language.

With the birth of our grandchildren, we recognize the significance of sharing our stories about their parents and our parents and grandparents. We become a vital link to their past, with our narratives and our wisdom, as they are to our future. In sharing ourselves, we are helping to establish a bridge to the world outside their nuclear family.

> My first-grade granddaughter was working on a project that involved knowing where her ancestors came from. She asked me about them, and I told her that they immigrated to the United States from Eastern Europe. I thought Russia, but my mother told me it was Russia/Poland, because during the late 1800s and early 1900s, the borders were changing. It was then that I realized that there is so much about my family history that is a blur to me, and if I wanted it continued and wanted my grandchildren to know about their past family life, I was the only one left who could tell them. And I didn't really remember much. The focus for our book came flooding back to me as I thought about the importance of writing family narratives as a gift to future generations. I wish I had paid more attention to the stories to tell my grandchildren. I want to share what I know, both in an oral and written tradition of storytelling.—MCL

If we want our grandchildren to know the richness of their ancestor connections, who they were and the principles they fought hard to maintain, it will be up to us to pass on their histories in our stories. Before the written word, the art of storytelling was the method through which culture, values, and history were transmitted. In much the same way, traditional fairy tales often came from a storyteller making his way cross country, stopping in town squares and weaving his yarns. What was passed on orally became a rich and cherished body of literature.

Each of our families has its own volumes of traditions and legends, values and spiritual beliefs, that have been handed down for generations. If we want these to come alive in the minds of our children and grandchildren, we must be committed to being their chronicler. Knowing we are linked to a past, bound to a secure present, and grounded in a historical timeline brings continuity to our lives. Celebrating our past through our narratives ensures that who we are—a composite of generations who came before—will live in the hearts of our adult children and grandchildren and the generations that come after.

LIST OF QUESTIONS TO REVIEW

What are the most satisfying qualities about your relationships with your adult children?

What was your concept of an ideal parent, and did the reality of parenting measure up to your expectations?

How would you describe your relationships with your adult children? How does that impact family relationships?

What generational differences, if any, affect the communication between you and your adult children?

To what extent will these interpersonal tensions ultimately affect the relationship with our adult children?

What special satisfaction do you get from grandparenting?

What role do you think you have in shaping your grandchildren's sense of self?

PERSONAL REFLECTIONS

_____

_____

_____

_____

_____

_____

_____

_____

_____

_____

_____

_____

_____

CHAPTER 5
The Richness of Sisterhood

Walking with a friend in the dark is better than walking
alone in the light.
—HELEN KELLER

The sixties were distinguished by a sociocultural shift from the prevailing conservative notions of the fifties. As women, we began to find our voice in the sixties. That voice spoke to the power and importance of our individuality—the individuality to determine our own destiny as well as to wield influence if we as individuals acted collectively. The women's movement, as it would come to be known in the seventies, birthed a newfound belief in *sisterhood*—a catalyst to promote women's issues and to celebrate women's friendships. It was within the framework of sisterhood that women developed the art of listening to each other, of solving the challenges of womanhood, and of rejoicing in each other's strengths. For centuries and across every continent, what had been instinctive for women to do—to seek connections with other women for socializing, for protection, for support—now represented a new armament to embolden and unify the power of women. How strange it all seemed that those historical connections, taken for granted and undervalued by women and by their communities, would now be our lottery ticket to have a seat at the table of life!

The women's movement changed all that we had come to accept. It was that very natural sense of connectedness that was being heralded as our lifeline to a world with equal status and with the right to make decisions about our own bodies and souls. Through sisterhood we had become empowered, socially and emotionally.

Now, fifty years later, with more time, maturity, and the capacity for self-examination, we are able to reflect on how integral those bonds of friendship are to our sense of well-being. We only have to listen to the voices of our *sisters* in their stories below to appreciate the strength of those bonds and the meaning they hold in our lives.

My understanding of the true nature of sisterhood took place on the plains of northwest Namibia among the tribal community of the Himbas. As I approached the small, clay-hutted village, I was struck by the beauty of the women and children who sat talking and laughing under the heat of the afternoon sun. I fell silent as our guide, a Himba male who served as our interpreter, introduced all the women as wives of the tribal chief, who that day had gone off to the "city," a place forbidden to his wives. The chief's eldest wife, with her wizened face and incredible smile, sat peacefully at the center. My initial reaction, colored by prejudices that were intricately woven into my Western values, was that these women were slaves to their culture. That they had lost their individual identities in their tribal braids and identical calfskin miniskirts, bare breasted and covered in clay "masks." I was angered by the thought that they were slaves to the tribal chieftain, forced to inhabit the same space with his other fifteen wives. I am sure that "barbaric" crossed my mind as my eyes flitted from face to face. I was angered by the thought that they were kept from being educated, from being set free to explore the world around them. These women did not even venture out into the neighboring city a mere forty miles away. It took no time for me to learn how wrong I was and how little I really knew about "sisterhood." These women were connected by a bond much greater than anything I had ever experienced, even with my dearest friends of fifty-plus years. These women spoke with one strong and determined voice. They spoke with confidence, a confidence that only comes from knowing that you are enveloped by the love and devotion of other women who understand your joys and the pain at your very core. They laughed at the "limited" nature of our friendships, of our families. The eldest wife, revered by all, seemed enveloped by the other wives' love and respect. I had learned that friendships and family encompassed these wives' entire world. For days, with the memory of those Himba women chiseled into the very fiber of my being, I thought about the extraordinary bonds of their sisterhood and the strength of that sisterhood—a moral compass for women who do not long for any other distractions in their lives.—CTS

Earlier in chapter 2, we examined life satisfaction. To better understand the true nature of life satisfaction at age sixty-plus, we need to examine not only the vital role friendships have played in our lives but also our own flexibility in adapting to the changing social dynamic affected by retirement, illness, death, and other life-altering transitions. Friendship is the glue that ultimately binds our lives inextricably to others. Our life stories, as well as those we find within this chapter, may prove to be a mirror for reflecting how and why these relationships have survived or faltered or failed.

The Meaning of Friendship: A Historical Perspective

It is not so surprising that we find that the earliest writings about friendship date back to the polemics of Aristotle and Cicero and that now, tens of centuries later, their discussions still serve as the foundation for our contemporary definitions. To the Greek philosopher Aristotle, friendship encompassed many elements—the enjoyment of a friend's company, the usefulness of the friendship, and, perhaps most importantly, a shared commitment to do good in the world. To Aristotle, each friend's recognition and acceptance of the goodness in the other and in humankind represented the singular feature of enduring friendships. Cicero, the Roman orator, shared Aristotle's notion of collective dedication to goodness and also identified virtue as the common bond between true and lasting friends.

How do you think this measures up to today's perceptions about friendship? Some students of sociology would argue that today, most friendships are influenced by external forces, such as class, age, gender, ethnicity, and occupation. This speaks to the somewhat involuntary and formal nature of friendships, and as over-sixty women, we may also, like Aristotle, choose our friends based on our shared moral commitments and common pleasures. This mutual acceptance, a feeling of simpatico in which our friend is a mirror to our own morality, is built on the intimacy of our relationships and a sense of trust that we nurture over time.

Interestingly, there is a clear relationship in the roots of the words "love" and "friendship" in Greek (*philos*, "friend," and *phileō*, "I love"), Latin (*amicus*, "friend," and *amō*, "I love"), and even Old English (*frēond*, "friend," and *frēon*, "to love"). It seems quite natural then that both Aristotle and Cicero, as well as social theorists throughout the ages, have rooted the ideals of friendship in the love for our friends and for the virtues they possess.

As young girls, we valued our friends because of shared interests—like being fashion queens in our mothers' discarded dresses and shoes. Life seemed so uncomplicated, didn't it? Through adolescence our girlfriends became confidantes and, at times, our rivals too. That teenage time of life! How we looked and whom we were with seemed *so* important. As young marrieds, we bonded to share our fears and our triumphs in motherhood and our anxieties over who we could have been. As we age, we recognize and are able to appreciate the real value of our "sisters": the women in our lives that allow us to be our naked selves. No need to dress up and pretend to be someone else like in our childhood years. No need to fit in and be accepted like in our adolescent years. No need to be validated like when we were young mothers. Today we can be who we are, accept what could have been but is no longer an option, and celebrate each and every moment we can share with people who bring meaning in our lives. Each one of my closest friends today has allowed me to cry and laugh unabashedly, to expose my weaknesses fearlessly, and to open my heart, unafraid of being vulnerable. Not only do I treasure those friendships, they are the nourishment of my soul. I have to thank my friends for allowing me to share with all the others that feel the same way as I do about our sisterhood and for honoring me with their friendship.—CTS

I don't sleep as soundly as I once did, so at night in the dark, I try magical techniques in hope of catching a few more winks before it is time to get up. Sometimes I recite Aesop's fables rewritten in French poetic verses by the fabulist La Fontaine, or mentally retrace my way home to Paris at the Place de l'Opera, meandering through beautiful, little-known streets. On other nights, I try to remember the names and faces of my twelfth-grade classmates. Occasionally, this complex system works...but not always. So the other night, a bright idea came to me. Why not try to recall the many pleasant happenings I have experienced in my life? Among the list that popped up was book club.

Yes, book club. I recalled the day D invited me to join you to discuss events that took place in World War II. I left that night thinking that I had given them a dose of information overload, so I was totally surprised and elated when later they invited me to join the illustrious, almost-forty-year-old Miami Beach book club. I was excited for many reasons. First, although I had studied classic English authors in school in London, I knew very few contemporary American writers, and I would never have discovered them on my own had it not been for the book club selections. Second, the timing was perfect, as my third child was back in school in Chicago, and I could finally give to reading the proper time it deserved. Third, I had left my friends and family when I left Paris but did not really feel an empty space while raising my three children and five grandchildren. Now only two live close by, though, so between Skype calls to Bilbao and Nashville, grabbing a good book is a treat that brings benefits. As a result of sleepless nights, my repertoire has increased. I travel with Cleopatra on the Nile River, follow the goldfinch on a mad trek through Europe, or read *Lolita* in Tehran. Finally, when I start to doze off, I feel ever obliged to my Miami Beach bookish friends.—MM

In the modern world, with the advent of industrialization, urbanization, and capitalism, the concept of friendship, an essential element that had sustained the traditional community, has been transformed. Face-to-face, interactive relationships oftentimes were exchanged for more exclusive and competitive ones. In the eighteenth century, people living and working in the village continued to be compelled to conduct themselves by the standards enforced by that community and were manipulated by the utilitarian nature of friendship: "How can your friendship benefit me?" Nobody could disappear into the woodwork.

Once the Industrial Revolution took hold, people migrated to the city, where they could easily become anonymous, attended to by no one, isolated, and alienated. Their long, tedious work hours and their mental and physical exhaustion prohibited them from reaching out for casual, feel-good kinds of friendships. Although many felt banished to obscurity, others enthusiastically embraced their newfound freedom—beyond the watchful eyes of family and community.

Early on, though, there were many estranged workers for whom it became essential to address their social needs, and they did this by forming trade organizations with compatriots from work. Thus industrialization gave birth to a culture of independence and, with it, a newly formed concept of friendship. Odd as it may sound to us today, it was the interplay between independence and the demand for mutual cooperation that created the worker's sense of well-being in the nineteenth century. With independence as its foundation, a new order of social organization was formed and became the core of early meaningful friendships.

In the twentieth century, merit was exchanged for companionship. Modern thinkers felt that out of companionship, friendship would grow. It worked quite simply. Companions based their initial attraction on the sense of "What, you too? I thought I was the only one"—a shared activity or interest. When someone then saw the same truth, friendship blossomed.

> I have always had a large number of women friends who have given life to the word friendship: a relationship of *choice* that is mutually enriching, involving intimacy and an unconditional acceptance of the other up to and including love. Life-long friendships carry a special luster because these friends knew you when and they love you still. I have counted on different friends for different kinds of support at different times of my life. Difficult personal periods put extra burden on friendships, but I have never misjudged or been let down. Early friendships had a distinct social flavor but evolved through the years as my needs changed. Some friendships are weighted intellectually; some spiritually; others emotionally. Each is unique and gives me something precious that I cherish. Rarely do my friends know each other. (I used to think that people would look around at my funeral and wonder who was there.) Living in a happy marriage with a large family limits the time I have to indulge my sisterhood, but there they are: for whatever I need, whenever I need it. They elevate me, even to myself. If we are judged in life by the company we keep, I will have no problems. As for the qualities in my woman friends that I most admire and have been influenced by, I would first mention independence of thought and action, being a freethinker, open to what's out there. It takes a great effort not to be influenced by the "group." My relationships have basically been one on one, an assortment of strong, capable women. The second quality I am drawn to is achievers who share my work ethic and who convert time into

substance. My friends are women who worked before retirement (or are still working), who continue to learn and grow. Women who talk about ideas rather than people. A third quality I admire in my friends is creativity and passion for something. My oldest and best friend is a pianist who inherited her musical talent from her mother. I was so jealous of that talent and tried hard to find one of my own. I even went back to college and took thirty-six hours of studio art, hoping that I had some latent talent. To my greatest disappointment, I didn't, and I have switched to being an "admirer" and "collector." Another quality my friends share is their "realness." I mean a lack of pretention, honesty I can count on, an intimacy that is safe and sacred. This is very good soil for a relationship to grow in and has helped me to be a good friend. I am extremely unimpressed by the vacations taken, the cars driven, the address, the fine jewelry. I am very impressed by who you are. I need my friends to be innately interesting and stimulating, and I try to be the same. Last, but maybe I should have mentioned this first, a friend should be a happy person. I like women who are happy with themselves, happy with their husbands, happy with their lives. I did learn from experience that you can't make another person happy, but you can share their happiness with them. I am happy when I'm with friends, but I am also happy when alone because my friends are within. I continue to be impacted by the joy of each unique friendship. And I think it's interesting that my husband really loves all of my friends and would call them his friends as well. He'll probably marry one after I am gone! In friendships, one plus one equals infinity. I am a different, better, smarter, and more evolving person because of my girlfriends. Keep it coming!—IG

We are struck here by how IG has thoughtfully woven together the influences from the classical as well as the modern thinkers—most likely without even knowing it.

Establishing the Stages of Friendships

The qualities—the desire for love, intimacy and support—that serve as our foundation for friendships are established with our very first relationship: the bond with our mother. It is within that mother-daughter relationship that each of us is able to develop our sense of self. The symbiosis of that mother-daughter relationship is critical. That safety net protects us in our early years from the vulnerability we could experience if left alone without that essential feeling of trust.

During the forties, fifties, and sixties, when we were young and establishing our roots as people, boys were taught to be independent and tough and be physically and emotionally self-sufficient. Because competition was supported, boys developed their sense of self from the ability to achieve power and status.

Daughters were given a different message from the very beginning. We were taught to model our behavior after our mothers, and we likely identified with them even as we matured and were launched into adulthood. As young girls, many of us were encouraged to be sweet, dependent, and, of course, selfless—always nurturing and responding to others' needs.

During elementary school years, we began to appreciate our own thoughts and ideas. Those of us who might have struggled in our early relationships with our mothers might have sought out substitutes who fulfilled our need to be nurtured and encouraged. We searched for other role models and were lucky if we found that needed sense of peace and safety we could not find in our own homes.

> Even when I was eight years old, I could not wait to get out of my house...both my parents were alcoholics, and we lived in perpetual chaos. I would leave my house early for school and then go to a friend's house afterward until I had to go home for dinner, and this went on for many years. There was little discussion about it with my friend or her mom, and it was just an open, welcoming door. I often went right into her room even when she was not home and waited until it was absolutely time to go. I did not feel lonely or upset. I had a place to be that was quiet and safe. There were many times when I did come home early that I found that my friend was waiting for me in my room, and we never questioned the need to be in each other's homes. Strange as I think about it now, I believe she was escaping as well...What I have learned from all of this is that I go to friends when I need help, never to my family of origin, whom I never could count on for anything. Friends are what have given me refuge over time, as well as food, shelter, and seeds of encouragement. I would be homeless if not for their generosity. I surprise myself when I think of my educational accomplishments and

my ability to trust others...I am forever grateful to those who gave me the strength to go on beyond just surviving...to thriving.—MH

The real challenge came as we began to develop as adolescents. Emerging with hormones storming, we tried to manage multiple relationships with other girls, with boys, and with our families. We were often left confused and conflicted. As young teenagers, we started to put ourselves in others' shoes. Because we were now mature enough to take on a third-person perspective, we were able to evaluate our interactions and work to better those relationships. At this stage, our relationships alternated between intimacy and rejection as we shifted our focus from our primary family unit to a circle of intimate friends. In our teen years, we learned that friendship linked us to those whom we wanted to be central to our lives.

> I had a very hard time when I moved into a new neighborhood to be closer to my extended family when I was fifteen. My parents were recently divorced, and really without much struggle, my mom allowed me to spend as much time as I wanted with my dad. It was the fifties... and my family looked nothing like Ozzie and Harriet's. I think I was one of the few people whose parents were divorced. To complicate things, I had matured early, and I know when the teachers saw me for the first time, they all assumed "trouble." The only thing I craved was normal. The girls I met right from the very beginning were very welcoming, and I easily became one of the most "popular" with both the boys and girls. I didn't invite my friends to my house, but my dad would let me sleep out on occasion when there was a pajama party or something. When my dad remarried, overnight I had the fabled wicked stepmother. As an only child, I was the only person around to take her orders. Although I felt I could escape to my crowd of friends during school hours, I was very cautious about going to other people's houses. I feel my friends' parents probably did not want them to be friends with me because, as the saying went, I came from a broken home. I was feeling confused about what it was about me that made my stepmom and maybe my friends' moms sense that I was not good enough. From where I stood, my friends were surrounded with lots of love and support. They tried to make me feel a part of things, but I felt I was an island sometimes.—Anonymous

In adolescence, we grappled with the notion of independence and separation and did battle with these conflicting goals as we strived to reach autonomy. Early conflicts with our mothers likely occurred. Themes of jealousy, envy, and dominance in our friendships were often hidden but may from time to time have skimmed the surface of our daily interactions.

Late adolescence was the time when many of our friendships matured as we began to understand empathy and were sensitive to the wishes of others. The quality of the friendships we were able to form as a child and adolescent had a strong impact on the friendships we made as adults.

Trust and reciprocity now became the foundations on which our friendships were built—friendships that hopefully would survive throughout our adult lives. These were quality connections. They were stable and mature connections. It was the constancy of these social supports that became the heart and soul of our most profound relationships with women. Late adolescence was the time when we began to feel comfortable in our individuality, to look for a mate, and to ponder the thought of planting roots for a family of our own. It was also the time that individual friendships grew and connected to make personal communities.

Clearly the stages of friendship run parallel to our stages of development. Once the initial bonding was established, the need for trust and intimacy became essential. With intimacy, though, may also come conflict and rejection. These feelings may wax and wane throughout our lives and our friendships. Conflict and rejection also speak to the depth and breadth of our relationships and add to the richness of each stage of our lives as we struggle and work to resolve the issues that arise in their wake. Young adulthood and the responsibilities of early parenting can draw us back to the familiarity, warmth, and acceptance of our primary relationship with our mother as well as set the stage for building a lifetime of relationships with other women who are sharing our experiences.

> Having a new baby at a very young age was completely frightening. I did not have the support of my husband, who expected me to do everything correctly. I remember burning the nipples I was sterilizing one evening and then just sitting down to cry. I probably was in some sort of undiagnosed postpartum depression. It was only through the help of some of my close friends that I think I got through this period of my life. Having women who already had babies giving me some ideas

and advice was more than helpful. It saved my life. Supportive women friends going through the same stage of life, sharing stories, and, most importantly, listening to frustrations can give you the kind of support you need to survive. I didn't want to tell my mother how hard this all was. I thought she might be too critical.—MCL

I, like other adults, looked to my friends to provide a reference point beyond my family with which to measure myself. It is a friend who helped me through difficult decision making. It is a friend who helped me heal the hurts of a broken relationship. It is a friend who smoothed the rough edges around the arguments I had with my parents. It is a friend who supported my need to be an independent thinker. Often my friends encouraged developing the parts of myself that were unknown to my family and perhaps even to me.—Anonymous

Friendships seem to be controlled by time and space and material resources. Constrained by these factors, there are likely to be differences in how our social groups organize into friendship relationships. There are likely to be differences in how the genders create friendship patterns. There are likely to be differences when age impacts the dynamics of our friendships. Nevertheless, in our mobile society, friendships as vehicles that significantly bind us to each other have increasingly become our social glue.

My best friend from New Orleans lost her seven-year struggle with ALS. My husband and I had been visiting her every two or three months because we never knew how long she had. Ironically, we found it to be an amazing experience—enriching, fulfilling, even happy. She was an amazing woman, as is her only child—a daughter. We were with her daughter until the day before her mother died. I received a box in the mail. It was copy of Anna Quindlen's memoir, *Lots of Candles, Plenty of Cake*. I cannot tell you what it felt like to open that box and know that my friend was gone and her daughter remembered me. I am not sure what it is a testimony to, but I am in tears. I realized the importance of handing down friendship a generation, making an effort to do that to ensure that relationship. I have tried to do that with my children as well. I have given them my friends.—IG

Finding the Meaning of Friendship

What are the qualities of women friends who most influenced your life, and why did they have such an impact?

> Having quite a few very good, longtime friends is something I greatly value. Whenever we are together, we can pick up where we left off—a wonderful feeling! Some friendships go back to elementary, junior high, and high school. It is wonderful to go through life with friends who share so many of the same or similar experiences.—ER

> When my husband was very ill and I was waiting for the surgeon to tell me his prognosis, my lifelong friend sat with me. When my husband died, she flew in from Maryland even though she has a fear of flying. When her mother was very ill, I was there to comfort her, and I will continue to do so. Good friends are those who communicate, are sincere, and try to be nonjudgmental. Mutual respect and trustworthiness are essential. They are there for you.—MB

After reading each of these impassioned reflections on friendship, we can better understand how difficult it is to define friendship with one broad brushstroke. For many women, the meaning of friendship is quite personal and taps into needs that are intrinsically tied to our culture, our personal history, our age, and our own internal image of what a friend represents. It may also tap into our desire to connect to women outside our family circle who, as friends, help us to discover and share hidden secrets, validate who we are, and help us confront our demons.

> I share a friendship with a woman who is both culturally and religiously very different than I am. We met twenty-four years ago and have been friends ever since. When thinking about the qualities of a person, I can say the most important thing about our relationship is that she is one of the few people I can be myself with and feel comfortable. We both have spiritual backgrounds so understand life differently than most, which adds to our acceptance and understanding of life and each other. We naturally are extremely considerate of one another's feelings and are most respectful in the way we express ourselves. I may say things that are critical to her,

but they are not said in an offensive manner. I learned a long time ago from masters in the art of communication that it is important to be positive and to use stories that illustrate a situation. My friend was insensitive and demanding of others, but when I used examples of other friends modeling those behaviors, over time she seems to have learned from their examples. I could tell her anything, and she lets me be me. We are tolerant, respectful, and considerate of each other, and it allows us to be what we are without playing games. There is an understanding and tolerance of who we are, and our energies are compatible.—Anonymous

Friendship is not one of those concepts where there is an agreed-upon, socially acknowledged criterion for what makes someone our friend. Basic to any significant relationship is the need to be valued and remembered. Some social scientists have actually attempted to formalize rules to define the friendship relationship, including things like giving help in time of need, respecting privacy and space, and keeping personal confidences. Whether we accept these rules or not, we do know that our definition of friendship is influenced by the roles we take with friends and how we see ourselves in those roles.

To add to our understanding of adult friendship, we can find recurring themes in women's literature and in our own narratives. They can be seen as universal themes that encourage us to build significant relationships by making ourselves available and responsible both as a giver and a receiver of our time and energy. The themes that highlight friendship go beyond convenience and obligation or the utility and pleasure that Aristotle spoke of. They address our ability to connect and even merge on an emotional level with a close friend as well as to separate without any loss of self. They address our willingness to be present, focused, and insightful enough to see a friend through her lens rather than our lens alone. They address our commitment to find the good that Aristotle thought essential. The depth of every relationship is enhanced each time we rejoice in a friend's achievements and accomplishments without feeling jealousy. Yet even if we succumb to jealousy, we have the courage to talk through our thoughts and feelings of inadequacy without the fear that we will, on some level, feel diminished as a person or as a friend.

The power of a friendship comes in knowing that there is someone who is willing to share life's many faces and is also able to honor confidentiality about our secret joys and sorrows. It is that quality of reciprocity in a relationship—an important commitment to receive and to give back—that is critical in women's friendships.

Life without friendships would be life without fresh air. Friends affirm life and raise the quality of lives in so many ways. Four years ago my husband had triple bypass surgery. Two days before, the doorbell rang, and standing before us were two very special people, our friends from Raleigh. They traveled 1,200 miles because they thought we needed a diversion from the life-threatening event that lay ahead. That is friendship. In 1992 Hurricane Andrew arrived in the middle of the night, and we rose to incredible devastation the following morning. We knew our way of life would be forever changed. As we walked out the door, we saw these two men coming toward us. They asked if we were safe, if we needed water, and if we needed any medicines. The logo on these shirts read IBM. That is corporate friendship.—Anonymous

Women friends have always been an important part of my life. In high school, I found it difficult to make friends but always had a couple of close girlfriends. When I arrived at college, I joined a sorority. This was probably the first time in my life that I belonged to a special group of friends and enjoyed sharing the camaraderie that goes with that. Doing things together, sharing thoughts, working on projects for the community—this all made me feel larger than myself and somehow became a significant part of life. Common interests, boyfriends, etc.— it made me feel good to be a part of it. I carried this working model into my married life. Things were difficult, and my relationship was rocky. My friends gave me the support I needed to pull through. My definition of friendship begins with a shared relationship where you are willing to listen to someone and care what happens in his or her life. It is a shared connection. A friend can envelop you in kindness and nurture you. While husbands, lovers, and children are also shared relationships, they seem to take place on a different plane. Women have a sensitivity for what you are experiencing in a different way. It's as if you are still in that sorority with your sisters. I actually think the role model for friendship was handed down to me by my mother. I haven't thought about it much, but she enjoyed her role in organizational work, her bridge and mah-jongg games, and the time spent with women in her family. I think she needed and gave support to others without any expectations. As I think of it, I think that somehow defines friendship for me. Friends have also influenced my life by helping me to see another perspective and allowing me to look at myself in a more positive way. I consider myself extremely lucky to have made and maintained so many women friends in my life. It always surprises me that my friends put up with me, because I know many consider me "high maintenance." Knowing that I am respected by women who I feel are so special gives me a sense of encouragement when I am down and the courage to try new things. It helps me define myself in a brighter light.—MCL

How different we are than our male counterparts! Men's relationships tend to develop around shared activities (e.g., work and sports) and not around shared emotional support. Remember that the earliest friendships among men came with industrialization and were rooted in the early trade societies. Women's friendships, on the other hand, were more cooperative in nature and emotionally supportive. Although both men and women may share the cultural norms of trust, commitment, and respect, female relationships are more emotionally intense. They are shaped by something quite different in our expectations of friends and by our emphasis on intimacy, loyalty, confidentiality, and an adherence to our rules of friendship.

How have your women friends, past or present, influenced how you define yourself and the quality of your friendships? Why?

When my father died and I left Northwestern University, Northwestern never left me. My close friends there never wanted me to feel left out and included me in parties, gossip, and conversation. They wrote and called and invited me to visit. They were steadfast, and I counted on them in those days for my "survival." Of course, I made new friends at home and reconnected with the old, but it was Margie and Lois and Carol and Linda and Joani who were always there for me. I have never forgotten how important "girlfriends" can be, and I have always tried to use that "Northwestern" model in my relationships with women for the rest of my life. I have always had good friends, and I believe I am a good friend. The remarkable thing to me is that the bonds I have made with women have not changed as we have aged. I think that one of the qualities besides loyalty that makes this possible is keeping a sense of humor in the face of *life*. I think having such positive relationships with both of my sisters has carried over into the close relationships I have had with other women throughout my life.—ETG

In recent years, there has been a renewed interest in both the physical and emotional responses of women to the stresses in their lives. An emerging behavioral theory has appeared on the horizon to challenge the legitimacy of the fight-or-flight response to stress exhibited in men. In men, the testosterone produced under stress seems to reduce the effects of oxytocin and promote the fight-or-flight response. This behavioral response in women is referred to as *tending and befriending* and is woven into the very fabric of how women create and maintain significant female relationships. When the hormone oxytocin is released as part of the response to stress in a woman, it buffers the fight-or-flight response and encourages her to tend to her children and to gather with other women in need. Thus the *tending* behavior draws on attachment and caregiving, which are akin to our earliest relationships. *Befriending* is what is at the core of building and maintaining the social networks essential for a sense of our emotional well-being.

There might have been times when we have responded to a spouse or partner's anger with our own hostility and defensiveness. Maybe he felt threatened in some way by our behavior and his anger escalated until he either won, no matter what the cost, or he retreated emotionally and physically. We are much more likely to defuse the stress with a female friend and do so with a nurturing response or an activity that ensures safety and intensifies connectedness.

Many of us have watched the men in our lives, as they get older, begin to welcome more emotional support and become more dependent on that support. They shift their focus from defining identity based on independence and power and control to one that is built on a growing need to enhance and sustain the most significant and meaningful emotional and supportive relationships in their lives. Quite different from men, we women seem to know instinctively from our childhood the significance of developing extensive and intense social networks. These social networks become the avenues for providing and receiving critical support throughout our lives and for discovering an abundance of fulfillment and satisfaction, especially as we age.

I visited the doctor for my annual checkup recently, which I always schedule around my birthday so as not to forget to do it. Had the routine blood work, and rather than just getting the okay to go on and enjoy my year, my doctor asked me to repeat the test. Within a day, the doctor called me to tell me she was concerned because one of the test levels showed that my count was below normal, and she scheduled an appointment with a hematologist. Although the doctor was not alarmed, just concerned, I e-mailed her after a day for some reassurance. I was feeling well. What could this mean? Her e-mail back was very reassuring. So I was just going to think positively. Nevertheless, I did share what was going on with two friends, who immediately told me to call them when I finished my appointment. One called the minute I walked into my home. Although I did not have time to return her call, I appreciated her thoughtfulness. I was so busy with work and a busy social schedule that I did not notice the other friend had not called. The next day I met with both of them. The friend who had not called was quick to tell me why she hadn't. Her husband is a cancer doctor, and when she told him I was seeing a hematologist about this problem, he suggested that she not call me since he thought her call would be intrusive. He told her that if I felt like talking, I would have called. My friend did not feel comfortable with his response, but she did give in and followed his suggestion. I could see his point. I got it. I got it because the true essence of a friendship is valuing the person and looking through their lens. The bonds of this friendship go over twenty to thirty years. But it is not just the years; it is also the sense of reciprocity that has been developed. They are always there for me whenever I have needed them and I for them. What an empowering feeling.—GH

That wonderful sense of belonging is fundamental to who we hope to have become as women and as to why we nurture our roots in both family and friendships. Maybe we see this need to belong as a relentless drive to form and maintain lasting and consequential relationships. Many perceive our social supports as the bookends that support and preserve our health and well-being. The intensity of our passion for identifying and committing to our role as a "BFF" (best friend forever) is a much stronger barometer of our emotional well-being than even income or our marital status.

I have learned a very significant lesson about friendship recently. I always felt that when a friend needed help, I wanted to be there for her in any way I could. But what I never realized was how important it is that a friend feels comfortable and safe enough to ask for help. I never understood just how strong the feeling of connectedness becomes when a friend calls because they need you. A friend recently was diagnosed with cancer and quickly realized that she would need help getting to her treatments. I was delighted that she valued our friendship enough and reached out to me. We need to remind ourselves that at the essence of friendship is a sense of reciprocity. That both the give and the take in a relationship give value to each of us and to that relationship.—Anonymous

I am lucky in maintaining close friendships with women I met in elementary school, college, and as a newly married. This is not an idle statement. I see and speak on the phone regularly with these women. Our husbands are very friendly. We socialize and travel together. Of course, part of this bond originates from living in a community in which I grew up. But more to the point, there is a sisterhood that is bound by loyalty. I know I can rely on my friends now, as I knew I could a short time into our relationship. You might ask if this leaves any room for new friendships. Absolutely! A shared travel experience or a newfound hobby, such as bridge, can bring a woman into your life that you grow to cherish. I don't think aging has redefined my friendships. It has only increased my awareness of their value.—MK

Those of us women who lack that sense of belonging are much more prone to depression and loneliness. Those with few social ties may even have an increased risk of dying. Amazing the power of women's friendships!

Friendships with Family

It probably should not come as a shock that for many of us over sixty, family members may represent at least 50 percent of our social support networks, and that proportion is even greater if we look at those who are our closest supporters.

> I am very fortunate that my children are also my friends. We may not see eye to eye on everything, but they understand me and know where I am coming from. We can discuss and share personal issues, and that feels good, knowing that I can count on them, and I am always here for them as well.—J

This bond is especially true for adult women and their aging mothers. The emotional ties that bind a mother and daughter can often be an enormous support for both as well as a source of conflict. No matter what the mother-daughter relationship is, this unique paradigm might have always served as the benchmark for our other relationships with women.

> My mom is my best friend. When I was about to deliver my first child, I was praying that my daughter would hold out as long as possible before delivery so my mom could be present, in town, when the baby was born. I just cannot imagine having a child without sharing that experience with my mom. I can only hope that my daughter will be my best friend like my mom is to me.—Anonymous

As aging women, we may be forced to lean more on family members for emotional, financial, and/or physical support. Consequently, our perceptions of ourselves as independent souls oftentimes give way to feelings of diminishing competence. When we find ourselves in this position, the friends we seek out and depend upon now—the new relationships or the ones we have treasured over our lifetime—tend to be women whom we perceive as closer to our imagined self rather than as the needy or dependent women our families may see us as. It may be that since it is extraordinarily difficult for us to terminate stressful family relationships, we find solace in having more control over the management of our women friendships. For that reason, we place great value on the role of friends.

> Old friends are more than family...even though we might have had less contact with them. We knew each other "back then" and "back when" and they continue to contribute to our identities as competent peers, despite our current circumstances.—S

When fifteen hundred people were monitored over a ten-year period, the findings were astonishing: close contact with family members had little effect on survival rates. But the more contact women had with a network of friends and confidantes, the longer they lived. Those of us who have nurtured friendships over a long period of time reduce our risk of dying by more than 50 percent. Other studies have also shown that the higher the level of engagement with friends, the lower the rate of cognitive decline. The concept that friends are more essential than family to our ability to cope and maintain optimism and self-esteem may be especially difficult to grasp for those of us who were raised in the mid-twentieth century on breast milk and family loyalty.

Although throughout our lives there have been roads we were able to travel alone, we nevertheless instinctively treasured the meaning of the journeys accompanied by female friends. During these transitional over-sixty years, we need to welcome new friends as well as to continue to make contact with those people who have added special import to our lives in the past. It is now that we should spend time with friends who inspire us, respect us, and accept us for who we are.

> I am not sure if time is fleeing faster than ever for me at this stage of my life, or if, at seventy-two, I have now taken on project after project and the hours of the day never seem to be long enough. I ask myself lately why I have the need to be so busy, and the answer seems to speak to values and role models that I have had within my family. Workdays were long for my father and grandmother, but they did not complain. It was just something that was necessary. They interacted more with family than friends and were supportive of each other throughout their lives. My days have usually been long as I feel an emotional high when

involved "in doing," sensing a feeling of accomplishment. On the other hand, I am beginning to appreciate a few very special women in my life with whom I can feel a sense of trust, an abundance of support, and an interest in my life situation. I value their input and look forward to the time I spend with them. I note that just recently, when asked to meet with friends for lunch, my immediate inner messages were very different than in the past. I began to think about the individuals I would meet with, knowing that they had similar values, a good sense of humor, and were fun. These friends shared many common interests. The opportunity was to meet now...not later...and why would I not want to get connected with special people who give me a reason to be?—GH

In every true friendship, there is an expectation of a fair exchange. We have to think about what we can offer in a friendship and what we wish to receive in return. Friendships are often both a social as well as cultural investment that ensure the feeling of stability in a growingly fragmented society. Long-lasting friendships offer each of us a mutual exchange, and this is especially true during times of crisis.

My husband died two years ago after a lengthy illness, and eight months later, after getting back to a seminormal and happy life, I discovered that I had lung cancer. (No, I never smoked a cigarette in my life. How unfair is that?) Fortunately, I didn't have any physical problems at all, which was important in the medical process. After having come through very toxic and aggressive treatment for lung cancer, I've learned a valuable lesson. Friends are what pull you through, with their constant being there for you, encouragement, and love. When I needed help, I asked, and someone always came through for me. Not only that, but when they were finished with their "shift," they wanted to know when they could come back again. Even though I had an aide, a friend was always there: taking me to a doctor's appointment and listening to what the doctor said so that I could have two pairs of ears, driving me to a treatment, sitting with me during the treatments, and then usually going to brunch or lunch. The time that we spent together was memorable. My friends were unselfish and generous with their time, and we had quality and important conversations. I'm so grateful to be over the worst and want to spend as much time as possible with friends—especially girlfriends. I feel richer for this experience, which I thought was going to be a nightmare.—CB

What is friendship? People who in times of hard or bad situations are there to help. I stayed at a friend's house when I had my cancer operation (so that my parents would not know). They took me to the hospital very early in the morning, and I recuperated in their house. And in another situation, a friend sat in the bedroom all day until they picked up my mother's dead body.—DG

CB was empowered by the support of both family and friends. But more importantly, she reached out and made each friend feel needed as a force in her battle with cancer. It was the power of being needed, an essential in the formula for a significant friendship, that bonded everyone together to give her a sense of security in facing her treatment. Her call for help allowed everyone to share in her experience. Her friendships filled her with love and filled her with hope.

The Meaning of Friendships as We Age

There is another dimension to women's friendships that we may not always be able to wrap our heads around, but it appears to become more pronounced as we age: social-emotional selectivity and adaptation. Sounds fairly esoteric, but it really isn't. Rather, selectivity and adaptation are things that free us to enjoy our friendships in our generative years.

As younger women, we never considered the element of time as we designed the adventures that would define our future. Friendships might have grown out of our school or work environments, for example. Oftentimes friendships were for convenience sake and limited by our stage in life. For the young, there is no need to think of time as a valued commodity; it seems there is an endless amount of it. Yet time is of the essence for aging women as we become focused on our ticking clock and our impending (though be it in the distant future) mortality! In order for us to be filled with emotional satisfaction, we search for how and with whom we will spend these days. The answers to how and with whom reside in each of us. As aging women, we appreciate that lasting friendships are as those defined by Aristotle: relationships enriched by the virtue of goodness.

By this time in our lives, we are savvy enough to recognize that the number of our meaningful relationships have likely decreased over the years, and not only as a result of loss or ill health as we might believe. What we know is that the decline in the numbers is more likely a result of selectivity, of focusing on the importance of interacting with those women who meet our life-cycle goals and share our same value systems.

> I am almost ashamed to tell my story about my friend, G...how I met her and what my initial reaction to her was. I hadn't even realized that I had changed my thinking over the years. I knew I did not always share the same interests as the women who had become my closest friends over time. I was pretty busy, though, with work and family, and I did not have much time left for friends. So when I spent the occasional day with them, I always had a good time catching up with all the latest things happening in their lives. My friends at work were the same age as my children, and although I loved spending time with them at work, our friendship did not go beyond our work hours. I certainly wasn't looking to make new friends either. I had become quite complacent. With more time on my hands, I quickly realized that there were only a few people with whom I wanted to socialize regularly. I do not know where my head was when I met G. Looking back on that first evening, I realized that my values were as superficial as some of the women I had complained about the most. I was focused on what she looked like. And what G valued was learning and growing and having new experiences. She was more in touch with what was happening than I was after living here for many years. But at first I did not see all that. Once I walked away from the party that evening, I realized a lot about myself. At sixty-five, I had more years behind me then ahead of me. How did I want to spend my days from then on? It was at that moment that I knew that G was going to be a treasured friend because she shared my same interests and my same goals for our aging years. Wow! How lucky I am that I gave her a chance. She has been someone who has turned out to be a mirror to who I want to be now. Once I could be honest with myself, I knew that I had to look for more friends like G...only this time I would embrace whomever shares my values without getting bogged down by those things that really do not matter in the end...like material

possessions. At my age, I am still learning a lesson about the meaning of friendship.—Anonymous

Almost around the same time I started teaching, I began running with two friends that are now my sweat sisters. Not only have we covered thousands and thousands of miles as well as conversation subjects over thirty years, but we have shared and rejoiced in our family celebrations and supported each other when tragedy struck...and oh yes, darkness fell on me in its most heartbreaking visit ten years ago when my daughter suddenly died. I looked for her in the full moon, that first night without S, and she was not there. I looked for her in the gorgeous sunrise, that first morning without S, and she wasn't there...I wrestled with G-d. I was mad. I was sad. There are no words to describe that raw pain...and yet my sweat sisters came to push me to run. We were training for a marathon in just a few days ahead. The day of the marathon came. It was pouring (heavy rain was a first, even though we had run many marathons). My tears and the raindrops became one, flooding the soil. In some sort of magical thinking, I stopped when I reached the finish line. I felt that by crossing it, I would have to accept the finality of life. My sweat sisters held my hands and gently pushed me through the finish line. I had carried S for nine months; now I carry her for the rest of my life in my heart.—MM

Thank you so much for persisting in your attempt to meet me, as well as for the lovely lunch we shared. I love being with you. You are such a fabulous role model for all of us who try to be good listeners, and you're a very special friend. I'm so glad you're my friend. The workshop was great today, and it was fun seeing some familiar faces as well. Again, thanks for just being *you*! Let's do lunch again soon. Love, HB

The friendship role we play and that others play in our lives impact our life satisfaction. The more emotionally satisfying these friendships are, the stronger our identities and our adaptation to aging will be.

The loss of a spouse or close friend generates a ripple effect that disturbs the continuity of our social connectedness. At this time, we again face that proverbial crossroads. As widows, a shadow is cast, even for those of us who boast of independence and self-sufficiency, since often we experience bouts of anxiety and depression. Yet we most appreciate and learn from those friends who have experienced their own losses and who are now giving encouragement and counsel. The ability to both *give* and *receive* support has kept widows engaged and enabled them to remain open to establishing new relationships.

One of the challenges of generativity may be our need to make adaptations in our social relationships as we strive to keep a sense of balance and replace relationships and social activities that have been lost. Widows and women who have divorced during these later years tend to intensify their friendships with unattached women to compensate for the loss of their husbands. Older women are more likely than older men to be widowed and live alone. It is critical then that, as women, we appreciate the wealth of emotional support that the bonds of friendship provide us.

> Friendship has been one of the most important things in my life. I have been fortunate to always have very dear friends, many of whom are still my friends today. One very important reason why I have a great need for a close girlfriend is because I have no sisters. I have a brother, but it is not the same. My relationship with a good friend is that I am able to be myself. I am able to share with a good friend everything that is going on in my life, because we have great respect and trust for one another. This has always given me much comfort, and I have always been able to turn to my friends for support. I have a very close friend whom I consider my sister. She lives in New York, and we have known each other since we were twelve. We lost touch for years, and when we met again, I found out that she had moved into my neighborhood, and both her kids were in the same classes as my children. It was a miracle. She guided me through a very bad time in 1980 when I was having serious personal problems. I always valued her opinion. Of course, it works both ways. To have a friend, one needs to be a friend. Six years ago, I was sixty-three years old and I went through a life-altering experience. My marriage ended in divorce, and I had to start out on my own. If it weren't for her, as well as a few other very good friends, I probably would have had a breakdown, and I would still be in that position today.—HG

The older we get, the more we are struck by the realization that our presence in the moment allows us to take notice of the people around us that offer substance and a sense of community. Perceptions of ourselves as aging women can be confirmed and reaffirmed through social interactions with friends for whom we feel a mutual respect and an affirmation of self-worth.

How does aging redefine your friendships with women?

> When I returned to my childhood home for a visit recently, I happened to reconnect with a friend whom I had not seen in twenty-five years. Our moms had been friends, and her mom had been the group "leader" in most of our childhood activities, like Girl Scouts, etc. As we were reminiscing, this old friend asked me a very poignant question that took me off guard: "Why didn't you help me when my mom was not kind to me?" And I thought to myself, wasn't every mother good like my mother? And I said to her, "I did not notice your mother was mean to you." And the woman looked back at me and was so relieved and so happy that it wasn't because I did not care about her.
> —MC

> Thank you for making me sit down and take some "leisure time" to write this. I can say that I have many more friends today than ever before. They are from all different areas that I am involved in, in my daily life—we share everyday experiences and stories of our wonderful families. I look forward to what life has for me and those I love and to enjoy and make every day count.—LT

> My Secret Success Recipe for Aging Well with Friends
> Directions:

> 1. Choose your ingredients well...organic if possible; some combination of farmed and wild makes life more interesting.
> 2. Measure carefully...too much or too little of any one ingredient may change the flavor...be flexible, as tastes vary.
> 3. Nurture over time...begin slowly on low temperature and gradually increase to a boil; patience, concern, and a watchful eye are needed to get it just right...approximately twenty-plus years or more...if one is lucky.

4. Take nothing for granted...keep ingredients fresh with new ideas gleamed from books, conversations, travel, attention to detail, an abundance of laughter, and little to no advice giving.
5. Be mindful of any necessary adjustments over time to reflect a change in taste buds. Discuss with honesty and respect.
6. Stir often with love.
7. Blend well.
8. Do not freeze.
9. Serve immediately, as time is precious.
10. Celebrate often with passion and compassion for the beauty of life and the uniqueness we each bring to the other.—GH

We have learned that friendships need time and space and resources to develop. They will be reshaped and formed and impacted throughout the years. As partners and family members die, friends begin to play an increasingly large role in daily life. Organizational life may take on new importance as older women wish to widen their social networks of support.

With age, we also find ourselves on a pathway to continued personal growth. A critical element in that growth is our ability to celebrate the changes within ourselves and the changes in our relationships. Yet we never can ignore that we are always traveling on this journey with our personal histories and countless experiences at our fingertips. When we stop to review our past, we have an entire life-span perspective and a wisdom that enhances all our interactions. Friendships are of enormous importance to the landscape of our lives, and their quality benefits from our life's travails.

Oftentimes, without even recognizing it, we are protected by layers of social support, layers that, upon examination, make us feel safe and validated. Those women who are closest to us and offer the most consistent and meaningful level of confirmation provide the innermost layer of support. We may share a lifetime of history with these individuals, or they may have come into our lives when we bonded on moral or "perspective of life" issues. The middle layer of relationships consists of those women who are important in our daily living but with whom we might not have reached that same special level of intimacy. The outside layer is composed of those friendships that encourage us at specific times along our journey. They represent the role players in our lives (e.g., coworkers, covolunteers). Although these layered relationships are dynamic and fluid, they often work in tandem with each other and provide needed continuity and stability.

It is important to stop and think about our own friendships with women in each of these circles. What are the contributions that each has made to our emotional health? If we think back to our early adult years, the circle of friendships might have been quite different. The women in our lives might have emerged from the outermost level and might have been there to give needed advice on helping us just get through the day with our small children or with our absentee husbands. Today, we have a different perspective. Friends are now cultivated, and they are cultivated patiently and deliberately over time. Today, we have the maturity and security to be attentive to friends' individual needs, not only to our own needs, and to define the parameters of confidentiality together.

> I believe for everyone who goes astray / Someone will come to show the way / I believe, I believe.
> —"I Believe" (1953)

The sense of believing and belonging are fundamental to who we have become. The need to belong is often translated into a drive to form and maintain enduring, positive interpersonal relationships. We have seen our friends, especially as we age, help to confirm our identity and bolster our self-esteem by providing a reflection of the world and a model for promoting change. We are convinced that there is importance in valuing the friendships we have cultivated over the years. *Yet increasingly at this stage in our development, we must be mindful of the opportunities to meet and nurture new friends also.*

> As time goes by and life unfolds, the practicality of being in one place and finding one's sense of purpose may bring greater distances to an already long-distance relationship. But the earliest memories of those I cherished remain as clear today as they did some sixty-plus years ago. The reality and constraints of time often make the idea of wishing to keep in touch a challenging endeavor. When walking along the beach, I often see pieces of driftwood and am fascinated by thoughts of their possible origins. Where have they been and how did they come to be where they lie today...still intact and purposeful? I see the qualities I value in friends as I examine these pieces of wood. I see the solidness

of their structure, the variations in their design as they have withstood the ravages of time. I imagine they were once shiny and rich in color. Even though today they may begin to seem dull and weathered, they still provide beauty and capture a special place within my heart. A meaningful friendship might not always have a long history like these branches I have gathered along the way. But I want it to be sturdy because of its emotional strength; something I can depend upon when necessary without feeling needy and weak. The awareness of this delicate balance—moral strength and yet an acceptance of life's fragile moments—has become so important at this stage of my life. The following quote from Albert Camus speaks to me: "Don't walk in front of me, I may not follow. Don't walk behind me, I may not lead. Walk beside me and be my friend."—GH

> **Thoughts to Remember:**
>
> 1. Identify the qualities we value in a friendship.
> 2. Reflect on the assets we bring to a friendship.
> 3. Examine the expectations we have of friendship.
> 4. Appreciate differences in our friends and in our friendships.
> 5. Acknowledge the significance of the 'giving' and 'taking' from each.
> 6. Be open to exploring new friendships.
> 7. Embrace the richness and power of friendships as they enhance our longevity and well-being.
> 8. Surround ourselves with emotionally satisfying friends.
> 9. Rejoice in the joy that friendships bring to our life each day.

In the very first chapter, we (the authors) spoke of how our friendship, and then our collaboration, began with a group of women created to address the "troubling" issues encompassing turning fifty years of age. After over twenty-one years of meeting once each month, our group has weathered many storms together. By sharing such an intensity of emotions, an enduring sense of sisterhood emerged that is reflected in the following e-mail sent by a member following a meeting.

My Dears,

Last night was amazing for me. I came to the meeting to share with you information I think every women needs to know. Have yourself examined after every mammogram. *Mammograms are not perfect,* and please, share this with others. Also share with those others that sisterhood is alive and well and better than ever! You offered so much insight, caring, and affection. I was truly overwhelmed and felt that I received much, much more than I could ever have given. Did we know way back then when we started on this journey together that we would share so many of life's experiences? Joys and sorrow, death, birth, courtship, illness, marriage, grandkids—*tzuris* (troubles) in a variety of colors—and be there to support and love each other through it all? I didn't know you would all come to mean so much to me. Everyone has been so kind and wants to help, and I know all of you really mean it. I also know that no one is just sitting around with nothing to do, waiting for me to call. I really don't like asking for help, but let's face it, there are lots of things I don't like. If I need you, I will call, I promise. You are the best and I love you.—LL

As we create our own narratives with stories about the meaning of friendships, we recognize how much we can learn and grow from our own memories and how much more clearly we see our lives unfold as the stories we write uncover issues that help us to appreciate the richness of our sisterhood.

LIST OF QUESTIONS TO REVIEW

What are the qualities of women friends who most influenced your life, and why did they have such an impact?

How have your women friends, past or present, influenced how you define yourself and the quality of your friendship? Why?

How does aging redefine your friendships with women?

PERSONAL REFLECTIONS

CHAPTER 6
Defining Our Place in Society

Luck and merit are traveling companions...
Allow them to coexist for you...at this stage.
—GOETHE

magine being viewed as "immoral, unfeminine, or an object of pity." Those were views expressed more than one hundred years ago in America about women who sought employment in a society and culture that believed the man was the provider and the woman the caretaker. Over our lifetime, women have succeeded in redefining a woman's place within society as a career woman, as a volunteer, and/or as a homemaker. Each of us is free, while balancing those options, to decide how to spend our leisure time and still preserve our significant relationships, raise healthy and happy children, and ensure strong family units.

At the time we were rearing our families, the societal standard was that a working mother became a threat to family life. A working mother became a negligent mother and an unavailable wife. Consequently, there were very small numbers of women who worked. Today, even when the majority of women who are employed are helping to support the family out of economic necessity, there are still groups in our society that contend that the earlier standard still holds true. In our generation, not only were there societal messages, but also our inner voices could not ignore the stress the demands of a family and a job placed on us as women.

How did societal messages affect our views of ourselves as career women and as wives and mothers?

Much has changed in a hundred years. Much has remained the same. The increased number of women in the workforce can be attributed to an increased respect for women's talents, a change in marital patterns, improvement in birth-control methods, longer life expectancy, and recent laws protecting working women. What women have been able to accomplish can be attributed to our incredible determination and our huge sacrifices.

Then and Now

Families operate within the context of the sociocultural expectations of the times. Our parents were affected by societal messages, both spoken and unspoken, and in turn conveyed those to us through behaviors and attitudes. Many of these are imprinted in our psyches, and even though changes have reshaped thinking in our communities, we may still be reticent to alter what we instill in our children and grandchildren.

Nineteenth-century beliefs spoke to the differences in nature between men and women. Women who sought change challenged those differences in the late nineteenth and twentieth centuries. In 1865, Vassar College opened its doors as an American institution of higher learning exclusively to give women the opportunity to receive an education. Other colleges soon followed. Once educated, women saw the need for equality, our past role as homemaker was to be redefined. Though we would now entertain the prospect of entering a profession, there were many more obstacles that still lay ahead.

In 1852 at age five, Christine (Kitty) Ladd-Franklin and her mother attended a lecture given by a well-known women's rights advocate, Elizabeth Oakes Smith, who said, "Women should be able to develop their talents to the fullest." Inspired by Oakes Smith, Christine would go on to graduate from Vassar in 1869. Encouraged by her father's unwavering belief in her potential to excel, she obeyed his counsel: "Work toward financial and personal independence. It is to your advantage and well-being to have some occupation and to be of some use in the world. Acquire a sense of independence and self-reliance, and with good health habits, you can take care of yourself." It was Ladd-Franklin's belief that women's limited role in science during her lifetime was a result of their lack of experience, self-definition, and a supportive environment. Yet she was the first woman to earn a PhD in mathematics from Johns Hopkins even though she needed special permission to sit for the classes for her studies and had to wait 44 years to receive it. She became the first woman professor of mathematics at Johns Hopkins. One of Christine's teachers, at Vassar wrote: "[Ann] was the most important woman scientist in America in the nineteenth century."

By 1897, local groups of women had formed the National Union of Women's Suffrage Societies. In 1919 the Sex Disqualification Removal Act, allowing women to become lawyers, veterans, and civil servants, was followed by the Nineteenth Amendment, giving women the right to vote. This opened the door for women's concerns to be heard in the political arena and affect legislation that shaped our future.

It was not unusual for women to have entered the workforce at the lowest level, both in status and pay, once we overcame restrictions as to job availability and the ridicule endured as part of our work experience. Jobs such as teaching, nursing, clerical work, social work, administrative support, and sales were all representative of the stereotypic occupational roles a woman could assume.

Things were very tough right after the Depression and my family needed the money, so I just quit my second year of junior high. My first job interview was when I was only fourteen. I told them I was eighteen. When asked what kinds of sales experience I had previously, I answered confidently, "Oh, soup to nuts!" Well, I did not get the job. However, the young man who had told me of this job was standing just outside the door when I left, and just then I heard a voice in the back of me saying, "That guy wants to hire you." After my first day on the job, they saw how good I was and asked me if I had a sister; well, I had a mother, and they hired both of us. We each earned eight dollars a week, and I was employed for the next eight months, selling and delivering merchandise in any weather and working till the store closed. That is until the truant office caught up with me. Education was very important to my mother, and I did return to school for a while. However, I worked at the same store, known for selling to the "best." Yet the people I worked for were horrible; they would yell at me often and then, after I was found crying in the back room, would offer me Mallomar bars and give me a smile, and I would stop crying and return to work. One day one of the nicer partners told me, "M, wherever you go, do not let them know how much you can do, as they will take advantage of you." I became a manager at age nineteen and so began a career in sales for the next forty-eight years for the same company, taking a few years off to raise two daughters. My mother was a spiritual person and saw me as her spirited child. She encouraged prayers daily and told me to forgive. It would make me stronger. She was also very controlling but our matriarch and a good woman. I married a man who was controlling as well. One day, after seeing a psychiatrist, he said this to me, and I have never forgotten it: "M, you are not your mother. You are you." This gave me strength and made me see I am an individual. At age seventy-six I received a gift of art supplies from my daughters and have since then become an artist, with paintings in several galleries in several states. I needed to be mentally strong and have faith in myself. I am a mentor for others who admire my art, my love of fine literature, and my love of learning. I am now almost ninety-six years old and feel very blessed.—MM

The era of good feelings ended in 1929 with the stock-market crash. For more than a hundred years, men had been defined by their work, and now millions were unemployed. Laws regarding employment were enacted to favor men over women. As times were difficult, some wives left the home and assisted husbands as "business partners without pay."

Dad had a grocery store—a mom-and-pop operation. Mom was his business partner for thirty-five years, never receiving a salary; It all went into the same pot. As children, we were the original "latchkey kids," having to fend for ourselves until Mom arrived to make dinner, help with homework, and do the laundry, all without the use of TV, cell phones, or alarm systems. We turned out pretty responsible after all.—AB

During World War II, gender roles changed again. Men went off to war, and employment for women was a national necessity. Once the war ended, men returned and wanted their jobs back, and women once again lost their newfound identity.

The fifties were a period of prosperity with an emphasis on family. New products entered the marketplace: vacuum cleaners, toasters, and washing machines, as well as TV dinners, baby formula, and cake mixes. Each one gave women more time. But now, with the increasing size of families, mothers were tied again to the home. Yet the seeds of rebellion for women were taking root. Betty Friedan's *The Feminine Mystique* fueled the feminist movement, and gender differences became a national focus. Although past eras were fraught with great turbulence and sacrifice, women made significant strides in creating a pathway for the next generation. The women of the seventies added unparalleled dimensions to our opportunities and to our perspective as to just how far-reaching our landscapes had become. It is to these women whom we owe a debt of gratitude—some our own grandmothers, mothers, and aunts.

It was during *The Feminine Mystique* review that I realized that I wanted to be a court reporter. That was in 1976. I was already working for a court-reporting firm, doing transcribing. I came home and asked my husband for "permission" to go to school, and he said okay, as long as I could still get all of the things done that I had been doing. What a dutiful wife. I have to say that he was very supportive when it came to my having to run to class. I started school. The teacher only taught two afternoons and nights a week. It was a real chore getting there from my house because the class started at four thirty in the afternoon and I had to fight awful highway traffic. As my typing speed increased, the time of the class got a little later, and then I ended up going around six thirty. Still awful traffic and stressful. I had to come home in the dark, all the while saying to myself, "Why am I doing this?" I was never so busy in my life. I kept my job at the court-reporting agency because I knew that when I graduated, I'd have a job there. So I was working part time, attending to the kids (then sixteen and thirteen), taking care of myself and my husband, and practicing a lot. There was no time for myself at all. It turned out to be the best thing I ever did because it was a wonderful career. School took me two years. I met R at the agency. We became friends and started our own firm in 1989. We had a great partnership. Of course, I had to give it up when I got my diagnosis of lung cancer, but I think it was time.—CB

In 1970, a new law was put into effect: women were to be paid the same wages as men for doing work of equal value. Three years later, the first women brokers were admitted to the stock exchange.

I am ninety-two now, and in some way I was a woman ahead of my times. At a pretty young age, I divorced, and in order to survive, I had to support myself. I had to withstand much ridicule because at that time women did not often act on behalf of their own well-being. I had typing skills and some experience working at various jobs as a young adult. I became a secretary to a man who worked on stock publications. I was so successful in helping him create a journal, a journal that became a standard for those who worked on Wall Street, that I soon was hired by another much-admired stockbroker. I worked for him for over thirty years. It was during this time that he encouraged me to become a stockbroker because he said he valued my communication and interpersonal skills. It was not unusual to hear from my clients, who continued well into their later years to either call or send letters thanking me for my guidance and personal attention to their financial needs. They thanked me for their ability to reach retirement age with a sense of security. I became the most successful working woman in my family of six sisters, and my many nieces always admired my guts and determination to do what I needed to do in order to move on with my life after a terribly trying divorce.—LL

By the late seventies, nearly 50 percent of all married women and 40 percent of all women over sixteen were working.

Influences That Affected Career Choices

Family Influences. Family influences were significant in guiding whether women in our generation would choose to work outside the home or not. Many factors determined how significant that influence was: our families' social and economic resources, the value our parents and extended families placed on work, and the messages they gave us regarding gender roles in the home and in the workplace. We repeatedly asked ourselves, "Are we expected to marry instead of going to college or to work? Is education available for both the males and females in our families?"

The degree of autonomy as we grew within the family structure was critical in shaping our career decisions. It was here in our families that we learned to make decisions. It was here we learned whether we needed to conform to strict rules or if we had the latitude to take risks and make mistakes along the way. Our thinking was also influenced by whether our parents liked or disliked their own chosen career paths, and whether they were fortunate enough to have the type of job they were best suited for or whether their jobs were merely a means to feed the family and pay the bills. Children's books, cartoons, movies, and the media exposed us to the kinds of choices available to us. Newspapers, radio, and television in the fifties and sixties portrayed women in homemaker roles, and that helped determine our life's course. Oddly, that portrayal has even continued to influence women in the twenty-first century.

Notwithstanding conventional views, there is a common thread that runs through many of our stories that goes beyond differences in gender roles while emphasizing the similarities in social influences that colored the messages our families gave us: life is uncertain, so we need to be thankful for what we have. For many, our parents and grandparents had pushed us to attain educational levels that were unattainable to them. They sacrificed so much so that we would have opportunities for an easier life. Some of our parents and grandparents struggled in a new land with new customs oftentimes misunderstood even by their own American family members. An accent could draw attention, could make them feel unaccepted. Yet parents in general were consumed with one hope, and that was that we could live the American dream: to have a good job, to own our own home, and to be a respected member of the community.

The career paths we have chosen originated as we transitioned from adolescence to young adulthood. According to Erikson, career development is one of the central-most challenges we face during the identity formation process. Thus, many of our career decisions were intertwined with our psychological separation from our parents and family of origin. The closer we were connected to our families, the harder it was to develop a clear sense of our own personhood. Our choice of careers, then, might have been based not only on our own distinct preferences but also on an emotional response to our parental expectations.

Who or what factors influenced you in choosing your career?

I had a lot of dreams when I went away to college. Maybe they were not all that realistic, but they were my dreams anyway. I felt so exhilarated being away from home and pursuing my dreams. In my sophomore year, my mom made it very clear that if I planned to finish at Northwestern, I would have to get a teaching degree along with the impractical degree I had been chasing. I had no choice. I wasn't independently wealthy. I couldn't go to my sister and disregard my mother's wishes. I felt like I was still a child with no will of my own.—CTS

Ever since my high school studies, I had a profound interest in science. I graduated in the top 5 percent of my class. I knew from early on that I wanted to go to college; however, in that era, preference was always given to boys—emphasizing the importance of the male family member getting a college degree. Thus, my dream of going directly to college after high school was derailed so that my brother could attend college. I began my nurse's training in a hospital but discontinued that training after two years because I wanted to fulfill my original plan of going to college and thus attaining a bachelor's degree in nursing. So I applied to the university and was accepted, and while there I met my husband. We had two children and relocated for about five years. But my marriage dissolved shortly after returning to Miami. I found myself with two young children to support on my own. And still without my nursing degree. My desire to become a nurse persisted; however, economic necessities came first. I worked as a waitress for two years simply to support my children and myself. I reapplied to college and was accepted, and all my previous credits were granted, and so I was able to complete my studies in two years. I graduated and began my nursing career at a hospital where I remained for thirty-six years. The privilege in becoming a nurse enabled me to serve in one of the most humane professions—caring for the sick. The benefits from the profession enabled me to put my two children through college, to buy two homes, and to travel extensively (oftentimes with family and friends), and my job provided me with the financial stability of a comfortable income and good benefits.—BP

Obviously, our separation from family influences and progress toward adulthood might have taken longer for some of us than for others. Even though theorists like Freud and Erickson may differ in describing the progression leading to identity development, they concur on the time in our lives during which significant progress should be made. They also agree that it is critical that maturing young adults balance parental influences with the power they perceive in others. By exploring religion, philosophy, vocational opportunities, and interpersonal relationships, we can develop our distinctiveness, create a power within, and expand a sense of inner stability. That balancing act is called *maturity*.

Tradition is integral for women over sixty. We were nurtured on the values our families instilled in us. The roles we came to value became our beacon. Yet there were also values that promoted gender inequality and impeded us from developing as totally independent women. As we look back at those early years of decision making, we recognize that, for many of us, the choices we made had little to do with our talents and more to do with societal expectations. For women, the domains of family and interpersonal relationships were central to the development of our identity. As in everything in our lives, those domains generated both positive and not so positive consequences.

A family trip turned into a lifetime experience in travel. My exposure to travel came to me when I was ten years old. I have now been in the travel business for over thirty years. The itch started when my mother took my sister and me to Greece for two months. As a child, I was wide- eyed and curious. Who knew that this would be the impetus of a career that was to come to me much later in life? After college and having a bachelor's degree in sociology, I was one of those who had no clue as to what to do after four years of education. I started in the banking industry and only lasted two years, always detesting the confined feeling of living my life in one place day after day. My break came to me in 1981, when a small charter airline was looking for reservationists. This was the real beginning of a travel career for me and became a permanent infusion in my life to help sustain my passion and happiness. I am currently with a company that encourages all of its contractors to work "when and where" they want. I now travel with iPad in hand and book cruises wherever I am. I can sit in the south of France and work. I can be in the mountains of Colorado and work. I can be sailing from Monte Carlo to Venice and work. As I grow older, I find that I can bring this travel career with me until I am in my eighties, health notwithstanding. I have been fortunate to have had travel be a part of my entire life. Working at this career has not been work at all. This has been a continuation of the childlike wonder and awe I feel every time I visit a new part of the world!—MKK

Born the third daughter in our family eighty years ago, I was raised by a very hard working dad and a caring, creative mom who cooked, baked, and made many of our clothes. My personal life reflects all that my parents imbued in me. I have been married for fifty-two years. I was a teacher for eighteen years, a career path filled with daily challenges and inner pleasures. I loved every day in the classroom. My husband shares my love of education, and he is presently attending our community college and earning his second baccalaureate degree at age seventy-seven. My father instilled a strong sense of reliance and a personal drive to excel. It was a family tradition that my dad took each of his daughters to New York City a few days after high school graduation. He and I rode the subway to the employment agency. He wished me well and said, "The Bronx is up and the Battery's down." Oh yes, and most important, "Get a job." Filled with self-confidence and a very strong desire to prove I was ready to face the future, I found a job at NYU, where I stayed for four years, working and taking college classes.—Anonymous

For many women of our generation, the available careers were pretty standard. Recent literature only confirmed what we had known for decades to be true: gender roles and attitudes shape our expectations and aspirations, and they inspire the career choices and decisions that promote our abilities.

Traditional Choice of Career

First of all, I never planned on a career when I was young. The goal was to get married and have children, and I didn't think much past that. The one thing I knew was that I did not want to be a working mother, as I had grown up with a working mother who was very involved with her business. She did not have time to sit down to dinner with my dad, my sister, and me. She was unable to attend school functions and was happy to give me her charge card so that I could do my own shopping. She was able to give of herself when she had time, and so it was not how much time but how well the time was spent. When it became clear that my marriage was on the rocks, and the children were in school and I had done my stint as a Brownie leader and PTA participant, it was time to look past tennis games. And so I began reading the want ads. Since I had always worked in my mother's office in the bookkeeping department, I seemed drawn in that direction. My first job was as a part-time bookkeeper in a flower shop. I remembered my mother's advice when I was still in high school that I should take a bookkeeping class rather than shorthand, as bookkeeping would be better than becoming a secretary. I might say my mother was my original mentor. I often talk to my mom up there to let her know I haven't forgotten her or any of her words of wisdom. Maybe it is time to send some of her words onto my grandchildren.—EB

I wanted to do three things when I grew up. As a child I was always playing with people's hair; I also wanted to be a teacher, and growing up, I had a gift for connecting spiritually with others. My mom was a psychic and a spiritual person as well. So I used these gifts as I became a hairdresser, a spiritual advisor, and a spiritual minister. I always knew I wanted to become a good person. I was in the top 10 percent of my class and a merit scholar. I was attractive and I was well liked, but there were times in my life when I did not feel secure. Through the years I had received acknowledgments of wrongs from others to me, allowing me to let go of past circumstances and to concentrate on and appreciate who I am. Through my work as a hairdresser, I have learned how to have my clientele, those seated in my chair, feel more important that I am at that moment. The person seated before me is now the queen, and when I am working on her hair, she has my full attention. My clients share stories with me, and they might have walked in feeling depressed, but because I am interested in them, they leave feeling better. I feel I have an extended family with my clients. I value this in my life. I remain humble and appreciative. I have learned we are all in a rightful place, and whatever is mine is there already. Knowing that, you learn to be accepting of others and yourself.—NS

I followed the path of so many others of my contemporaries and that of an older sister, entering the field of education. Practically everyone I knew who was going on to college was in the field as well. I attended school and worked to pay for the cost of this degree. Upon graduating, finding a job was not too difficult. It paid a decent salary, and I felt satisfied, as I enjoyed working with children in elementary education. After several years of teaching, one of my good friends, also a teacher, announced that she was going to go for a master's degree. I decided to join her. This degree led to a higher salary and more opportunities for growth in the field. I was married without children. The hours were good and the vacation time was excellent. It was a job that was well respected, and I was very satisfied.—RE

Nontraditional Choice of Career

I had not yet understood that a career in museum work was a possibility. In those days there were practically no women museum directors, and most of the important curators were men. From the first art history classes taught by brilliant art historians at Barnard College and Columbia my freshman year, with its assignments to study and write about works of art in all the city's great museums, I was hooked. I knew I wanted to get closer to and handle those works, learn and write about more art and artists of the past, and meet and work with artists of the present. I wanted to travel widely in scholarly pursuits that would bring me together with colleagues in the many places that compose the world of art internationally. My expectations were fulfilled in the more than thirty years I worked in museums. They are still being fulfilled now as I work as an independent art consultant and curator.—DC

DEFINING OUR PLACE IN SOCIETY

A few years ago, I had a major wake-up call. While taking an art class, a teacher said to me, "What do you do the rest of the week when you are not in my class or preparing for my class?" I told her I was a professional volunteer. She turned to me and said, "You should not be spending time going to meetings, running around, etc. You have a gift, and you are the only one who can make the art you are making." I realized I didn't want to turn eighty without being immersed in creating art, living the life I was meant to live. Ultimately this teacher became a mentor, encouraging me to apply to art school and to develop a creative practice. I came to the realization that I needed the structure of going to school full time to make a radical shift in my life. I received an e-mail announcing a new joint program offering a MFA in applied craft and design. It was synchronicity! I pulled together a portfolio and submitted a lengthy, thought-provoking application. I was ecstatic when I received the acceptance, because I had wondered whether they would take someone my age. I have learned it is never too late to start doing. Age can be an excuse regardless of how old you are. It should not stand in your way. In the past three years, I have exposed new layers of my own identity, peeling off some old material as I bring the new to the surface. When I am steeped in the work, boundaries of time and place dissolve. Patterns and rhythms emerge that connect me with the higher creative force. The repeating hand-eye rhythm is my meditation. The work is a giant puzzle; I crave the process of assembling the pattern. I become the process of assembling the pattern. I have invented a new approach in my work and my life.—AC

Besides the effect of family on career choice, teachers and other professionals might also have impacted our decisions.

As a clinical social worker for much of my adult life, I feel gratified in knowing that I have been able to really help some people. Years ago, I had a young boy for a client. He was a teenager in the throes of puberty. He was somewhat hostile and not very verbal. Multiple issues impacted his family, and he was lost in the shuffle. I tried everything I could think of to get through to him, to no avail. Finally, I threatened to kick his ass all the way to California and back for daring to throw himself away. Somehow this got his attention. He went to summer school, graduated from college, went to graduate school, and became a journalist in California. You never know what's going to work, but it sure feels good when something does.—RE

Choosing a field for ourselves as we searched deep to find the right fit helped us uncover our own vision. Those of us that discovered this within ourselves were best equipped to mentor others. It was the power of our own expectations of ourselves that seemed to be the strongest predictor of the choices we made regarding a career, much more so than past performances and achievements.

In the end, we became the executor of our own career "trust." In so doing, we became the executor over our belief in ourselves and thus exercised control over the events that led us to make decisions about what career we would ultimately choose. Women of our generation made those decisions based on what we knew to be true. If we knew then what the world and we would come to know about our potential, many of us might gladly have changed careers.

Looking back on my career choice today, I have few regrets. However, I do think about the different careers that I had not pictured myself doing at that time...but now, having the confidence I have in my adult years, I could have well imagined myself becoming a TV interviewer. It makes such sense to reflect and note the differences in time periods, with TV having just come into being at the time I entered my teaching career. Timing is often a part of our choice making in life. If I were to rate myself then as my chief executive of my beliefs about my capabilities, I would have given myself a six on a scale of ten.—GKH

The one thing that I value most is that I became a teacher and made a difference in many children's lives. Working in low-Income areas has shaped my life as a teacher for the past twenty years. So many children come to school today with so much extra baggage. As a teacher I felt it was up to me to give the students the confidence to succeed—not just on a standardized test but in life—and to believe in themselves.

Becoming a teacher was by far the only thing that made me who I am today.—AH

After a divorce, with three young children, I built an interior landscape business that grew to thirty people and was sold to a public company after fifteen years. The success, through much hard work, was a stepping-stone to growth. I had several mentors that taught me some business principles and gave me a strong arm to lean on. It was difficult juggling the business, family, and social activities without much support. Again, the confidence factor that I could do it was huge. I feel this confidence, as well as my ability to get along well with people, has been a reason for my success.—CS

The biggest thing I learned from my second job is that you can do things you've never done, never had an interest in, and knew nothing about. You just have to jump in and do it! And you just may find out that you do it really well. It's so nice to discover new things about yourself. I loved that feeling and keep looking for it again and again.—IG

Beginning to work as an artist is a little hard to define because the impetus, training, and motivation begin very early on and form a smooth continuum from childhood play to serious exploration and thought as an adult. I expected and hoped to be an "important" and "influential" artist. At various points in my art studies, I asked myself, "Am I an artist yet?" The transformation was very gradual. I knew always that I could do only what seemed genuine to me, that truly interested me and moved me to get out of bed in the morning. A Miami gallery owner once said to me, "I like your work very much, but no one will buy the work of a woman artist because you'll quit to get married and have children and won't continue to produce, maintaining the value of your work." Thanks, Gorilla Girls, Women's Caucus for Art, the National Women's Museum in Washington, and many others for exposing those conditions and helping to change them. Women are well represented in the art world now. I gradually realized that the only goals worth pursuing in art or in life are not to be "important" but to be genuine and to live and work in a way that is true to oneself. Art has been a lifesaver, a reliable constant in my life. I have created some work that has given others pleasure and stimulated thought, but I think I have been most "influential" as a role model. During my twenty-two years of teaching bronze casting and running a foundry, I realized that being an older woman, fit and strong but not particularly impressive physically, empowers young women and young men to believe that they, too, can do it. For students with any self-doubt, I feel that I provide encouragement.—FT

After college I became a first- and second-grade teacher in Harlem in New York City. My parents thought it wise to prepare to have a secure, well-paying job. It was the first job that I had that could be called an occupation. It was a challenge and a big undertaking for a very green girl. I was a dreamer in college and wanted to be a bohemian, writing or painting in romantic, inspiring places with a clone of Hemingway or Picasso. Like most aspirants, I had neither the skills nor insight nor perspective, although I pecked at both. But I happily married my Prince Charming and then chafed at the limitations of not dreaming and creating, just mentally and physically being a housewife, although I loved my husband and kids dearly. To keep me being me, I started to paint as an amateur, taking painting classes and an anatomy class for artists. It was a discovery. At the same time, I designed packages for my husband's business and realized the ins and outs of producing, from artwork to printer to die cutter, and the costs of production. I had real-world contact with grownups in various fields. It was engaging, but the art bug got hold. I was very lucky to grow up and live in New York, to develop while looking and absorbing the greatest art in the world. I went to all the museums and art galleries and painted in earnest until it all came together. I witnessed abstract impressionism from the start and drank it all in. We moved to the backwater of Miami Beach, and it was an adjustment for the whole family. When I joined the ArtCenter on Lincoln Road, painting, exhibiting, selling, and being with other artists. I loved it and settled in for thirteen years until the occupancy rules of the ArtCenter changed to make way for other artists. Since my husband's illnesses, to be out in the world, I've become a docent at the museum at the University of Miami. They trained us in art history, which turned a new leaf. It's human contact and how we feel about others' creations and expression of the human spirit. It's also back to teaching.—CG

Expect the Unexpected

Let us not forget how serendipity could affect our career paths. Imagine how a chance event can be life changing, redirecting many of our career choices. Chance events can be perceived as marker events. Taking a class because it was the only one available and finding you like the subject matter—a chance event. Meeting someone at a networking event who then recruits you for a job, or being encouraged by someone in your past to try out a new idea—chance events. But chance is not the sole agent. To make the process work, we have to be endowed with certain characteristics, such as resiliency, flexibility, motivation, and self-confidence, and be blessed with the support of interested and committed family and/ or friends. As the following stories demonstrate, it is critical to be aware of our personal strengths as well as our weaknesses and to be malleable as the challenges present themselves. As Louis Pasteur stated in 1854, "Chance favors only the prepared mind." We have earned our own preparedness through our accumulated life experiences.

> The expression "life happens" is exactly what happened to me. Through a friend I became a part-time legal secretary, then a full-time one. Then, through another friend, I became a mortgage loan officer and, through that same friend, the branch manager at the same savings and loan company. I then followed her to become a real estate salesperson, having gotten my license, and then I became VP for the same contractor, preparing units for closing. Along came a savings and loan debacle, and we were out a business. So what to do now? The height of boredom set in and I volunteered for my condominium, but I could never feel comfortable or go to meetings since that same builder for whom I worked to build the place I lived in was of course being sued, as were most builders. Along came another friend, and we began a mystery shopping service otherwise known as "Rat Fink, Inc." After my friend's passing, I went back

to work for H&R Block part time. In retrospect I must really like numbers, as my finale as a bookkeeper is still going on as I volunteer for a theater company.—EB

As a senior in high school, I was enrolled in Miami University with every intention of attending to obtain a degree in elementary education. I always loved children and was even the president of Future Teachers of America at our high school. However, it was not to be. One of my cousins was married to an oral surgeon, and he asked me why I wasn't interested in dental hygiene as a career. Well, quite honestly, I never knew what a hygienist did, for in Youngstown, Ohio, in 1959, I had never met a hygienist. I had spent many hours in a dental chair, unfortunately, but had never been treated by anyone other than my dentist. Both my dentist and cousin explained the job description of a hygienist and offered me a job prior to my even applying! I did not attend Miami of Ohio and instead attended Ohio State University, since it was one of the few universities that offered a dental hygiene curriculum in Ohio. I was in the dental hygiene education program at OSU, which was a four-year program and would allow me to not only work in an office, but also to teach in the school system. I received a dental hygiene certificate after three years, which was another option, took boards, and got married. I worked for two and a half years full time in a dental office before my first child was born. In the early sixties, my family was very opposed to my leaving my child, so I didn't work. In 1970 I moved to Miami with my husband and three children. I was going to go back to college but instead studied for my Florida dental hygiene boards, passed them, and went back to work part time on and off for twenty-five years. It was a very satisfying career and allowed me to be my own person instead of S's wife and my children's mother (which wasn't so bad either). I worked for some very wonderful dentists and met some wonderful people. Dental hygiene was a very flexible career for me.—DZ

For someone who graduated college still thinking, "I just want to be a good wife and mother and contribute to the community," with no career desires or plans, I now look back and count some nine different careers in just under fifty years. Each of them brought surprises, and each of them taught me lessons about myself. After college and only a few months of volunteering and playing tennis, I realized I needed to do something more with my life. Having been recruited by IBM while in college, I decided to embark on a career in the computer world. This was in 1963, the early days of business computing, and though I enjoyed the challenge, it did not keep me sufficiently busy to hold my interest. Besides, late that year I met the man I would marry, and so I quit. Then I was recruited to teach at a private girls' school, where I learned a lot about my personality: I'm a "goals" person, not a "process" person, so I didn't like being told how I had to teach. I also discovered that, while I was fine with students who were not terribly gifted, I had no patience whatsoever for those who didn't care. For the next eight years, marriage, motherhood, and volunteering in the community took up all my time. Then came the divorce and the necessity to find a paying job. I went to work for public television, where I discovered my talent for marketing, raising money, and—later—for interviewing. While it was acknowledged that I did brilliantly in that job—even being recommended for a like one in Washington—it was ultimately my inability to "go along to get along" that spelled the end of that career. I decided I was meant to be a capitalist, and I approached my father about working with him in real estate development, a job that lasted a good deal longer and provided a measure of satisfaction, though I was still under someone else's direction all the time. In 1983, I was asked to write for a local newspaper, and I developed a career as a print journalist, doing feature stories, interviews, restaurant reviews, and an opinion column. A chance conversation with a woman whose son was a radio talk host and who told me how good she thought I would be at that led me to pursue what became my favorite career—one where I was in control and could voice my opinions freely, investigate all the things that interested me, and use my interviewing talents. I loved every minute and especially enjoyed occupying the top rating in the market. Alas, I got caught in a power struggle at the station and lost the job, but it soon was replaced by a career as an author. Perhaps the most important thing I learned in my radio and writing careers was how to listen and how to make people feel that I cared about what they were saying. I often was impressed by the favorable and grateful comments of those I interviewed. A genuine interest in people makes the difference. One of the people I had interviewed on the radio was the consul general for South Africa, and as a result, I was invited by his government to visit the country. I wanted to know what South Africans thought about their country, not just what American newsmen thought. My first book, which ultimately became a source book on South Africa, was published in 1990, followed in 1992 by a biographical collection of stories about the only white and one of the only women witch doctors in Africa. When my father died in 1992, I took over the running of his real estate management company (which I still do today) and managing the care of my mother, who had developed Alzheimer's. My last career is as the head of a company specializing in online education and has resulted in my serving as council chairman of an international medical school I founded in conjunction with the government of Samoa, in the South Pacific. This job has taken more patience, perseverance, and sheer stubbornness than anything else I've ever done. We've become internationally accredited and have thirty-six graduates (as of July 2012), and that is cause for pride.—TG

I am a seventy-two-year-old wife, mother, and grandmother. I was raised to marry a doctor, pure and simple. And I did it. For me, the doctor was a freshman in medical school, so I had to work in order to support us. Qualified to teach English, I became a teacher at a beautiful private school in New Orleans. I did not, however, consider this a career. Not at all. It was what I did while my husband was learning or interning or being a resident at Charity Hospital. I worked very hard as a teacher, and I loved the kids and literature. I wasn't ambitious, however, and neither sought nor accepted promotion. I had three children a year apart and didn't want any extra responsibility. I never took my work seriously; it was just what I did for thirteen years! My husband had the career. My experience teaching was certainly a maturing one from which I gained a sense of self and confidence as an individual, not half of a couple. It was that experience that gave me the independence and later the voice to become separated at the age of thirty-six and later divorced. My second career was in the field of law, first as an administrator and then as a writer, director, and producer of documentary videos for lawyers. Again, my motivations were purely financial. I was a now-single mother with a big mortgage in need of supporting three teenage children. The job sort of fell on my plate, and I took it. Did I ever consider the range of possibilities available? No. Did I consider going back to school? No, I couldn't afford that. Did I have a burning passion? No. Somehow, my employer noticed my English background and offered me a golden opportunity. My work involved traveling, interviewing, writing, editing, research, and production. Though the pressure was often overwhelming, I liked dealing with people, hearing their story, listening to their pain. I thought I was working for *60 Minutes*, and I felt creative and independent because I worked alone.—IG

I began my second working career later than many. My first was raising seven children. The second actually began as an answer to financial need, and I was unprepared, therefore surprised, when my life changed so radically. My liberal arts education with a theater major did not include a career in education. The principal of my children's school suggested that I substitute teach for him. I was at once paralyzed with fear. I could not imagine myself in front of a classroom and prayed that my psychology minor would help. I picked up the books three weeks before my first day, convinced that these elementary students knew more than I did. When I was greeted by the class clown with "Wow! This is going to be a good day!" the challenge was on. I was thirty-six years old and just learning that I liked a challenge. (As if my kids were not enough!) The second thing was that I knew far more than they did, and that maturity is a wonderful thing. I completed some teacher prep courses, found myself working at two schools for long assignments, and decided to take an offer to teach sixth grade in one of my schools. That year proved valuable in many ways. There were twenty-seven students in the class, and at least seven were exhibiting a variety of learning problems. At that time, the research was sparse in that area, and it was up to me to creatively figure things out, do the research, and assist parents in understanding the situation. We moved to Miami, where my husband had accepted a position to open a school of social work. A fellowship opened up unexpectedly, allowing me to obtain a master's degree in special education. I then began my lifelong career of working in the world of special needs students and wounded parents. At this point I hoped to be a force for change, working with peers, administrators, students, and parents in a challenging field of education. That meant more studies to keep up with the research; indeed, I continued to study for the next thirty years and am still doing so. The years spent in my newly chosen career proved satisfying in many ways. Not just in my own personal growth, but in sharing my passion with family and friends.—RB

Gender Differences in Building Careers

In today's world it is important to realize two important building blocks for success: (1) interpersonal relationships *and* (2) the collective attributes of being a businesswoman.—EH

Anecdotally, we know that men and women exhibit very different approaches to career decision making. There is relatively little solid data that examines the experiences of women who reach the highest levels in a variety of professions. Nevertheless, we do know that in the areas of trust and social networking, men and women exhibit totally different behaviors. In a rare study, women entrepreneurs in Sweden embraced personal networking in order to build and nurture relationships, not to advance their careers. For women in general, trust grows out of our personal relationships, our respect and admiration for the positive attributes individuals exhibit. For men, networking is all about a collective identity for doing business and furthering careers. Consequently, men do not have the same trust issues as women because, for the most part, there have been no intense personal relationships cultivated.

Because as women we may be more emotionally invested, it is conceivable that we might withdraw from challenging situations because we do not want to risk losing the interpersonal trust we have gained in our group. The dilemma for us may come in mixing our personal and professional networking groups. Many of today's young professional women are taught early in their careers to voice their opinions in order to be better prepared to compete for executive positions of leadership. Our conception of interpersonal trust might be one reason why women tend to head small companies and why they often succeed in middle-management positions.

Older Americans: Still Part of Our Workforce

Today, there are a record 7.2 million Americans age sixty-five and older that are active participants in the workforce, and that is double the number of fifteen years ago. As we know all too well, there are many life events that factor into this increase. Many seniors have remained in the workforce because of economic reasons. Between 2015 and 2040, there will be a 67 percent increase in the population of people sixty-five and over. Since 2007 and the Great Recession, there has been a 25 percent increase in older Americans who are employed.

The Great Recession dashed hopes of retirement at sixty-five as many saw their 401k nest eggs drastically diminish. With the bottom dropping out of the housing market, an increase in oil prices, and added portions of saved dollars going for health-care costs, retirement was no longer a viable option for many seniors. Increases in age requirements for Social Security and Medicare were put in place. The boomer population is eligible for benefits at age sixty-six, while those born after 1957 are not eligible until age sixty-seven. With no pension, delayed benefits, increased health costs, and deferred Medicare, working appears to be a most reasonable alternative.

In addition, many older adults have been subject to the rise in investment fraud as well as targets for identity theft.

> I had a successful career in a service industry when I became a victim of investment fraud. I found myself back at work to make ends meet. I had rent to pay and needed food and the bare necessities of life. I was sixty-two and armed with several advanced degrees and thirty years of work experience, but I could not get any interviews related to my skills. I was very frustrated and desperate. Soon I became depressed. I finally found a minimum-wage job and was grateful I could pay my rent.—Anonymous

More than half of our senior population continues to work to stay active and involved. Increasingly, older women are employed as caretakers for the elderly. In a recent interview on National Public Radio, an eighty-year-old woman, using the skills she acquired after thirty years in the field, spoke of the benefits of feeling needed and making a difference for herself and the people for whom she is caring.

While many employers subtly attempt to push out older workers and replace them with those who command lower wages, others like national pharmacy chains celebrate the experienced employee by developing innovative programs to retain them in their corporate world. One of these programs transfers older pharmacists to Florida in the winter months to help relieve the high demands of the snowbird communities. It's a win-win situation for both the retirement communities and those pharmacists who want to continue to work and are delighted that they are in a warmer community away from the ravages of the cold winter months. How impressive it is to see the courage of employers who value age and experience.

A Changing Picture Emerges Once Again

> Seeing women in the workforce is the new norm, as natural as texting
> or surfing the web and doing both at the same time in this, the twenty-
> first century.—Anonymous

Those of us who chose a career are more than likely now in some phase of retirement. We are watching our children and grandchildren, the women of today and tomorrow, immersed in quite a different work world than we were in more than forty years ago. The stereotypical messages about women's roles and capabilities as we entered the workforce are no longer pervasive in corporate settings. Advancement for women of all ages in careers previously dominated by men is a now an everyday occurrence. Since 1984, the number of women in graduate schools has exceeded the number of men. While the enrollment number has increased, the pay scale for women in careers such as mathematics and engineering remain lower than for men. Business magazines and books now written for both genders are beginning to note the successes of women. The advocacy of our past generations has contributed to this, and that accomplishment should not be forgotten.

I am always amazed when I look at the achievements of my forty-four-year-old daughter. Although she politely acknowledges that the world has radically changed in medicine over the past fifty years since my husband entered medical school, I wonder if she truly comprehends the magnitude of the struggles that preceded those changes. She does not think it unusual that she is in her job. When my husband began medical school, there were four women in his class. Only half of those graduated with him. My daughter's class boasted nearly 50 percent women. All graduated. In my law school class in the mideighties, one-third of the class were females. Today, 50 percent are women. Why would young professional women even stop to think about the world for women fifty years ago? They are too busy meeting the challenges of doing it all: career, husband, children, community.—CTS

Nevertheless, even today, women are inclined to choose female-dominated careers and appear to be more flexible in terms of gender-role-influenced career choices than their male counterparts. Yet how we measure success in any career must be adapted to quantify those qualities that women bring to the table. Measurements of job performance need to be expanded to be more constructive and personally meaningful for women. If employers promoted job performance scales that measured collaborative relationships, nonhierarchical modes of social organization, flexible work arrangements, and other broader criteria, they would have evidence-based findings that could promote personal development and optimal productivity for women in the workplace, no matter their age.

Gender stereotyping in occupations is still present, although less than that reported in the past. Adolescent and adult males tend to stereotype more about occupations than females do, and older adults do so more than younger adults. Despite what may be seen as increasing flexibility about women's roles in the workplace, there are significant negative consequences when women engage in what males might term *deviant gender-role behavior*: women who excel in academic endeavors or in work performance. All this is not surprising if we study magazines, newspapers, television, and children's books. There the roles of men and women are still portrayed in a traditional manner.

RETIREMENT

Life is what happens when you're busy making other plans.—
JOHN LENNON

As we age, retirement is one of those life-altering events that compel us to step back and reflect. When we set goals for ourselves and look toward the future, especially at this time, we are more apt to be successful at handling this life transition.

I worked for them as a paralegal, and when my second spouse died, I was most happy to have a meaningful job, one that paid well and had a supportive atmosphere. As the economy weakened, it was obvious business was slower than usual, and therefore that affected my job responsibilities. One day one of the partners asked to speak to me. It was then that I was given a one-day notice: the choice of working part time for an hourly pay that was quite low, or not working at all. I said I would think about it and let them know. When I walked into the office the following day, I said, "Today is my last day." Do I think they were surprised? No, as I believe they knew I did not need to work. Although I had not planned to retire, as I look back on this months later, I was more emotionally ready than I thought. Today, I have no schedule and no set hours I must follow. Consequently, I am practically stress free. I have always loved animals and now volunteer four days a week at the Humane Society in my area. I feel that I am there to help give the animals (dogs) a second chance. Most of these animals have come here as they have been surrendered for one reason or another by their former caretakers. I now socialize them to prepare them for their next family, which I hope will be one of permanence. For me, too, I am helping each dog as if it were in an orphanage. I recently took a risk and adopted a dog that had been high energy with three former owners. He and I seemed to be a good pair. I found my energy partner. We run together, and this dog is the easiest mate, as whatever I do is fine. As I age, he, too, is aging and has mellowed as well, with adjustments and time. I visit the dog park in my condo, and I feel I have a whole new social world, seeking others and feeling

I can come home and not be alone. And most of all, I have read that seeing such goodness in an animal lowers blood pressure and helps longevity. *I am all for it...*—SS

Throughout our working years, we juggled many aspects of our lives so that our families and friendships were not sacrificed along the way. We were adept at managing our time and responsibilities. When we retired by choice, we took a deep breath and escaped from the structure that oftentimes held us prisoner. We forget that the choice of an equally dynamic life, albeit different from the adventures or misadventures of a career, is possible.

It is important to be mindful of our mental and physical state of being, our personal associations, our expectations, and our support systems in order to guard against isolation and prolonged solitude. Many neurologists say isolation and solitude may cause early onset of dementia. What we may fail to recognize is that retirement can be the time to set new goals to fulfill the dreams we might have had on hold. For some, retirement may come filled with excitement and a commitment to new adventures. For others, it may be numbing—a period of our lives when we fear we may experience anxieties regarding personal well-being and financial, health, and housing concerns.

What were your expectations of retirement? What plan, if any, did you make for this time in your life?

We stand at this new juncture discarding the routines that are no longer relevant and necessary and replacing them with a novel set of priorities. While we may not be in control of the continuous ticking of time, we can do whatever is in our power to recharge our individual batteries. Why do we feel so empowered at an age when our culture is quick to put us out to pasture? Because we represent a cohort of women over sixty who are living ten to thirty years longer than any other generation before, and we are beneficiaries of discoveries in medicine that have resulted in cures unknown to our parents and their parents. We are committed to changing our cultural view of retirement. It is a time to rediscover the world. A time to accept the challenges of aging and loudly protest, "We are not afraid of getting older!" We must begin to think outside ourselves and be curious about people, and to stay connected to those activities that maintain and enrich our significant relationships.

213

What positive qualities about yourself have you discovered since retirement?

> Retirement is the most fun time I have ever had. Retirement...what a sweet word to my ears. Retirement is that stage in life when you can enjoy the fruits of your toils and labors. It is synonymous with freedom. Of course, not everyone feels this way when they get to retirement. All I can say to those who reach retirement age is that it is just another chapter where you can make it victorious or disastrous. It all boils down to attitude. For example, I see retirement as a stage where every month I see a paycheck whether I work or not. I love it. It is not about having a lot of money. It really is about what we do with it. I am at a stage where I can appreciate the decisions I have made in the past. I do the best that I can. I do plan to grab every day of my retirement by its horns and make the best of it. Nothing can keep me from my highest good. When I feel down, as we all do sometimes, I pinch myself and remind myself that I need an attitude check. I then ask for divine intervention, breathe deeply, relax, and seek the beauty in nature. Laughter is also good. So I might just rent a funny movie, go for a short walk, call the kids or grandkids, and wait patiently for the emotional imbalance to pass. No doubt, retirement does bring some challenges, but I know that with the right attitude, the best is yet to come!—PP

There are others for whom their entire lives were centered on their careers. Yet retirement can become a catalyst for personal growth, a time for soul searching, and an attempt to reorganize one's life.

> Finding balance was never an issue for me, especially since I was married and had no children. Work took priority. It is at this juncture that longtime marriages may be ending, and one is faced with what to do with the newfound time. Never having devoted myself to my spouse or other family and friends, work became my primary focus, overtaking much of my time, beginning with checking in at my computer for messages and then gradually allowing my day to become filled with work instead of pleasure. Then I would make a list of the work I had to do the following week. Then later in the

day I would recheck all these activities. This practice grew, as did many of my obsessions about work and my need to prove myself,. Boundaries seemed to fade away...Did I really know who I was, or did I become identified by my work? My relationships with my family and friends began to decline. There was a paucity of time to cultivate and enjoy relationships that matter. In the end no one is getting the best version of you. When I did leave the job, there was little I knew of myself. Although I know that I am talented, intelligent, and have an abundance of energy, I realize that I did not have to be so extreme.—IG

For many, retirement is about rediscovery and the appreciations of those parts of ourselves that have been dormant for years.

I retired rather suddenly eight years ago, following a thirty-nine-year, full-time banking career. In 2004, my employer closed the loan center where I worked I decided to retire, since I was sixty years old, had (and still have) a working spouse, and also felt pretty sure that I did not want to subject myself to the torture of learning a new job in another company with all it would entail. Our financial situation being secure, I chose complete retirement. In any event, with retirement looming in approximately ninety days, panic set in. I do not participate in sports, nor did I have any particular hobbies. I do not cook or clean (yes, I'm a princess). How would I handle retirement? Would I be lonely? How would I fill my days? Lying on the couch and eating bonbons? Certainly not (I hoped)! One of my sisters (three years younger but already retired from teaching) was concerned as well about my impending adjustment. She had taken a course after she retired, and she recommended it for me. She also told me that I had to search out and develop new friendships, since many of my friends were either still working or lived out of town. I took her advice. I signed up for the weekly class mentioned above, and I also finally joined a gym. I knew that by going to the gym three or more mornings per week, I would be giving my day the structure it needed. I also searched out new female friends. At about the same time that I retired, a book club was started in my neighborhood. This has enabled me to make many new friendships among my neighbors and to read many good books as well. I also started playing mah-jongg (channeling my mother, perhaps), and that introduced me to more new "lady friends" and provided many fun-filled hours. I was lonely at first—but soon got over it. Having a cat for company helped; he and I spent many quality hours together, although he tended to nap more than I did. I also let my "travel genie" out of the bottle. I have always loved traveling but had always been restrained by "vacation days" at work. With this no longer being the case, I have spent the last almost nine years traveling the world. I stay in Florida during the winter months to welcome friends and family who visit, but as soon as the heat and humidity set in, off I go as much as possible, with my husband, sisters, friends, or, more recently, alone. So—what advice would I give others about retirement based on my experiences?

1. Join a gym.
2. Get a pet.
3. Search out new friends.
4. Take a class.
5. Expand your current hobbies.
6. Join a book club.
7. Learn a board game.
8. Take a nap.—RL

As we face the prospect of retirement, we gain an important sense of control over our lives by planning around our financial, health, lifestyle, and psychosocial concerns. The beauty of this phase of our lives is that choices are still available to us—personal choices on how to focus our daily lives, especially if we are in good health and mobile.

I worked in a large department store until the store closed, forcing me to retire. So at eighty-five, I began volunteering at an agency on aging. I whispered to the other workers that I was eighty-five, and they took me under their wing immediately. The other workers are delightful. The program offers compensation to seniors who have been victimized because of their age. It makes me sick when I think about the crimes that are being perpetrated on the elderly. The agency pays for my travel expenses, and it gives me the opportunity to deal with the voids in my life, such as the loss of my son. But basically I am a happy person. I have to be a part of the world. I have always been since childhood. At ninety-one, I enjoy an active life and am still volunteering services to the community.—RL

Planning has increased the psychological well-being of many retirees.

I set little objectives for myself that I like.—Anonymous

I actively seek ways to accomplish the things I wanted to do. —Anonymous

I feel I am able to face challenges that may arise in pursuing my goals. —Anonymous

I always make plans as it gives me something to look forward to, yet my spouse cannot stand to make plans. He prefers to take one day at a time. I begin packing for a trip weeks in advance, yet my spouse can pack at a moment's notice. For him, the best barometer of goal setting is relishing any given moment on any given day. My goal-setting approach seemed to have been shaped by observing a friend's sudden illness, being well one day and having a stroke another. It was at this point that I realized I could take a sabbatical and travel and see the world or remain static. A decision and an action followed. Upon returning after a one-year leave, I felt psychologically renewed and decided to remain in teaching and continue to this day on a part-time basis, freeing me up to take classes of my own and pursue travel and other activities that enrich my life. This pattern was not one I ascribed to when a young woman. Today I am more focused as to what is important to me: having a purpose as well as having fun, and recognizing that I deserve this for myself. A friend shared this phrase with me, and I enjoy reminding myself of it often: "Life is not a dress rehearsal." I have much more that I want to do. What am I waiting for?—J

Successful retirement demonstrates the advantages to skillfully teaching ourselves to set, plan, pursue, and realize our personal goals. As women, we must not only deal with our own retirement plans. At the same time, we may also be dealing with the shift in responsibilities within our own relationships with aging parents, spouses, or partners. But with all the changes looming in front of us, there are always the newly discovered opportunities that give us the energy to move forward. Even if life presents us with forces beyond our control, our accumulated years have afforded us the vision to see far beyond what is just at hand. With that newfound power, we have the tools to keep planning, in the present time, for our futures.

When retiring from a career, many of us find ourselves asking those common questions of ourselves: "What will I do with the newfound time on my hands? Will I purchase a recreational vehicle and travel to places yet unvisited? Will I purchase a cabin in the woods for my second home? Will I volunteer or mentor others in my field of work? Will I develop a hobby, or enjoy the hobby I have sorely neglected?"

> One afternoon after enjoying a book club discussion on finances, I realized that I was not well versed on the subject, and that began to have an effect on my sense of self. I became overwhelmed with an urgent concern to learn as much as I could to prepare for this new stage of my life. I never took care of the bills or took an interest in our investments. In fact, most of those decisions were made by my husband. I decided to meet with my spouse and have a heart-to-heart talk about our financial situation. I was worried whether I would have the amount of monies we would need to remain in our home or if we would have to have smaller quarters. I wondered if we should own or rent. I also worried if we could afford long-term health care. A few short months after the talk, my husband became quite ill. Our children live in another state, and now I became the sole caretaker. After months of caring for him, I became depressed. My friends helped me to contact social service resources, and with the help of our financial professional, we reviewed my insurance coverage and my entire financial picture in order to understand my options. I was more scared than at any other time in my life, but with all this support, I found strength to continue to do what I needed to do. I am so glad that I had asked for a crash course—Retirement 101—BM

My husband and I worked for forty years on the authorship business that we created. We compiled over 125 directories filled with helpful information and guidance on a wide variety of subjects for the benefit of thousands of appreciative people. Since we retired, I spend lots more time keeping in shape by going to the gym, power walking, doing yoga, and definitely keeping up with my lifetime sport, tennis—still playing singles! I also enjoy taking care of my garden. After all the hard work, I get such satisfaction seeing what I created. In addition, I am a student of the practice of holistic healing. I count my blessings every day. I am so very grateful.—BW

I had been a teacher for almost thirty years when I was asked if I would consider retirement. I was aware of my peers putting in for retirement but never thought about it much for myself. I loved my job. I loved helping my learning-disabled students to succeed. I also loved socializing with my staff. I am a people person and enjoyed engaging in dialogue. If I retired, where would I get this feeling of fulfillment? Did I know enough other people who were not working to socialize with during the day? How would I spend my days? I had to make my decision by April 1. I was always told by others who retired, "You will know when the time is right." I really did not know! It was a very difficult decision, but ultimately I chose to retire. I have *never* regretted it. It was the best decision for me. It allowed me to become free. Free to discover more of my interests. Free to spend time with people I choose. Free for the first time in my life to just be! I became a grandmother and offered to help out two days a week. What a joy! Words cannot express the feelings that grew as the bond with these little beings grew. I would not trade that for anything. However, I also need some brain stimulation and people time. I began volunteer work but did not find it very fulfilling, so I am in the process of seeking a new venue. I enjoy going to museums, shows, or just walking and exploring. I see friends for "game time" and play canasta and mah-jongg. It is great to just sit and read a book, cook, surf the Internet, or just be outside on a beautiful day. It is a great feeling to wake up and do what you want, when you want, since I have spent so many years nurturing others and being on a tight schedule. Do I miss teaching? Yes, but I now get fulfillment by helping students after school. It is great to feel needed and helpful.—BG

I was young during World War II. After the war I was given many opportunities to develop my intellectual curiosity. I had many careers that were quite successful, but I reflect now that I was quite passive during those years. Now I have time on my hands, and I began to ask myself, "What is my real purpose?" I decided to share my war experiences after fifty years of silence. It was time to share my story with the younger generations. I feel that in sharing my story, I can impart my belief that the differences in each of us need to be respected, reflected upon, and shared with an appreciation of how each of us can make the world more human, kind, and loving, a world where hatred is banned.—B

When I was younger, I had the responsibility of a family and did not work until the children were in middle school. I gave myself to them and their school. My only leisure time was once-a-week bowling in a ladies' league and a once-a-week mah-jongg and/or canasta game. Then a divorce, a remarriage, and no leisure time as I continued to work with my new husband. Now I have all the leisure time I want. My children are married with children of their own or careers, and my husband died nine years ago. I retired shortly thereafter and devote myself to my interests in the arts, friendships, and my condo association as their board president. I look forward to what life has for me and for those I love and to enjoy and make every day count. Life throws many different options your way. You have to learn to handle them, good or bad. To me, the glass is always half full, not half empty. Keep yourself busy. Give good to others and you will be a bigger person for it. I hope my son, two daughters, and six grandchildren have seen what I have done with my life, and I hope they will follow in a similar path.—LT

So often we can achieve increased serenity when we set new goals we hope will satisfy our needs. If we are able to accept things that cannot be changed and have confidence in life and in our future, we will attain an enduring sense of hope.

Over the last five years or more, the economic environment has been very volatile for many of us. Thus, retirement and unemployment may not be an option without a steady income to maintain our sense of security. With ten thousand baby boomers turning sixty-five each day, *encore jobs* for people who retire and return to work are commonplace. Retirees are creating a demand. Areas of technology, health care, and travel are offering opportunities for employment. Second employment may come with fewer hours and less responsibility, yet with the benefits of earning power and job satisfaction. We also should not minimize the importance of the sense of connection to others that employment offers, that sense of being a part of something greater than ourselves.

Whether we look for encore employment or explore a host of activities to satisfy our needs as we age, our landscape may become more complicated if we decide to move to a warmer or more desirable locale. Even if this is just for a few months, the challenge to meet new friends, adjust to a new living space, and find activities that will fill our days can be perplexing. Oftentimes, we do this without the support of family, and although the change can be very exciting and even stimulating, it can also upset the balance we have worked to achieve in the first sixty-plus years of our lives. By engaging the same tools—*set, plan, pursue, and achieve*—we rediscover who we are and how we want to spend the rest of our lives.

VOLUNTEERING

We make a living by what we get. We make a life by what we give.—Sir Winston Churchill

Volunteering has historically been one of the few formal roles available to older adults after exiting the workforce. With advancing age, we understand that we need to begin to reprioritize our goals as we confront the potential of reduced activities and social interactions and, with those, diminished emotional connections. Volunteering offers us the opportunity for a commitment that enhances our quality of life. The richness and meaning these experiences provide cannot be underestimated.

Volunteering can be defined in two ways. The formal definition implies an activity that one engages in without being coerced and, at most, only minimally compensated. As defined this way, volunteering is usually structured by an organization and directed toward a community concern. Informal volunteering activities also are pursuits that are not coerced and are unpaid, but they are personally directed, not structured by organizational goals and objectives. Examples of informal volunteering activities may be caregiving, contributing financial support, offering a supportive phone call, or performing a neighborly task.

Early influences of volunteering for many of us often began with our families. Volunteering was a part of the natural order of things, especially if we lived in a household that took time to feed others on Thanksgiving and Christmas, brought used toys and clothing to secondhand stores, or worked weekend shifts in our community hospital.

> My family's involvement both as volunteers and as philanthropists in the community was of great influence upon my life. I still remember the wonderful feeling of contribution when I collected for the March of Dimes at age six, knowing I was helping children less fortunate than I. It was simply natural for me to take my place in the community alongside my parents, and I take pride in reflecting on the number of successful projects I started for a number of cultural organizations.—TG

> My mom was the "Ann Landers" of our neighborhood, and Daddy was a hardworking and generous man in our community. In my early forties, I had a huge health scare that resulted in surgery. From that date forward, I began to organize *bikur cholim* at our synagogue. It means "to visit the sick." This group of caring men and women work with the rabbi to do whatever is needed for someone who is ill, in the hospital, or shut in. I have made a lot of soups, meals, hospital visits, calls, etc. to bring people comfort. I now have a daughter living in Los Angeles who has five children. Besides being a doting mother and wife, she recently started *bikur cholim* in her community. She told me how influenced she was by what I did and is very excited with her own initiative to help others. We have always been very generous in our community. Our children are extremely devoted to their city. Our son just served as president of his federation, and our daughter is doing acts of kindness all over Los Angeles. I know that our seven grandchildren, who are surrounded by messages, will make the world a better place and will fill their hearts with the pleasure one receives

when making others better. I hope as our grandchildren mature, they will be able to "carry on" the messages of *tikkun olam* (repairing the world).—SC

Others learned this skill in schools by participating in service clubs, for example. Often, giving of our time was a cultural expectation. It became a learned behavior if we were fortunate enough to be a beneficiary of role models who became our mentors. The late Marilyn Smith, a remarkable leader in the Miami community, wrote a wonderful piece on the pride of being a volunteer:

> There are a vast number of other things I'd love to do, but for me right now the action is here as a volunteer. It is my choice, and it is my pleasure. Don't be misled. It's not all altruistic, or payment of "Jewish dues." Where else can one find the potential for such outstanding personal enhancement; the superb opportunity to risk, to learn and grow; the possibility of sharing unique events with special human beings; the occasion to participate in raising funds and rendering decisions that impact Jewish life here, in Israel, in the world at large? Where else can one feel so congruent, working in a professional capacity with no monetary compensation for something so positive and important as the perpetuation of the dreams and values of our people?

Growing up in the fifties and sixties, we had a keen awareness of the responsibility we had as a nation to help bring peace to a world suffering from the devastation of wars. Many of our aunts, uncles, cousins, and parents were involved in these war efforts here and abroad.

In 1941, with the start of US involvement in World War II, President Franklin D. Roosevelt announced the new Series E defense bond. Following the attack on Pearl Harbor, defense bonds became known as war savings bonds, or informally as war bonds. War stamps were also introduced in small denominations.

> I can well remember the fun of the Stamp Day program that was established in many schools. My parents were happy to give me the small coins to purchase these war stamps to do my part. By purchasing

these stamps, we could then save enough to buy a savings bond. I can still recall those little books, and if I look hard enough, I would imagine I could find one in my stacks of remembrances. I can also recall the ads on the radio for Lassie and Superman regarding the importance of buying a savings bond. Through this school program, ninety thousand jeeps were purchased to be used when needed.—GH

Each one of us is capable of giving of ourselves with time or money. With those contributions we are privileged to become change agents as volunteers answering the needs of our society. Volunteering does not restrict anyone because of age or educational level. For some, volunteering has been a way of life while raising children or having a career. For others, the present allows us to have a first-time experience. We have arrived at a time in our lives, especially once we have retired and are less likely to be the principal caretaker for small children, when our priorities are changing. Reaching out and giving back is the essence of generativity. We are capable of embracing new challenges, and we now have the time to dedicate ourselves to those challenges.

Volunteering can be both static and dynamic. It is static as we home in on the organizations or causes with which we want to be associated. Yet it is also a dynamic process where we interact with others, oftentimes learning new things, setting new goals, and together sharing the benefits of our personal resources—our wisdom and experiences.

What role has volunteerism played in your life, both as a giver and receiver? Who, if anyone, inspired you to do this work?

I had intended to be a psychologist, but as a result of some misunderstanding by the school media, I became a medical doctor instead. And I never regretted it, although I wish I could have practiced longer. Most of the time as a doctor I worked as a volunteer, and I still do. It seemed perfect for me, because I wanted to raise my children (when I retired, I said, "My patients can get another doctor, but my children cannot get another mother"). Being a volunteer has kept me doing what I love to do, which is taking care of patients, but I still have the hours that allowed me to drive the kids to school and be at their sports events, ballet recitals, etc. I got the best of both worlds (but certainly not the money).—NL

What better way to prove my love of people than by my volunteering efforts? Perhaps my greatest contribution to a cause was when I spent three years with two women to build a trauma center by selling bricks. We raised a large sum of money while we ran most of the daily operations in order to realize the building of this much-needed facility. On the lighter side, we were in Pasadena attending our national college championship game in the Rose Bowl. At my son's urging, we sought out a site where volunteers were working on a parade float. Before long I found myself sitting on a large pail that previously held roses, measuring stems and removing thorns. Was I proud to see our little float from South Pasadena pass by the cheering crowds on New Year's Day. Working on the parade was definitely on my "bucket list" or, as I prefer, my "saucepan list."—Anonymous

Volunteering was a natural part of being a young wife, a mother, and a homemaker. All my friends were becoming involved in service organizations, and it was a way for me to find satisfaction by contributing to a worthwhile cause, feeling connected to others my age, and expressing my interests and the traditions instilled by my mother, who was committed to charity work. Today I continue to be dedicated to my work with young children, giving hundreds of hours to train teachers and childcare workers. I cannot even explain how fulfilled I feel to have made a real contribution, and that gives me a deep satisfaction.—MCL

In my early years, I varied my volunteer activities between my kids and my personal causes, attending PTA and various other school activities and volunteering in my son's kindergarten class as a room mother, helping with school parties. I did not get much satisfaction but did it anyway. As a past early-childhood teacher at a nursery school in New York, when asked to help with a reading-readiness program, I accepted. I worked with two students, giving one an hour a week and the other a half-hour session. What I noticed was that I found myself looking at the clock and could not wait for the hour to end. So it was at the end of the term that I decided that the patience I once had was gone and that if I had to earn money, teaching was no longer going to be the profession that spoke to my needs.—ER

We must never forget that the art of volunteering also extends to those of us who care for our grandchildren, helping out a single parent or providing some loving babysitting. We all agree that although these times may test our creativity, our patience, and our communication skills, they also afford us an opportunity to share family traditions with family stories. At the same time, our grandchildren are instructing us on how to manage the mysteries of technology in the twenty-first century.

When I retired from work, I knew that I had to stay actively involved not only in helping to care for my grandchildren but by finding something I could do that would keep me in touch with young people. I was lucky enough to find a position where I spend two times a week at a high school helping students master their literacy skills. I find it challenging and stimulating. I know that I am helping those students who may not have people around them who are knowledgeable in grammar and writing skills. I find that I get the same thrill I did when I was a teacher when a student gets a good grade on an exam I helped them with or when a student is accepted into college.—DS

"To whom much has been given"...I feel I have a good life and need and want to give something back to the community.—PK

In 1835, the historian Alexis de Tocqueville wrote a book titled Democracy in America, in which he raised volunteerism to the level of civic engagement. In the late eighties, President George H. W. Bush affirmed in his campaign for presidency that he would "keep America moving forward, always forward—for a better America, for an endless enduring dream and a thousand points of light." After winning the 1988 presidential election, he defined those "thousand points of light" in his inaugural address, elevating the importance of volunteerism to an integral part of the national agenda:

> I have spoken of a thousand points of light, of all the community organizations that are spread like stars throughout the nation, doing good. We will work hand in hand, encouraging, sometimes leading, sometimes being led, rewarding. We will work on this in the White House, in the Cabinet agencies. I will go to the people and the programs that are the brighter points of light, and I will ask every member of my government to become involved. The old ideas are new again because they are not old, they are timeless: duty, sacrifice, commitment, and a patriotism that finds its expression in taking part and pitching in.

Volunteering in later life not only strengthens society but simultaneously improves the lives of older adults who question their usefulness to others and increases their feelings of being needed and valued. Score is a volunteer organization that involves frequently untapped human capital: the aging adult with extraordinary experience who counsels new entrepreneurs.

Although the exact amount of volunteering needed to produce the following results is unknown, there are studies that suggest that older adults do benefit in terms of:

1. Personal well-being
2. Physical health
3. Psychosocial resources

This is especially important in a population such as ours that often encounters messages of devaluation from our society, which prizes youth, beauty, and physical strength.

The University of Miami, recognizing the tremendous resource in the Holocaust survivors in the local community, created a volunteer project that assigned one college student volunteer to a Holocaust survivor for a year of learning about each other. For the aging survivor, the benefit of the program was to promote a sense of hope for the world and gratitude in knowing that the interviewers were now silent witnesses of the past.

Estimates from the 2014 population survey show that 25.3 percent of adults sixty-five and older (22 percent of men and 28 percent of women) are engaged in volunteering.

> I have had the amazing opportunity of volunteering one half an hour a week in a school setting where I just listen to children who may be at risk. My successful interaction with one child in particular fills me with incredible pride. The first time I met with this young boy, he had just lost his mom. I told him that I had lost my father. I shared with him that one day after my dad died, I walked out on my terrace and glanced up at the sky. There I saw the brightest star. I told him that I knew that star was my dad, and I began to speak to him. I asked the young boy if he ever looked up to the stars, and when he said he did, I suggested he find the brightest star and speak to his dad about things. He loved the idea, and it gave him a way to cope with his loss. This shared experience gave him a reason to continue to come and speak with me. This really allowed us to bond. What a priceless experience.—BW

Philanthropy and Women Entrepreneurs

Women business owners in the United States are more likely than male entrepreneurs to participate in volunteer activities and to encourage their employees to volunteer.

> My business partner was fifteen years older than I and was a fine role model in her patient and calm manner. We laughed a lot and learned how to manage a business together. It was almost like a marriage. I have been exposed to many professional women through organizations, and they have been mentors and role models. By participating in community service, I have gained the appreciation of how fortunate I am to be on the giving end. I have served on a board that advocates for the personal empowerment and economic self-sufficiency of women and have had many valuable insights and growth through this experience.—CS

I feel my greatest strength as a leader—and I have served at the head of any number of volunteer and professional organizations—is valuing and promoting the ideas and suggestions of everyone involved, no matter what his or her position. This is not just about "consensus building"; it is rather about making team members feel they all have an important role to play, ensuring that all opinions are heard and considered. It is gratifying to see people respond to this and to take greater interest in whatever the project happens to be.—TG

I have spent my entire adult life volunteering in my community. I never really appreciated how any of the programs I devoted my time to affected my personal well-being until I was in Poland serving as a chaperone on a trip with teens who were exploring the horrors of the Holocaust. Unexpectedly, I was faced with one of my most challenging life experiences, and my companions and my peers quieted my fears and allowed me to focus on my immediate preparation to return to America. When I received the message that my husband was hospitalized and was deathly ill, everyone on my bus went into a Code Red mentality, taking charge of what I needed. Airplane reservations were made by one individual; another took charge of taking me to the airport and supplying me with the necessary change and small bills I might need to travel. They allowed me to concentrate on getting home on time. Their energy was comforting and helped me not to give up hope. To this day, nine years later, I can recall with vivid memory how endearing and caring they were to me. What we shared were years as volunteers in a program we all treasured and shared together.—GKH

We have learned that volunteering lowers depression levels for those over sixty-five. These findings suggest that, once again, social integration is a positive outgrowth of volunteering.

Some say that I am the consummate volunteer. I have been volunteering throughout my many careers, affording me the opportunity to serve my community well. For over fifteen years, I was able to fulfill my commitment to serve others, volunteering for the Boy Scouts and Girl Scouts of America while organizing events for hundreds of campers. With my ability to speak four languages, and presently studying a fifth, I took on a new occupation after retiring: visiting elderly residents at a facility that is both a hospital and residential home to hundreds of people. In Cuba I was a professor of piano, theory, and music. Now I am using my skills as a "friendly visitor" in this setting weekly. We discuss current events in politics and fashion. These discussions allow these people to interact, be heard, and voice their opinions. I also visit nonverbal residents who are in critical condition, allowing me to interact with residents every week. I will say that there is something unique about each person, and being a volunteer has allowed me to strengthen my commitment to doing good work. It also has given me a sense of purpose and has blossomed into a whole new chapter in my life.—MV

So who is counting? Recently, I recall reading an e-mail at about one o'clock in the morning and began laughing aloud, surprisingly not awakening my spouse. I was laughing because the e-mail was asking me if I was fulfilling my ten acts of commitment to study and to do good deeds, a commitment that I had personally pledged at a holiday service on New Year's. I was laughing not because I did not think the question a good one but because for days I had been preparing a holiday feast honoring the Holocaust survivors who have become mentors to me. What I did realize is that no matter how exhausted I was, my time was valued and appreciated. It is these feelings that provide a level of immense personal satisfaction and pleasure and, I strongly believe, add to my sense of being physically and mentally healthy.—GKH

The variety of programs is limitless. Often people choose programs that are similar to their careers, such as working with children if one was a teacher or working with special needs children or adults if one has had special training.—RB

When the children were growing up, I never had time to think about me. I was so involved with taking care of them and everyone else. Now that I have the time to think about me, I need to learn how to do that...I really need to concentrate on what I want for me, and how to do that feels undeserving or foreign...but I am going to work on it.—HW

Although we see that there are untold benefits for those older adults who volunteer, there are also factors that contribute to lower rates of volunteerism among older populations: (1) as older adults are separated from educational institutions and workplace environments, they are less likely to be presented with volunteer opportunities, and (2) older adults may be less likely to be asked to volunteer, and being asked is a major route to volunteering.

Thoughts to Remember:

1. Set, plan, pursue and achieve your personal goals.
2. Share the importance of balancing your career and your personal life.
3. Apply the abilities learned from your work experience (i.e., resiliency, flexibility, decision-making, risk-taking) to present decision-making.
4. Appreciate your contribution to the acceptance and respect women have in the work force history today
5. Use your skills and talents to mentor the next generation in career and volunteer activities.
6. Honor the decision to become a volunteer.
7. Identify the many interests, talents and life experiences you have to share with others
8. Appreciate the uniqueness of your role as a volunteer and inspire others to participate with you.
9. Serve as a " Guardian of History" by sharing individual stories of both career and volunteering. Remember helping others reinforces a sense of purpose and one's usefulness to others.

Volunteering promotes positive growth for ourselves and for all those we have touched. This thread runs through the women's stories, and binds us together while recognizing that we are a part of something larger than ourselves.

As a volunteer worker in an ALF in our community, I have the privilege of interacting with incredible residents. One in particular is a 105-year-old woman whom I visit. I know my visits are important, as she has just a few family members who are still living, and they live far away and in other states. She is infirm, very much alone, and wonders why, if suffering is inevitable at such an advanced age, does God not just let people die? Why does she have to keep on going? Why does she need to live so long? I really do not have an answer for that, but I looked at her and asked if she would like to speak with the clergyman in the facility, who might be able to help her find an answer. Subsequently, he visited and wonderfully, gently, and compassionately spoke with her and shared with her that evidently God feels she still has so much more purpose and value to give to the world, and that it's just not her time to go as yet. In relating this conversation to me at our next visit, we shared with each other how very much we mean to one another, and that's what it's really all about. I told her, "As much as you appreciate my visiting you each week, it is I who gain so much from our visits. You are an extraordinary woman who has given so much to the world, and I have learned and continue to learn so much from you. You have changed my life in many ways and have truly been a blessing to everyone who has known you. It would be so sad for me if you were not here. I need these visits as much as you do." The woman responded that she does perk up and feel so good whenever I visit, and in the time we spend together, she enjoys very much sharing her many varied and wonderful life experiences. She said, "H, I feel so invigorated when you come to see me. I look forward to our time together, and I can't thank you enough for caring about me. I love you."—HB

When we reflect upon one of our gender differences as women leaders, it is that of making connections and valuing the relationships we build as priorities. We desire equal pay for equal opportunities while valuing the humanness involved in the business of doing business with another, on any level. In doing business, the relationships we build are priorities (source: National Foundation for Women Business

Owners). This is not just about "consensus building"; it is, rather, about making team members feel they all have an important role to play and ensuring that all opinions are heard and considered. It is gratifying to see people respond to this and to take greater interest in whatever the project happens to be. Before so many women entered the workforce, this country ran on the tireless efforts of the many women who volunteered for any number of cultural, educational, religious, or social organizations. There we not only learned good business practices, marketing, finance, organization, and public relations but also leadership—how most effectively to get people working together for a common cause—and the joy of seeing projects succeed. This is an incredibly valuable set of lessons, one being missed by those who go directly from college into a paid career.—TG

As the ultimate volunteer, what does it all mean to you, especially at this time in your life? I think that this quote from Ralph Waldo Emerson sums up what motivates me and likely others to volunteer: "It is one of the most beautiful compensations of this life that no man can sincerely try to help another without helping himself." As I reflect on my life and what I have hoped to accomplish, I realize that it goes beyond raising a family or living life to the fullest. Yes, I've done all that and feel satisfied. I've always been actively involved with several organizations and long ago decided that it wasn't enough to just be a member; something in me wanted me to take on leadership positions. Now that I've reached the age of retirement and have lots of time on my hands, volunteering seems to be my ultimate driving force. As I became involved in Jewish studies and Torah, I learned that tzedakah is the highest of all commandments—that giving to the poor is an obligation. Yet I found myself volunteering not because I must but because of the satisfaction that it brought me. I found that I felt better about myself by using my time to help the community and others that weren't as fortunate. I am about to embark on a volunteer project called "Take Stock in Children." Imagine the satisfaction of being involved in a program that will give a child the opportunity to further his/her education with a college degree. Maybe we take it for granted that our children will automatically go to college, but for a low-income family, it can never be possible without a full scholarship. I know I will feel proud knowing that I helped one child reach this goal. What else is gained by my volunteering? I've made many new friends through all the organizations I've joined. I've met people whose goals are similar to mine. I realize that many service organizations would cease to exist were it not for the many volunteers who are involved. So where do I see myself in the future? To give back to the community for all I've gained from it? To continue to be the volunteer who is always able to find the time when tzedakah is needed. To continue to grow as a worthy individual fulfilling the commandments of Torah.—EB

LIST OF QUESTIONS TO REVIEW

Who or what factors influenced you in choosing your career?

What were your expectations of retirement? What plan, if any, did you make for this time in your life?

What positive qualities about yourselves have you discovered since retirement?

What role has volunteerism played in your life, both as a giver and receiver? Who, if anyone, inspired you to do this work?

PERSONAL REFLECTIONS

_____
_____
_____
_____
_____
_____
_____
_____
_____
_____
_____
_____
_____
_____
_____
_____
_____
_____
_____
_____
_____

_____

_____
_____
_____
_____
_____
_____
_____
_____
_____
_____
_____
_____
_____
_____
_____
_____
_____
_____
_____
_____
_____
_____
_____
_____
_____
_____

CHAPTER 7
Finding Our Present Voice

I am what I am today because of the choices I made yesterday.
—ELEANOR ROOSEVELT

*Why would I turn back the hands of time when
my own have so much character?*
—LETITIA BALDRIGE

Aging, like childhood, comes in stages. It is developmental. As we age, we bring along the sum total of life's experiences to the here and now. These experiences affect how we live out our present.

The voices of many women have shared how one's earliest experiences help to shape not only our personalities but our relationships, our actions, and our values as well. With each new experience, we have learned. With each new experience, we have grown. With each new experience, we have changed. Some of the changes have been difficult, and some of the experiences we could have lived without. Nonetheless, those earlier years set the stage for the genuine depth of joy we all have the capacity to feel in our *twilight years.*

I just can't get enough of myself.—LO

I am my own best friend.—JK

Our present voice, to be authentic, should speak of acceptance.
—Anonymous

When we approached adolescence, we were ready to move out into the world with a newfound sense of independence. Our parents were hopeful that we had internalized the lessons they had taught us. As we entered the adult world, many of us chose a life partner; some of us chose a lifetime career. But we still had not achieved the full potential of our *voice* as women in the midst of the twentieth century.

In each generation, women have had to speak up and fight so their voices could be heard. In 1428, Joan of Arc, acting by divine guidance, succeeded in winning the respect of Charles VII and in convincing him to grant her the authority to lead the French army into victorious battle over the English. The suffragettes of the early twentieth century succeeded because they spoke out and marched to demand the right to vote. And Rosa Parks succeeded when her voice resounded as she courageously sat in defiance of hatred and discrimination. Collectively then, as women, we have propelled one another to a higher ground.

We finally have a chance to make meaning of who we have become intellectually, emotionally, and spiritually now that we are rooted in the *twilight* of our lives. It is a time of reflection and introspection.

How have our reflections from our past impacted how we see ourselves today?

> On contemplating the ninth- and twelfth-grade graduation polls:
> Were we really this shallow? Voting on Darling Dimples? Best Legs? Most Freckles? Looking back, I can see some more substantial categories: Brainiest, Friendliest, Most Athletic (I'm pretty sure no one went on to make *that* a career). But as I think about my life fifty-plus years later, I confess to feeling a failure. I never lived up to those votes of confidence from my classmates, who twice voted me Most Likely to Succeed. Today I experience a real, deep-rooted discomfort when asked about my life, my "career," my, ummm, place in the world. I mumble, deflect, obfuscate, blabber, clam up, anything but give a straight answer that is "I am a nonperson." Even my mom (yes, at age ninety-eight) recently implied that I "do" nothing—this in conversation with my sister, a veterinarian/thirty-year businesswoman/equestrienne. So these poll categories now haunt me. When I first thought about them all these years later, I thought I would get to point out how laughable

they would now seem. But they have caused me to be introspective and confront these bad feelings. I suppose in our heart of hearts, when we are young, we each feel a little bit "exceptional"—I know my early school years were full of small and even a few big triumphs. But I peaked early, I guess (something my husband and brothers like to remind me of), and to find myself feeling the opposite of a "success" is more than a little painful. So I float along, lamenting not having made a difference in the world and, at seventy, not having the talent or energy to rise out of this rut.—NHR

I am a doer. I don't think about tomorrow. Every day I'm celebrating.—E

At first, getting older was frightening. Then I came to the realization that when I opened my eyes each morning and smelled the coffee brewing, I knew that it was to be another beautiful day. Having been able to retire with my husband has made my life joyous. My younger years were spent working, taking care of my family and home, and making a place for us in our community. Consequently I knew that at retirement I would have to have something useful to do. So getting older has been more than I could have asked for. In addition to enjoying my family, I have time to volunteer. My husband and I run a program to feed three to four hundred homeless at the Chapman Center once a month. In addition I volunteer at Mt. Sinai Medical Center and also take educational courses to feed the mind. It is a wonderful feeling to be useful as one gets older.—LF

I learned to be content with my situation and my losses. I try to be positive even when life seems to be challenging and people are disappointing. I will continue to travel, learn new things, and volunteer in the community. I consider change as inevitable. And I care less about what others think about me. I have less fear of computers and repair small things around the house. Time is very important, so I spend less time on superficial activities.—MB

My life is a riches-to-rags-and-back-again story. At a very early age, I loved to sing and dance and was never without a pencil in my hand.

Drawing was my passion, but I also did some off-Broadway acting. I am happy to see that nowadays children who show talent are encouraged to further their ambitions. Unfortunately, difficult times and my father dying at an early age prevented me from doing what I wanted to do. However, I always had my pencil. My dream of becoming an artist changed when I found out that I was color-blind—or actually it is really color deficient. I gave up my art, and since I married at an early age and became a mother, all other thoughts left my mind. I worked for the recreation department and then left to go into the produce business with my husband. At forty-five years of age, my doctor and his nurse literally forced me to go to an art class. The teacher encouraged me to start again where I had left off so many years ago. Color was always my problem, and I kept giving up. Somehow I decided that I did not like thinking of myself as a quitter. I felt that I could teach myself how to work with color intellectually. It took me a great many years, but I eventually got to where I did outdoor shows. I became a signature member of prestigious art organizations. I also was happy to do demonstrations for students from the early grades up to those at the university. I always made a point to tell youngsters that I am color-blind and that if they want to do something badly enough and had obstacles standing in their way, they just had to try harder as I did to overcome them.—RK

Throughout the past chapters, we have examined our important developmental stages, friendships, career, and other lifestyle choices we have made. We answered questions that might have compelled us to reveal some hidden treasures from our past. Looking back in order to look ahead has real purpose. We may mourn over past decisions. We may look at some of our choices and wonder how and why we made them. We may celebrate small but meaningful triumphs we are most proud of. Looking at the past has an important value for us in the present.

I am one hundred years old right now, and I cannot do some of the same things that I used to do, like attend concerts or the ballet or go to my favorite Lincoln Road mall because I don't drive anymore. But I can go shopping because I do have a wonderful aide; I am able to walk pretty well and sleep well. I have macular degeneration, but

I still have one good eye. I have a wonderful family who checks in with me daily, and a daughter who lives nearby and calls me each morning and night and about six times a day. (And I call her about twelve times a day.) My daughter told me that she will never let me be forgetful. It's hard sometimes, but I go with the flow; it's also easier said than done. I grew up in a household that was very musical. My mother was a marvelous pianist, and I learned to play at age six, and I played along with her when she traveled throughout the state of Pennsylvania performing. I was also head of many of the music activities in my junior high school, and I will remember that each day when classes were dismissed, I was the one who played the marching song upon dismissal. I still have my 1932 medal that I received for my musical excellence as accompanist on the piano for our band, and I still wear it proudly today. My parents danced all the time, and I can remember when we were going to bed, they were dancing around the living room. I love all kinds of good big band music...Cab Calloway, Benny Goodman. NPR has many of these programs, but I do not like the music they play today. I even won the first Charleston contest in school. Before TV we had radio, and we used to listen to boxing with Joe Louis, music, and comedy. We were fortunate that my daughter was accepted to Brandeis and did receive a scholarship. I liked what the university stood for. The university was the only Jewish university that was nonsectarian; all religions were accepted. No pictures were necessary on the application for identification, and Arab and Israeli students lived together in the dorms. I have worked diligently for over sixty years raising money for books for the Brandeis library and all that that school has stood for. I created a chapter for the Brandeis women in Miami over sixty years ago and attend their study groups regularly to this day. Recently they honored me with a surprise party for my centennial birthday. When I was young, my mother introduced me to many crafts and said, "What the eye can see, the hand can do," so I started a craft group for women in my building about twenty years ago. Using these skills, we began with twenty women and are now five, but we meet every Wednesday afternoon to knit, crochet, or sew veterans' lap robes and baby blankets, which we send to a hospital in Israel or to people at a cancer center. I have always enjoyed making scrapbooks, and for over ten years I have made birthday cards from pictures that I cut and paste from magazines for my family.—ITD

Focus on survival with an objective of the success of my children defined my life and, whether I realized it or not, was the source of my drive over the past twenty-four years. I was a single mother of three young children, abandoned by a husband who destroyed our finances and then disappeared. I did not have any living family members for help and support. Despite my personal internal agony, I knew that I had to put that pain aside and focus on my children, repairing their wounded hearts and guiding their success in life as well as providing the financial support for this to happen. Total focus on that objective, the success and recovery of my children, drove all of my actions. I devised complicated matrices of activities to ensure that each child was at Boy Scouts, football, cheerleading, cross-country, track, student council, French club, school musical rehearsals, religion class, etc. on time and with the appropriate equipment and attitude. I pursued opportunities for challenge and higher salaries at work in a field dominated by men, predominately by men with law degrees. I butted into the "glass ceiling" and broke through, becoming a top executive at the headquarters level of a powerful government agency managing many of those male attorneys across the country. My success at work was not particularly important to me as an ego booster but instead meant I had the financial ability to continue to ensure that my children had the means for pursuing their dreams. Each of my children succeeded as a scholar, an athlete, a leader, a lover of fine arts, and a complete and compassionate human being. As my third child neared university graduation, I began to evaluate my quality of existence. Despite my financial success, I realized that I wasn't living an existence that was healthy or happy. I decided to retire and turn my focus inward. For the first three months, I slept until afternoon, knowing that I did not have to do anything at all. I never even for a moment missed my former work life. I resumed oil painting, a love of mine that had been on hold for the past forty years. I swim laps for forty minutes and take long walks almost every day with the objective of paring down some of the extra me that appeared during

> my years as supermom. I really believe that sixty is the new forty. I am emerging as a woman of many dimensions, not solely a mom (well, maybe mom emeritus). I recently challenged myself by going on a transatlantic cruise solo and spending several days on my own in Amsterdam at the end of the cruise. To my surprise I found myself enjoying the company of some very interesting men (not attorneys) to whom I was a glamorous, intelligent, entertaining woman in my own right as opposed to the focused mom I have been for the past thirty-three years. I reflect on the reality of aging, and for many, many years, I was an observer of life as a woman rather than a participant, outside of being a mom. I feel that I have many adventures ahead of me.—DC

Aging is something that comes gradually. It doesn't spring up one morning and we wake up old. Over the years, we come to look at ourselves in a different way. Some may say, "I'm old." Some may say, "I feel like I'm getting old." Still others may say, "I know I'm getting old, but I don't feel it." There will be changes along the way that may involve adjustments. But we have learned aging is a constant and requires inner strength to adapt to all its variables. Now is the time when the skills we have acquired and honed the last sixty-plus years come into play as we search to find our present voices.

> I look at where I am today, and at the same time, I look at where I've come from. It's been a long, hard journey, but I think that's what life is about. I look at much younger women; I look at children. At each stage there are difficulties to conquer. But when I look at myself, I see a person who has already met many of these challenges, and I know that whatever comes my way, I'll be able to handle it. To me that is the experience we bring to this time in our lives. We understand that challenge is a given; it's just what we do with it that makes the difference.—Anonymous

The next generation of women will learn from their own experiences as we have from ours. Yet consider the evolution of our own voices and how our knowledge and wisdom can be passed on in a way that could be significant to future women over sixty.

What Is Our Present Voice?

In an article in *Psychology Today* (Jan. 12, 2010), Susan Nolen-Hoeksema, while summarizing some of her findings, observed that women, more than men, are prepared for aging. Why? She attributes our preparedness to having spent years refining our psychological strengths and relational skills in managing the complexities of our families and communities. Nolem-Hoeksema is quite optimistic: "Old age is not just about surviving; it's about flourishing!" She adds that older women are better able than younger women to cope effectively with stress.

Dr. Mark Agronin, in his book *How We Age*, also discusses the advantages and disadvantages that come with aging and how we are better able to cope as we look with vision and pragmatism at what is within our control. Although many of us do not always look at aging with a positive slant, we have the tools in hand to give rise to resilient and powerful present voices and to our ability to make this third of our life both fulfilling and meaningful.

Definition of Voice

Do our voices take on a different tone or timbre as aging women? Are we freer in expressing ourselves to others, no longer worrying as much about what others may think? We are using the metaphor of voice to symbolize a woman's sense of self—her feeling of self-worth, her power of self-reflection, and her ability to take action on behalf of herself and others.

> I live in a kibbutz. Religion is bridge. I am involved in creative writing, dance, art, and a book club. Although there are differences from what I am used to, change seems to agree with my well-being.—Anonymous

Our voices are a mixture of our inner thoughts and how those thoughts affect how we respond to the world around us. Our voices weave from the past to the present, connecting us historically, socially, culturally, and spiritually with those who have helped to give voice to our present.

> I have a direct line to G-d. I am feeling blessed.—DO

> What are the reasons that I have maintained a positive attitude? First and foremost, I have been lucky:

1. To have had good health all my life.
2. To have had a loving family.
3. To have had three good men in my life and a fourth kind to me now.
4. To have maintained long-term relationships with dear friends.
5. To have formed new bonds with exercise, bridge, tennis, book club, and social club and the people I have met here.
6. To have had an education, enabling me to be independent.
7. To have inherited enough to supplement my income, which considerably enhanced my lifestyle.
8. To enjoy a closeness to my sisters and their husbands and my daughter and my grandson.

Secondly, I live in a great place for interaction with lots to do here physically and intellectually. So I am appreciative of my good fortune but apprehensive at this age because I see friends failing. But so far, so good!—BGC

It is hard for me to believe that I am eighty-five years old. I never thought along the way what my life would be like at this age. I met my husband when I was seventeen and married when I was nineteen. Marrying was the defining decision of my life. My husband had a tremendous enthusiasm and a lust for life, and together we shared sixty-two years of growing older together. Aging was not a thought that determined how I lived. I learned to make adjustments that were necessary according to health and circumstances. Sports always played an important part in our lives. We were avid skiers and tennis players. Golf came into our lives after my husband had two knee replacements and I had a new hip. It became, and still is, an important part of my life. Fortunately along the way we had bought a vacation home. When circumstances indicated it was time to retire, there was the perfect place to make a new life. We eased into it. Sold our home. Slowly closed our business and relocated. Luckily it was a place my children loved and visited as often as possible. My grandchildren consider it their second home. I very quickly became involved in my third career. After taking courses at the local public-access TV station, I became a producer and worked there for the next fifteen years. The people I met and the challenge of new experiences kept me very much in touch with the real world. Everything changed when my husband was diagnosed with cancer, and after a long courageous battle with cancer, he passed away. And so began another chapter in my life. There is no way to put it into words to have part of your life forever gone. What lives on is the family we created and that they in turn have created. It is with great pride and joy that I watch my grandchildren find their places in the world. And they are my legacy.—PC

I am unique. I am adorable. I make people laugh and I make people feel good and I have an existential view of life. I think that life is just a big game. We are liberal Democrats, and my children understand it and embrace it. I understand that I stand for gay rights and feminism. I understand that we need to make our own choices, and I understand that we have to take care of poor people. But I am aware that America does have bad things that it has done. We sit at the dinner table with all the kids and grandchildren and my son-in-law (who is a Republican). We have been together as a family for twenty years, and they have heard our conversations over the years and come around to some of our beliefs. I do not really believe in God since I had a friend who lost a child to crib death and a very good friend that committed suicide. There seems to be no rhyme or reason to it. I guess this ties into my feelings about religion, too. I do believe in my heritage. My heritage is first. Temple provides a community. On 9/11 I wanted to go because I wanted to be with community, to sit beside my friends and family and peers. I do not know why I am here. We live until we die. I do not want to die any time soon. But I am going to live as best as I can while I am here. The idea of love is very important to me. I did not have love when I was little. My mother and father divorced. My sister made my mother into an Auntie Mame so we could stand her, but she was not a responsible mother. I adored my sister, who was twelve years older and was like a princess. My mother slept around, she gambled, and she owned a liquor store that she only had to work in during the summer and at Christmas. My mother got married many times, and I felt like I was more like a burden to her. No one ever said that to me, but it was like I was discarded. At sixteen I became pregnant, and I felt love toward him. I married, and it was not until my friend heard me speak and mentioned depression and the possibility of divorce that I had an aha moment. On the phone my friend said, "I have never heard you sound so defeated." I thought, "No one is going to defeat me!" Then I divorced when my daughter was three. There is stored energy in the love for the people who count. I cannot be bothered with superfluous relationships or activities. I was involved in a women's group when my child was young. But now I like to be alone. I love to read. I like my own company. I shy away from being involved in activities. I do not have the energy, and I need to store my energies for that which counts: my friends, my family, and myself. There was an age when I would have wanted to be a fundraiser, but that does not matter to me anymore. There are a number of things that are depressing, that I do not find that important anymore. My friends can call me because they know that I will be home and share. My friends visit, and they know that they can share something good or bad, but I am always there. I like to needlepoint and I used to like to cook, but since my husband's illness, my priorities have changed. For over twenty-five years I learned how to take care of myself when I went to North Carolina while my husband was working here. I learned to go into a restaurant and sit by myself. I learned to go to the movies alone if I wanted. I learned to walk into a party without a spouse. I learned to go out to dinner with people and to make sure to give them a credit card so that I would be treating because they were always treating me. It was growing up. Having to stand up for yourself. I do not think we are leaving the world in such a good way. We are the last generation to have it easy. I see my daughter watching over her children and worrying over them. At first I thought it was so overblown, but I do not feel that anymore. I think there are real scary things out there these children face. I was fixed up. To the person whom I was fixed up with, I was five foot two, and when my hair is combed, I was adorable. I swept him off his feet. I am adorable. Near the end, my mother and father were friends. They made sure that they were together when I married again. They sat at the same table, and I have always thanked them because we could finally look like most normal people. I know how to be very self-confident. I know how to be a good friend. I know how to be a loving person, because I know how to make people feel comfortable when they are around me. I have had a best friend for sixty years. I met her in fifth grade. I am proud to be her friend. She is smart. She is pretty. And I have a history with her. I rode on her coattails. I have trained myself to be smart and educated. And when my friend's son was in an accident, I took over for my friend during the crisis. I knew what she would want and was able to take care of her wishes. When my friend had breast cancer, I told her I was going to North Carolina in three days. Because there was honesty between us, she asked that I not go. And I did not go. I think I know what is important to me. It is about time.—MH

I am a lucky girl. I was born into an affluent family, and my parents were madly in love. My father was a developer where I was born. I attended FSU for one year and then married when I was eighteen. I continued my education at the University of Miami for one year but never graduated. I always felt a need to educate myself and have done so through the years. When the computer came out, I made it my business to learn everything I could and am most proud of the fact that in my age group, I am the only one who does. My "friends" on Facebook and Twitter and those I e-mail are usually more of my daughter's friends. One of my first jobs was as a travel writer for *Showcase Magazine*, where I interviewed celebrities and wrote monthly articles. I landed a job on a local TV show with KB and was his "girl friday" for eight years until he died. I really had a good life. My husband supported me in everything I did and never tried to stop me. He was always proud of me, and whatever I tried, he believed I could do. I took acting classes with my daughter at the Playhouse, and I had small parts in movies made there, including a part in *A Hole in the Head* with Frank Sinatra. I served on the grand jury for two years and have served on many community boards. My husband was a pharmacist and had many stores and real estate holdings. He was active in Miami Beach politics and served the community. I worked along with him and always felt I was his partner. We traveled extensively all over the world, loved to entertain, and had many common interests, including loving to dance. I have always been very energetic, and at eighty-nine I don't feel old now. I continue to work overseeing our business interests. I spend a lot of time and energy with my children and grandchildren, and I will soon become a great-grandmother. My goal is to be alive to see my great-grandson. We have a very close family. I played tennis until I fell at age eighty-one. For me, the most horrible thing is not being able to drive, and having to depend on someone else. I think for my age I look pretty good. When asked what I am most proud of being married to BG."—SG

The book that inspired many of us, *The Feminine Mystique*, by Betty Friedan, has been reissued more than thirty-five years after it was first published, and yet its message is still relevant. Much of what we read then about equality and our right to choose is still valid for us and for our daughters and their daughters. Friedan wrote in 1963 that women spent half a century fighting for their rights and the next half wondering whether they wanted them at all. Her words were quite *prophetic*: *"Rights have a dull sound to people who have grown up after they have been won."*

Today, we see our daughters and granddaughters competing for jobs on or near the same footing as men without giving any thought to the struggles that preceded them. In a recent article in the *New York Times*, Janet Maslin wrote that she had arrived at the *Times* because of the opportunities that Friedan's book created. "I wish I had known how much I owed her," she said. Many of us feel a sense of gratitude for the opportunities made possible by the powerful force of the women who played an extraordinary role in changing our world and in giving us the gift of owning and appreciating our present voice.

In America, I see strong women. It is important to me to be independent and not to depend upon others. Each day I rise at 5:30 a.m. and do my exercises on my treadmill. I attend the community center twice a week and have worked for the past seven years giving manicures and pedicures three and half days a week. As one of six children and the oldest, I often helped with my siblings. This is a role I still value today, as I am a caretaker and have been all my life. Today, I care for my neighbors, my brothers, and my sisters and am so thankful that I am able to continue in this capacity. I am not a fighter nor a complainer. My first marriage ended in divorce, and I had a two-month-old. I did remarry and had a forty-two-year marriage. I learned that in marriage, it is important to talk, each giving and taking from the other. Each day my inner voice speaks of thoughts of how our family got out without getting harmed and reminds me of how lucky we are. I feel blessed today with two sons and their families. As a mother, I am still concerned for them and speak to them often just to know they are okay. It is good to hear their voices nightly. In reflecting once again, the many circumstances helped to make who I am today. I remain positive and remind myself of being both a blessing and of having many blessings.—EH

The religious values my parents instilled in me and their example has had a strong impact on my personality and who I am today. Growing up in a culture that is different from my parents' culture has taught me to be tolerant and to have humility. Being a child of refugees has taught me not to take anything for granted. It has taught me to be very grateful for the freedom we enjoy as Americans. As a woman I also value and appreciate the opportunities we have in education and to be self-reliant. I married an American, and that has been culturally quite challenging. I have been fortunate to have had the opportunity to be a stay-at-home mom. I feel that women today have two jobs. They have a career and they are also raising children. My husband is now retired, but I continue to work because I enjoy what I do. I work in Jewish education, which has always been my passion. My husband is very helpful and supportive, especially because it helps us financially. Throughout our marriage we have been very supportive of each other and respect each other. In spite of inevitable difficulties in life, our love has helped us to grow in our marriage. Learning has always been my passion. I learn from the wisdom of our sages, and I try to apply that to my life. As I am getting older, I think it is more important to have a healthy diet, sleep well, exercise, and maintain a healthy social life. It now requires more effort on my part to balance all that I want to do. In reflection about my life, I would say that my mom, who passed away when I was ten years old, has had the greatest impact on what I am today. She is my role model, and even though I was very young when she died, her spirit lives on in me. She is always there as a source of strength. She was a devoted, kind, and loving mother. I always try to listen to my voice, and the voice of my mother speaks silently to me and tells me to do the right thing. I have found that gives me contentment. My mother was a wise woman. I wish I could have spent more time with her and learned from her. I miss her, and it is a sadness that will always remain with me. I think keeping busy helps me to deal with my sadness. In retrospect I believe the most important lesson in life is to have a positive attitude, be a good listener, and be open to change.—AK

It is our inner voices—those private thoughts that speak only to us—that enable us to intensify our sense of awareness. It is those voices that help us to move forward and accept possible change or to stand back and reflect on our past experiences. Our present voice not only speaks to us of what we have become, it helps us to look back on the past in a very different way. Naturally, we all have regrets. Many of our regrets concern lost connections, words spoken in haste or anger, and unfulfilled dreams of what we could have been. We berate ourselves: if only we had made better decisions, acted with more confidence, or seized the moment to make an unfulfilled idea a reality.

I remember how my extremely talented mother told me that in her youth she wanted to go out on the road with a band. Her parents would not allow her to do this (in her day children usually listened to their parents). She always spoke about that and about not being able to afford a college education. Later, after she married and had two children, she developed and led a choral group that took her all over the state, performing and raising money for a charitable organization. Later she used her intelligence and skills to write books in braille for the blind, paint pictures, become a wonderful golfer, and finally, in her seventies, go to college to take courses in music and theater. The semester she made four A's was extremely gratifying to her. She wrote music and skits and had the admiration of all my friends. We participated in her shows and special birthday skits and attended her luncheons. As brilliant and talented as she was, my mother always wanted and asked for reaffirmation of her skills and work. I fear that I did not give her as much appreciation as she wanted or tell her enough how much I thought of her. This is my regret, and I see it so clearly now as I age and want my own children to express my value. If my mother were here today, I would like to tell her how much I really did appreciate her value, her successes, and the positive influences she had on my life. Each time I view a painting that she has made, read one of her old scripts, or talk about her with my friends who knew her, it brings up so many positive memories and sadness of how much I miss her.—MCL

Our Present Voice through Achievements

It is with our present voice that we also consider our past achievements, our accomplishments that celebrate who we are and how we arrived at this place and time in our lives.

What are the things you have achieved in your lifetime that you are most proud of?

When I think of the accomplishments that I have had something to do with, I need to let you know that I don't think any accomplishment that I have been part of can be claimed by me alone. Part of belonging to a religious order is that we value community, teamwork, and partnerships as our way of working toward ends that match our values. When I moved to Miami to work at a community center, I was looking forward to working with regular folks as opposed to nuns (whom I dearly love) because I needed a change. I took on becoming the financial director, and due to my efforts, the agency was congratulated for its financial management. I pursued a master's of divinity that was a theological degree, which I loved. I wanted that degree because I was asked by many of our nuns to meet with them for spiritual direction, and I knew that I did not want to respond to these requests without having a thorough background in spirituality. I have never counted the numbers of people I have directed over the years or the number of retreats that I have directed, but I consider it to have been a privilege (more than an accomplishment) to do this work.—SRB

Beyond my family and my grandchildren, I have achieved a good reputation and respect in my communities and am valued as a leader, of which I am very proud. It is the by-product of hard work, integrity, and dependability, I think.—EH

I am most proud of having a wonderful family, a devoted husband, two lovely daughters, two sons-in-law, and four great-grandchildren whom I love very much. I am most proud of having dear friends whom I have been connected to since grade school. Later on, I had new friends who lived in Illinois while I had a career. They are all in touch with me regularly. I am most proud of having a long and meaningful career where I was given many opportunities to develop programs, teach thousands of students, and serve my community in many areas related to education, both religious and secular.—MB

When I think back on my life's achievements, at first glance I don't think of them as anything more than usual. I raised three children, I must say successfully, and did it during times of strife, stress, and the problems that many women of our generation had to deal with. Having married young, my children were born when what would be characterized today as way too young to be a wife and mother. I passionately tried my best to be what I considered a "good mother," the best I knew how. Thinking back on those times, this was quite an achievement. I can think of nothing that matters more to me. My next big achievement was to finish college and graduate school, despite raising a family and despite my self-doubt and my negative thinking that this would not be possible. It goes to show me that I had courage and strength way beyond what I gave myself credit for.—MCL

Education has always been important to me, and I have passed that on to my children. Both of my sons have college degrees; neither one works in the field of his major studies, but they have a base of knowledge and the ability to think critically. A college degree, in my view, wasn't just about making money; the point of it was the education and the life experience. I asked my sons what advice I gave them that has stuck with them. Here are my two favorites: "If you keep making that face, it will freeze like that!" and "Question authority." (I probably should have waited until my son was out of high school to teach that one.) What I have learned through the years is to take life as it comes. No point in fretting about what may happen in the future, no sense in regretting the past. Neither of those can be changed. We take the good with the bad and just keep moving forward!—JR

Taking care of two ill parents and setting up a beautiful booth at a major antique show and bringing people beauty. I do not have a deep emotional life; instead I love beautiful objects and laughing.—DG

Being happily married for over fifty-eight years and having three wonderful, caring, and loving children and seven fabulous grandchildren.—Anonymous

I remember when my mother went off to visit her relatives and left my brother and me for a week. Since both of us were working, I made my brother help with the housekeeping chores. Upon my mother's return, he bitterly complained that I had him do women's work. He got a lot of sympathy from our mother, and I got a tongue-lashing: "Don't you know, what you had him do was not his job but yours. And do not ever do that again." With this one action, our family dynamic changed. Do not get me wrong; I cannot analyze all the facets of our triangle. I know, however, that I felt stepped upon and put in my place—in the corner where a woman "ought to reside," according to even my mother. Years later, my husband and I married. After a number of months of being married, working, and rushing home to be ready with a hot dinner for my beloved, I began to feel the stress. I remembered that I was trained to be a homemaker! So with my husband's approval, I quit my job. Then A and then S were born, and I thrived at being a wife and mother. All was well being a stay-at-home mom and raising our two children until the ideals of feminism started to garner my attention. I became more despondent as I realized that it seemed my lot in life was to be a wife and mother. I wanted more. I felt that I was living the life of a third-class citizen. I wanted to assert myself, prove myself, and be successful! I always had a lot of ambition and was a self-starter. I felt that there was plenty more to me to give and it was time to prove myself. I will never forget the following incident as long as I live. One day I approached my husband to discuss my thoughts, feelings, and ambitions. Ever the gentleman, he listened to all my explanations, my pleas, and my ambitions and then gave his thoughts to the matter. First, he said that he was shocked that I was not happy. He reluctantly agreed to changes under the following stipulations: I must find sufficient help to run the household so that the transition to me working would be seamless. Second, he was not going to help me in my quest—that was the worst news I could receive. I thought, how was I going to have his slippers ready each evening? Dinner served and my children in their PJs? I gave up. So what did I learn from this? Plenty! First, being a woman, I struggled hard against being summarily dismissed as a second-class citizen to the man/boy of the house. Or the class. Or the workplace. Second, I was damaged by the traditional oppression levied against girls from my earliest age. Third, in the majority of my married life, I never had the strength to assert myself against my husband. It was only in the nineties that my husband began to soften his attitude toward my wishes. For example, he supported my efforts to sponsor and resettle Russian refugee families. He admired my desire to get the Russian children reconnected to their Jewish heritage. He was awestruck at my driven support to provide assistance to the small Jewish community of Bendery in Moldova (former Soviet Union, or FSU). All my efforts to support Jewish communities and refugees from the FSU were supported by my husband. This was brought home to me the day he mounted an article from the local paper about my involvement in the Jewish community. *He* was proud of *me*. Finally I am now entering my third phase of life, according to *Prime Time*, by Jane Fonda. Finally I feel happy that I have made a mark not only on my life and my immediate family's lives but also on my local community—and yes, if I may be so bold, on the world on a microscale. Through my support and tenacity, I have seen children from the FSU that have gone through the programs I have set up to reconnect to their heritage. I have become involved in establishing a

Reform Jewish presence in Hamburg. I have continued the support of a struggling Jewish community in Bendery. I have reestablished my family connection to family in Argentina. Life has been a wonderful experience. I bless our G-d.—EGF

I've come a long way, baby, from those early days as a youngster living on a poultry farm in upstate New York. My roots run deep, very deep, with the messages and values I gained from each experience. As a young girl, I was taunted with anti-Semitic slurs on my way home from school as well as faced with the harshness of racial injustices living in the South. Early losses of loved family members helped me to take note that life is not fair, that one has numbered days and each day counts. My days are never long enough to complete all I wish to do. These themes in my background have informed my choices for my two careers and my volunteer activities that have directed me all my life. I have listened wisely to myself. Teaching has provided many connections with my former students. Social work as a career has provided a phenomenal experience in using my abilities of empathy and compassion to instill hope and self-confidence when life presented challenges needing skilled guidance and direction. Individuals have taught me that no matter the depth of pain, minds and bodies may heal over time when there is support. My choice of a marriage of forty-nine years to someone who is positive has served me well in getting the most out of what life offers in people, in places to visit, and in things to do. I have learned through him the importance of maintaining a sense of humor and to thoroughly enjoy the element of surprise. Life is most precious, and my voice tells me to appreciate each and every moment, as there have been many moments in the past few years that have been of great concern, giving me a reason to pause and a need for silent prayers. My concern is in not knowing how long this present feeling of security will last and yet I know that my inner voice may have to take over. If truth be told, I have been spoiled, and there are presently fleeting thoughts of the possibility of loss and of changes. However, I know how important it is to keep reminding myself of my ability to be the choral director of the voices I want to hear. Right now I value my moments...of peace within, love, and security.—GH

Since early childhood I have had to be responsible, help my mother with my younger siblings, and be financially independent as soon as possible. Without a father in the home, and growing up during World War II in Europe, I learned at an early age to take responsibility.—NL

I have achieved a very loving relationship with my husband, children and grandchildren, and many relatives and friends.—JK

I am most proud of saving my mother and my younger brother from certain death.—AO

Our Present Voice through Our Silence and Losses

Although loss may present itself at any age, it is at this juncture that we are confronted with our own vulnerability and a more in-your-face kind of awareness. Our present voice speaks to facing loss: loss of friends and relatives, loss of health, loss of relationships, and sometimes loss of memory. The sense of finality and unbearable loss as we brought closure to our relationship with parents, partners, and our dearest friends can trigger a reawakening—a sense of awe and respect and even a sense of freedom.

My mother was a labor lawyer in the forties and fifties while other mothers were home baking cookies. She taught me the value of hard work, "feminism," and that using your brain is more important than batting your eyelashes. My parents divorced when I was thirteen, but I always maintained a strong and loving relationship with my father. He was all kindness and gentility, traits that I hope I have inherited. After high school I went to the University of Buffalo, of all strange places. But after my freshman year, I returned home because of family illness. After that a standard university did not seem interesting to me, so I went to a college of medical technology and became a registered medical technologist for several years. I actually met my first husband when I was working at a doctor's office. I married just short of my twenty-second birthday to an attorney who was fourteen years my senior. My first child came two years later and ultimately carried the diagnosis of retardation and autism. At that time, autism was almost unheard of—one in ten thousand children shouldered the diagnosis. It was a tremendous struggle, as the theory of the day was that the child was withdrawing from the world because of a "refrigerator mother." It took years of psychotherapy for me to get past the unwarranted guilt. After I had children, I no longer worked and was basically a housewife and mother. One night my husband and I were in a backgammon tournament and I ran into an old high school boyfriend. Not bragging, but he and I were both exceptionally bright students. He asked me what wonderful things I was doing with my life, and I became flustered. His comment made me think about my mother and her respect for education. And it was at that time I went back to college, and I would consider that evening as a significant turning point and the beginning of a new road minimally traveled. At the age of thirty-nine, I became a widow. My second child at that time, P, was fourteen and A, seventeen. Not only was I a very young widow and single parent, but I was dealing with the conundrums of finding adequate education for A as well as helping P get through his adolescent years with as few scars as possible. I remarried three years later to a man who was the antithesis of my first spouse. He was fun loving, exciting, and passionate and taught me how to once again love life. Unfortunately, he was a compulsive gambler, and the marriage ended. Shortly thereafter, I found that I had breast cancer. A double mastectomy, chemo, and reconstruction followed. More recently, three years ago, I was diagnosed with an aneurysm in my aorta. A stent was placed, but shortly thereafter I developed an ischemic colon. Two colostomies followed with ultimate reversals. Needless to say, I am a strong person who has weathered many storms and has come out stronger and braver than I ever thought possible.—Anonymous

I don't associate my number with my age, so I reject that idea about aging. My parents have been gone for about twenty years now, and I have had this fantastic freedom, maybe because they weren't here anymore to comment on what I was doing. It was such a relief and a release, and at the same time, I found myself sifting through the values I had learned from them because I knew I was an accumulation of those values in all the years we had spent together. I had this push and pull...

to be free, and yet I couldn't ignore my heritage. At the same time, I feel closer to them than I ever have. I think what happened was I had to give myself permission to be who I was, and I couldn't when I was little for whatever the reasons were. When I was little, I was shy and silent. Now I'm still shy, but there are some days when I just will not be quiet. Now I'm learning to speak in public at Toastmasters, and one of the things I enjoy is mentoring youngsters that are in my class. I wanted to be working with kids since I have no children. This is my way of staying fresh and generational. I do what I can do by letting them see my vulnerabilities and, when I speak, letting them see some of the skills I have for speaking. I give them time to ask questions. It is important to just have fun with the world and have fun with people, because I believe in letting people know, "You're dear to me." When I meet you and I can connect with you personally, that is great, but we are not stopping to smell the roses. What I've come to learn is that I need to value myself.—WS

Knowledge that we have the ability to make sound choices helps us to balance the eventuality of losses with an enthusiasm that comes with mastering new things and unearthing personal resources that might have lain dormant.

Why did it happen to me? Other women, yes, but not me. I was too young, not ready (not that I would ever be ready). It's amazing how your life seems to change at the drop of a hat. I'm bright, highly educated, and a world traveler. I knew my life wasn't over. I was aware of my newfound responsibilities, but all the tears shed doing the most mundane activities was just not me. Throwing out the garbage, which I never did before, walking down the hallways of "our" condo, and hearing love songs on the radio were just a part of what set off a waterfall of emotions. Fast-forward five years— alone still but not miserable. My most flagrant mistake during the past few years was to compare each guy I met to my husband. I met good men, but he was glamorized in my mind. Life was certainly not perfect, not even close, but I wanted to remember only the good. Absolutely not realistic. As a matter of fact, not even logical. Keeping busy was my key to survival. Getting out of the apartment and seeing people each day was so necessary in order to maintain my sanity. To this day I continue to work (part time). Working with children and young teachers keeps my perspective balanced. Basic suggestions that worked for me were:

1. Go to new restaurants and try different food that you ordinarily would not order.
2. Shop at different stores.
3. Watch new television programs and read books that will stimulate your thought processes.
4. Open your mind to activities that might be exciting if given the opportunity.
5. Smile at people in your environment. Nobody wants to associate with a grouchy person.
6. Don't be a loner. If you acquire that label, you indeed will be alone.—HR

Getting married at age nineteen shaped the way I was at that time—which was to be dependent on my husband for most things. I feel I went from my parents' house to my own house, with little time to grow up as a mature woman. Having children was certainly a game changer, and with little experience at that time, my views of parenting have changed, but not in time to make those changes with my children. I would have given them more of myself and would have been more attentive to their needs as individuals. My husband's death changed my life drastically but changed me slowly. I had to learn to be self-sufficient, to call upon assistance whenever needed and in whatever areas the help was wanted, and I had to make my own decisions, the biggest challenge of all. Living independently for many years, I have grown as a person and have become a more self-reliant individual. The older I get, the more I can feel that doing as I please is okay.—ER

After my husband passed away, I had a lady friend who was twenty years younger than I who counseled me to "reinvent myself" by getting involved in different things. I will never forget her. It was the best advice I could have received. Every time I heard of something interesting an organization was involved in, I joined. I made many wonderful friends and became very involved in the community.—Anonymous

My relationship was like no other. My whole life was like an adventure. As a couple we did everything together. Decisions together. My husband was ill for over a year. You just have to make it the best for the person each day. You have to just face it, and if it had been me, he would have done the same thing. Now I am by myself in a big house. I am responsible for everything. I am not here to complain or criticize. I muddle through.—RV

At this time I am facing some difficult times dealing with a husband who has Alzheimer's disease. However, I look back on my life with pride... proud of my family and my career, of being able to counsel others with their problems. As I age, I spend my time exercising, attending ballet concerts with friends, and going to the theater with my husband. I am eighty-three years young. RJ

Awakened from a deep sleep, my hand reaches out to an empty space. My partner of more than sixty-two years is gone. With whom can I share my interests, cares, concerns? Who will calm the deeply hidden fears? Who will encourage my hopes, goals, dreams? Despite greatly advanced years, the hormones still surge. No one to share the emotional and physical needs. And then I say a prayer of thanks for two honorable, bright, devoted, loving children. For the very few friends left from way back when. In the past three years, it has been my privilege and pleasure to meet several new people, each of whom has made my days brighter. Hopefully, the future will continue to be filled with many more inspiring people. I want my family to know I love them unconditionally and forever. This doesn't mean I like or agree with everything they do. I have confidence that everything good they undertake, they can and will do well. The more self-reliant I am, the greater my sense of well-being. Perhaps it is only a dream. I'd like to find a suitable traveling companion.—EB

In our later years, our voice takes on a more authentic quality, as we no longer feel the need to silence ourselves. Many women over sixty feel that (1) we have earned the right to say and do what we want; (2) we will not live according to the expectations others place on us; and (3) we do not have to gain anyone else's approval anymore. We are our own persons.

Right now I'm seventy-five years old and I want to say what I want to say, so recently I said something that I felt was helpful. I told my grandson that he was totally indifferent to me and my feelings were hurt. My son gave me a dirty look but I didn't care. When I was thirteen years old, I said I'm gonna do whatever I want. When I'm thirteen, I'll wear lipstick and nobody's gonna tell me what to do. And there are still people telling me what to do.—CB

I feel like I should live my life according to what I want for me, but I am so used to being the person the world (or at least my friends and family) can depend upon. Sometimes I want to say no, but I just can't disappoint. It's not in my nature not to be a pleaser. Whenever I do make a decision that I feel is right but that others would disagree with, I feel guilty. I have to talk myself into my thought process and provide many defensive statements to justify what I have decided. And then I still feel guilty.—ML

I wish all the young people I know could have taken a lesson from a young student I met who developed a research project designed around his living within an adult congregate facility for a period of months, observing as well as participating in the activities chosen by the residents daily. It is not surprising that he enjoyed good conversations with many well-informed adults who might not have had time to join discussion groups earlier in their lives, as they might have been employed or caring for families, but who now had the pleasure of time to pursue areas of interest such as painting, politics, dancing, and theater. He also learned that he started out by being a member of the younger generation who believed aging is a sedentary period in life, a time one fills with gossip and naps...Much to his surprise, he discovered people with humor,

> curiosity, and a desire for companionship. He discovered people with a zest for living, which can sometimes be exhausting.—Anonymous

While we may not be willing to be held prisoner by others' expectations, age helps us to understand compromise better than we ever have before. Our knowledge has helped us to use discretion in decision making, to measure our words after careful thought, and, most importantly, to choose when to remain silent. Our inner voices from childhood may still be very strong no matter what our age, but oftentimes that voice is silenced because of our understanding that the meaning of our words may somehow be misconstrued. Therefore, we run the risk that our voices will go unheard.

> I have a huge fear of speaking my mind or sharing my feelings about another person. I often still hear a father's harsh voice...a voice from years ago..."Remain silent." I remained silent so I could be safe that way, for fear that I might be slapped or spoken to harshly. That would make me feel so uncomfortable that I would feel numbed.—PW

> I realized recently that at seventy-three, I have the right to speak up! Not only did I have the right, but I also had the ability to empower myself if no one helped me along the way. I had the ability to own the feelings that went along with the words.—RS

Sometimes our strengths, not only our fears, emerge out of our silence. For Holocaust survivors, the recovery of their voices is priceless.

> It is important for me to be involved; less time for regular thoughts...—RR

> It is important to be joyful about what is...to lighten up. To enjoy every day you are here and to remember our past...and be kind and loving with each other.—Anonymous

As women over sixty, the silence may help us to listen more attentively to others and thereby come to understand others as well as ourselves.

I was leading a group of parents recently, and while I was speaking, a woman stood up and loudly questioned me and proceeded to attack my presentation. I had not met her expectations. Several people came to my defense, feeling the need to put her in her place. Strangely I felt quite calm, recognizing her disappointment and anger at having taken the time to attend a program that did not meet her expectations. I then suggested that she might choose to leave while I completed the program. At that moment I had come to appreciate my own skills that have grown out of my introspection, tolerance, and recognition of individual differences. I have learned that it is best to listen, to observe, and to remind myself that everything is not about me and that there is someone else who is in the picture as well whom I need to respect. It is amazing the self-respect I have earned within.—GKH

Our Present Voice and Facing the Inevitability of Change

We may find ourselves confronting a devastating change in our lives as our spouses or partners face an illness that may impair them physically, mentally, or both. This is something extraordinarily difficult to prepare for emotionally. When it happens, we often feel overwhelmed by these transformations, as they appear to begin to chip away at the very foundation of our relationships. Illness may necessitate a drastic shift in power, and now not only do we become the primary caretaker, but we also become the master of the house. Many women of our generation started out dependent first on our family of origin only then to quite naturally take on that same role with our mate. It may be that not only will we have to learn new skills of caretaking but also to take control of financial matters that have been managed faithfully in the hands of our partners. How do we do this seamlessly so our loved ones do not feel threatened or emasculated? How do we maintain their dignity? How do we keep ourselves afloat?

Each of us has a unique and intimate perspective on our significant relationships; therefore, we need to begin this difficult journey first by trusting in ourselves and in our knowledge and understanding of the nature of that relationship. We need to harness our anxieties (difficult as that can be) and have confidence in ourselves and in our ability to manage the situation. This does not mean that we have to face these responsibilities alone or, to protect the dignity of our loved one, shut ourselves off from the outside world and feel isolated. It is helpful to remember that many of those who are in our inner circle also share in a commitment to the well-being of our loved one.

The following is a list of suggestions that may serve as a springboard to help us in developing effective coping strategies for the future.

1. We can begin a conversation with the significant people in our lives about the challenges that aging brings and start to identify together the possible alternatives for meeting those challenges. Ongoing conversations encourage us to be open and comfortable with what may be a taboo subject. Obviously, it would be best to have those discussions before the changes in health become apparent; nevertheless, oftentimes, for a variety of reasons, we might not have gotten around to having them until the problem is already on our doorstep.

2. Although we may be the individuals who have the ultimate responsibility for the primary caretaking role, we have to reach out and create a strong support network. Building a connection with people who are committed to providing us a sanctuary to retreat to, as well as who wish to be active participants in the care, is indispensable to our own mental health and that of our family and friends.

3. Seeking out professional help does not signal weakness. Adapting to changes may be very painful, and we may feel a great deal of anger and guilt that, for many reasons, we simply cannot express to family members or even our closest friends. Sharing these feelings with a third party who has knowledge of the problem and insight as to how to cope can provide us with critical strategies, emotional support, and encouragement.

4. Whether we have the help of a professional or not, it is essential that we take the time to explore the range of emotions we are experiencing and how those feelings could impact the level of supportive care we will need to provide. It is critical that we are honest with ourselves and recognize our own needs—the personal need for privacy, autonomy, and even the need to *escape*. Balancing those needs with the needs of our loved ones is the key to keeping our focus and our energies on providing tender and effective care.

5. Routine brings structure for both our partners and ourselves. Controlling the environment promotes everyone's sense of safety.

6. Although we may find it very difficult to accept, our loved ones have the right of self-determination while they are competent to make decisions on their own behalf. The key for us is to be able to listen— listen to what they are saying and then focus on what they are not saying. It is essential also to listen to what they want without those wants being confounded by our emotions or our religious and ethical beliefs. Providing an environment that does not compromise one's safety, self-esteem, independence, and most of all dignity is the essence of nurturing care.

Sometimes I wake up in the middle of the night and look over at my husband and wonder what I will do when he cannot be left alone and he won't be able to take care of himself. I know that I shouldn't be thinking about me. I should be thinking about how he must be feeling about what he has already lost in his life. He is less mobile lately, so no more driving and no more going out even walking on his own. I am so afraid he will fall and I won't be there to help him up. Worse than that, he could break his hip or hit his head. So he has become a prisoner in his own house and dependent on me to take him out into the world. I do not resent that, but I am sure he does. He is so angry with me for taking away his independence. But it seems that it happened so quickly after he was diagnosed. We still haven't had a discussion about anything, so I am not sure what his expectations are. We never had any secrets before. Now it seems that everything is a secret. Even our daughters seem to dance around the issue. They do call me and ask how we are doing. They are wonderful and available. It is even more difficult for our friends to be with us, although they try very hard to include us when all the couples go somewhere that is not too difficult for us to access. When I am up in the night, I wonder about our future, and that is frightening. I hope I will do better than I think I will.—Anonymous

No matter what methods we use to relate successfully to others, we may want to listen to the voice within saying, "Do not care for others at the expense of losing yourself." As women, we have the option to say no. We count, too.

In taking care of my sick mother, I realized that I have to make sure that I don't abandon myself in the process. In the beginning, I felt I had to respond to her every need and desire. A call for lunch meant I had to cancel a doctor's appointment. I felt guilty if I couldn't do everything she needed. Then I came to the realization that I couldn't lose myself in the process. I learned that I could still be the "good" daughter and also take care of myself.—JG

The very thought about ending my marriage, *getting a divorce*, made me physically ill and an emotional basket case. Yet in thinking about what shaped my present reality, I believe it was my divorce that led to the events that forever changed my life. In my midtwenties with two small children at home...and my husband drove our car to work...I was left to figure out how to get to the grocery store. We bought a big old used Buick, and I finally learned to drive. The car was an absolutely battered wreck before I felt that I could actually head out on the roads and the "wreck" could be replaced. Buying a brand-new yellow Camaro was the first major decision and major purchase that *I actually made on my own,* using money that I earned with my part-time jobs. This was a heady experience! It was about this time that my marriage started to fall apart. Maybe it was because I could now assert a little independence. Maybe we just outgrew each other. But it took another few months before I asked him to leave, and then only when I was positive that he was unfaithful and lying about it. The initial separation made me very aware of how dependent on others I had really been. Meanwhile, I thought long and hard about my future, what would happen to my children and me. I hated the thought of becoming a divorcee, a word with very bad connotations in the sixties. Also, I wasn't 100 percent sure that I could make it on my own—I had been so sheltered by my family and then my husband. I never failed at anything before and hated admitting failure at marriage. I began to doubt my ability to make good decisions; after all, I chose to marry this guy. I dreaded telling my parents that their "good" daughter had messed up "big time." I never confided in my parents as to how really terrible my home situation was, thinking that this was my business to handle. But I needed money for a lawyer, so I swallowed my pride and told them only that the marriage wasn't working and we both wanted out. My dad sent me to an attorney that he kept on retainer, and I unburdened myself with the particulars of the situation. I really believed that what I told him was privileged, but by the time I arrived home, my folks had heard the whole story. I threatened to have the attorney disbarred, which so totally unnerved my father that he gave me a good deal of money to seek my own lawyer and forget about this betrayal. It was the first time I asserted myself to my parents. It was the first time I actually felt power. It felt good. I gained self-confidence. I could begin to believe in myself. I hired an attorney of *my* choosing. I applied for and got a wonderful job as chief pharmacist in a rehabilitation hospital. As a department head, I was earning enough to pay the mortgage on my house, cover my car payments, and send my kids to a private school. My ex never paid the child support payments that the court ordered, and alimony was not awarded because I had a higher academic degree than he, and therefore I was expected to be the bigger earner. This turned out to be a blessing. Living alone, I began to learn to trust my instincts. I could manage my own life. I could take certain risks, not always play it safe. I was finally growing up. I threw myself into the dating scene, trying to make up for what I had missed by not staying single through college. I worked hard, and being a single mom is not easy, but I was living on my terms, and that felt wonderful. Finally, through a cousin, I met my wonderful husband of the last forty-two years. He was exciting, mature, and very handsome. He was a great dancer, and we had fun together. It turned out that he had a very hard time obtaining his final divorce decree. So we lived together for two years, traveled, lived out of the United States, and had a baby together before we could get married. All of the above would have been unthinkable in my former persona. When we married, because my ex never supported the kids, the court granted him immediate adoption of my "abandoned children." We moved to Florida and started a new family comprising my first two kids, our baby, two of his kids (one natural, one adopted), and finally, another baby girl. This in addition to four grown children from his first marriage. We were the parents of ten children. My "new life" defied everything that I was taught as a young girl, mainly that the more alike you are, the better the chances of marital success. Our politics, core religious beliefs, personalities, and ages (twenty-two years apart) should have made us incompatible. Yet this marriage works despite the fact that he was a country boy and I was a city girl; he learned at the school of hard knocks and I was an academic; he was well traveled and I had never left Philadelphia; he was adventurous, loved challenging sports, and flew his own plane while I was an avid reader, a romantic daydreamer, timid, and a nonathlete. During our marriage we developed common ground: we both learned to ski, we traveled and had adventures, we raised a family. We lived abroad and gave our children a broader view of life than I could ever have imagined in my youth. I never returned to the practice of pharmacy. My time and talents were spent on my family and on volunteering. I have had a wonderful life and want to give back and share the wealth with those less fortunate. Supporting the state of Israel, its viability and success as a nation, is important to us as Israeli citizens. We have a family charity started by one of our sons to take care of neglected, abused, and abandoned Jewish children. We love the creative arts—visual, music, and dance—and I am willing to work to keep the arts alive. I am blessed to be able to do these things. Last, I did not follow my parents' example of child-rearing. I learned to allow my children to make their own decisions and their own mistakes. Many times I wanted to shield them from mistakes—but I gave them space to grow. I encouraged them to travel, to try new things, to explore the world. They grew to a diverse, strong, assertive, self-reliant group of adults, different from us and different from one another. Among them are a teacher, an artist, a rabbi, a military officer, and parents. They are Jewish, Israeli, Christian, and just plain American. They follow their own stars. They are great people. I am proud of them. I feel that I did a good job. The divorce did change my life forever. For the better. It was a blessing in disguise.—SS

We know there is a finite period of time remaining. We have to make sure that the decisions we make for ourselves will bring meaning to our lives.

I am very happy with the "me of today." I have no regrets, and the only reason I would like to go back twenty years would be that I could look forward to twenty more years of living.—NK

While buying makeup in a major department store, I met a sales associate who had just turned seventy. The woman told me she had just worked there for one year. "You mean they actually hired you at age sixty-nine?" I asked. "Yes," she said, which totally surprised me. She told me this was her sixth career and that she decided that working was something that helped her to conserve her savings while maintaining her current lifestyle. Her voice was one of confidence, using old skills to develop new ones—even after age sixty-five!—AK

Relationships: Cultural and Spiritual Implications

Subconsciously, we are still, even at our age, hooked into the "voices" of our parents and inspired to act based on our earliest cultural and spiritual influences. JW set a personal goal to honor the memory of her father by standing as an equal member of her faith.

What place do religion and spirituality play in your life today?

"I did it, I did it perfectly." Could the congregation see the grin on my face as I walked back to my seat? Back in my seat, my thoughts were on my father. Would he have been proud or dismayed? He cared little about my Jewish education. Women in the village in southern Poland where he lived until fourteen received no religious education and were an invisible presence in the shul (synagogue). Curiously, he had no problem with women (i.e., me) getting a secular education after he assimilated to life in western Massachusetts. He paid my tuition through a doctorate and was proud of my academic accomplishments. But my ignorance of Hebrew, Jewish law, and history was never discussed. I was a woman. So why would I want to know? It was not hard to make a kosher home and observe the holidays after marriage. I just had to imitate my mother. But mimicry did not convey literacy. Despite numerous college and adult education religion courses, I was functionally illiterate. Then I had an adult bat mitzvah. Maybe this would demolish the wall that stood between me and the learned, the ones who could read and understand Hebrew. Would I become one of them? It didn't happen. Oh, my D'var (discussion of the Torah portion) was well received; indeed, it was published in a Boston Federation newsletter. I sensed my departed father's hand on my shoulder. "What are you doing?" he whispered. "You shouldn't be here. You are a woman. Why are you reading from the Torah? You don't even know what you are reading. You don't even know Hebrew. Sit down and let those who are learned chant." But my father's whispers were right. The bat mitzvah did not bestow the mantle of literacy. Maybe I needed to read the Torah again. I knew how to pronounce the words. Would their meaning infiltrate my brain? So encouraged by our congregation, I volunteered to read every few months. But each time I failed. I made mistakes: looked at the words I thought I knew and did not recognize them, failed to sing the correct phrase signaling that the sentence ended. Shame and relief were the only things I took away when the reading was over. I had to learn Hebrew. How many more years could I wait? How many more years would I live? So I found a teacher, a demanding teacher. What she taught me besides Hebrew grammar was an appreciation for contemporary Hebrew literature and the joy and astonishment of translating the Bible. So I decided to try chanting the Torah again, now that I was studying Hebrew. Finally I understood that chanting wasn't arbitrary but grammar itself. It told the listener, "Pay attention. This is an important statement" or "You can doze now, just filling in some details." And then I read. The congregation disappeared. There were only the parchment, the words, the story told for three thousand years and still being told. An eternity of words. An eternity of readers. Finally I was among them. I think my father would have been proud.—JW

Thank you for allowing me the opportunity to share with you and others not just what the sixties mean to a woman who is aging but also the seventies and eighties. When I read the first question pertaining to spirituality and the part it has played in my life, it took me back to when I was ten years old and castigating my best four-legged friend, Jeff: he shouldn't step on the cracks in the sidewalk because God created the ants that were crawling there and that was their home. As I grew through my teens, I attended religious school and was somewhat turned off as we read a book called Hillel, which gave me nothing realistic to hold on to. Seeing my mother and others close to me being challenged by different illnesses, it led me to believe that, although God is good, there are nasty things in life that cannot be controlled. I often asked, "Why?" and never really got a rabbi to answer the question. Over the years, I was exposed to "this thing called God." One book after another, one year after another, I began to understand what is missing in our world today. I taught religious school for twenty-two years, and my goal was not to make sure the children understood the twenty-three pages they were given to read but that they were free to ask questions and be accepting of that which God has graciously given us. Fifth grade is a very challenging grade; the first three months, you have children in your class who are lost, and the next five months give you the opportunity to put them in touch with all of God's creativity. I was the administrator of a home for battered and abused children and was able to secure ballet lessons for the girls and tennis for the boys provided by Killian High School students. They built courts, secured rackets, erected basketball hoops, and learned what it was to share the goodness of the life they had been given. Encyclopedias and books galore were also supplied by volunteers. At the same time, I became a companion to my best friend, Susan, who was battling terminal cancer. I comforted her by doing all the things that would have been done for her had she been put in a nursing facility. Her soon-to-be-ex-husband signed legal papers giving me the authority to raise her ten-year-old and fifteen-year-old daughters, along with my own two, while I was still working. He was as remote as the two blocks between us would allow. And his pockets were empty. My then-husband, who was twenty-two years my senior, found it difficult to work, and therefore I picked up the rest of my responsibilities, working four jobs at one time and keeping the family going. God taught me to take care of those who cannot help themselves, either physically or mentally. What does aging mean to me? For the first time in twenty-five years, I have been able to make a choice of going to a symphony or a park or to plant my flowers, and somehow or other, God has offered me the opportunity to break down the outer walls that my ninety-year-old neighbor across the street had put up forty years ago. We are celebrating her birthday this month. Aging has not changed who I am, the choices I make, the people I take care of, or the praise I give to God. The legacy I wish to leave has been fulfilled by two daughters, one a pediatrician and the other a talent agent. My grandchildren have learned discipline from their parents, and my children have exhibited great independence and great drive. Totally different, their goals are totally different, and they arrive at their destinations by knowing never to quit.—JG

Our Present Voice and Its Relationship to Work

For many of us, our job is often our voice to the world outside the safety of our family and close friends. Because of our ability as women to connect when we feel comfortable to trust, we are able to give voice to our coworkers and cement relationships with those very important individuals with whom we spend many hours per week. Often we do not know how we influence others, and when we are fortunate enough to be told, how much more blessed we are to be the giver and the receiver as well.

Dear P,

Each day and every day, I have an attitude of gratitude, a glass not half full but full as can be...Why is my outlook so positive? I was born to the most wonderful, caring, loving parents that came from the blackness of hell of the Holocaust of World War II. Mother was orphaned at fourteen and father at seventeen. My mother was saved by Henrietta Zold, my father by his own lonesome self. Having lost their entire family in the concentration camp, reinventing a family unit and having my brother and me was like breathing life into their soul. My father was the most generous man, kind, smart, and very good-looking. He would give the shirt off his back to those in need... and so would my mom. We were poor but also rich at heart, sharing with friends and neighbors what food was rationed to us. In the year of 1955, the Red Cross found my mother's sister alive and well in America. They had been apart since 1938. We arrived in 1961... So here I am...not taking anything for granted, appreciating all of the bountifulness that surrounded us—our local grocery stores, department stores, the Florida sun, the flowers...and of course my own growing family...including the helpfulness of my coworkers at my job, like P. Each day I have a lengthy drive to work with time to think, and much of that is being thankful for the car that will get me to work, for the ability to work, for a life with none of the fear and hell that my family endured. My outlook on life comes from a different perspective. Therefore I am truly feeling blessed and thankful...

Grateful I am,
T

Dear T,

Thank you so much for sharing your story with me and for coming to me last week and telling me how much you love each and every day and coming into the office and working with me, our staff, and fellow Realtors...Your words made me feel so grateful and appreciative that you took the time to sit with me and to say thank you and share your feelings...it was a true blessing and will stay with me forever. You are and have always been an incredible lady...and I am thrilled that you came into my life.

Best regards always,
P

Our Present Voice Reflected in Our Physical Appearance

It is time now to recognize and accept who we are in the present. We are not the selves we were twenty, ten, or even five years ago. We look in the mirror and can see the physical changes that age has created. We recognize that we may not be as quick in our reaction time or remember things as swiftly. We know we have changed.

Our present voice, in order to be a positive one, must take into account all the changes that aging brings and accept those changes as an integral part of our present reality. For many, it may take years to be open and honest enough to discover all the positive qualities we can claim as defining our me of today. This is not true for every aging woman.

I am not concerned with a few wrinkles or the physical signs of aging. To me, I feel so lucky to have arrived at my age. I am happy that I have had the health and good fortune and some newfound wisdom to appreciate all the wonderful things that life has brought me. I experienced the death of a parent when I was a teen, so I feel so grateful to have had the opportunity of being an in-law, a grandparent. I guess that I cannot spend too much time worrying about how old I look. The signs of age would be visible even if my face were smooth and flawless. I know that I do not have time to worry about my looks when there is a laundry list of things I need to do to improve what is beneath my skin at the heart of who I am.—CTS

I was always proud to tell how old I was because everyone guessed that I was ten years younger than my given age. And then one morning, when I was in my fifties, I walked into a store and the clerk said, "Hello, ma'am. What can I do for you?" In shock, I walked out thinking, "Well, I guess it's finally happened. I'm starting to look old." In my sixties and early seventies, I was working at a job that I loved; however, for the first time I felt uncomfortable telling my age because most people were much younger than I. For the first time, I withheld telling my age, saying, "Every woman has to have her secrets." Then one day, as I walked into my office, everyone greeted me with "Surprise! Happy birthday!" and they sang "How old are you now?" I couldn't just make it up, so I told them the truth—and they all applauded. They said, "You should be proud to know you are able to work and do all the wonderful things you do." Today, as I see every new wrinkle and every age spot, I really couldn't care less, because that's who I am and I'm just very accepting. I think back to hearing a lecture many years ago by the renowned psychiatrist Elizabeth Kubler-Ross, noted for her work on death and dying.

She presented a poetic metaphor of how we, like the mountains, gain beauty over time; mountains are chiseled by the rain and by windstorms crashing upon them. We earn every wrinkle through the storms of our own lives over time.—AM

The one good thing about getting older is that your waist can be wherever you want it to be.—LWS

Our Present Voice Enhanced by Shared Experiences

Coming together with our own community of women and retelling our personal stories creates a platform for us to share our present and future goals. That connection allows us to explore, share, and incorporate new ideas we hear into our own voices.

When I was young and just beginning to get started in service to the community, I was introduced to an exemplary community leader who led by her fine example. In reflecting back some thirty years, I realized that I gained inner strength from her presence as demonstrated through her teachings...not in books but through actions. I admired her knowledge, her open-mindedness, her never-ending ability to be and remain humble throughout life, and her ability to be gender blind and to accept herself and others in all of their many roles. I clearly remind myself of these values when I am in charge of meetings. She often was the only woman among many men in boardrooms, making decisions for an entire community. In my opinion she created the original recipe for power using the very basic of ingredients of honesty, selflessness, kindness, knowledge, and a desire to make positive changes for all peoples. What she really valued was the bond of her community of sisters...her sisterhood. Not having a daughter of her own, many of us considered ourselves lucky to be "officially adopted" by her. It was at her funeral that several of her "adopted daughters" spoke of the heritage she has left for them and how proud they are to have been among her "chosen." Living into her nineties, she had a zest for and interest in each of us. Even now that her voice can no longer be heard, her words remain a powerful source of inspiration and guidance to those who knew and admired her.—GH

Until we are mentored by others who believe in us, or we find inner resources to mentor ourselves, it may take many years to feel a sense of security and the courage to reinvent ourselves. *When we are open to possibilities, we are more open to opportunities.*

> I know my husband and mentor would be happy to know I am still very much involved with using my voice to stand up for myself and others when the time is right. My focus is currently on helping to raise large sums of money for scholarships at a university for first-generation Americans. I have been encouraged to use my skills in all facets of my life, and although I have had loving and brilliant mentors, I do give myself credit for synching the inner and the outer voices in blending what was needed for my successes.—Anonymous

> In 1962, I had broken up with a man I had dated. I was very lonesome and really didn't have any friends. My daughter suggested I take some courses at the university. I signed up for an art class and met some very nice people. My daughter was making decorative clothes for children, and I was introduced to a woman who came and bought some things for her granddaughter. Later I ran into her at a drugstore, and we started talking. We went out for lunch a few times, and then I told her about the class I was taking and that we were going on a field trip to New York. She then joined the class and the trip. Through her I met a whole new group of people. We went to concerts and shows and more trips with this art teacher. I don't go to the art class anymore, but I do take a class on politics and have met more people. So I keep busy and am very grateful to my daughter for the push.—VG

In earlier years, our inner voice might not have felt safe in speaking up, especially if we felt we might have hurt another's feelings or negatively affected a cause we held dearly. Our inner and outer voices might have been in conflict, as one might have wanted to speak, while the other was filled with fear or uncertainty. Yet with aging, we have stockpiled experiences, amassed wisdom, and gained the confidence to trust in our own judgment and in our own decision-making skills. With aging, we are now comfortable enough to stand by our principles and to affirm the *leader* within.

Recently I was meeting with a group of peers when one woman chose to speak. She was interrupted as she was speaking, which broke her train of thought. Surprisingly, she took charge in announcing her problem. "I am speaking now and need time to think clearly, and although it may take me time to get my thoughts out, I cannot think when you interrupt me. I would appreciate it if you can wait until I finish what I am saying." Immediately the woman apologized, and there was utter silence. I must admit, I was thinking, "Good for her." Yes, she had the courage to say what she needed to others, and I saw this as a major change in her growth and identity. I learned a lot from that interaction, and I feel it has added a different level of trust between us. This person helped me to be more in tune with other people's needs.—BMR

I learned the hard way, after my husband died, that I have a hell of a backbone. I grew up overnight when having to confront a situation in settling a family estate. My mom used to say, "Don't trust anyone when it comes to money. If anyone has a proposition, let them earn your trust." Dad used to say I should be happy with what I do and should need to be the best at what I do. I am grateful for everything they taught me. I even had the brains to marry a second time to a Southern gentleman who taught our daughters not to depend on men. Be educated in something, and learn to stand on your own feet. If there is one lesson I would want my grandchildren to know, it is don't ever doubt your guts, and be receptive to learning. I realized through these recent experiences that I am not stupid and am capable of making major decisions. If I have a regret, it is in not being able to tell my parents how much I benefitted from how much they taught.—JV

Lessons learned from miscalculations, errors, and omissions were: don't assume anything, do not take anyone for granted, and always apologize for offenses.—Anonymous

There is power in one voice, and much more power when many of our voices join together for a common cause.

> Every Tuesday morning, when my spouse was fishing, I met with six or eight other ladies for philosophical discussions that sometimes became quite heated but were always interesting and fun. These women were from all walks of life, but all had written scripts for the old soap operas people listened to on the radio in the forties and fifties. As diverse as we were, we had one common interest, and that was to make the world a better place. We would meet at one person's house, a former nurse. It was natural for her to do what she could to help the wounded deer that she found at her doorstep. Each week there were a number of deer dying, and this bothered me. I began questioning and learning of wild dogs using them as prey. The number dying became alarming to me. I knew something had to be done by someone and decided that someone was going to be me. Within weeks we began an organization of people who wanted to keep Key deer from becoming extinct. It was as if the people were all waiting at the starting gate for the gun (in this case the meeting announcement) to go off. We began to see the results of our efforts. There are now six to eight hundred deer roaming the islands. We also were able to give scholarships to students who were interested in preserving the environment. It has been a gratifying adventure, and I learned an important lesson: it only takes one person to get things going in the right direction. Some say I was lucky. I think it was meant to be.—MG

More and more, as we hear from women in their sixties and beyond, we begin to celebrate the small things and to recognize how satisfied we are with day-to-day gratifications. We understand that, even if we live to a ripe old age, we have lived more of our lives than we have left. We accept where we are on the timeline and realize that *now* counts! When we were young, we did not think about these things too much. *Now* is for discovering or rediscovering parts of ourselves that may be emerging, the known as well as the unknown talents that might have lain dormant for years as we attended to raising a family, promoting our careers, or just being who we were at that time in our lives.

There is a sense of newfound freedom in the air!

I am energized by a beautiful day with sunshine and a breeze and walking early in the day with my husband and walking alone at other times in my neighborhood, meeting neighbors with their children and/or dogs. Also, I find time with friends and volunteering with students very special. As for insights that come with age, I understand that most people are wrapped up in their own issues, and I try not to make a "big deal" out of incidents that occur, take offense, or put others on the defensive. I believe that most people I meet think that I am friendly and agreeable, and I think so too! I am definitely less patient than I was twenty or thirty years ago. I still like to meet new people and exchange ideas. However, I'm not willing to spend time with those who I feel have closed minds, even when we agree. My goal now is to *stay alive*! I hope to remain as healthy as possible to be able to participate in the activities of my family, my friends, and my community, and to keep voting for people who believe as I do..."early and often," of course!—DS

I'm just about seventy-three years old and am crazy about this time of life. I have on my bulletin board a photograph of my mother, along with this quote that, long ago, was in my hometown newspaper: "Count your blessings. Don't look at the next person and compare your life." Beautiful, right? I cherish those blessings that have come with love and work. Now, just recently, I feel I am in a newly defined time, one that is removed from daily work and caretaking of children and, more recently, of my parents, too. I am my own girl more than ever. Here is what matters to me: being kind whenever the opportunity appears, and looking for where kindness is needed. You know, at this age, we aren't the center, and that is so okay—or rather, our work is to make that okay. That doesn't mean we don't get irritated or feel a judgment rising...but our job is to squish that and move on. Who needs you? Go there. The small things can have the same value as the big ones—the hello, the compliment, the listening. And I think that's just another way, really, of taking care of yourself. My goal for the years ahead: to wake up in the morning and begin to feel the daily joy of life. To close the door to the bedroom so my dear heart of a husband can sleep a little later. To let the cat in, put the coffee on, go outside to pick up the papers and look up at the remains of the moon, and to count my lucky stars as I go back inside and slip into the day.—MS

Time and good health are, in my opinion, two of our most precious commodities, and yet all the money in the world can't buy either one. If it could, Steve Jobs would not only still be alive, he could live forever. I'm never lonely because I truly enjoy and make use of my alone time. The words "I'm bored" have never come out of my mouth. If I were under house arrest, I could keep myself busy indefinitely. If I had a supply of flour, yeast, yarn, fabric, beads, books, newspapers, a landline, and my dog...well, I'll probably never be under house arrest. But nevertheless, my hands are always busy working on some creative endeavor or turning the pages of the endless supply of actual books that I get at the actual public library. I also try to always have something to look forward to. It can be as simple as having a sleepover with my grandchildren, or having a few friends over for lunch or dinner, or teaching bread making in my kitchen, or taking a wherever-the-wind-blows driving trip in Europe, or planning a silly theme party for fifty or sixty friends, or laying out fabrics for my next patchwork quilt. I don't own a computer, iPad, smartphone, or any other electronic device. Sometimes I go a week without even thinking about turning on the TV. Frankly those things would take too much time away from all the above and more. In my opinion, the more gadgets people have, the less they communicate. Somehow, without all that stuff, I'm always busy keeping touch and spending quality time with my friends and manage to stay fairly well informed. I know I'm a dinosaur, but it works for me. Perhaps someday I'll catch up to the twentieth century but probably never the twenty-first. I don't want to. If I did, I would. Until I was twenty-one, my life was better than good, although I didn't give my life much value while I was actually living it.—FM

I feel, at age seventy-seven, that life is now a gift. I have outlived both my mother and my only brother, three of my grandparents, and will soon outlive my father and maternal grandmother as well. This increases my awareness of the rapid passage of time. It also means that my voice is much more patient and understanding than when I was younger. I am less judgmental and tend to take setbacks more in stride. I am more relaxed since I retired at age seventy-five. I did love my job, especially assisting clients who became friends and friends who became clients with financial matters and finding satisfactory solutions to various problems. But I also felt that I wanted to spend more time doing things that I enjoy and spending more time with my husband, whom I love. This includes travel, music, reading, taking courses, gardening, learning more about art, and even trying to create art. I now notice the blooming of every flower and the visits of backyard birds, and I photograph the most beautiful. I spend more time in the garden and am trying to grow vegetables. I have started oil painting, using as subjects photographs I have taken of places we have traveled to previously. I remember the color of the sea, the mountains, the umbrellas, the peeling paint on the facades, the Italian landscape, and the Norwegian fjords. The memories return as I paint; I now dream the colors. I am still interested in politics and the developments and changes to Miami Beach, a city I have loved ever since my childhood. I think my voice is strong but one of fairness. It continues to be difficult to visualize the future and what will be best for the residents, business owners, and generations to come in this fascinating city. My attitude toward age has changed. When I was in my thirties, I thought fifty was really quite old. And in my sixties I thought eighty was definitely "old age." However, eighty is just around the corner and no longer seems very ancient. I suspect my voice, my views, will continue to change. Life is a continuum, and though the demands of a young family and the stress of work are behind me, the importance of family and friendship is stronger than ever. As I continue to age, perhaps religion will be more important to me. Right now in this gift of time, my family, friends, and good health are of the greatest importance.—JM

When I realize where I am in the span of life, it is very surprising to me. My husband is living in the community he lived in all his life, and we came back here for him to begin his private medical practice. How did forty-seven years pass so quickly? It is as if I'm on a train. Every ten years is ten miles and an ever-shifting scene—the first ten changing diapers and creating enduring friendships that have lasted forty-seven years and, more than that, a family of three children who have created wonderful families of their own. I have five very different grandchildren, but all enjoy being together for different events. The love for each of our children sometimes is overwhelming for me, and I could cry with joy and do. I have been married almost fifty-two years to the man I fell in love with while still an intern. How blessed—a girl growing up in a small town in East Tennessee has lived forty-seven years in beautiful, sunny South Florida. From mountains to oceans!—JJ

What energizes you in the present?

I believe my long life (ninety-eight years) has many contributions. A faith in God. Since a little child, a love for books. At thirteen years I read Zane Grey, Seltzer, and Alexandre Dumas, among some of the adult books I enjoyed. I worked hard since age twelve, and I started painting at age seventy-six. No lessons. Hoping it would be therapy for me after the loss of my husband. Having two wonderful daughters and one wonderful son-in-law are my greatest blessings. Their love sustains me. Adopting a cat is a big help due to the calming effect on me. The affection he gives is such an added gift and so enjoyable. Painting and reading every day keep my mind and imagination active. And I love every minute of it. Using my imagination in both keeps me alert. I meet interesting people through my books, and also I go to exciting places. What a joy! And I am never lonely due to my books. Always having the desire to learn more and more keeps me going. A sense of humor is most important, and I thank God for this additional gift. But most of all is the beautiful gift of a beautiful apartment to live in great comfort the rest of my life. With no financial worries due to the generosity of my daughter, I am surrounded by love.—MM

A realization came to me one day...something like..."You know, when the children were growing up, I never had time to think about me. I was so involved with taking care of them and everyone else...Now that I have the time to think of me, it does not feel that comfortable, and I need to learn how to do that. I really need to concentrate on what I want for me, and how to do that feels undeserving or foreign, but I am going to work on it."—HW

Early in life, I learned to be a survivor, and I believe that has greatly contributed to my emotional and spiritual happiness. In tough times and in times of bliss, I took the punches as they rolled in and made the best of it. Perception, perception, perception is everything. If we only look at the negative things in life, believe me, you will only get more of it. It is a universal principle. I certainly do not want to be a magnet for negativity. I want to always be high on life. I never took recreational drugs or drank. I have always practiced the art of positive thinking coupled with spirituality. I love living because life is worth living. If you think I am living in an unreal bubble, I ask you to look at the alternative and then tell me which one is better. *Remember, a good life is better lived forward.* I plan to continue setting new goals, even if it is to paint my bathroom cabinets. Goals are so important! Friends are so important! Praying is so important! Love is so important! The Internet is so important! I feel I can still learn so much. I don't know how to play any instrument, but I want to learn how to play the American Indian flute. I think music is so important, especially if it elevates us to a higher spiritual level. One other thing: I realize that physically I am not as young as I was or even that my looks are not as I used to be, but who cares? Beauty and strength are an inside job.—PP

I think the most important lessons I have learned from life revolve around the fact that I married too young and too impulsively, without really knowing the man whom I chose to be my partner. It was all about chemistry when I was nineteen years old and a need to escape a promised engagement to another man I did not love. That drove me to make an impulsive decision that would affect my life for twenty-eight years. I was also too young to have four children quickly and didn't really think about the sacrifices needed, although I had wonderful parents who set an example of family being primary in your life. I didn't have enough knowledge about child-rearing, although I would go to the library and read Gesell and Ilg every time my child reached another stage that I did not understand. That was very helpful. Another driving fact in my life has always been financial insecurity, as I had no money of my own. This has made me realize the importance of being educated and equipped to support oneself if one had to be on his/her own without being dependent on a man. That lack of security also led me to make poor decisions regarding other relationships after my divorce. My granddaughters are smarter in that respect and understand the pitfalls of being totally financially dependent on their life partner. Although I did go back to college eventually and earned a master's degree, I never was able to earn enough money to support a secure lifestyle on my own. All are hard lessons to learn. But for the most part, life has turned out well for me, through much effort and utilizing resources to heal my regrets and internal turmoil during rough periods of my life.—Anonymous

Basically I am a happy person. I do not project my personal upsets onto others. I do that behind closed doors. I have to be a part of the world. I always have been since childhood. In our family, anger was never tolerated for any length of time. I realize that I am too verbal and opinionated when I am annoyed. I am a road racer. I drive on cruise control. I am no prude, but it disgusts me how women dress today.—RL

I like being athletic. I am happy to be a faithful, flexible, trustworthy, and good-natured friend to many, including of course my family. I also find great contentment when I find myself with alone time.—MP

Thoughts to Remember:

1. Reflect and interpret our past and grow as a student of the present.
2. Listen and be open to the voices within and those outside our inner circle.
3. Celebrate our accomplishments and the meaning they brought to our lives and encourage enthusiasm and knowledge wherever we can.
4. Recognize the talents and skills we have developed in our 60+ years as self-evaluation is healthy.
5. Identify the regrets we have and how those regrets can be acted on today.
6. Discover a new sense of personal freedom and excitement about the future as we put closure on the unbearable pain of loss.
7. Uncover the leader within each of us.
8. Be resilient and capitalize on our experiences in order to adapt to the changes we face.
9. Be willing to stand by our principles and the truths revealed to us through our life's experiences.
10. Continue to remain engaged with others and HAVE FUN!!!
11. Take care of your needs but not at the expense of others.
12. Stay as independent as we can and when we need help, ask.

Having recently celebrated my seventy-fifth birthday, I tend to believe that my years of experience and history probably equal wisdom. Like most grandparents, I have a belief that my insight and knowledge could provide useful wisdom for my twenty-seven-year-old, adventurous grandson. He recently sent an e mail to his family members, informing us that he intended to seek better ski conditions by climbing to and skiing on an off-limits mountain area while in the Andes of Argentina. I received this unsettling message the same day I was attending a workshop on treating obsessive-compulsive behaviors. As a former skier, I understand the perils of off-limits, off-trail skiing, even for the best of skiers. I even had known a young person who died in such risky behavior. The workshop lecturer gave the attendees an exercise: to write the worst possible thought they could have for someone they love. Many of the therapists refused. The thought was uncomfortable for me as well; to write it seemed almost impossible, but I did. I was able to control or stop my obsessive anxiety about my grandson's safety as I read my own words. I let go of the "worst possible thought" along with my anxiety. There was nothing I could do to affect the outcome. This is a *reaffirmation*, yet I must learn again and again: live in the present, one moment to the next.—BMR

My inner voice at seventy-four announces a note of thankfulness each morning as I remind myself of how lucky I am to wake up to the sounds of a bird or the radio, to the sunlight of a new day, or to the routine of hearing my spouse breathing next to me, which, when younger, I took for granted. Recently, my inner thoughts are about fear of the unknown, of how I may manage if something happens to our couplehood and how very different life would be. However, my voice reminds me to think of today and how to make this day the best it can be. I think about the positivity of the present moment. I adopted a message from a recent obituary that stated, "There are no rear-view mirrors. The best is yet to come. Let's live life as we always imagined it could be." Soon thereafter, I was happy to hear my spouse suggest we take weekly dancing classes with a small group of friends. I immediately thought he was joking, because we had earlier attempts that were less than successful. Now we are dancing as fast as we can. We can laugh at ourselves and appreciate laughter as a special ingredient that we each take from these moments. My voice says this is good for our mental and physical health. There is tenderness. There is showmanship and a sense of peacefulness. We recognize that while we both have responsibilities, those too have changed, and we have more time to focus on "the individual and the couple." We enjoy celebrating the richness of our times together as well as time alone.—Anonymous

As a structured person, I seem to thrive on action and on having some routine, which becomes my outline, giving me a purpose. I tend to judge my day on how much I have gotten done but know that some of my best days are not about checking off my lists but being involved with others and sharing valued activities that speak to me, such as conducting a workshop with peers on the importance of group work, or being a part of an ongoing support group of women learning to define boundaries for ourselves, through which I also learn about myself through others' eyes. My inner voice knows that I have creative ideas and leadership abilities, yet I may no longer need to lead, to be in charge. I am just wanting to be a part of the group with less responsibility to make things happen—and this is okay. I am ready for others to step up to the plate to lead. Am I tired? Sometimes. But it is more about relinquishing how I spend my time. Successful aging is a work in progress, and my voice reminds me to take notice of the attitude of those older than I who are vitally interested in life. I am inspired daily by their stories. I hear young adults praise my list of activities and my ability to continue to work, and my inner voice is telling me that they think of me as "old," disinterested in learning new things. I fight hard to be kind in my responses, as I wish to remind them that life is not over until it is over! On the other hand, I hope that in some small way, I can influence their opinions on what older people are still able to accomplish.—GKH

It is not often that I search my soul with a critical eye...the critical eye that burrows deep until my essence is unearthed and stares back, bold as a naked light bulb, no reflections, no shades that can cover what really lives there. When I was younger, I was afraid to explore to see if I had "inner strengths." I was afraid to see who I really was for fear that I would be so disappointed in all the weaknesses, which would be a stark reminder of messages of what I still needed to accomplish. Afraid to discover if what I thought were my motives in life were authentic. Afraid when I reached my bottom I would find piles of should-haves, would-haves...disillusionment and betrayals to who and what I wanted to be. When my father died, I worried that my core had died also. I was unsure if I had a moral compass that could be my guide. I closed out sorrow. And it was fear that kept me away when youth gave me so much energy to live my life. My mistake in those earlier years was that I did not have faith in my inner goodness. My mistake was that I did not have faith that I was strong enough to survive on my own. My mistake was that I did not have faith in my future. My mistake was that I did not have faith that I was worthy of meaningful connections with others. My mistake was that I had no faith that I was strong enough to confront people with whom I disagreed. My mistake was that I didn't really hear what people were saying to me. On the surface I am sure that others saw me as whole. Yet I thought that I was broken. Today, emboldened by years and by relationships, by my reflections of the world so vibrant with diversity and by a stronger belief in myself and my personal successes, I employ that critical eye and feel comforted by the inner strengths that I now see...that helped to guide me as a wife, as a parent, as a grandmother, as a daughter, as a sister, as a friend, and as a social worker and that will help to guide me from now on.

I value that...

I learned to be a caring daughter and to feel strong in character, not swallowed up in my mother's sadness and negativity.

I learned to encompass the incredible lessons my mother taught me, even if she did not live by them, of how to be a loving woman with a strong sense of core values that my family could live by.

I learned not to be disappointed that my mother did not always live by those lessons.

I learned to appreciate that I was a spiritual human being that took comfort in feeling that there was some greater order in the world and that I had a community that was my support and identity.

I learned to cherish the opportunity to be a parent, respect who my children are, and feel incredible pride in launching them and watching them soar.

I learned to be independent and feel empowered by my ability to move outside my comfort zone and still be loved and respected.

I learned to be a wife that could feel secure enough in who I was to sacrifice my own identity sometimes to be a true helpmate.

I learned to take pride in being a friend who was honest, loyal, and comfortable in sharing myself.

I learned to be a person who was transported and energized when I was learning something new.

I learned how important it was to feel more complete when I was able to make a small difference in someone else's life.

I learned the beauty in being able to communicate in a way so that others wanted to listen.

I learned to listen and feel secure even if I was wrong.

I learned that alone was not another word for lonely.

I learned that I could still feel good about myself even if I were on the outside looking in.

I learned that being an adult meant that I had to step back and not take myself so seriously if I wanted to be taken seriously by others.

I learned that no one, including me, expects perfection anymore.

I learned it is okay to do the best that you can even if that falls short of what your expectations of yourself might have been.

I learned to love and respect who I am and genuinely feel that I am a worthy human being who can and has made even the slightest difference in this world.—CTS

Now established in the stage of generativity, we are persuaded by our age and experience to place ourselves front and center in this universe, taking advantage of the length of our days and prioritizing just how we want those days to be spent. With a confidence that has grown out of our collective experiences and shared wisdom, we are women whose *present voices* have the potential to reverberate throughout the generations.

LIST OF QUESTIONS TO REVIEW

How have our reflections from our past impacted how we see ourselves today?

What are the things you have achieved in your lifetime that you are most proud of?

What energizes you in the present?

What role do religion and spirituality play in your life today?

PERSONAL REFLECTIONS

_____

_____

_____

_____

_____

_____

_____

_____

_____

_____

_____

_____

_____

_____

_____

_____

_____

_____

_____

_____

_____

_____

_____

_____

_____

_____

CHAPTER 8
Building Our Living Legacy

Wealth...Not what you accumulate but what you share.
—M. Osceola

*How far you go in life depends on your being tender with
the young, compassionate with the aged, sympathetic
with the starving, and tolerant of the weak and the strong.
Because someday in life you will have been all of these.*
—George Washington Carver

W e find ourselves now at a critical juncture in the book. We all have been on a life-enhancing voyage. In each chapter, we, like you, have been inspired by the voices of women who have spoken out, many of whom have been courageous enough to share poignant stories of their struggles and their triumphs. In each chapter, we, like you, have had the opportunity to reflect on our own struggles and triumphs in answer to the chapter questions that have guided us in creating the groundwork for our own personal narratives. What we have learned from each of the stages and the critical influences of our friendships and careers is that we are a composite of all those significant pieces of our personal puzzle. Many of us might not have given much thought to what relevance each of the pieces had in our concept of who we are today. Many of us might not have placed value in the reminiscences as a storyline, *our* storyline, and just how influential those recollections have become now in enriching us as women over sixty.

As we tried to re-create our earliest memories, we began to see where we acquired the very building blocks with which we consciously or subconsciously constructed the foundations of our core values. It is likely that we were not surprised at the influences from our parents, grandparents, and other extended family members. But maybe we did not realize just how precious those core values were until we were challenged to reflect on our lives.

Bruce Feiler, in *The Secrets of Happy Families*, writes, "The more children know about their family's story, the stronger their sense of control over their lives, the higher their self-esteem, the more successfully they believe their family functions... Their larger family story helps them understand that they are a part of something bigger." If we were not convinced before, maybe knowing how important our stories are to the health of our extended families will be the impetus to complete the task of composing our personal stories and shaping our legacies. Our narratives, the storylines we have now patiently constructed chapter by chapter, are only the first step in the generative process. The legacy we write based on the insights revealed in our narratives will be the cornerstone for creating our world that we leave behind.

A legacy is something, often thought to be a physical possession, handed down from an ancestor or from the past. We are about to reshape that definition. We are all about to create our legacies while we are alive. *What we are going to pass on to our loved ones are intangibles—our personal, family, and cultural histories, our beliefs and value systems.* We are going to hand down something of ourselves, a collection of things that we have chosen that reflect what we discovered and what is a mirror to our soul.

What are your life goals for the next years?

> To remain healthy, not be judgmental, and to stay in touch with my friends and family. Yes, these are my current goals.—BHK

> My goals have never changed—never in my life. I am serious of purpose. If you knew me at fourteen, you would see the same person—but a little less rigid, I hope. That is Miami versus Philadelphia too. We are more open here and not so concerned about lineage. I still want to be the best mother, wife, daughter, friend, and leader I can be, and I will do whatever it takes to get there. I am on call for every need/person/ commitment 24-7 (and my husband is too). I put my heart and soul into everything I do. My goal has always been to do the right thing and

to be productive. Leadership has never been my goal, but it is a quality with which I have been blessed—as I am always willing to stand up for what I think is right, and to listen to others in the process. I know that happiness is also a skill. And I know how blessed I am—so I need to continue to produce and not to get lazy. I cannot change the world— but I can help improve our community. And I would like to exercise more!—EH

Much to my dismay, I never really had plans or goals that were long range. Completing college, getting married, having a family—those were givens, not specifics. I have always felt I shortchanged myself because of that, but then again, if I had emotionally or intellectually been able to create those (or different) goals, I think I might have. Therefore, now, as a senior citizen, I also have no specific goals to reach other than to remain active with my volunteer work and to stay as healthy as I can. Enjoying my family and friends and continuing involvement in the community seem to be the ultimate activities at this time—while there's still time to be engaged.—ER

My goal is to ride the crest of the wave of my profession and balance my life, taking more time to smell the roses. (George Bernard Shaw said, "You see things; and you say 'Why?' But I dream things that never were; and I say 'Why not?'") I just got the first 3-D mammogram machine in Miami. It was very expensive, but at this point my salary is secondary to continuing to provide the best possible service to my patients. I am taking more time off in the summer when other doctors can cover my practice. I also want to teach new radiologists the importance of knowing more of the clinical side of breast health and disease.—NK

My life goals:
- To be healthy and content
- To be with people whom I enjoy being with
- To be content with my life as it is now
- To continue to be physically active

—Anonymous

In the more than four hundred narratives we collected, women challenged us with their personal truths as they contemplated the significance of their memories and the emotional impact those had on their lives. Their insights served as an impetus for us to retrace our own remarkable paths. First, we gave voice to our stories. As with many of our memories, those stories were now painstakingly filtered through the thousands of experiences imprinted into the fiber of our years. Those stories today may take on a more profound meaning than what we might have initially recollected. We may now have brought closure to unfinished business with family members and friends because looking back with wisdom and maturity slowly dismantled our most rigid boundaries.

Why now do we begin to think about our legacy? It is not merely that our stiffening joints remind us that the road ahead is shorter than the one we have traveled. Or that we are watching some of our oldest and dearest loved ones grapple with loss of memory or frustration and anger at not being the people they once were. Throughout the decades we have gathered stories, often unwittingly, that come to reflect the significant life lessons that became our moral compass.

Remember that we are, by virtue of our stage in life, the keepers of the meaning. The key that unlocks the treasure trove of meanings we have unearthed is our narrative. Today those stories record our living legacy; they are what we have come to see as the relevance of our lives. Through the process of sharing our stories, the depth of our messages and the connections we forge are intensified. With sharing comes the promise of future connections and of continued self-exploration. By recounting the stories, we are sharing our moral inheritance with the most significant people in our lives—our family, friends, neighbors, coworkers. Most importantly, shaping our legacies also gives each of us a revitalized set of guidelines for today and for the years that lie ahead.

In a stunning TED Talk, Andrew Solomon, PhD, a writer and a two-time winner of the National Book Award for nonfiction, celebrates the opportunities that allow us to transform the worst events of our lives into our "narratives of triumph." For Solomon, stories are the foundations of our identities. They bring change, not by making what is wrong right, but rather by valuing the wrongs as precious gifts in building our unique selves. Nevertheless, we do not want to minimize how treacherous the road to enlightenment can be. We often get stuck wallowing in self-pity over the wrongs that are done to us—especially in our childhood. It might take the majority of those sixty-plus years to, as Solomon says so eloquently, "forge the meaning of our lives."

I wrote my book to celebrate yesterday's accomplishments and today's opportunities, a time to be grateful for family and friends, for good times and good fortune. What I meant by "yesterday's accomplishments" is that I had a very difficult young life but was able to survive the negatives and celebrate my accomplishments through the years. And I felt the necessity to write down my experiences so that my family and future additional family to come would know what it takes to turn the negative experiences into positive opportunities to live a happy, fulfilling, wonderful life. I first related about my mother's death soon after I was born. She suffered from leukemia. I had a sister who was ten years old. She was taken in by one of my mother's sisters. My father did not have the means to care for me, so I was placed in an orphan home, where I lived until I was six years old, at which time I was taken into a foster home of a wonderful older couple that came from the same small shtetl in Russia that my parents came from. I lived a somewhat normal life with them until I was fourteen years old, at which time my father had a massive heart attack and died. My mother's sister made arrangements for me to go live with my older sister, who had married a Peruvian and lived in Lima, Peru, and from then on, my whole life changed. I was all of fifteen years old. I met my future husband and, at the age of seventeen, was married and began my own family, and new life, in Peru. I had four children and struggled through the first few years, but little by little, through small opportunities, I lived a very good life. My husband was a wonderful person, a good father, and a very good provider. After writing my book, my children, although they knew parts of my life, didn't realize the trials and tribulations that I went through to come to this day. They were thankful that I shared some events that they were not aware of and how I was able to overcome and become the independent woman I am today. In writing this book, I have learned to forgive and forget but most of all to have had the pleasure of love. To love my husband, to love my children, to love my friends that I've made over the years, and to share my life story with them. I was married for fifty-three years and lost my husband eight years ago, and this legacy that I have left behind will forever give me comfort.

I recommend that anyone who has a story to tell, whether short or long, sad or happy, should share it with his/her loved ones. It is a cleansing process that will make you feel fulfilled.—SGG

I went through the first fifty years of my life angry with my mom for what I perceived as her abandonment of me after my dad died when I was fourteen. Throughout those first years after his death, she was so lost in her own grief that she was not tuned in to where and with whom I was going. I never doubted she loved me, but her loss was so great that she had difficulty righting herself. My older sisters tried all they could, but they were dealing with their own pain and confusion. I quickly fell into a pattern, and my friends and their families became my stability. It was easy to say "Poor me," and I replayed that tune incessantly well into my twenties. It was very easy to place blame. All my insecurities. All my anxieties. I was a kid—so it could not possibly have been my fault. There were no grief counselors. At the time I grew up, no one ever even talked about death. When I stopped to take a breath, I felt isolated and all alone. So I never stopped. As an adult I could no longer put the blame for any failures or missteps on the death of my dad. I had to take responsibility for my actions. It was then that I learned that my coin had two sides: yes, at a critical time in my life, my dad died. Yet his lessons continued to live on in me by my successes. I honored him by my achievements. The other side of the coin was the lesson his death had certainly taught me: carpe diem. Make each day count. I understood pity now was for those who did not have fourteen years with my dad and a lifetime with a mother that taught me invaluable lessons about being a mother, grandmother, wife, and sister.—CTS

Even the stories that speak to the pain and disappointment in ourselves and in others are critical to tell. In the retelling, we discover how valuing our wrongs as precious gifts propels us toward the unlimited possibility of changed attitudes and new beginnings. In the twenty-first-century world of texts and e-mails, just recounting our legacy could very well, as an additional benefit, reintroduce the art of storytelling to generations who have somehow abandoned the art of verbal communication.

The Seven Merits to Writing a Living Legacy

Exploring our personal histories has proven to have both pleasant and unpleasant emotional moments. As we weave together those that are most relevant to the life lessons that transformed us, we are crafting our living legacies. Oftentimes our loved ones compose our legacies after we have died. The beauty of writing our own stories is that it affords each of us the opportunity to give voice to our own legacy while we are alive and still vital.

> How many times have I thought, "If only I could ask my mom!" My mother was a wonderful storyteller who bedazzled her grandchildren with her wonderful tales of the small village in Eastern Europe she left as a child. I left her to tell the stories. I was too busy and distracted by the business of everyday life to show much interest in those details. As I age, I recognize how valuable those stories are. As I am choosing my own stories to share with my family, I see how many holes there are in my storyline. I wish I could ask her to fill in those holes. That has convinced me that I am going to leave my children and grandchildren a storybook with as few missing pages as possible.—CTS

Rather than having our loved ones be frustrated by their lack of information, we have the obligation to be the resource for the questions our families have not even thought to ask. We have to anticipate or even direct (something many of us are very adept at doing) what our families will want to know. If we were ever worried that we would not have enough to fill our days as we age, here is a project that will not only occupy our time but will bring the personal reward of sharing what will be their inheritance and their lasting connection to family and community.

Sharing a legacy is not simply telling our stories. It can be a window into the past and a pathway to a rich and significant future.

The following are the seven merits in building a meaningful living legacy.

1. Maintaining Our Pathways of Communication

Even as some boast of their proficiency at texting and e-mailing, we recognize that those modern tools have made communication a series of sound bites, of abbreviated thoughts. They only provide hints of activities and no real insight into anyone's feelings or emotions. In fact, that may be one of the reasons for their popularity—they are an artificial barrier to connecting. Although we might have adapted to technology in order to maintain our relationships, this mode of communication still remains foreign to us and oftentimes leaves us devoid of any of the feelings of connection we had come to enjoy in the past. The depth of feeling and substance of thought could cause seismic cracks that open new pathways to communicating hidden thoughts and profound emotions—a lasting gift to the next generations.

> My "legacy" would be defined by the impact I have had on the people I love and that love me. It's quite difficult to consider that I have a legacy, but I can sum it up as such:
> Remember me as a loving daughter.
> Remember me as a devoted sister.
> Remember me as a *true* mother who loved unconditionally and infinitely.
> Remember me if you care to.
> —Anonymous

> There are no beliefs and values I would pass down that I haven't already instilled in my family. I would continue to pass on the importance of respect and kindness to my daughter who is my family. We share the traditions of a small family unit that consist of time spent together, openness, communication without limits and love. Family means everything and the one thing that I hold closest to my heart is the connection I have with mine. Everything else in life seems unimportant next to that. SB

> I am leaving my daughters the following gifts:
> A kind heart
> A curious mind
> A thirst for knowledge
> A sense of humor
> A love for books
> A love of family
> —MM

2. Imparting a Foundation of Values

How many times have we been told by the younger generation not to lecture about things they already know? Yet to know something does not mean the same as adopting and integrating that thing as part of our daily behavior. Our narratives chronicle our fundamental values. Our stories reveal how those values have been shaped and reshaped and reside in our every action.

> *"If I am not for myself, who will be for me? But if I am only for myself, who am I? And if not now, when?"* (Rabbi Hillel) I don't think I understood the significance and profound depth of this message until fairly recently in my life. We so often hear about the importance of self-esteem, but for many women, especially those of my generation, our own self-worth was much less important than how we thought of and cared for others. However, they are not mutually exclusive, and that is so important for women to understand. We can take care of ourselves and be concerned with our growth and development, not to the exclusion of others, but as part of who we are. During the early years of my marriage and raising children, I often felt burdened by the responsibility. I always felt that I wasn't doing things well enough or good enough. I always felt that I didn't really matter. I could miss an event—who would notice? I could skip someone else's simcha (celebration)—what difference would I make? I remember once venturing to tell a friend of my insecurities about not being a good enough mother to my infant son. She rebuked me, saying that I should be ashamed to be ungrateful for my beautiful, healthy son. I was so very grateful but so unsure of how to manage the awesome responsibility ahead of me, and so sure I was unworthy. Needless to say, I didn't share those feelings again until many years later in therapy. When I had been widowed for a number of years, I decided it was time to allow some love and light into my life. A very dear aunt continued to encourage me to "get back into the scene." As I did so, with little hope of success, a wonderful friend of mine asked me if, along with "putting the word out" and changing my mindset, I was also praying to Hashem (G-d) to send me someone special. I replied, "That's all Hashem has to worry about, my ancient love life? Each Shabbat (Sabbath) I do pray for the health of my children and grandchildren, and for peace to come to Israel." She was surprised and reminded me

that if I wasn't including G-d in the equation, what was that about? And if I wasn't asking for myself, who would? I went home, and that Shabbat I did include a prayer that if finding someone special was in G-d's plan for me, I was ready. Ten days later I met the man to whom I am now happily married. People remark that there's something different about the way I look. I chuckle because I think I look the same, only I am truly happy. That happiness shows, and it's better than any makeup, face cream, or spa treatment!. It's never too late to dream. So take care of yourself. It's not selfish; it's kind. Find wonderful and supportive friends, because you deserve that. Surround yourself with people who share your values and who make you stretch to be the best that you can be while accepting you now. Life is a process; we are all unfinished and are developing every day. You will make mistakes, so learn from them. Don't beat yourself up, just figure out what you don't want to do next time. Find meaning in your life. Find your passion and seek it. Be healthy and take care of yourself, because when you do, then you can be there for those you love. Every day, remind yourself that you are worth your efforts. When you accept that, others will too. And start now!—JL

I have often thought of the legacy I would like to leave my children. Hopefully, they will always remember a mother who loved them dearly above all else. My children saw a single mother who created a business that was very different from what was in existence at that time. They witnessed hard work, inventiveness, and the ability to overcome obstacles, and they learned to never give up. They were taught the lesson that if they put their minds to something, they could be successful and independent. Hopefully, these values will endure in them and they will pass them on to the next generation. Finally, I now can look amazedly at my wonderful grandchildren, the rewards of my life. I want them to know how important they are and to always reach a little farther than they think they can.—MB

3. Making Our Values Live and Last
Values may become platitudes if they are not integral to our actions. Haven't we all felt the power of those quizzical looks from friends and family when we have spoken passionately about something we value—maybe a political or religious or

social value? Are they wondering if we are just giving lip service to those values? We then have to ask ourselves, "Do my daily actions reflect the sincerity of these passions?" Recounting our past may give credence to what might have been seen merely as lofty platitudes.

My values speak of my place of birth, the parents who raised me, the opportunities afforded me, and the lessons I learned from each. I am thankful to live in America, a democratic society, and feel strongly that as an individual I have a responsibility to contribute to making this world a better place, one day at a time. I do so by voicing my opinion to newspapers, magazines, organizations, or friends to address issues that are important to me and others. This sense of freedom is comforting, and I appreciate those women who came before me and who fought for the equality of rights for all people. I value the family I was born into and the love and safety provided by my parents. Equally important were the many unspoken messages I observed, as when Dad left to go to work each day. There were few complaints, long, hard days, and little time for fun. I knew my father provided us not only with the basics but had an interest in reading, in listening to opera, and in playing handball, taking what little time he had for mind and body before it was fashionable. Mom's devotion to connections with family, her sense of humor, and her fun-loving nature provided much love. Her making do with little excesses taught me to appreciate and value the time we spend with those we love, offering more meaning than a new trinket or toy or new dress, which is disposable. We had what was essential, each other. When I lost my dad as a young adult, I never lost the value he placed on education, nor the principles of kindness and honesty by which he lived. I then chose a spouse with similar values and one who injects humor into our lives daily, and I value the nearly fifty years of marriage we have had together. I sometimes adjust to change slowly but work hard to remind myself that change may offer many opportunities for further growth, even at seventy-plus. There are no guarantees in life, but I value my instincts and belief in myself and take the paths that speak to me at the time, and when and if changes are necessary, I do take what is in my control and go forth with a lot of faith in a higher power than myself. I value, treasure, and continue to learn from both the positive and negative connections I have made with others over a lifetime.—GH

It was our son who taught me an important lesson about being true to my values. I decided to go to law school when my children were teenagers. At the time it seemed like a natural progression from the work I was doing as a social worker. By the second year, I was pretty certain that I was never going to practice law; with twenty hours left, I decided that I had had enough and quit. At the same time, our son was starting his final semester of high school. My husband and I had always stressed the importance of education, and we were so proud that he had done so well and had been accepted early decision to college. He had truly been an outstanding kid. He was always so responsible and mature. So naturally, when graduation rolled around, we wanted to give him something special that would signify all his achievements. A few days after we asked him to think about what he might imagine that gift would be, he told us he had decided. He turned to me and said, "Mom, I would like my gift to be that you finish law school. Our whole lives you have preached that a good education was the most important gift we can give ourselves. You always preached that you should always finish what you start. What if I told you in my junior year of college that I wanted to drop out? I had learned all I that I needed to. You would be appalled. Well, now you have to practice what you preach." The day I graduated law school was one of the most meaningful days of my life. Not because of the law school degree, but because I had proven to my children that one of our greatest achievements is to live the values we preach.—CTS

Long ago, when the state of Israel was not even yet "sweet sixteen" and I was a couple of years older than the state, I traveled twenty-one days on a ship from my country, Argentina, to Israel to participate in a one-year program of youth leadership. That rich experience influenced me throughout my life. Among the great leaders that we were fortunate to meet was David Ben Gurion, who visited us in our kibbutz, and I vividly remember him, short with white, disheveled hair, telling us in an authoritarian and yet grandfatherly way, "Young girls like you will go back to your countries. Never forget the Hebrew language. It will be a 'Kesher v'Gesher' (a connection and a bridge) with this land." I promised myself I would not forget this newly acquired language. In fact his words became imprinted in my DNA. Many years went by. I got married, came to the United States, and had three wonderful children. Over the years I went back to Israel as a tourist, as a volunteer in the army, and to a hospital in Yaffo as a volunteer with the B'nai B'rith, bringing along my family. Once, I temporarily replaced a Hebrew teacher at Temple Beth Shalom for what was supposed to be just a couple of weeks and is now reaching thirty years. I found a most satisfying meaning in this sacred work, helping children connect with their Jewish identity, getting them closer to Israel, and inspiring them to love its language. Ten years ago my daughter suddenly died. I had carried S for nine months; now I carry her for the rest of my life in my heart, and she, of all my children, was the one that shared the passion for Israel...so with her in my heart, "we" walked the Israel National Trail over seven hundred miles from Tel Dan to Taba. "Together" we crossed the Negev, Ben Gurion's late-life pride project...years later "we" ran the Kineret Marathon, and "we" participated in the March of the Living, going from the darkness of the Holocaust to the light of the Promised Land with thousands of young people. What energizes me today at seventy is looming around the corner: more projects where I combine running, walking, volunteer work, and Eretz Israel.—MM

4. Strengthening Connections

My legacy is about connection. For me everything is a connection. Real connections. Core connections that you have with your family and with your community. I continue to feel connected to my parents. I feel connected to my sister and to my aunt, who was a very important part of my life. Connections transcend physical life. In these connections are the roots of every part of me, and they have nurtured the person I have become. I want my grandchildren to have respect for all people. I want them to believe that all people deserve respect. I do not ever want them to feel that they are better. Each human being is unique and someone from whom they can always learn something new. I hope they are learning that from my husband. Oftentimes they are annoyed that he is stopping to talk to people. But someday I expect that they will remember the genuine interest he has shown in others and his respect for their differences. We have shared the story with them about the importance of family and community. While on safari we watched a young water buffalo wander off from its herd—either testing out his independence or in search of another grazing area. He was unaware of a pride of lionesses nearby. Even a water buffalo is vulnerable when alone without his herd. Even animals may not have the proper respect for the meaning of community. The pride killed that water buffalo. The other water buffalo could not protect him. Our commitment to community gives us strength, and its strength gives us roots and purpose. I came from a family that valued that. From the strength of the community, we can make a difference if we allow others to mentor us.—KG

Not one of us exists in a vacuum. Our legacies become the channel through which we can teach about the significance of our connection to family and community. Just like the young water buffalo detached from his herd and testing his independence, many of us also strayed in the hopes of finding a more meaningful life. We have often lost sight of how important those roots were that came from our families and communities. Sharing those experiences, even admitting we made major mistakes, levels the playing field between the younger generations and ourselves. It is amazing how approachable we become when we admit to the errors of our ways. Creating that bond gives us the perfect entrée to demonstrating, in a personal way, our reliance on our shared paths.

I was married and worked closely with my husband for many years before we divorced amicably. I am now happily remarried. All this has shown me there is hope and great strength. One day I attended a ceremony for a boy turning thirteen, a child of a friend of mine. I couldn't help but feel sorry for myself, thinking how I, too, have a son his age but because of issues of mental health, my son could not be celebrating with all of us. I was able to be there for this young man and his family, but as I drove home in the car with one of my friends, I totally lost it. I began to sob and couldn't stop crying. I was feeling so sorry for myself. My friend turned to me and said, "I'm tired of hearing and seeing you cry. You have children that need you, and you have to pull yourself together." I really thought that she didn't understand my problems. We went home, and I continued to feel sorry for myself. But when I got up in the morning, I went to my friend's house and thanked her for making me look at myself. I realized that I have courage and strength. My friend always believed this about me, and that's why she was able to confront me. I appreciate the gift of true friendship that she gave to me—a friendship of directness, honesty, and a true feeling of what I meant to her. She believed in me totally, and I needed to believe in myself. There are so many things that occur in people's lives that could be of help to others when they are faced with the same situation. Fortunately, I have helped many people who have been in that place and who have called me to see if I could point them in the right direction, and hopefully they gained some strength and knowledge. I have grown and have learned.—BS

When it comes to legacy, for me, my legacy is for my children. I want my children to have the experience creating their families as I had. I want them to be giving to their children so that they have at the end of their day the same kind of fulfillment looking at their children as I have looking at my children. That is what defines my happiness. When I look at my children, I have a feeling of accomplishment. I have a feeling I did it. I have children whom I brought up to be the people I wanted them to be. I had my mother, who is somehow always in my dreams, in my visions or illusions—who is my mentor and has been my whole life, and who instilled such values in me. The value of the money I will leave has very little meaning. My mother left me with no money. To have a family is the most sacred thing to have in your life. Your sibling, if you are lucky enough to have one, is the most valuable partner you have in your life. To have an alliance of family to hold onto who come from the same place is such an important asset to facing the outside world. With that sibling, you always have someone to have your back. No matter what happened in life, my mom felt her children were the most important things. The last words she said to me before I left her hospital bed were

"What are you still doing here? You have little children. Go take care of your little children. Do not take care of me. I am being taken care of." I am so disturbed by people who are my age and who do not speak to one family member or another. I believe that inside that sucks the life out of you I want my children to understand clearly that there are things that are more important than yourself. I feel that needs to be handed down to the next generation. Each of us is not that important. Everyone can be substituted. It depends what you bring to the "job" of living. If you have a soul within you, that defines you. If you do not have it, you can do the "job," but will you be remembered? I am not sure. The very defining sentence for me is "You are only as happy as your most unhappy child on any God-given day"—that is the story I live by. That is how I function.—VB

It is important to send the message that there is no shame in reaching out to others, admitting our vulnerabilities—our weaknesses—and accepting help from those who truly care about us. Connections to our family, friends, and communities are a gift we should encourage our loved ones to treasure.

5. Continuity: From Past to Future

We should not envision our legacies as static and one-dimensional, something we write that is read and then placed upon the shelf to be reread as a memoir on occasion by generations to follow. Our legacies should be dynamic and part of an ongoing conversation we have that will continue long after we die. The legacies should reflect our role as the *keepers of the meaning*, and their words should resonate with the wisdom entrusted to us for safe keeping by our parents and their parents and, too, with our own wisdom grown out of our years. They should reflect the past, the present, and all our hopes for the future. Legacies can help women appreciate that they are links in the chain that carries critical life lessons from one generation to the next. If the link is broken or damaged, continuity is at risk.

It is funny that you ask me to write about what I want to leave behind... worldly possessions don't mean much, but they are a reminder of who I am and where I have been. Memories fade, as do voices and touch. Therefore I want to leave pictures, video recordings, and some things that I have worn, perhaps jewelry, or a favorite robe that feels like me when my daughter or grandchild wraps herself in it. My life lessons have been put so eloquently into a PowerPoint presentation that my daughter, Kim, showed at my seventieth birthday party at her home. I am blessed to have a caring, thoughtful, and talented daughter who I guess learned my life lessons during her forty-five years. This is what she wrote.

Rule 1: Honor History. Know where you came from, and honor your parents, grandparents, siblings, and extended family and all their memories and stories.

Rule 2: Value Family. Always tell those you love "I love you." Know in your heart that they will not disappoint you.

Rule 3: Travel the World. Meet new people and see how the rest of the world lives. Count your blessings when you drink clean water at home. Experience the unexpected and learn from it. Finish checking off the places in my book, *A Thousand Places to See before I Die*, and have a fantastic time going there. If you don't finish the book, pass it on to your daughters or Joe's boys.

Rule 4: Silence Is Not Always Golden. Stand up for what you believe in. Stand up for choice. Be fierce like Dava, the comic book character in *Robin #49* (1998). As a Jew, never be a Jew of silence.

Rule 5: Sing. Oh yes, I am wise / But it's wisdom born of pain / Yes, I've paid the price / But look how much I gained / If I have to, I can do anything / I am strong / I am invincible / I am woman.

Rule 6: Carpe Diem. Seize the day or a moment in time. Put aside all differences, all fear, all worries and just go for it.—DGLC

6. An Opportunity to Review the Stages in Our Lives and Find Relevance in Our Stories

Retelling our stories in preparation for writing our legacies encourages us to recall who the significant individuals were in our lives and what core values they instilled in us. Most importantly, these stories prepare us for the new path we are about to forge. We have learned a lot about ourselves as our minds journeyed through our past. Each step might have conjured up an explosion of memories, causing us to pause and consider their relevance in our lives now. We ask if their underlying lessons are something we wish to share. Do they add significance to our personal tapestry?

With my bright round red nose lit up and my antlers straight, I had zipped myself into my reindeer outfit and headed for Mac's Club Deuce, a landmark bar in South Beach, Florida. I eventually had to end up at the event that I had planned to lure South Beach partiers into "Christmas in August." The club was already decorated with trees, snow, wreaths, and all the colors of the Christmas season. I decided it would be a good idea to do a little preparty advertising dressed as a reindeer. So here I was, an alcoholic in a perfect role, a costume; if I walked oddly, it was because the feet were too large. I was totally covered. I was hidden. My alcoholism was hidden. I kept telling myself not to drink too much. I still had to go to the club. It was nine o'clock. Lots of red straws were being placed in front of me as people kept buying me free drinks. Everyone knew who it was under the reindeer outfit; my drinking spoke for itself. I loved the bars, the smoke, the noise, the drunken banter, everyone trying to be someone or something—even a reindeer...I had to leave. Calling a cab, I headed for a local club. I was very unsteady on my feet. I entered through the back door to avoid the owners as the beautiful people of South Beach started to arrive. Checking with my girlfriend in the business office, we had a quick "shot" together. I headed downstairs. The mirrored balls were spinning as people skated on our fake ice and threw snowballs with our fake snow. The music was loud. I was drunk. The room was pulsating. People were everywhere. I pretended to dance with some people on the dance floor. I was in a "gray out," waving to the owners. They were happy. The bar was three deep. It was smoky; the smell of pot wafted through the air. Going to the ladies' room, I hid out for about an hour in one of the stalls. I found my favorite bartender, and she slid me White Russians until 3:00 a.m. I left for home, changed into jeans, and headed for my favorite dive bar near my apartment. I drank in this loud, smoky, bottom-of-the-pit bar until they closed. I slept for two hours and faced the ugly mirror of myself again another day. It was becoming harder to look at myself each morning. My prayer became, "Just don't let me wake up." A friend bet me I could not stay sober for a week. He had my red $100. I did not think I could, but at the end of the week and after being in and out of AA for seven years, I faced a major decision...I had seven days sober. As I write, I now have twenty-four years sober and realize that it was not just the alcohol, but I loved everything about alcohol. I was an excitement junkie for the noise, smoke, fights, loud music, gambling, all the pretty people. Until the day I realized none of it was real. Today my legacy is to bring hope to young women and every female who enters the doors of AA thinking that her life is over because she cannot be in the "fast, exciting lane." I share the reality of the truth of life without alcohol and drugs, helping each woman find her own special beauty and talents. As Robert Frost put it so beautifully, "Two roads diverged in a wood, and I— / I took the one less traveled by, / And that has made all the difference."—LB

Undoubtedly, the opportunity to study for a semester in Israel during my junior year in college is the singular event that most shaped the direction of my life. Brandeis University's Jacob Hiatt Program offered students the opportunity to pursue interests in modern Jewish history, sociology, and politics through a combination of classroom instruction, travel throughout the country, and experiential learning by meeting with the country's emerging leaders as well as working alongside professionals in various fields. I must admit that I signed up for the Hiatt Program for all the wrong reasons. At Brandeis on a full need-based scholarship, I could not afford a summer trip to Europe like many of my peers. I desperately wanted to see the historical sites and art that I had studied about in my humanities classes, and the Jacob Hiatt Program ended with a three-week trip throughout Europe. I could apply my scholarship to the cost of the program; it was my ticket to Europe. What I did not expect were the overwhelming feelings I experienced as I departed the plane at Lod Airport, now Ben Gurion Airport. I felt compelled to kneel and kiss the tarmac. I was home. The Jacob Hiatt Program was a life-changing experience. I developed a deep and abiding love of Israel. I decided to become a social worker after shadowing a social worker in Jerusalem, and I finally felt comfortable and proud in my Jewish skin wherever I went. While studying in Israel, I first heard Hillel's famous quote: "If I am not for myself, who will be for me? But if I am only for myself, who am I? And if not now, when?" Imprinted in my mind, Hillel's words often gave me the impetus and courage as a young woman to take leadership roles in the Jewish community as well as to initiate new programs from scratch in my professional life. Hillel's words also led me to attend rallies on behalf of Soviet Jewry, and that is where I sat beside a friend while waiting for the rally to begin. Somehow the conversation came around to his telling me about his "perfect" daughter, who faced difficulties in college. I can still hear him saying to me, "A, when your children are the least lovable, you have to love them the most." Additionally, my father had always told me "to never give up" in looking for a solution to a problem and used his story as a young child to illustrate his point. In 1915, he contracted polio as a preschooler, and he explained that if his parents had not gone from doctor to doctor until they'd found an orthopedist willing to operate on his withered leg, he would never have been able to walk. My friend's words, combined with my father's advice, helped me deal with those moments in life that seemed bleak and insurmountable, particularly my search to find an appropriate educational setting for my learning-disabled son, especially where none existed at the time in Miami in the Jewish world. The Department of Jewish Special Education was the result of a grass-roots survey of the need for such services and funding obtained through the Central Agency of Jewish Education. The knowledge I gained in promoting educational opportunities for learning-disabled students prepared me with a valuable skill when I became a guidance and college counselor at a local private and competitive high school. Every day I dealt with stress-related issues, both with students and their parents. In consulting about one of my students with a local pediatric psychiatrist, I happened to ask him his suggestions for maintaining good emotional health. His response, added to the previous lessons I learned, is what I would like to pass along to my grandchildren. He said simply, "Know yourself—your strengths and weaknesses—and structure your life around them." He continued, "Concentrate on what you love and do best, lower your expectations in stretching beyond your limits on what is most difficult for you, and learn to work hard." In the end, I hope that my grandchildren find fulfillment in their life's work, always take joy and pride in their Jewish heritage, and work hard, using their strengths to enrich their lives and those of their spouses and children and others around them.—AR

7. Guideline for Life

What may surprise us as we formulate our legacies is that we are actually also creating a blueprint for living out the remainder of our lives. Upon reflection, we understand that "our yesterdays came too soon" (JS), and by taking an important step forward, we must now make peace with what was. There is a new sense of urgency that pushes us to appreciate what we have and recognize that what we do not have, we are likely never to have. Instead of feeling defeated because the concept of aging has itself made us question our ability to function energetically in the present, we should feel invigorated by the idea that our future is uncertain and that we are now positioned to complete all unfinished tasks. For many of us, that could well consume all our waking hours for the next thirty-plus years.

> *As you set out for Ithaca*
> *hope the voyage is a long one,*
> *full of adventure, full of discovery.*
> —C. P. Cavafy

It is through the "journey" that we leave our legacy. We hope those who follow us will learn from our triumphs and mistakes.
How did we meet the challenge of achievement?
Are we accepting and supportive of others' ideas and efforts?
Can we be sure that the needs of others take precedence over ours when they should?
If, in my professional and personal journey, I carved a positive niche in each of these three areas, I would hope my life would have meaning to others.
Keep Ithaca always in your mind.
Arriving there is what you're destined for.
However, as I live the challenge of old age, I know there is yet another facet of legacy. One does not arrive at Ithaca. We continue to create again and again solutions to the challenges of the journey. Don't avoid the journey in old age—capture, endure, and cherish it. How freeing this concept is!—PE

It is understandable how being a baby boomer and a child of the sixties would influence and frame my thoughts on aging. The quest for personal freedom, the chutzpah to experiment, the sense of adventure, the need to know and explore…the small burst of exhilaration at finding out what the roots of your hair feel like blowing with abandon in a convertible at 120 mph. To live on the edge, in a myriad of countries, constantly allowing your instincts to soar. Learning to allow your eyes to be wide open and allow your spirit to rise. Coming to terms with what makes you exhilarated. Continuously defining your own purpose and desires, always careful to allow your senses to be alert, as you relied on "vibes" and perceptions. Trusting that the strangers you'd encounter would be worthwhile and possibly result in the colorful compilation of people you accumulate and cherish forever. Of course, everyone does not stay on board. We aren't forever young, and not everyone is worth having for the duration of the stay. For the moments that we are most alive, those are the people who stimulate our imaginations, spur our creative directions, and encourage us. To be creative requires an inner trust and childlike quality. To me this is key in remaining fresh and somewhat ageless. I always have believed that we are a compilation of our experiences. We bring each adventure with us to the next place. In keeping positive, we realize there aren't too many happenings in which a lesson isn't learned or sometimes a red flag isn't raised. Having lived in creative avant garde communities from Berkeley to the West Village in New York, I was lucky to be surrounded by intellectuals, poets, writers, artists, sculptors, architects, and students. The days were hungry. We wanted to know and feel what was out there. Create the rest. No one was too involved in pregnancy time clocks or clocks at all. It was only later, when we found ourselves in the throes of lucrative jobs, that our wrists were embellished with Rolexes and the cars we drove were fast and fabulous. Being surrounded by intelligent people who create gave way to the process of always being in a state of imagining. Not aging. As long as we kept up with healthy living, we could take something from nothing to an outcome that was new and original. Without toxicity from distractors, there is always a new way to see things. Whenever you're surrounded by "new," it is harder to buy into "old." Break up your routine. Take a class, learn something offbeat, travel a different road. As Bob Dylan said, "He who is not busy being born is busy dying."—LK

The How To's of Writing Our Legacies

Hopefully, we now have successfully established why writing a living legacy has merit. The exercise may seem a daunting one—one beyond our capabilities. But we have the tools at our fingertips. They are found in the volumes of recorded and unrecorded solutions we have fashioned to the daunting challenges we have faced. They are found in our answers to the questions detailed in the earlier chapters. It would be helpful to examine each of our answers again and determine the life lesson we have gleaned from each experience.

We (the authors) also found it extremely helpful to share our stories, exploring the past with close friends. The questions they raised seemed to stimulate our search for an even deeper meaning in those earlier reminiscences. Photo albums, old letters, and other family treasures all helped to jog our memories and enhance our recollections.

Many of us do not have the confidence in knowing exactly where to begin writing about our lives. This is not about perfecting the written word. The most important thing is what you say, not how you say it. All that is really necessary is making sure that the words reflect how you really feel, because those are the messages imprinted in the minds and influencing the actions of generations to follow.

> Since I have no grandchildren, I can only hope that the principles I have taught my children will have directed their lives. Honesty, integrity, responsibility, compassion, education, charity, reliabillity, sharing, do unto others, and above all love and laughter! I hope these have made an impact and influenced not just my family but those who have known me through these many wondrous years!—BJ

Legacies

As a guide, we are sharing with you our initial attempts at writing our legacies. We have gathered our thoughts and tried to put them out there in order to see how they actually resonate within. We have used the seven guidelines to help structure and organize what we have written. We are sure there will be further iterations as we continue to expand our insight into ourselves and into our worlds. This is a *living* legacy. We need to feel comfortable in changing or widening the scope of this gift we are bequeathing. The impact of our words will be memories shared from generation to generation. That is our role as *keepers of the meaning*.

Shakespeare: All the world's a stage...

A community supervisor once asked me if I ever thought of being on stage...and although I never took that to be a serious thought, I have recently reviewed this with a much more serious vein in thinking about my legacy. I have been on stage from the moment of birth... as I deeply believe life is a one-time performance, lived and relived through periods of great transformations involving the many aspects of theater—be it drama, comedy, or a musical—often involving great storytelling with themes of love and loss, of courage, and despair, and of resiliency. My coproducers and codirectors in life were my loving parents, who are responsible for staging my successes early in life. It was my paternal grandmother, Yetta, who arrived in America seeking freedom in the early twenties who was my silent agent extraordinaire, a title unbeknownst to her but richly deserved.

When I was ten, she moved to Florida. I enjoyed many, many hours visiting her small efficiency, surrounded by her photos; her newspaper, *The Forward*; her Shabbat candles; and a small sofa and kitchen table just large enough for us to eat, talk, and play casino. It is still hard to believe from this setting that this little lady had once been penniless, then married, raised a family of four children, was widowed early, and became a successful farmer. A businesswoman before her time. In the many hours I spent with her as a young girl, I admired her sense of independence, her connections to family, and her pride in being a "pioneer woman." I was present when collections were made weekly from her tzedakah box for charitable giving. I admired the importance she placed on family, and her gentle manner. I have tried to emulate her sense of spirituality, as it is always with me and brings tears to my eyes upon thinking about her now, tears of respect and love.

She, like my parents, demonstrated the values of honesty and the importance of being responsible and dependable and working hard for that which you think is important. They each demonstrated acts of loving kindness and sacrifice in helping others and stressed the importance of being humble in all we do, as we are but specks in the realm of a very large universe yet capable of making positive differences.

My two sisters, Barbara and Heidi, have always been a part of my performances, even if just lending a supportive role. They have taught me no matter how similar or different we may be as individuals, we are family and are there for each other with love. They have demonstrated to me that they are both resilient and determined women and are survivors of losses and of great powers for success.

To my three sons, J. D., Brett, and Geoffrey, these are the principles I have admired and attempted to live by and hope to have passed onto you, hopefully to admire and imitate to this day as well.

My life has been centered around my family first and foremost, my friends, and my community here and around the world. As I matured from a young adult into an older adult, I came upon a quote in one of my classes, which has been so much a part of who I am. It was Rabbi Tarfon, in *Pirke Avot* (a very special book on ethics), who stated, "It is not your obligation to complete the work of perfecting the world, but you are not free to desist from it either."

I chose teaching and social work as careers. When I taught young people, I enjoyed helping them grow and think for themselves, to read and explore the arts and drama, and to put on plays and learn about life, which then helped me as a parent...I was actively involved as a parent while you each attended school, and I am enjoying the time I spend with my grandchildren in their classes as well, when given an opportunity, making sure the education each receives is the best it can be. In my next career as a social worker, I still am thoroughly involved in helping people appreciate all of their many skills and talents, hoping to help them believe in themselves...become problem solvers and decision makers as well as risk takers, as I attempted to do with you. I have become a mentor to many and take pride in knowing (through their notes and calls...often years later) that their lives have been made better by my compassion for them...Most of the time

I will not know of my results, but I want you to know that as long as I feel I was there for someone and did my best, I am pleased and honored to have been given the chance to be a part of their lives... Other times I know I have not made a good connection, but I have done my best and accept that not everyone will connect with me as not everyone will like me. This is sometimes hard to accept, but it is realistic.

So in life, I believe we each find our calling—or many callings, as with me—but be the best you can be at whatever is that chosen area, and be receptive to learning and change. Nothing remains the same. Each day brings new beginnings.

Over the years, I have thought about the answer to this question: "Who is rich?" Through my many years of living, I appreciate the simple but deep response that was given to me, and now I give to each of you: "One who is happy with what he has."

As a people person, I have a tremendous number of friends from my earliest days of elementary school to the present, yet not all can be a best friend. Time and energy as well as emotional resources define our days. Sometimes I am overbooked and need to regroup for quiet time. Choose wisely, and allow yourself to share with those special people you need for you.

I have treasured many of these associations in a book club for over thirty-eight years, in a support group with like-minded woman for over eighteen years, in a peer group, and in many of the organizations that stand for the values I feel are important in life. Within each I have learned a lot about myself as well—my faults as well as my leadership abilities.

My commitment to action, be it political or social action, to right the wrongs of this world began many years ago with my involvement in organizations for creating positive change, especially in the GMJF, on a march in Washington, chairing committees on domestic violence and the abuse of women, and traveling to Poland and Israel with Holocaust survivors and teens on a program called March of the Living. It is in that last endeavor that I learned so much about life. It is my hope that each of you will continue the work of the survivors in creating love versus hate within our world and to honor them by remembering them and our past while creating a more tolerant and peaceful future. Social injustices anywhere should not be tolerated in our lifetime. My work began when I was an at-home mom and all of you were very young. Now I hope you will continue this work.

For me, life has centered around my relationships, especially as a parent. Sometimes my performances as a *mom* were of high drama, receiving poor reviews, especially by me. For those times, I hope my deep regrets will be accepted. With the gift of time, I became more tolerant and patient and less authoritarian. I know I was not always loving; yet this is one of the key qualities that my grandmother instilled in me. I failed on some occasions, but not often. In my reruns, I hope I have proven my love for each of you. Know that I will always want to be there for you.

My hope is for all three of you and my two gifted daughters-in-law, Elana and Olga, to remain close with each other for the good times as well as the difficult ones; to be curious, to love, to laugh, and to plan a lifetime of achievement for yourselves and others. Travel often, especially when in your most physically fit shape.

Remember that relationships with all ages, from the youngest person to your oldest acquaintance, are worthy and deserve your respect. Honesty goes both ways, and when one must give a critique of another or disagree with another, the human element of respect for others' opinions and differing ideas needs always to be present—no matter how difficult. Relationships take time and work. Make them work for each of you, and when it is time to end a relationship, do it with dignity, leaving room to renew if desired. Trust your own judgment, and follow your instincts. Knowing how good each of you is as an individual makes me proud to say you are my sons.

I value the love, deep respect, and trust Dad and I have shared with each other, our immediate family, and extended family. With Dad we had never-ending action, magic, travel, trains, games, and an abundance of laughter—ingredients I hope you instill in each of your lives. May our grandchildren, Jack, Eden, Stella, and Evita, enjoy the stories of your pasts—at least those that you are able to share; there were several that may be in question (nothing too, too bad but some not to be wanted for my grandchildren).

When I am no longer here, I would want you to think about my performance as one that was always a work in progress, and I hope you will give it a lifetime achievement award as I tried my best to be the best. Yes, I have accumulated plenty of "stuff," but it is a reminder of the essence of each person from whom I received an object that I treasure. And until that time that I need to toss those objects, they act as connectors to my past and the wonderful souls with whom I have connected. Some have been designated for each grandchild with open choosing when they visit.

I give to you what your dad inscribed to me on my wedding band: With all my love for always.

Your Loving Mom
—GKH

"When tomorrow comes, this day will be gone forever. In its place is something that you have left behind…Let it be something good."—Anonymous

It has taken many years, much self-reflection, and the wisdom only age can bring to even begin to make meaning of the above quote. And even now, in what might be called the twilight of my life, I still have trouble making each day count, although I am improving. It has been a long journey, and as I continue to live and grow, I try daily to reflect on all I have to be grateful for. And that reflection led me to believe, despite my complaints, that I have had a wonderful life.

Through the years I have had more than the usual amount of fantastic friends, friends who supported me through a nasty divorce, raising my children, and overall helping me look at my life with a more positive attitude when I felt down. Sometimes I wonder what I have done to deserve the love and friendship given to me.

I am grateful to my good friends who introduced me to such things as camping trips in the mountains and allowed me to accompany them on fabulous trips to the great Northwest, hiking beautiful trails and seeing the sights of our wonderful national parks. These are some of my most treasured memories.

Hiking the trails of the Rocky Mountains now, I am grateful that with two bad knees, I can still make it. I go a little slower now, but it gives me more time to take in the beauty that surrounds me. I know I have grown because I am happy to be doing this and not too upset that I cannot do what I used to.

Today I am grateful for the opportunity to be working in a career that brings meaning to my life. As a social worker and early-childhood educator, my work allows me to provide guidance and training to professionals who work with our community's most vulnerable and needy children, giving my life purpose.

I can't leave this page without saying how grateful I am for my good health. As I see friends depart, I hope I can maintain a high degree of physical and mental health until the end.

My life, according to my mother, started in a hospital where for ten days she wondered who the screaming baby in the nursery was and how she felt sorry for that poor mother. Of course, that scream belonged to none other than her own little darling. I remember as I was growing up that my mother was high strung and didn't take things in stride, always worrying about some impending catastrophic event. I'm sure I was a challenge for her, always questioning, always ready for an argument. I remember once at the age of around five (I don't actually remember this—only what my mother used to say), when my mother asked me to come in from outside, I defiantly stuck my tongue out at her. When my father arrived that evening and she recounted the day's event, he asked me, "Did you stick your tongue out at your mother?" My response was, "Oh no, Daddy, I just stuck it out in the sun to dry!" So no wonder my mother might have had some difficulty with me, which I think remained the status quo through my adolescence.

My mother was a beautiful, talented, and brilliant woman. She would have preferred a job in theater or as a singer. Her own grandmother was said to have been an opera singer in Europe. She was raised in a family of five siblings during the worst depression this country has ever seen. As a poor girl, she made the best of things, going to school in her gym suit. After high school she went to Hebrew normal school but eventually landed a job at Schraft's candy store as a bookkeeper. I guess for a high-strung mother, I might not have been the right fit, active from the start and perhaps what today would be called a challenging child. A first child, born during the war in a tense historical period to a hardworking family, I do believe my parents tried hard to give me what I wanted and to make sure I was not lacking. I remember stories about receiving a Shirley Temple doll that cost fifty dollars in a time when my father only made fifty dollars per week. I believe my parents tried their best to give their children what they could. I know they both loved me and my brother passionately and did the best they could for us. On my mother's side, I was the first grandchild. We were very close with my grandparents and spent many weekends sleeping at their home. Three and a half years after my birth, my brother was born. He was a beautiful and also talented child who could sing Al Jolson songs as though he were Al Jolson. Everyone wanted to hear him sing at family gatherings, so of course he took the limelight.

My father was a hardworking man who was very close to his family. Busy working when I was growing up, in later years, after retirement, he couldn't do enough for me and my children. He took up cooking as a hobby and was always baking or cooking for us. My book club friends still remember his "Lindy's" cheesecake that he made every time the members came to my home.

I always saw myself as one with no talent, perpetuating this belief throughout my life. At extended family dinners, I was encouraged to mouth the words when the singing began. In elementary school, I was smart but always worried about getting things right, always anxious about performance. During my growing-up years, I saw little of my father. He worked in his contracting business by day and at a local factory making some kind of war materials at night. It was a time of difficulty, not only for our family but for the nation. Two of my younger uncles served in the army, one in Japan and one in Germany. I am sure this caused much stress.

I was a shy child with few friends who loved to listen to my mother read fairy tales. I spent my elementary years in the library making books my friends and living vicariously through the stories of the protagonists. I still believe in stories and get great pleasure in reading. This is a gift my mother gave me, as I still believe in happy endings and the possibility of hope for the future. To this day I am an avid reader and encourage reading to all children. I especially loved reading to my grandchildren as they were growing up.

We had to move to Florida just as I was beginning high school, which took me away from any stability I had found. Living in a small two-bedroom apartment with my mother and brother while my father stayed up north to work, I started at a school where "snowbirds" were basically unwanted. I did not have the skills needed to make a lot of friends and floundered around for three years before I left for college.

Once at college, I was initiated into a sorority where, for the first time in my life, I had friends who were my "sisters." Belonging to a group was a meaningful part of my life. Although most of the connections are now lost, the good feelings of those connections seemed to be the precursors of my later abilities to relate to others. Today I am most fortunate to have a wonderful group of true friends who have supported me emotionally during my entire adult life.

After having two small children and a difficult divorce, I was lucky enough to meet a man who would become my husband and who raised my sons as his own. We have a daughter whom we both adore and who has given us much joy. For me, it's always been about family. This is the essence of life and a message I hope I have passed on to my children.

I have always been a passionate person with a drive to succeed in every endeavor. Fearful of failure, I pushed myself to do my best and never give up. After dropping out of college to get married, I eventually went back to school and earned a bachelor's degree, followed by an MSW and eventually a PhD. For me, this was a defining moment.

Raising my children, I strived to be the best mother I could. I believe despite all the difficulties I encountered, my three children grew up with fine moral principles and the ability to work hard for their respective goals. All three are wonderful parents and collectively have raised seven of my grandchildren with good value systems and wonderful work ethics.

I think of my children and grandchildren and watch how they live their lives. The boys are devoted fathers and care deeply about their families. My daughter, a single mother with two small girls, juggles between work and home, trying to provide the support that her children need, emotionally and financially. Each of them, in their own ways, contributes to the betterment of society. If that is my legacy, what more can I ask for?

My grandchildren have always been a major focus of my life. I love to be with them and have tried to enjoy every moment that we share together. I had the joy of being present at two of their births. I try to provide experiences with them, to the best of my ability, that will be meaningful in the present and provide fond memories of me when I am gone. I think of my parents and grandparents and forever hold them in my heart. They were not perfect, but the stories about them provide insight into who I am and what I have passed down. I try to share the stories of my past and my parents' past. It is only a partial oral history, but it's the most I have. Today, no doubt, everything will be recorded technologically and kept for posterity. I have fleeting glances of albums of beautiful greeting cards my mother had pasted in a photograph book, her old photos, and memories of strong bonds with my extended family on both my mother's and my father's side. To this day, my cousins and I feel the importance of seeing one another, although we are geographically far, and share wonderful stories we remember about our lives as children.

A legacy is created by one's life. Even as we live, we are forever creating our legacies by the way that we live. Our deeds, our words, our contributions—all are part of who we are.

I believe that my parents provided me with a good value system, the love of learning, and the ability to enjoy life. While this might have been peppered with a little neurosis, I feel strong and able to face life's challenges. I pray I will be healthy to the end of my days and able to continue to give to others. My passion and love for children has led me to a career in social work and early-childhood education, where I continue to put my efforts in the hope that all children will have a good start in life. I hope I can continue to do this for as long as possible, as it provides meaning to my life.
—MCL

Within each of us, oftentimes tucked away out of the conscious reach of everyday thoughts, lies the essence of the legacy we hope to leave of our lives. Maybe we do not want to think about it, as we may believe it portends the finale, our closing act. Strange as it may sound, I remember very clearly the moment I began to design the first square of the patchwork quilt that would be my life's legacy—a dynamic blend of stitching, revealing all its flaws and inconsistencies. I was a woman in my early forties with so many dreams, a family I treasured, and much to accomplish.

Why was I thinking about my legacy? It is a simple story. I was attending a funeral of a woman I hardly knew. My husband had asked me to attend. It was an incredibly beautiful spring day, and like so many that time of year, the sun was shining brilliantly. Odd, how clearly I can remember that day. I sat at the back of the funeral home as the family took its place next to her casket. I was lost in my own thoughts when the rabbi began his eulogy. Almost thirty years later, the memory of his words still resonates within me. His eulogy described a woman whose appearance—the magnificence of her clothing, the importance of how she presented herself to the community—was the essence he captured that day, the "legacy" she would leave behind for her children and grandchildren who sat there listening. It was the first time that I had ever thought about what someone might say about me at my funeral. It was the first time I had ever thought about what I wanted to be said about me.

That very day I began asking myself those "soul-searching" questions. I only hoped there would be more to say than that I had put away a magnificent Chanel suit for my burial, or that people always confused me as the sister of my youngest child. One's legacy as a woman, a wife, a mother and grandmother, a sister, and so many other important roles it takes a lifetime to create is always a work in progress until we die. As others my age and younger search to find solutions for sagging eyelids and jowls, for crow's feet circling eyes and mouths, for "squishy arms and necks" (as my granddaughter calls them), I am still stuck deep in my soul doing repairs. A "nip and tuck" of my spirit, I often think.

My legacy—a quilt of a dizzying assortment of colors and shapes—does not only grow out of my devotion to family and causes or out of the successes in my career. My legacy also grows out of the struggles at the core of who I am. A core fashioned by the deft hands of a strong-willed yet loving mom. Of a father's words of wisdom silenced at the cusp of my teens. Of the love and adoration of two amazingly talented sisters. Of a husband whose love for his family and zest for people and places has taken me on the most extravagant journey of a lifetime. Of two incredibly gifted children and grandchildren who are generous of spirit and have taught me what really matters in life. And of a gaggle of exceptionally talented women who have honored me with their friendship. My legacy also grows out of the struggles at the core of who I wanted to be and how I anguished over how to get there.

My legacy is a series of connections, some randomly linked, others strategically attached, stitched and restitched to each other to support it and protect it from the helter-skelter of life's experiences. Through my Hebrew name, I was connected to my maternal grandmother. But it was not just simply her name that was our bond. My mother's stories spoke of her sincerity, of her ability to extend herself beyond her comfort level and make others around her feel safe and protected. Her role was to give comfort to all the souls she touched with her kindness. The peasants for whom she sewed and those for whom she baked set aside their prejudices and welcomed her in. Even as a young child, I felt a spiritual connection with her and seemed to sense, long before Brian Weiss introduced me to regression therapy as a window to our past, that I was responsible for embodying her legacy into the future. I felt so proud to have been asked to carry that mantle, although I am not sure I was ever able to feel I did it true justice.

My parents created a household where music, literature, theater, and education were an integral part of our daily life. Although in my father's words, "Your mother is always to be treated like a china doll on a pedestal," he nevertheless was the first voice in my life that spoke passionately for equal opportunity for women—primarily for his three daughters. The three of us grew up believing that we could have a meaningful career and still create loving and caring homes. We could do it all. I certainly took my father's words to heart as I spent many years of my adult life studying and retooling my skills, never forgetting the meaning of family and its importance with every breath I took. I never felt conflicted, as my husband, children, and I seemed to move in tandem. Maybe it is my life through rose-colored glasses, but somehow I always felt that we were an integrated whole.

After my dad died when I was fourteen, my connection was to my older sister, Edie. My mother withdrew; her grief consumed her for years. Together my sister and I struggled to try to keep the semblance of family alive, learning along the way. It was my connection to her that kept me upright, never noticing as a self-centered teen that she was struggling herself to just keep afloat. My closest girlfriend and her parents enveloped me, never allowing me to feel sorry for myself or feel different or feel alone. All my friends surrounded me and protected me, although they were not really aware of how critical they were to my survival. Somehow the need to rekindle those relationships has brought meaning once again as we approached seventy. From those early years, I learned how essential women's friendships were to me and have spent my life nurturing those relationships.

It was my connection to my husband that marked the true beginning of my life as an adult, the haze of grief and sadness set off to the side as together we made way for an adventure. He gave me the encouragement to look at living with an enthusiasm and positivity I had never known before. He helped me to understand that I alone was the master of my own successes and achievements. And yet I always felt so safe, as I knew he had my back and would always be there to catch me when I stumbled or fell. We were both far from perfect, but there was always a genuine respect for the gifts that the other possessed, and each of our strengths meshed perfectly as we forged our ever-changing path.

My legacy was also born out of the connection to my students those early days in April 1968, when we huddled together, stunned by the news of Martin Luther King's death and unsure of what would now be each of our paths for the future. It was fashioned by the million people we walked beside down Pennsylvania Avenue in Washington, DC, that day in 1972, with our son, sitting on our shoulders, as we shared the goal that the Vietnam War must end. It was sustained by the connection to that football player, harnessed to the machine turning ever so slowly in the spinal cord unit, that gave me time to talk with him about his past and how who he had become would influence our present. It was shaped as I stood, flowers in hand, watching new Americans uncertain about their decision to abandon their roots begin again in a strange and mysterious country. It was molded as I walked across the stage to receive my law degree at forty-four to the applause of a loving and supportive family and friends. It was transformed as I watched my husband proudly hood each of our children—our son, Scott, and daughter, Deanna—as well as our son-in-law, Michael, and pass the mantle to them so that they could now make their own personal contributions to medicine and to the betterment of their patients. It was created at the sight of each of my grandchildren, Andrew and Sophie, at birth as I wished for them all the excitement and promise the world had given me, each of them carrying forward the names of their incredible great-grandparents and the rich legacy those names brought with them.

As I have looked back and reexamined all these relationships, these connections, I recognize that my legacy is merely an extension of all the messages about values, character, and the choices we have to make received from all those significant people who have indelibly influenced my life. I can see that what I am is just a distributer of goods—the goods of the human soul. I did not create those goods. I am the jobber of goods—like my maternal grandfather. The goods were crafted by my grandmother, my parents, my siblings, my husband and children, and the many people I have met along the way.

Maybe it was through my work as a teacher and social worker that I was able to channel the essence of my grandmother's being. My father used to say of her that without any degrees, she instinctively knew how best to counsel people about their life decisions, how best to listen compassionately to other people's pain, how best to withstand adversity and land flat on her feet. I am still a work in progress but have always used her skill set as a guiding light, sometimes more successfully than at other times. But her lessons were so inspirational.

Maybe it was through parenting that I was able to channel the essence of my grandmother. Again, my children will tell you that I had many shortcomings, but I tried to always be there to listen and to give advice—solicited and unsolicited. But I do believe that they always knew that I was by their sides, along with their dad, to weather the storm—and we had quite a few. But it was my grandmother's instinctive faith in the human spirit, surging through every fiber of my being, that allowed me not to be discouraged or change direction. We are a loving and caring family, and our loyalty and respect for each other to seek his/her own challenges has given us all, including our grandchildren, the sense that we stand united.

My legacy, like my life, I guess, continues to be a work in progress. When I was a young parent, I am certain I would have wanted to be remembered as a devoted and selfless mother, wife, sister, daughter, friend, professional. I would have wanted to be remembered as energetic and compassionate, as a team player and as a team leader. I would have wanted to be remembered as a champion of our community, as a proud caretaker of its values and ethics. I would have wanted my children to feel pride in my commitments and to believe that by living according to those commitments, I was leaving the world a better place.

In my fifties, with children on their own and beginning over in a new city, I would have like to be remembered as someone who was comfortable enough to meet the challenges of starting one's life over again, of accepting that a leadership role in my community was something in my past. The pressure to do it all was obviated by the pressure to do what it took to find a safe place and be satisfied, a place the children could still call home and find solace from the trials of becoming independent adults, and where work was a comfortable place to still make a small difference.

Now as I reach my seventies, I have circled back to reinforce the stitching on my well-worn quilt—my enthusiasm for learning, the importance of nurturing those you love, a respect for others and for myself, and the significance of passing on the meaning fostered by my parents and sisters, who were the cornerstones of the family I have spent a lifetime working to construct.

Who could have ever asked for more than to travel the world with a husband that was the master at it? Oftentimes just a half step behind, I was always delighted at the world he uncovered before me. Every place was a wonderland because he made it that way. His love for people and new experiences was infectious, and the children, their partners, grandchildren, and I are constantly swept up into the excitement of every new day. I continue to respect his unselfishness to his patients and his kindness and compassion to them. He has always set an extraordinary example for us all to live by.

Who could have ever asked more than to be blessed with my two loving and devoted children, Scott and Deanna? From the time they were small and we forged our way south, we were a strong and committed unit to each other and to our community. Scott and Dee taught me to love so deeply in a way I could have never imagined. They delighted me with their excitement over every new thing we learned together. I could not help but feel their every pain, only I am sure I felt it more profoundly because I could not always make it better. Today they are extraordinary human beings filled with compassion and an unselfish devotion to their careers, to their phenomenal partners, Mike and Robert, and to our incredible grandchildren, Andrew and Sophie—the children I never could have imagined loving more than my own two.

For friends and family who know me the best, I apologize for being too passionate about things that others might have felt unimportant and for wanting to live by principles that were probably way beyond my reach. But I would like to believe that I did everything because I truly wanted to make this world a more loving and caring place and to forge lasting and meaningful connections based on an abiding love and compassion for every human being.

—CTS

<u>Thoughts to Remember</u>: To make the process as "stress free" as possible, we have provided a list of guidelines that hopefully will help in processing the information we all want to share:

1. Identify the significant moments along our developmental timeline that speak to the opportunities and the disappointments that may have influenced the changes in our lives.
2. Identify the traditions and rituals that were significant and why they were so important.
3. Identify the significant people and what contributions they made to each one of us.
4. Identify the lessons and values learned and why it is so important to pass them on to others.
5. Identify what were the historical events or periods that were significant in defining us.
6. Identify our interests and what makes them so significant.
7. Identify the significant choices we made and how those choices may have changed the landscape of our lives.
8. Identify our achievements and failures and what lessons can be learned about ourselves.

LIST OF QUESTIONS TO REVIEW

What are your life goals for the next years?

What beliefs and values do you want to hand down to others?

How would like others to remember you?

PERSONAL REFLECTIONS

CHAPTER 9
Changing the Landscape of Aging

And make this moment last,
Because the best of times is now,
Is now, is now.
—La Cage Aux Folles

And then the knowledge comes to me that I have space
within me for a second, timeless, larger life.
—R. M. Rilke

T he sixty-plus woman of today is being swept up in the rapid changes that are redefining the landscape of aging. Less than thirty years ago, approximately 6 percent of the population of the United States was sixty-five years and older. In 2010, that figure doubled and is expected to reach 20 percent by the year 2050. What may be both surprising and encouraging is that the fastest-growing segment in America is the elderly eighty-five years and older, and that population has also doubled since 1985.

Recently, I moved out of state to be closer to my children and relocated happily in an adult independent living facility. I have meaningful activities throughout the week: writing, art, political science, and music classes, to name a few. When I was congratulated recently upon reaching my ninety-second birthday, I said that I am among the young here. We recently celebrated a man's birthday who was 103 and another who was 101. EB

No question that the boomer generation and beyond are living longer. In 1950 life expectancy for women was seventy-one years as compared to 2010, when it reached eighty-one years. So the latest refrain adopted by energetic older adults that "seventy is the new sixty" is more than hyperbole.

With a twelve percent strength in numbers comes power for older Americans. It would be foolish to sit back and allow the world around us to interpret the changes and legislate our future when we can be the masters of our own destiny.

The growing numbers of energetic and competent elderly in the population will no doubt have a tremendous impact not only on the psyche of those of us who are aging but on the perceptions of the younger generations whose views have dominated societal values and the social construct of our country. Older women have decried society for abandoning them, for characterizing them as useless or, even worse, invisible. In order to compete, women over sixty have had to continually refurbish aging parts, retool skills, and re-create images. It's exhausting! But does any of it actually change thinking?

> Recently, more and more, I have been thinking about the past and how I will spend the rest of my life. I grew up in a time when women were struggling with equality in the workplace, so I feel lucky I was able to work as an art director and then in management as a creative director and vice-president of communication and branding— and most of all that I worked to age seventy in a very young and changing field. I do wish my last job had turned out differently and I could have stayed there a few more years. Starting something new at seventy is difficult. On the other hand, the job was extremely time consuming—I worked until eight or nine many nights, came home, and often did work past midnight. I worked most every weekend, and taking vacations with our very exhausting schedule was tough. So now I have more time with my husband, who is ten years older than me but still works (lucky man). We see friends a lot more—and since our first grandson was born right after I left my job, I have the opportunity to see him a lot and be part of his life (something that would have been difficult with my former job). All of this is good and appreciated, but it's not enough. Some of my friends lunch daily, go to movies during the day, and travel quite a bit. That's not how I see myself spending the future. While I enjoy movies and theater and

meeting friends for lunch or dinner, it is not the main event. It is only topping on the cake. And while travel sounds great, I hate to fly and am only interested in a modest amount of travel now. What would make me happy is some meaningful work. I know that there are many people in my position—people are living longer and having healthier lives, and frankly, many need to work. I have watched great progress over the years (though more is still needed), from the civil rights movement to the women's movement and the gay right movement; now I hope for a comparable surge for elder work rights. I remember my mother, after she was widowed for the second time in her late sixties, was still strong and able; she used to talk about the "golden years" and how they weren't golden. Now I can see what she meant, and I wish she were alive so I could tell her that I understand—I don't think I conveyed that when she was alive. I don't think young people really "get it." Recently a close friend was on a very difficult ten-day hike in Corsica and disappeared. He was seventy, a psychiatrist who had a practice in New York and one in New Jersey, traveled all over the world, climbed mountains, ran marathons, and hiked in unusual and strange places. When the search was ended and his death assumed, his family said that he had done everything, and if he lived, he would just be doing things over again. That made me sad—I know they were saying that to make themselves feel better, but I never knew anyone so full of life—and there is always so much more—we just need to figure out what more is and how to do it. I think my friend could have told us. Looking back, I can take some satisfaction in what I have accomplished, but there is also dissatisfaction: I wish I had done better, gone farther, been more successful. Now I am seventy-two—I am healthy, strong, have lots of energy, and want to stay relevant. It is more important for me to look forward and find new ways to be productive. I do not want to waste the time I have left.—SC

One cannot discount that many of us approach the final third of our lives with an awareness of our vulnerability. As we age, we may be facing losses: loss of mental acuity, loss of physical capability, loss of partners. With aging there may be lifestyle changes. We may "age out" of certain activities simply because we do not have the same amount of energy we had in previous years. Because of external forces beyond our control (e.g., employer restrictions, changing economies, workforce dynamics favoring younger employees), we may not be able to continue in careers that had provided meaning and purpose in our lives. This may leave us feeling negative, lost, and depressed.

"Searching"
It takes a village
To raise a child
True or false you say?
Who is right or who is wrong
Who will grow wicked
Who will wax strong?
Choosing heaven or hell, who can foretell?
From the same eternal seed
Love or hate can spring
Twisting, turning as it spins
Into a whirling ring
How to disperse the dangerous clouds
Before a village sinks
Searching, searching for an answer
For that elusive link.
—AO

Yet as Brene Brown, PhD. (2011) has acknowledged, vulnerability is both the "core of difficult emotions" such as "fear, grief, and disappointment" as well as "the birth-place of wonderful ones like love, empathy, innovation, and creativity." She goes on to write, "When we shut ourselves off from vulnerability, we distance ourselves from the experiences that bring purpose and meaning to our lives."

When someone our age is given a cancer diagnosis, it might be easier for us to just lie down on the couch and remain there. How vulnerable we feel when we are given the treatment options and the myriad of consequent side effects that come with them. Yet "giving up the good fight" has never been a part of my DNA, because I am not a quitter by nature. At those times when I can muster my energy and go out and feel connected to friends and family who bring meaning to my everyday life, I feel most centered. I value those connections I have with my women friends who have been my lifeline forever. My life has been fairly complicated, so I value the fact that I have lifelong friends who have stuck by me. I value that we can still learn so much from each other. I value that I have the time to share my stories with my family and friends so that they can understand where I came from, what I have learned, and how all that influences my decisions. Most importantly, I realize how crucial it is to make the most of the hours, or even minutes, when I can escape from feelings of vulnerability and open myself up to the challenge of making every hour and minute meaningful. Making my life meaningful now is my top priority. So when I visit the doctor, I take charge of my care. I ask the questions that my husband and children may be too afraid to ask. I want to know the facts. The chemotherapy treatment has become a metaphor for my life. I spend my days now "infusing" my life with significant moments that can enrich who I am and the relationships I hold most dear. I used to be so fearful and isolated, but now I have opened myself to everyone's love and the opportunity of having them with me and even help me if I need that help.—Anonymous

Consequently, as we reach the upper limits of our timelines, each of us has an opportunity to make critical choices about how we wish to spend our remaining time on this earth. If we heed Dr. Brown's words, we should embrace the vulnerabilities that result as part and parcel of the aging process with the passion, enthusiasm, and energy that have been our hallmarks throughout our lives.

Maybe it would be useful to first look beyond our own internal battle: how we as a sixty-plus sisterhood survive this next third of our lives. Central to understanding the phenomenon of society's discrimination of older adults, we need to examine the basic foundations of our belief system. Our country was built on the principles of Puritanism. The ideals of independence and individual rights are based in the culture brought to our shores by the Puritan settlers. Their core principles colored the essence of the rights created in our Constitution. Because we place great value on being independent and self-sufficient, young adults are naturally elevated to a higher status because they have the greatest opportunity and energy to be self-reliant.

Unfortunately, those principles also influence the American view of aging. The loss of independence is oftentimes associated with aging adults and thus diminishes their power and respect in the greater community. Simple as it seems, many researchers studying the aging adult cite this rationale for how we view the aged in this country and why our treatment of older people is so different than in most other cultures. In societies where communal responsibility is sacrosanct, the aged are revered.

With that in mind, we can next examine the distinction between "old" and "aging." Is this distinction merely one of semantics, or is there an actual demonstrable difference? For us, aging refers to a process...and old is where we find ourselves at the end of that process. Old connotes finality. Old reflects our mortality. And most important, it is quite possible that we might never get to old! Aging is a dynamic process and could, if we allowed it, speak to our persistent effort to evolve. After all, aren't we *aging* our entire lives?

Why then does society view aging as a negative?

Should it not be our task to reconstruct the societal model of aging and restore the respect preceding generations had for their matriarchs? Should we not take control of the narrative on aging? Isn't that what the more than four hundred women's stories did? For most, *old* was not part of their narratives. Rather they shared the wisdom they had gathered from living.

> Old is when you give up! Aging has to do with the mind and the body.—E

> "Life is like a hot bath: the longer you stay in, the more wrinkles you get!" Hope we get lots of wrinkles!—PK

> We don't stop playing because we grow old, we grow old because we stop playing.—George Bernard Shaw

It may be surprising to you, as it was to us, that research on aging has dispelled the myth that healthy adjustment to aging is largely dependent on economic security and mental and physical health. Other myths have also dominated the dialogue on aging. For example, older women are thought to be

1. not as competent as younger women,
2. concerned with ideas that are outdated and inconsequential, and
3. fragile and compromised.

I am one hundred years old right now. I am discouraged with the politics of today in America. I always voted for the person rather than the party. Today it seems so unfair that neither side can work together. My country, America, displayed the Statue of Liberty, the welcoming of immigrants. I feel so bad about the hatred of people to people in this world today. There seems to be no respect for the president of the United States, and he is brilliant. Murders are reported on a daily basis, as well as the lack of gun control laws. The environment is in trouble, there are no jobs, and people are hungry. It is now hard to look on the bright side. Honesty and fairness are what is important to me. Today I have to be satisfied. I have my wonderful children and grandchildren; I have a few friends in my building; and I have my activities—including my weekly nail appointment and a caretaker who reminds me each day as she leaves, "Miss I, be careful. " So I do use my chair/walker but look forward to Sunday when I take charge.—ITD

Studies have demonstrated that characteristics such as *resiliency* and *connectedness* are far greater determinants of well-being in aging adults.

As we round out our lives, connecting with those who were there at the beginning has been fulfilling. I love the unique space we've created, one we can visit day or night. In good times and bad. In sickness and health.—TS

I think there is something nice about reconnecting with folks with whom one had a history.—LFG

Connor and Davidson (2003) have devised a scale that measures resiliency in older populations. Those individuals who displayed a sense of "personal control and goal orientation," an ability to adapt and tolerate negativity, a demonstration of leadership and a "trust in their own instincts," and a capacity for "coping through spirituality" tended to exhibit "optimism, successful aging, social engagement, and fewer cognitive complaints." Throughout this book, we have seen how celebrating extraordinary relationships serves as a promoter of healthy aging.

> You should surround yourself with friends that can make you better—people who nurture your soul. Seek out friends that are kinder, smarter, and more thoughtful than yourself. You need the ability to listen and to give the gift of curiosity. A true friend inspires you to be the best self that you can be. There are lots of heartbreaks in the world. You need to be with your friends during all kinds of travails and difficulties.—Anonymous

Igniting our memories by recalling events and relationships is critical to successful aging. These memories are created when thousands of neurons fire in a unique pattern. Focusing on the memory reinforces and strengthens the pattern. The more often the memory is activated, the stronger and more permanent the bonds are in the pattern. As we challenge ourselves and our aging brains with new experiences and with the task of remembering the old ones, we promote not only the reshaping and growth of our brain's neural network but also an optimistic view of our potential as women and of the powerful networks we have established with our friends and family.

We believe that essential to our adjustment to aging is acknowledging that the *future is the present*. Once we recognize the sense of immediacy inherent in this statement, we become the architects of our own landscape of aging. The attitudes that inspire the design for our landscape also will govern our successes. Although at times we may get mired in thoughts such as "Where will I be for the milestones in our family's life?" we first have to appreciate how lucky we are to have made it to our age, as many friends and family members have not been as fortunate. With that recognition comes a responsibility to make the most of the choices we make.

> Today is my present and is shaped by both the good and the bad of my life's experiences. As I age, I am comfortable with who I am. I have much less time ahead, so I spend time enjoying each day with friends, plan time alone, play bridge several times a week (including tournaments), and enjoy the game of mah-jongg. As an avid reader since childhood, I enjoy a good book or see a good movie and plan dinners with friends. I thoroughly enjoy time with my ten-year-old great-nephew and his enthusiasm, which I hope serves him for the rest

of his life. I've become very mellow, and everything I thought should be on my soapbox no longer exists. I am no longer opinionated, even though I do have opinions. What made the difference for the change? I have had many experiences that are more serious than most people, so I do not stress about less important things. Just let everyone live their lives, and let me live mine. For younger people I can understand the striving for the better things in their lives; as I got older, I realized I was never assertive, competitive, or wanting to reach the top plateau of anything, but as I reflect, I understand myself and I'm okay with who I am. My son David died at age sixteen of cancer. At age thirty-six, I was diagnosed with stage II melanoma and then twelve years ago, at age fifty-eight, with stage II breast cancer. Therefore I do not worry about things I have no control over. I realized at a young age my family was dysfunctional, and it helped me learn to cope with life. We are who we are, and old age only accentuates all of our personality characteristics. I see myself as a small part in the universe. I have never been the center. I am not so important in this universe that I should demean anyone or look down on anyone or think that I am more important than anyone. I allow myself ten minutes of self-pity if I'm feeling sorry for myself, and I tell myself I am wasting my time. I am an observant person by nature and grew up seeing unbelievable poverty in the Orient, where I grew up as a child in the fifties, and I saw and realized how lucky I was then. Today as I look out upon the ocean from a beautiful apartment and have clothes in my closet and food in my belly, knowing many people are starving, I always have to recognize how lucky I am, because I feel I have so much.—CJS

At this age health issues may limit certain activities. We can still continue to express ideas and experiences.—BS

We are looked over and considered to be worthless! Our thoughts are not valued or considered to be interesting...I would like to be noticed for someone who can contribute to society from time to time...Aging in itself is not the problem, it's how we deal with the aches and pain! And the limits our bodies have to deal with at this time...I think I'm most proud of raising our children, but I do believe in luck and believe we were very lucky! I don't believe there is anything one can do about getting old except to keep trying to stay well and looking good.—MB

I think we are so busy trying to stay young, but no matter what we do, we are going to grow old. When I tell someone how old I am, if they are younger, their first response is "You look much younger!" My response is that this is what sixty-eight looks like now. Sixty *is not* the new forty. Let's talk more about what happens as you age. Having watched both my mother and mother-in-law age, I am very aware of what is in store for me.—GM

Redesigning the Landscape of Aging: For Ourselves and For Others

When we look back at the feminist movement of the sixties and seventies, the goals addressed fundamental barriers to the rights of women, from family life to the workplace. Because of their well-defined focus, feminists were able to empower women's lives by dismantling the historical acceptance of a patriarchal society that devalued both political and personal equality for women. We believe that it is time to tweak the sensibilities of our current society, to raise the consciousness of our youth-driven culture that regards the aging woman as *invisible*.

When I think about the landscape of aging, I am thinking about the comparison between older women and older men. The comparison is very straightforward in our lifetime. Older women are compared to old rags or older rags. Or become invisible beings. While older men are compared to cheese—the older the cheese the better. It is very unfair treatment by our society. It is a vision that is inherently wrong. There really are no differences between old men and old women. They are both old. The values and practices of the society we live in are determined by the young. The young are running the scene. In the past, people our age used to vanish very slowly from the picture, and then they were dead. But thanks to modern medicine, we are still around. All of a sudden, industry started to cater to our needs. All of a sudden, you listen to the TV and you hear about Viagra. Twenty years ago there were no advertisements for older people. We are being

345

recognized. As long as the younger generation is running the show and everything is geared toward youth and toward being thin and thinner, toward beauty in any form or shape or enhancement of beauty, we must face the fact that we do not stand a chance. We can only have a legacy about what we have to say, not about how we look. We should not be tempted to give in to beauty regimens, to put on this or that to look younger, or to wear short sleeves because the wings of our upper arms are going to fly in the wind. I do not think so. I think differently. I am sixty-four, but I have never defined myself by how I looked. When I was younger, I probably was better than I am now, but I refuse to be defined by my looks. You do not define men by their looks. I am not sure what it takes to change what is a male-oriented society, but we as women have to demand that we are not judged by what we look like but rather by what we have to say, by who we are, by the roles we fulfill in our capacity as mothers, as girlfriends. We have to define ourselves and not leave our definition to others. Older men, especially those with money, get everything they want in the world. For men, age is not a problem. But men are working in a different realm. I do not want to be remembered by my family, and by my daughters in particular, as a beautiful old woman when I die. I want to be remembered by what I said, by what I did, by what I stressed in my life that was important to me. That is my main goal.—VB

To make changes, we need to galvanize the growing population of women over sixty. Just as the leadership in the sixties and seventies streamlined their goals to win support, we need to craft a strategy that is simple and speaks to our strengths and to our value in society. Our campaign will likely not take women to the streets with placards. We are not sure that that would even resonate with our base. Rather, we need to seek out like-minded women who are willing to band together and speak out to dispel the myths of aging and to address how *women of age* are continuing to evolve.

How would you change the landscape of aging for women in our current society?

First of all, our society needs to accept that life is finite. We cannot just wake up one day and realize we are old; we must prepare ourselves for aging.

1. Start exercising at least four to five days a week.
2. Do not let yourself gain more than ten pounds, and try to go back to your weight at age forty.
3. Eat well (healthy).
4. Take care of mind and spirit: meditate, practice yoga.
5. Find a goal you love and then pursue it.
6. Know that you are born alone and will die alone; don't expect that your husband or children will fill your needs. Make new friends if your old ones are no longer here or are too depressing. Never forget or stop dreaming.—NK

To quote an oft-repeated saying, "Today is a gift life gives us; that is why we call it the present." Underlying our strategy to redefine aging for other aging women and younger women alike is the recognition that women over sixty have learned to find meaning and fulfillment in each day of our lives. To redefine aging, we have to value, as VB said, how a lifetime of experiences has transformed us into a force to be reckoned with. To redefine aging, we have to celebrate our wrinkles and what they symbolize: who we are as independent thinkers, resistant to societal pressures and wise to how to successfully cope with life. With that transformation, we have evolved into more confident, resilient, adaptable women who are grateful for all we have learned. These collective attitudes have earned us the right to gain the respect we so deserve and to be the principal architects in designing a productive and fulfilling landscape for the future of our own generation of women and those women who follow behind. *The beauty of this design is that as women we tend to be most creative when working in tandem with other women, blending ideas, and sharing perspectives. With connectivity and cooperation will come the power to make change.*

Creating Our Mission Statement:
FOR POSITIVE AGING, BEGIN TO PLAN YOUR NEXT PHASE IN LIFE WITH THE END (NOT THE ULTIMATE END) IN MIND:

1. **Who is the person you want to be (your character)?**
2. **What do you want to do (your contributions and achievements)?**
3. **What are the principles and values upon which your being and doing are based?**

Persuaded by the importance of organizing our thoughts and of converting those thoughts into an articulated approach to living, we have penned our own mission statement that we think may promote the most meaningful tomorrows.

We will work to continue the paths that have brought success to our lives and to resurface our well-traveled roads in order to revitalize our efforts

1. **to value ourselves, to be valued by others, and to promote the importance of valuing others;**
2. **to welcome people into our lives and to strive to be the people whom others want in their lives;**
3. **to feel a sense of purpose and by our actions make a difference in the lives of our family, friends, and community;**
4. **to appreciate our connections to those we love and to live life to its fullest, making every day count;**
5. **to strive to be mentally healthy and physically fit;**
6. **to learn to accept our own limitations and those that are placed upon us;**
7. **to appreciate the difference between what is and what is not within our control; and**
8. **to value our history, respect our individual differences, practice spirituality, and foster a love of learning.**
   —GKH, MCL, CTS

Thoughts to Remember: Eighteen Essential Elements to Positive Aging
The answers given to the three questions regarding our personal mission statements on aging are meant to create the framework for what we believe to be eighteen essential elements necessary to redesign the landscape of aging for not only ourselves but for other women over sixty as well.

> Vision without action is just a dream, action without vision just passes the time, and vision with action can change the world.—Nelson Mandela

In order to effect a change, our generation of women must promote the synergy between fulfilling our dreams to emerge from invisibility and transforming our personal landscape into a landscape of positive aging. Endeavors that celebrate the wisdom of women over sixty, a dedication to creating a world that values a search for meaning, and a commitment to family, friends, career, and community provide the necessary groundwork for that transformation.

As we read through the list of the elements below, let us see how many of them are already integral to our lives and which of the others could be easily incorporated.

<u>Thoughts to Remember</u>:

1. Chronicle our evolution as women and nourish our narratives with ongoing self-reflection and self-evaluation.
2. Recognize that we are no longer the center of everyone's world and be ok with that.
3. Be grateful that we are alive.
4. Embody the belief that "the future is our present" and live each moment of each day.
5. Learn from the past but do not obsess on it.
6. Have faith in ourselves and in our own judgment.
7. Give ourselves permission to ask for what we need.
8. Accept that mistakes are opportunities from which we can learn.
9. Let go of unrealistic expectations of ourselves and others.
10. Welcome change as inevitable and not as something to fear.
11. Continue to sustain supportive relationships.
12. Be open to new supportive relationships.
13. Challenge ourselves to a new task that stimulates our brain.
14. Limit relationships, thoughts and activities that are no longer satisfying or healthy.
15. Do things for others that have purpose and meaning.
16. Explore our spiritual side.
17. Take action to make our thoughts known.
18. Remember if we are not steadfast in rejoicing in our own worthiness, we cannot fault others for not taking up our battle.

The Promise of Visibility

When we began writing this book, we never dreamed that at the end we would find ourselves where we are right at this moment. There were some things we knew quite well at the beginning. We believed that women would be willing to take the time and make the effort to explore their pasts as a means of uncovering the long and sometimes winding pathway to their present voice. With only a little coaxing, we found that the many women who wrote were very open. Yet we were astounded at just how positive the responses were.

We felt quite certain that once each of us discovered how rich and expansive our histories were that we could be inspired to share the lessons we had learned through our legacies with those individuals. What we never imagined was that by rewinding those stories over and over again in our minds, they would be a catalyst for change. We have come through the process much more focused, self-aware, and complete than when we started. Each woman who shared her narrative in a voice that resonated courage, candor, and insight had something of value to teach us. What we initially relied upon was what the three of us had learned in helping others untangle the mysteries of their lives. Now we were discovering that in the course of sharing our narratives and the narratives of all those voices, we had initiated some important changes within each of us.

These changes have come in many different forms. They have for the women who revealed to us their own personal struggles. They have helped bring closure to relationships that needed repair. Surprisingly, it made no difference if we were separated from those people through death, because the renovation came from deep within ourselves. It impacted how we would look at our relationships and ourselves in the future.

For others of us, the exploration into the past unearthed some of the skeletons in our closets! Once these were revealed, many of us felt a newfound sense of liberation. No more masks; no more deceptions. With age and an insight into the meaning and consequences of our own histories, we could now begin to trace the origins of our strengths and our weaknesses and deal with them head on.

> When one door closes, another door opens. But we often look so long and so regretfully upon the closed door that we do not see the ones which open for us.—Alexander Graham Bell

We wrote this book with the notion that at age sixty-plus, as we stood facing the challenges of growing older, we could benefit from exploring, through the writing of our narratives, who we were and how we could improve our own personal landscape of aging. We initially saw this as a private journey. It took us many months before we appreciated how monumental the potential effect of remembering, recounting, and communicating our stories with other women could be on the collective landscape of aging. We now have a network of women—women who do not even know each other but who can identify in each other and in themselves that sense of belonging, that sense of validation, that sense of shared history. The individual messages on aging have been clearly articulated. Nevertheless, it is the connectedness of our messages and the richness we value in those messages that potentially could make our sphere of influence multiply. Sharing ideas can only help to create social supports and a sense of community that can exponentially grow our influence as aging women.

Our stories debunked the myth that women over sixty have no alternative but to become invisible in a society that worships youth. Enlightened by the truths we have encountered in each other's words and emboldened by the discoveries that come with wisdom, experience, and singularity of purpose as *keepers of the meaning,* we have the possibility of creating a platform of ideas that could transform how others regard our generation of women.

- *The responsibility for changing the landscape lies within us individually and as part of a community.*
- *The responsibility for changing the landscape lies within us and our refusal to back down as others try to diminish our power.*
- *The responsibility for changing the landscape lies within us and our acceptance of our limitations, not as failures but as a privilege of reaching our age.*

We are repaving our road to well-being according to our own needs, according to our own dreams.

> It is my belief that "aging has a different connotation with the progression of plateaus within the life cycle." Beginning with childhood, aging might be defined as a goal, an aspiration, an ambition; for example, I can't wait until I am old enough—to ride a bicycle...to go to school...to become

a teenager...to become an adult...to enter high school...to drive a car...
to go to college. The next plateau when "aging" is defined as a challenge
or a dare is the entry into marriage and parenthood; now we want the
aging process to take a lengthy sabbatical! The children should see us
as "young"...our bodies must remain firm and slender; our faces should
be without lines; our teeth and hair should be perfect; we should be
athletic, indefatigable, knowledgeable, and attractive to our mate.
Then an empty nest, a time of reflection, and now the "aging" process
is defined as an obstacle course! Looking in the magnifying mirror is
a reality check. I never knew gravity did this. What happened to my
twenty-twenty vision? Of course I can hear you, why do you ask? We'll
babysit for a night but not for a week. Doctor appointments are very
prominent on the calendar. Aches and pains. A daily hurdle to remain
positive and upbeat! The final stage is when "aging" can be defined as
a comfort zone, a security blanket, or a dependable friend. Any part
of each day when one needs an excuse, there is a pat answer! Living
beyond eighty or ninety (much more common now than ever before),
any shortcoming can be attributed to age! I am so sorry, I forgot; I
didn't mean to get angry, I meant to say...forgive me...I forgot to hang
up the phone...I didn't hear the phone, the TV was too loud. I have, I
could have, I didn't! *Aging is a gift and a blessing. Enjoy it each and every
day!*—BDJ

Only our voices can change the perceptions of the world, and those voices have
to reverberate with commitment and determination. We no longer are obligated
to accept the societal messages conveyed through print, electronic, and new-age
media. The stage of generativity gives us the power to embrace our new role as
the matriarchs to younger generations and as the caretakers of the values that will
serve as the legacies to enrich the lives of our children and the children who follow.
With generativity comes an extension of our social radius. After having balanced
an immersion in our family and/or our career for much of our earlier years, our
focus now is directed outward toward community building, mentoring, and caring for all that the world and we have created. In Erikson's last phase, the integrity
stage, we fight a sense of despair at growing older by recalling past circumstances
with a new perspective and understanding. By reintegrating those memories, we
have a newfound appreciation of who we are.

Although we all are likely to face certain inevitabilities, such as health issues and potential financial uncertainties, each woman begins this last phase of her life with quality-of-life choices to make that can affect how we approach today and each day forward. Our narratives create a road map through our past and help us discover markers—for example, family "scripts" and unresolved issues—that can redirect our future.

It is the sisterhood of women over sixty who have explored their past that has inspired us. As we read and unearth our own pasts, we, too, will be encouraged to contribute our voice to that chorus of women. As the chorus grows, the potential to stand tall and demand recognition, to be counted as valued and valuable, will also grow. And maybe then a full chorus of women with rich and synchronized voices will defy the negative landscape of aging that permeates our culture. Maybe that chorus of voices will no longer be branded *invisible*, and a new vibrant and fertile landscape will replace it!

LIST OF QUESTIONS TO REVIEW

How would you change the landscape of aging for women in our society?

What are the things you value about yourself that will contribute to a positive view aging?

PERSONAL REFLECTIONS

_____

_____

_____

_____

_____

_____

_____

_____

_____

_____

_____

_____

_____

_____

_____

_____

_____

_____

_____

_____

_____

_____

_____

_____

_____

_____

_____

BIBLIOGRAPHY

____. 1951. "The Younger Generation." *Time*, November 5.

Adams, R. G., and R. Blieszer. 1995, Nov.–Dec. "Aging Well with Friends and Family." *American Behavioral Scientist* 39 (2): 209–24.

Agronin, M. 2011. *How We Age: A Doctor's Journey into the Heart of Growing Old.* Cambridge, MA: Da Capo Press.

Allport, G. 1961. *Pattern and Growth in Personality.* New York: Holt, Rinehart, and Winston.

Anderson, M. I. 2000. *Thinking about Women: Sociological Perspectives on Sex and Gender.* 5th ed. Needham Heights, MA: Allyn & Bacon Publisher.

Antonucci, T., and H. Akiyama. 1987. "Social Networks in Adult Life and a Preliminary Examination of the Convoy Model." *Journal of Gerontology* 42 (5): 519–27.

Antonucci, T. C., and H. Akiyama. 1995. "Convoys of Social Relations: Family and Friendship within a Life-Span Context." In *Handbook of Aging and the Family*, edited by R. Bleiszner, V. H. Bedford and V. Bedford. Westport, CT: Greenwood Publishing Group.

Averick, L. S. 1996. *Don't Call Me Mom: How to Improve Your In-Law Relationships.* Hollywood, FL: Lifetime Books.

Baltes, P. B., and M. M. Baltes, eds. 1993. *Successful Aging: Perspectives from the Behavioral Sciences.* New York: Cambridge University Press.

Bates, U., F. Denmark, V. Held, D. Helly, S. Hune, S. Lees, S. Pomeroy, C. Somerville, and S. Zalk. 1995. *Women's Realities, Women's Choices: An Introduction to Women's Studies.* 2nd ed. New York: Oxford University Press.

Baumeister, R., and M. R. Leary. 1995. "The Need to Belong: Desire for Interpersonal Attachments as a Fundamental Human Motivation." *Psychological Bulletin* 11: 497–529.

Belenky, M. F., B. M. Clinchy, N. R. Goldgerger, and J. M. Tarule. 1986. *Woman's Ways of Knowing: The Development of Self, Voice and Mind*. New York: Basic Books.

Berkman, L. F., and S. L. Syme. (1979) 2001. "Social Relationships and Health: Berkman and Syme." *Advances in Mind-Body Medicine* 17 (1): 5–7.

Bernstein, E. 2012. "Want Great Marriage Advice? Ask a Divorced Person." *Wall Street Journal*, July 24.

Binstock, R., and L. George, eds. 2010. *Handbook of Aging and Social Science*. 7th ed. San Diego, CA: Academic Press.

Blair, P. D. 2005. *The Next Fifty Years: A Guide for Women at Midlife and Beyond*. Charlottesville, VA: Hampton Roads Publishing Company.

Borysenko, J. 1990. *Guilt is the Teacher, Love is the Lesson*. New York: Warner Books.

Boston Women's Health Book Collective. 1998. *Our Bodies, Ourselves for the New Century*. New York: Touchstone.

Bowen, M. 1978. *Family Therapy in Clinical Practice*. New York: Gardner.

Brazelton, T. B., and J. Sparrow. 2006. *Touchpoints: Birth to Three Years*. Cambridge, MA: Da Capo Press.

Brazelton, T. B., and J. Sparrow. 2008. *Touchpoints: Three to Six*. Cambridge, MA: Da Capo Press.

Brown, B. 2010. "The Power of Vulnerability." Video file. http: www.ted.com/talks/ brene_brown_on_vulnerability?language=en.

Brown, L. 2011. *The Art of Talking: A Handbook of Marital Communication*. http://www.udemy.com.

Burditt, K. S., L. M. Miller, and E. S. Lefkowitz. 2009. "Tensions in the Parent and Adult Child Relationship: Links to Solidarity and Ambivalence." *Psychology and Aging* 24 (2): 287–95.

Butler, R. 1980. "Ageism: A Forward." *Journal of Social Issues* 36 (2): 2–11.

———. 2002. "The Study of Productive Aging." *The Journals of Gerontology*. Series B, *Psychological Sciences and Social Sciences* 57 (6): S323.

Butler, R. N., and M. Lewis. 1986. *Love and Sex after 40: A Guide for Men and Women for Their Mid and Later Years*. New York: Harper and Row.

Cabeza, R., L. Nyberg, and D. Park. 2005. *Cognitive Neuroscience of Aging: Linking Cognitive and Cerebral Aging*. Oxford: Oxford University Press.

Calasanti, T. M., and K. F. Slevin. 2001. *Gender, Social Inequalities, and Aging*. Lanham, MD: AltaMira Press.

———, 2006. *Age Matters: Realigning Feminist Thinking*. New York: Routledge.

Cameron, J., and M. Bryan. 1992. *The Artist's Way: A Spiritual Path to Higher Creativity*. New York: G. P. Putnam's Sons.

Carey, J. R., and S. Zou. 2007. "Theories of Life-Span and Aging." In *Physiological Basis of Aging and Geriatrics*, edited by P. S. Timiras. 4th ed. Boca Raton, FL: CRC Press.

Carnegie, D. 1981. *How to Win Friends and Influence People*. Revised edition. New York: Simon & Schuster.

Carson, L. 1996. *The Essential Grandparent: A Guide to Making a Difference*. Deerfield Beach, FL: Health Communications.

Carstensen, L. 1991. "Selectivity Theory: Social Activity in Life-Span Context." *Annual Review of Gerontology and Geriatrics* 11 (11): 195–214.

Carstensen, L. L., D. M. Isaacowitz, and S. T. Charles. 1999. "Taking Time Seriously: A Theory of Socio-Emotional Selectivity." *American Psychologist* 54: 165–81.

Carstensen, L., and C. Lockenhoff. 2003. "Aging, Emotion, and Evolution: The Bigger Picture." *Annals of the New York Academy of Sciences* 1000: 152–79.

Chopra, D. 1993. *Ageless Body, Timeless Mind.* New York: Harmony Books.

Cnaan, R. A., F. Handy, and M. Wadsworth. 1996. "Defining Who Is a Volunteer: Conceptual and Empirical Considerations." *Nonprofit and Voluntary Sector Quarterly* 25: 364–83.

Cohen, G. D. 2006. *The Mature Mind: The Positive Power of the Aging Brain.* New York: Basic Books.

Coleman, J. 1988. "Social Capital in the Creation of Human Capital." *American Journal of Sociology* 94: 95–120.

Coleman, P. G., C. Ivani-Chalian, and M. Robinson. 1998. "The Story Continues: Persistence of Life Themes in Old Age." *Aging and Society* 18 (4): 389–419.

Connor, K.M. and J. R. Davidson. 2003. "Development of a New Resiliency Scale: the Collor-Davidson Resilience Scale (CD-RISC). *Depress Anxiety.* 16(2):76-82.

Cooley, D. 2009. "The Inner Voice of Self-Leadership." *Dissertation Abstracts International, Section B: The Sciences and Engineering* 69 (9-B): 5821.

Coontz, S. 2013. "Why Gender Equality Stalled." *New York Times Sunday Review,* February 17.

Cormier, H. C. 2004. "Women's Experiences of Loss of Voice and Sense of Self." *Dissertation Abstracts International Section A: Humanities and Social Sciences* 65 (5-A): 1660.

Covey, S. R. 1989. *The 7 Habits of Highly Effective People: Powerful Lessons in Personal Change*. New York: Simon & Schuster.

Crowley, C., and H. S. Lodge. 2004. *Younger Next Year for Women*. New York: Workman Publisher.

Cruikshank, M. 2009. *Learning to Be Old: Gender, Culture and Aging*. New York: Rowman & Littlefield Publishers.

Daffner, K. R. 2010. "Promoting Successful Cognitive Aging: A Comprehensive Review." *Journal of Alzheimer's Disease* 19 (4): 1101–22.

Davis, N. D., E. Cole, and E. D. Rothblum, eds. 1993. *Faces of Women Aging*. Philadelphia: Haworth Press.

Depp, C. A., and D. V. Jeste. 2006. "Definitions and Predictors of a Successful Aging: A Comprehensive Review of Larger Quantitative Studies." *The American Journal of Geriatric Psychiatry* 14 (1): 6–20.

de Tocqueville, A. 1835. *Democracy in America*. London: Saunder and Otley.

DeRougemont, D. 1983. *Love in the Western World*. Princeton, NJ: Princeton University Press.

Diener, E., D. Wirtz, W. Tov, C. Kim-Prieto, D. Choi, S. Oishi, and R. Biswas-Diener. 2009. "New Measures of Well-Being: Flourishing and Positive and Negative Feelings." *Social Indicators Research* 39: 247–56.

Diener, R. 2009. "New Measures of Well-Being: Flourishing and Positive and Negative Feelings." *Social Indicators Research* 39: 247–56.

Egan, G. 1977. *You and Me: The Skills of Communication and Relating to Others*. Monterey, CA: Brooks/Cole Publishing Company.

Elwood, C. 2008. *The Lucky Few: Between the Greatest Generation and the Baby Boom*. Dordrecht, Netherlands: Springer Science.

Erikson, E. 1994. *Identity and the Life Cycle*. New York: W. W. Norton & Company.

_____. 1950. *Childhood and Society*. New York: W. W. Norton & Company.

Erikson, E. H., J. M. Erikson, and H. Q. Kivnick. 1986. *Vital Involvement in Old Age*. New York: W. W. Norton & Company.

Erikson, J. M. 1997. *The Life Cycle Completed*. New York: W. W. Norton & Company.

Feiler, B. 2013. *The Secrets of Happy Families*. New York: William Morrow.

Felmlee, D., and A. Muraco. 2009. "Norms among Older Adults." *Research on Aging* 31 (3): 318–44.

Fisher, B. J., and D. K. Specht. 1999. "Successful Aging and Creativity in Later Life." *Journal of Aging Studies* 13 (4): 457–72.

Fisher, R., W. Ury, and B. Patton. 1991. *Getting to Yes: Negotiating Agreement without Giving In*. New York: Penguin Books.

Fogler, J., and L. Stern. 1994. *Improving Your Memory: How to Remember What You're Starting to Forget*, rev. ed. Baltimore: The John Hopkins University Press.

Foster-Bey, J., R. Grimm, and N. Dietz. 2007. "Keeping Baby Boomers Volunteering: A Research Brief on Volunteer Retention and Turnover." Washington, DC: Corporation for National and Community Service, Office of Research and Policy Development.

Fraiberg, S. H. 1959. *The Magic Years*. New York: Charles Scribner's Sons.

Frankl, V. E. 1948. *Man's Search for Meaning*. New York: Beacon Press.

Freud, S. 1905. *Three Essays on the Theory of Sexuality*. Vienna, Austria: Franz Deuticke.

Frey, D., and J. Carlock. 1989. *Enhancing Self-Esteem*, 2nd ed. Muncie, IN: Accelerated Development.

Friedan, B. 1998. *The Second Stage*. Boston: Harvard University Press.

Friedman, M. 1993. *What Are Friends For?: Feminist Perspectives on Personal Relationships and Moral Theory*. Ithaca, NY: Cornell University Press.

Fulghum, R. 1988. *All I Really Need to Know I Learned in Kindergarten*. New York: Ballantine Books.

Furumoto, L. 1992. "Joining Separate Spheres: Christine Ladd-Franklin, Woman Scientist (1847–1930)." *American Psychologist* 47 (2).

Giles-Simms L. C., G. F. Glonek, M. Luszcz, and G. R. Andrews. 2005. "Effect of Social Networks on 10-Year Survival in Very Old Australians: The Australian Longitudinal Study of Aging." *Journal of Epidemiology and Community Health* 59 (7): 574–79.

Gilligan, C. 1936. *In a Different Voice: Psychological Theory and Women's Development*. Cambridge, MA: Harvard University Press.

Gottman, J. M. 1999. *The Seven Principles for Making Marriage Work*. New York: Harmony Books.

Gottman, J. M., and N. Silver. 1995. *Why Marriages Succeed or Fail: And How You Can Make Yours Last*. New York: Simon & Schuster.

Graham, B, ed. 2010. *Eye of My Heart: 27 Writers Reveal the Hidden Pleasures and Perils of Being a Grandmother*. New York: Harper.

Greater Miami Jewish Federation. 1993. *Women's Division Directory*. Miami, FL: Greater Miami Jewish Federation.

Guber, P. 2011. *Tell to Win: Connect, Persuade, and Triumph with the Hidden Power of the Story*. New York: Crown Publishing.

Gulette, M. M. 1997. *Declining to Decline: Cultural Combat and the Politics of the Midlife*. Charlottesville, VA: University Press of Virginia.

Hall, G. S. 1904. *Adolescence: Its Psychology and Its Relations to Physiology, Anthropology, Sociology, Sex, Crime, Religion and Education*. New York: D. Appleton & Company.

Hamilton, H. E., ed. 1999. *Language and Communication in Old Age: Multidisciplinary Perspectives (Issues in Aging)*. New York: Routledge.

Hanson, R. 2013. *Hardwiring Happiness: The New Brain Science of Contentment, Calm, and Confidence*. San Francisco: Potter/Ten Speed/Harmony.

Heilbrun, C. G. 1977. *The Last Gift of Time: Life Beyond Sixty*. New York: Ballantine Books.

Heiman, J. R., and J. Lopiccola. 1976. *Becoming Orgasmic: A Sexual and Personal Growth Program for Women*. New York: Simon & Schuster.

Heschel, A. J. 1976. *God in Search of Man: A Philosophy of Judaism*. New York: Farrar, Straus and Giroux.

Hill, R. D. 2008. *Seven Strategies for Positive Aging*. New York: W. W. Norton & Company.

Highe, J. 2008. *The Modern Grandparents' Guide*. London: Piatkus Books Publisher.

Hite, S. 1981. *The Hite Report: A Nationwide Study of Female Sexuality*. New York: Seven Stories Press.

Hoffman, A. 2013. *Survival Lessons*. New York: Workman's Publishing.

Hollis, J. 2005. *Finding Meaning in the Second Half of Life*. New York: Gotham Books.

_____. 2009. *What Matters Most: Living a More Considered Life*. New York: Gotham Books.

Holt-Lunstad, J., T. B. Smith, and J. B. Layton. 2010. "Social Relationships and Mortality Risks: A Meta-Analysis Review." *PLOS Medicine* 7 (7): 1–20.

Hom, S. K. 2007. *Life's Big Little Moments: Grandmothers and Grandchildren*. New York: Sterling Publishing.

Howe, N. 2014. "The Silent Generation: The Lucky Few." *Forbes*, July 30.

Hurd, L. C. 1999. "We're Not Old: Older Women's Negotiation of Aging and Oldness." *Journal of Aging Studies* 13 (4): 419–39.

Jacob, R. H. 1979. *Integrating Displaced Homemakers into the Economy*. Wellesley, MA: Wellesley College Center for Research on Women.

James, J. B., and N. Zarrett. 2006. "Ego Integrity in the Lives of Older Women." *Journal of Adult Development* 13 (2): 61–75.

Jong-Fast, M. 2010. "Growing up with Ma Jong." *Wall Street Journal*, November 6–7.

Jordan, J. V., ed. 1997. *Women's Growth in Diversity: More Writings from the Stone Center*. New York: Guilford Press.

Jordan, J. V., A. G. Kaplan, J. B. Miller, I. P. Stiver, and J. L. Surrey. 1991. *Women in Growth and Connection: Writings from the Stone Center*. New York: Guilford Press.

Kabat-Zinn, J. 2011. *Mindfulness for Beginners: Reclaiming the Present Moment and Your Life*. Louisville, CO: Sounds True.

Kaufman, S. R. 1986. *The Ageless Self: Sources of Meaning in Late Life*. Madison, WI: University of Wisconsin Press.

Kettermann, S. M. 2000. *The 12 Rules of Grandparenting: A New Look at Traditional Roles…And How to Break Them*. New York: Checkmark Books.

Kim, J., and M. Pai. 2010. "Volunteering and Trajectories of Depression." *Journal of Aging and Health* 22: 84–105.

King-Cooper, J. L. 1996. "Explorations in Voice: Women's Psychosocial Development." *Dissertation Abstracts International, Section A: Humanities and Social Sciences* 56 (7-A): 2904.

Kinsey. C., W. R. Pomeroy., and C. E. Martin. 1958, Sexual Behavior in the Human Female. Philadelphia, PA: W.B. Saunders.

Kinsey. C., W. R. Pomeroy., and C. E. Martin. 1948. *Sexual Behavior in the Human Male.* Philadelphia, PA: W.B. Saumders.

Kirpatric, M., ed. 2002. *Women's Sexual Development: Explorations of Inner Space.* New York: Plenum Press.

Klinenberg, E. 2013. *Going Solo: The Extraordinary Rise and Surprising Appeal of Living Alone.* London: Penguin Books.

Krasnow, I. 2014. *Sex After...Women Share How Intimacy Changes as Life Changes.* Rutherford, NJ: Gotham Publishers.

Kubler-Ross, E. 1969. *On Death and Dying.* New York: Routledge, Taylor and Francis Group.

La Ban, E. 2009. *The Grandparents Handbook.* Philadelphia: Quirk Books.

Lee, G. R., and C. L. Shehan. 1989. Social Relations and the Self-Esteem of Older Persons. *Research on Aging* 11 (4): 427–42.

Leiblum, S., and J. Sachs. 2002. *Getting the Sex You Want: A Woman's Guide to Becoming Proud, Passionate and Pleased in Bed.* New York: Crown Publishing.

Lerner, H. 1994. *The Dance of Deception: A guide to Authenticity and Truth-Telling in Women's Relationships.* New York: Harper Collins.

Levine, S. 1997. *A Year to Live: How to Live This Year as if It Were Your Last.* New York: Bell Tower.

Levine, S. B. 2005. *Inventing the Rest of Our Lives: Women in Second Adulthood*. New York: Penguin Group.

Levinson, D. J. 1996. *The Season of a Woman's Life*. New York: Ballantine Books.

Levy, B. R., M. D. Slade, S. R. Kunkel, and S. V. Kasl. 2002. "Longevity Increased by Positive Self-Perceptions of Aging." *Journal of Personality and Social Psychology* 83: 261–270.

Li, Y., and K. F. Ferraro. 2005. "Volunteering and Depression in Later Life: Social Benefit or Selection Processes?" *Journal of Health and Social Behavior* 46: 68–84.

Livingston, G. L. 2008. *Too Soon Old, Too Late Old: Thirty Things You Need to Know Now*. Philadelphia: Da Capo Press.

Lund, D. 2003. "Grandchildren Give Us Hope for Immortality." *Pittsburgh Post-Gazette*, September 7.

Markus, H., and P. Nurius. 1986. "Possible Selves." *American Psychologist* 41: 954–69.

Maslin, J. 2013. "Looking Back at a Domestic Cri de Coeur: On Reading a Treatise 50 Years Late." *New York Times*, February 19: 1C.

Maslow, A. H. 1954. *Motivation and Personality*. New York: Harper.

Masters, W.H. and V.E. Johnson (1966). *Human Sexual Response*. New York: Bantam Books.

McEwen, B. S. 2005. "Stressed or Stressed Out: What Is the Difference?" *Journal of Psychiatry and Neuroscience* 30 (5): 315–8.

Morrow-Howell, N., J. Hinterlong, P. A. Rozario, and F. Tang. 2003. "Effects of Volunteering on the Well-Being of Older Adults." *Journal of Gerontology: Social Sciences* 58: S137–45.

Morrow-Howell, N., S. Hong, and F. Tang. 2009. "Who Benefits from Volunteering? Variations in Perceived Benefits." *The Gerontologist* 49: 91–102.

Musick, M. A., A. R. Herzog, and J. S. House. 1999. "Volunteering and Mortality among Older Adults: Findings from a National Sample." *Journals of Gerontology: Psychological Sciences and Social Sciences* 54B: S173–80.

Musick, M. A., and J. Wilson. 2003. "Volunteering and Depression: The Role of Psychological and Social Resources in Different Age Groups." *Social Science and Medicine* 56: 259–69.

Nolem-Hoeksema, S. 2010. *The Power of Women: Harness Your Unique Strengths at Home, at Work, and in Your Community*. New York: Times Books.

Northrup, C. 2015. *Goddesses Never Age: The Secret Prescription for Radiance, Vitality and Well-Being*. New York: Hays House.

Nuland, S. B. 2008. *The Art of Aging: A Doctor's Prescription for Well-Being*. New York: Random House.

Nussbaum, J. F., and J. Coupland. 2004. *Handbook of Communication and Aging Research*, 2nd ed. Mahwah, NJ: Lawrence Erlbaum Associates.

Nussbaum, J., L. Pecchioni, J. Robinson, and T. Thompson. 2000. *Communication and Aging*, 2nd ed. Mahwah, NJ: Lawrence Erlbaum Associates.

O'Grady, D. 1994. *Taking the Fear Out of Change*. Holbrook, MA: Bob Adams Publisher.

O'Hanlon, B. 2000. *Do One Thing Different*. New York: William Morrow & Company.

Olson, E. 2013. "Score, a Nonprofit Association That Provides Business Counseling: Turning Hobbies into Profits, with a Little Help." *New York Times*, May 15.

Pahl, R. 2000. *On Friendship*. Cambridge, UK: Polity.

Paston, B. N. 2010. *How to Be the Perfect Grandma: Rules of the Game*. Naperville, IL: Sourcebooks.

Peel, N. M., R. J. McClure, and H. P. Bartlett. 2005. "Behavioral Determinants of Healthy Aging." *American Journal of Preventive Medicine* 28 (3): 298–304.

"Planning and Living the New Retirement." 2015. *Wall Street Journal, Encore Section*, October 19.

Prager, D. 1998. *Happiness Is a Serious Problem*. New York: Harper Collins Press.

Ratey, J. J. 2001. *A User's Guide to the Brain: Perception, Attentions, and the Four Theaters of the Brain*. New York: Vintage Books.

Richards, M., R. Hardy, and M. E. J. Wadsworth. 2003. Does Active Leisure Time Protect Cognition? *Social Science and Medicine* 56 (4): 785–92.

Rosin, H. 2012. *The End of Men and the Rise of Women*. New York: Penguin Group.

Rossiter, M. 1982. *Women Scientists in America, Struggles and Strategies to 1940*. Baltimore: Johns Hopkins University Press.

Rountree, C. 1997. *On Women Turning 60: Embracing the Age of Fulfillment*. New York: Harmony Books.

Rowe, J. W., and R. L. Kahn. 1997. Successful Aging. *The Gerontologist* 37: 433–40.

Satir, V. 1988. *The New Peoplemaking*. Mountainview, CA: Science and Behavior Books.

Schacter-Shalomi, Z., and R. Miller. 1995. *From Age-ing to Sage-ing: A Profound New Vision of Growing Older*. New York: Grand Central Publishing.

Schnarch, D. 2009. *Intimacy and Desire: Awaken the Passion in Your Relationship*. New York: Beaufort Books.

_____. 2009. *Passionate Marriage: Love, Sex and Intimacy in Emotionally Committed Relationships*. New York: Beaufort Books.

Schneider, K. 2013. "For Modern Retirees, There's No Place Like Home." *New York Times*, March 13.

Schuessler, J. 2013. "Looking Back at a Domestic Cri de Coeur: Criticisms of a Classic Abound." *New York Times*, February 19.

Seligman, M. 2002. *Authentic Happiness: Using the New Positive Psychology to Realize Your Potential for Lasting Fulfillment*. New York: Free Press.

Seligman, M. and M. Csikszentmihalyi. 2000. "Positive Psychology: An Introduction." *American Psychologist* 55(1):5-14.

_____. 2011. *Flourish: A Visionary New Understanding of Happiness and Well-Being*. New York: Simon & Schuster.

Sheehy, G. 1955. *New Passages: Mapping Your Life across Time*. New York: Random House.

_____. 1974. *Passages: Predictable Crises of Adult Life*. New York: P. Sutton.

_____. 2006. *Sex and the Seasoned Woman: Pursuing the Passionate Life*. New York: Ballantine Books.

Siebert, D., E. J. Mutran, and D. C. Reitzes. 1999. "Friendship and Social Support: The Importance of Role Identity to Aging Adults." *Social Work* 44 (6): 522–33.

Snowden, D. 2001. *Aging with Grace*. New York: Random House.

Solberg, V. S., G. E. Good, A. R. Fischer, S. D. Brown, and D. Nord. 1995. "Career Decision-Making and Career Search Activities: Relative Effects of Career Search Self-Efficacy and Human Agency." *Journal of Counseling Psychology* 42 (4): 448–4

Solomon, A. 2014. "How the Worst Moments in Our Lives Make Us Who We Are," video file. Accessed October 22, 2016. https://www.ted.com/talks/andrew_solomon_how_the_worst_moments_in_our_lives_make_us_who_we_are?language=en.

Steinem, G. 1994. *Moving beyond Words*. New York: Simon & Schuster.

Stewart, J. K. 2015. "The Gray Divorcee." *Chicago Tribune*, February 28.

Tang, F. 2006. "What Resources Are Needed for Volunteerism?: A Life Course Perspective." *Journal of Applied Gerontology* 25: 375–90.

Tang, F., E. H. Choi, and N. Morrow-Howell. 2010. "Organizational Support and Volunteering Benefits for Older Adults." *Gerontologist* 50: 1–10.

Tannen, D. 1990. *You Just Don't Understand*. New York: Ballantine Books.

_____. 1994. *Talking from 9 to 5*. New York: William Morrow & Company.

Taylor, S. E., L. C. Klein, B. P. Lewis, T. L. Gruenewald, R. A. R. Gurung, and J. A. Updegraff. 2000. "Biobehavioral Responses to Stress in Females: Tend-and-Befriend, not Fight-or-Flight." *Psychological Review* 107 (3): 410–29.

Telushkin, J. 1991. *Jewish Literacy*. New York: William Morrow & Company.

Timiras, P. S. 2007. *Physiological Basis of Aging and Geriatrics*, 4th ed. Boca Raton, FL: CRC Press.

Trafford, A. 2009. *As Time Goes By*. New York: Basic Books.

Twerski, A. 2007. *Happiness and the Human Spirit*. Woodstock, VT: Jewish Lights Publishing.

Ussher, J. M. 1997. *Fantasies of Femininity: Reframing the Boundaries of Sex*. New Brunswick, NJ: Rutgers University Press.

Vaillant, G. E. 2003. *Aging Well*. New York: Little, Brown and Company.

Viorst, J. 1986. *Necessary Losses*. New York: Ballantine Books.

Viscott, D. 1976. *The Language of Feelings*. New York: Simon & Schuster.

Walker, M. V., ed. 1999. *Mother Time: Women, Aging and Ethics*. Boston: Rowman & Littlefield.

Wallerstein, J. S., and S. Blakeslee. 1995. *The Good Marriage: How and Why Love Lasts*. Boston: Houghton Mifflin.

Walsh, F., and M. McGoldrick, eds. 1991. *Living Beyond Loss*. New York: W. W. Norton & Company.

Walter, M., B. Carter, P. Papp, and O. Silverstein. 1988. *The Invisible Web: Gender Patterns in Family Relationships*. New York: Guilford Press.

Westheimer, R., A. Grunebaum, and P. Lehu. 2011. *Sexually Speaking: What Every Woman Needs to Know about Sexual Health*. Hoboken, NJ: John Wiley & Sons.

Westheimer, R., and S. Kaplan. 1998. *Grandparenthood*. New York: Routledge.

Williams, E. N., E. Soeprapto, K. Like, P. Touradji, S. Hess, and C. E. Hill. 1998. "Perceptions of Serendipity: Career Paths of Prominent Academic Women in Counseling Psychology." *Journal of Counseling Psychology* 45 (4): 379–89.

Wilson J., and M. Musick. 1997. "Who Cares? Toward an Integrated Theory of Volunteer Work." *American Sociological Review* 62: 694.

Zastrow, C., and K. Kirst-Ashman. 2001. *Understanding Human Behavior and the Social Environment*, 5th ed. Monterey, CA: Brooks/Cole Publishing.

Zullo, K., and A. Zullo. 1992. *A Boomer's Guide to Grandparenting*. Kansas City, MO: Andrews McMeel Publishing.

WEB REFERENCES

AARP, https://join.aarp.org/aarp-tdp-g-12/

Administration on Aging, http://www.aoa.gov

Alzheimer's Association, http://alz.org/join_the_cause_donate.asp?

Chautauqua Institute (adult learning), http://www.ciweb.org

Eldercare. http://www.eldercare.gov *Learn about financial, employment, legal, and caregiving help for seniors*

Good Health Habits at Age 60 and Beyond, http://familydoctor.org/familydoctor/en/seniors/staying-healthy/good-health-habits-at-age-60-and-beyond.html

Healthy Women, http://www.healthywomen.org/content/article/health-your-60s

National Association of Area Agencies on Aging: n4a **http://www.n4a.org/**

National Center for Assisted Living, https://www.ahcancal.org/ncal/Pages/index.aspx

National Center on Elder Abuse, www.ncea.aoa.gov

National Council on Aging, https://www.ncoa.org/

NHS Choices: Live well. Women's health 60-plus http://www.nhs.uk/service-search

National Institute on Aging, National Institutes of Health, https://www.nia.nih.gov/

Osher Lifelong Learning Institutes, osherfoundation.org *Online courses for women over sixty* http://www.osherfoundation.org/index.php?olli

Prevention, http://www.prevention.com/health/healthy-living/7-things-every-woman-in-her-60s-should-do/ slide/1

Road Scholar, http://www.roadscholar.org

SCORE. https://www.score.org/

Senior Brains, http://www.seniorbrains.com

Sixty and me, http:// www.sixtyandme.com

The Budget Fashionista, http://www.thebudgetfashionista.com/

US Bureau of Labor Statistics—Division of Labor Force Statistics https://www.dol.gov/

WebMD.com: Women's Health http://www.webmd.com/**women**/frequently-asked-**questions**-about -**womens-health**

Women's Guide to Aging, http://www.womensguidetoaging.com

Women's Health: Sex & Intimacy - WebMD **http://www.webmd.com/women/guide/womens-health-sex-intimacy**

AUTHOR BIOGRAPHIES

Gail K. Harris, MEd, LCSW; Marilyn C. Lesser, PhD, LCSW; and Cynthia T. Soloway, JD, MSSW, MA, have spent their forty-year careers in education and social work using various therapeutic techniques to help women from all walks of life. Along the way, they have encountered a wide variety of issues women face, including the challenges of parenting, relationships, career and aging, and surviving loss, divorce, and abuse.

All three live in Miami, Florida, and are married with children and grandchildren.

Made in the USA
Middletown, DE
08 August 2021

45628566R00236